TO

MW00412427

# JOSEPH SMITH

## A Biography

OTHER BOOKS BY THE AUTHOR

*Porter Rockwell: A Biography* (1986)

*Rockwell: U.S. Marshal, A Novel* (1987)

*The Porter Rockwell Chronicles, Vol. 1* (1999)

*The Porter Rockwell Chronicles, Vol. 2* (2000)

*The Porter Rockwell Chronicles, Vol. 3* (2001)

*The Porter Rockwell Chronicles, Vol. 4* (2002)

*Hübener vs Hitler* (2003; 2nd edition 2004)

# JOSEPH SMITH

## A Biography

## Richard Lloyd Dewey

STRATFORD
**BOOKS**

ISBN: 0-929753-15-1
*Joseph Smith: A Biography*
by Richard Lloyd Dewey

Stratford Books, Inc.
Eastern States Office
4303 37th Road North
Arlington, VA 22207

Stratford Books, Inc.
Western States Office
P.O. Box 1371
Provo, UT 84603-1371

Dust jacket front cover photo:
Stan MacBean from Photographic Solutions

Dust jacket back cover painting:
*Joseph Smith* © 1997 by David Lindsley. Used by permission.

First edition: October 2005

This book is printed on acid-free paper.

Printed in the United States of America

The Book of Mormon was first printed in Grandin's Book Store in Palmyra, New York, 1830. The first edition may have been printed in different leathers, but at least some were bound in marbled calfskin, using an oil-soaking technique to give it texture and color. Others were bound with patches of leather, and still others may have been bound in pigskin, similar to the pigskin-bound replica depicted on the dust jacket of this book. Joseph owned a pair of spectacles, but they were not for functional use, as the glass lenses were plain glass and were stored in an etched silver case.

*To those who first introduced the author*
*to the Joseph Smith story:*

*Paul Helms*
*Duane Derfler*
*Melvin Kent Brown*

*and others who provided early information and inspiration:*

*Roger Gorringer*
*Robert K. Oscarson*
*Kim Haws*
*Mr. Brenchley*
*Drew Hansen*
*Fred Hartkopf*
*Douglas Clyde Vertel*
*Thayne Thomas*
*Blake Butterfield*
*Warren Geitche*

*James and Susan Harris*
*Jerry Harris*
*Charles Harris*
*Dave and Ann Campbell*
*Scott Campbell*
*Larry Brown*
*Doug Campbell*
*Sam Brown*
*James Noblitt*
*Robert and Betty Drubay*
*Bill and Virginia Brown*

# P R E F A C E

IN all five published volumes of Joseph Smith's journals, as well as his numerous letters, he generally used a scribe. He handwrote only some letters and notes and parts of his journal during 1832 and 1835. Most other writings he dictated to his scribes. One portion of his journal, and possibly others, he did not even dictate: it was written solely by his scribes in the first person as though he had written it but probably with his supervision—from December 21, 1842, through June 27, 1844. That portion was authored by Willard Richards. During this period some pages from others' diaries, including George Albert Smith's, were also added to Joseph's in the first person as though he had written them.

As for his own writing, Joseph felt held back by his inabilities, calling it "total darkness of paper, pen, and ink." Furthermore, he labeled English as "a crooked, broken, scattered, and imperfect language," which made writing for him a "little, narrow prison." Nevertheless, his commitment to record his history is admirable, and using scribes was the most practicable way.

This biography utilizes his journals and letters as the backbone of telling his story, without citing specific page numbers that would flood readers with thousands of footnotes. Most other research for this volume came from the author's previous work, *Porter Rockwell: A Biography*. In the second edition of this volume, endnotes will be added in some cases, for sources utilized from outside of Joseph's journals. They are purposely eliminated in this "reader-friendly" first edition, to make it less cumbersome and more readable for the general public.

The author is indebted to the librarians and staff of the Church Archives of the Historians' Office for The Church of Jesus Christ of Latter-day Saints in Salt Lake City and the Harold B. Lee Library at Brigham Young University in Provo, Utah, for providing materials used for this volume, which were originally researched for the author's above-listed work. He is also indebted to the many historians who have worked and written for years on the life of Joseph Smith, and he has found valuable gems of information from the footnotes and bibliographies of their works, which represent countless years of research. And finally, the author wishes to acknowledge the assistance and help of Faith Thompson, proofreader; Amy Tolley, typist; Vance Hawkins, typesetter and designer; and the staff of production assistants and living research sources who provided invaluable service and information for the author on *Porter Rockwell: A Biography*, whose names are there credited, which facilitated much of the research for this volume.

# PART I

# Vermont, New York, and Pennsylvania

# CHAPTER 1

JOSEPH Smith has a history unparalleled in inspiration, intrigue, and controversy. His followers went on to establish by the 21st century the seventh largest Christian religion in the United States, with even more members of the Church of Jesus Christ of Latter-day Saints outside U.S. borders. His life was steeped in controversy, and Latter-day Saints believe that it was his detractors and enemies who made him controversial, because his actions, as viewed and written about by thousands of early Saints in their journals, showed him as a man who, although flawed, was gifted, charismatic, extremely likeable and charming and, from numerous firsthand accounts, downright heroic.

Growing up in Sharon, Vermont, until about age 10, and then upstate New York, Joseph blended in well with farm folk neighbors. But when events of religious significance began to unfold through him, he found himself the target of unusual interest, with enemies claiming, to begin with, that he and his family were "riff-raff." Before that, however, his family name was connected with an unusually solid reputation. His ancestors were stalwarts of their communities, and even his own parents sacrificed greatly to repay debts when a certain business project went awry. That business venture may have occurred during the period in Joseph Sr.'s life in which he was a partner in a small merchandise store at Randolph, Vermont, that did a modest amount of exporting overseas. From that one venture they were left "in indigent circumstances."

That circumstance came about when Joseph's father, Joseph Sr., invested heavily in ginseng, grown wild in Vermont, to sell to China. He was offered only 70% of its value and therefore passed on the offer, later to secure booking of the ginseng on a ship to China, along with an agent to sell it. When that agent, the son of a man named Stevens, returned from China, he announced the money was gone. Later, while drunk, the same young man admitted to Joseph's uncle, Stephen Mack, that he had absconded with it, leaving the Smiths' high and dry to the tune of $1,800. So the Smiths, choosing to honor their obligations, sold their farm at half its value, for $800, and Lucy Mack, Joseph's mother, pitched in her $1,000 wedding present money to pay off the rest, leaving them destitute.

Now without a farm they moved to Royalton for a few months, then to Sharon, Vermont, where they rented Lucy's father's farm in the hills above White River. Although it was poor land, they worked it hard. It was here that Joseph was born on December 23, 1805, under the heritage of tremendous sacrifice and honor, coupled with extreme toil.

Joseph was born two years after his sister Sophronia, and five and six years after his two brothers, Hyrum and Alvin, were born at Tunbridge at the farm they had lost.

Children and adults alike worked feverishly to eke out a living for years.

Soon they realized the land was worthless and moved from one farm to another, while finding other odd jobs to survive. From Sharon they returned to Tunbridge, where Joseph's brother Samuel Harrison was born in 1807. Almost immediately they moved to nearby Royalton, Vermont. Two other brothers were born there—Ephraim in 1810 (who died 11 days later) and William in 1811. All three of these last boys shared the same birthday—March 13.

It was there in Royalton that Joseph began school on Dewey Hill, taught by Deacon Jonathon Rinney.

At age five, in 1811, the family moved to Lebanon, New Hampshire. In Lucy Mack Smith's account, *The History of Joseph Smith by His Mother: the Unabridged Original Version* (Stratford Books 2005), she reports that their lives improved, especially in the realm of education as they found good schools for the children. While Hyrum went to Moore's academy in Hanover, the others, including Joseph, attended a common school nearby. (This information, and much of the material used for this book, comes from Lucy's original version. Other versions of the book have since been abridged.)

Just when things were finally looking up for the family, a plague hit them—right before Joseph's eighth birthday. Hundreds of people were taken with typhoid fever, including all the Smith children. Their skin looked horrid, they became delirious, contracting high fevers, and their tongues turned black. There was no cure for the dreaded disease. According to Lucy's account, Sophronia was given up for dead by the doctors, but through the prayers of Lucy and her husband, the girl lived, convincing Lucy that God lived, that he took a personal interest in people, and that he actually answered prayers.

Joseph had the disease two weeks, but from it his health would spiral downhill in other aspects—he developed an excruciating pain in his shoulder. Typical of abusive and just plain bad medical practices of the day, a Dr. Parker treated him with a hot shovel and bone liniment, despite Joseph insisting he had not injured his shoulder. Later they would learn the pain had come not from injury, but from a large abscess. When it was lanced, it finally began to heal, but then the pain shifted to his leg. For two weeks, says Lucy, Joseph lay in bed in severe distress. Hyrum stayed with him constantly, rubbing his leg to attempt to comfort him—the first recorded incident of Hyrum's close friendship with his brother.

Although the pain increased, Joseph was fortunate to receive the services of a doctor who had learned revolutionary techniques of bone surgery. But first were other attempts by another doctor. Nathan Smith, a renowned surgeon from Dartmouth College at Hanover, made an eight-inch cut in his left leg, which relieved the pain for a while—but only until the leg began to heal. Then the doctor operated a second time with no positive results. Finally he returned a third time with another doctor, named Perkins, and eleven other doctors, possibly students or residents from Dartmouth. While they would eventually perform the leg-saving miracle, their first idea was simplistic and reactionary—they decided to amputate. When they came to perform the operation, one of the doctors commented, "My poor boy, we have come again."

But the doctors were surprised at the boy's resoluteness. Despite his tender age, he refused to have the operation. They insisted, but he still refused. At this unexpected impasse, his mother finally came to the rescue—she persuaded them to not amputate—but to remove only the infected part of the bone.

Despite the doctors' orders, young Joseph refused to be bound and told them that he needed only his father to hold him. He also refused liquor to soften the pain. Finally he ordered his mother away from the cabin so she would not be emotionally tortured by the scene. He recalled the example of his parents—remembering them praying over his sister—and felt God would assist him. The operation consisted of boring holes into both sides of the bone and breaking off pieces with forceps. When he screamed at the first piece of bone that was broken off, Lucy came running inside, but he yelled for her to again leave. Finally, the third piece was broken away, and Lucy could not contain herself. She returned again, only to see Joseph white as a sheet, his leg cut open, and his bed soaked in blood.

The operation was a success, but he lost much weight and had to use crutches for at least three years. He would later say that when he was 12 it was extremely painful for him to walk long distances, which exhausted him. Thereafter, he would limp slightly the rest of his life. About two years later he was sent to his uncle Jesse at Salem, confident the ocean air would enhance the healing process. There he stayed for an unknown length of time, but likely was initiated into the world of, or at least saw from a distance, the riches and sophistication of high society—with its art, literature, clothing, furnishings, and foods, which he would appreciate in his later years. No more is known of Joseph's early years except that he recovered completely and was tall for his age. He was also redheaded as a lad and retained some of that color in his later years.

After an entire year of fighting with typhoid fever, the family moved again, their state once again indigent, due undoubtedly to the sickness itself draining the parents and directing what energy they had left away from farm work. Their next stopping-off spot was Norwich, Vermont, where they began sharecropping for Esquire Moredock. They survived by selling fruit while their first, second, and third years' crops failed—the latter from a summer frost and an ensuing slight famine.

Two years later, in 1814, when Joseph was 10, the family packed up again and took flight to greener pastures to start life anew. Their father heard of a newly settled community in western New York where wheat would grow from easily tilled, soft-soiled land.

That new home: Palmyra, New York, where Joseph Jr. would receive life-altering experiences that would spin his entire family's life in a new direction and even turn their whole community upside down. And from it Joseph would change the lives of millions of people.

C H A 2 T E R

B EFORE making the move, Joseph's father first hired a driver named Caleb Howard to take him to Palmyra. Upon reaching there, Joseph Sr. trusted once again, as he expected himself to be trusted—he paid Howard in advance to move the rest of the family. He did in fact show up for them, but just as Lucy and her children were about to ride away with Howard, several creditors appeared on the scene, demanding more money from Lucy—even though they had been carefully paid in full. Once again Lucy and Joseph Sr. had sacrificed to pay their debts, following the example their parents had set for them. Lucy challenged these men, pointing out how they had been paid in full and had even earlier admitted so, but now they were changing their story, trying to eke out every last dime, no matter how undeserved. Lucy realized she could not afford to pay the driver Howard to wait, so she paid the creditors the $150. A neighbor saw the injustice and volunteered to raise the funds, but Lucy proudly refused. The family of seven children, from ages four to seventeen, finally embarked on their journey with Lucy's mother Lydia.

On the trip their wagon overturned. Lydia received fairly serious injuries, enough to cause her death two years later. She was let off at Royalton at a son's residence, which had been her destination.

Another disaster that impeded their progress to Palmyra was dealing with their driver Howard, who was abusive to all the children—most especially to Joseph Jr. Howard spent the money Joseph Sr. had advanced him, mostly at inns along the way, drinking and gambling. Perhaps not entirely sober, he was irresponsible with their goods and, more importantly, with his passengers—he insisted some of the Smith children travel with a family named Gates heading their direction. The reason: Howard liked the Gates' daughters and had them sit on his buckboard. Not having room for the 10-year-old Joseph with his lame leg, he split up the Smith family by tossing Joseph off the buckboard and forcing him to walk for miles, even though he was unable to keep up with the wagon. Joseph's older brothers confronted Howard, but he fought the young teens back with the butt of his whip, knocking them down.

At Utica, New York, Howard threw the Smith family goods into the street and was about to drive away when Lucy shouted to the townspeople that Howard was stealing their wagon and property. Lucy then fired Howard on the spot, but because of the denunciation, she was able to keep the wagon and retrieve her property scattered in the street. She and the boys then reunited—Joseph limped into town on crutches, and the Gates family arrived with her other children. Together again, the Smith family drove the wagon themselves the rest of the way.

However, being destitute from the fraudulent creditors, the Smiths were out of money and had to trade all their goods and even their clothing to survive the rest of the journey. When they arrived in Palmyra they had only two cents and no worldly goods.

This was the sixth community in which they had settled and the eighth home they would establish, once again completely broke but full of faith in the future.

When they arrived, Palmyra was a rugged little town of only 600 people, nestled in log cabins among a couple stores. A year later the Eerie Canal would begin construction right through their township, connecting the Great Lakes with New York City, revolutionizing commerce along the way.

The family had a meeting and decided to buy good property. But they realized it would have to be a family effort. The three oldest boys (Hyrum, Alvin, and Joseph) grabbed whatever odd jobs came their way—farming, well-digging, trapping and fishing—while Lucy developed her artistry by painting oilcloth as table covers to sell. On their front door hung a sign, "Cake and Beer Shop," in which they sold root beer, pies, and gingerbread. They also sold goods from a handcart in town whenever there was a public event. It is possible they had a shop in the area, other than their home, that sold root beer, boiled eggs, gingerbread, and other items.

They finally bought their land—they made a contract for 100 acres in Manchester, New York, two miles south, and made most of the first payment within a year. Thinking they had claim to the property, they saved as much as they could, paid all they thought was needed, and moved onto the land after two years of living in Palmyra. In their new home they lived just south of the county line between Ontario County (home to Manchester) and Wayne County (home to Palmyra), so they were officially residents of Manchester, New York.

Unlike their rented Vermont farm, this soil was fertile. Joseph Jr.'s brother William stated they cleared 60 acres "of the heaviest timber I ever saw." They also obtained maple sugar from 1,200 to 1,500 maple trees. Lucy adds they averaged half a ton of sugar per year, and that one season they won the county prize for the most maple syrup produced—a tedious, difficult task of collecting numerous barrels of tree sap and boiling it down, producing one gallon of maple syrup from every 30–40 gallons of sap. They also sold wood from their property, farm produce—specifically vegetables—and crafted and sold brooms and baskets and cakes. Joseph's father worked as a cooper, which he had learned from his father Asael. Lucy worked as a community doctor, possibly not for money but simply to help the community.

Lucy believed her husband was receiving inspired visions or dreams, which had begun in Vermont as early as 1811. This apparently helped prepare her to accept her son Joseph's later reports. It was now 1816 and Joseph was still 10 years old. One such dream, among seven different ones Joseph's father had, convinced his wife that the local preachers had no special knowledge of heavenly things. (Asael, Joseph Sr.'s father, had held a similar conviction.) The dream itself consisted of a spirit leading Joseph Sr. through a forest of dead trees, which he interpreted as the earth without spiritual guidance. Joseph Sr. then found a box of food but was kept from eating it by beasts, which he and his wife interpreted as ministers of the day.

A second dream has similarities to Lehi's dream in the later published Book of Mormon. The dream has Joseph Sr. being led to a tree bearing white fruit and bringing his family to it. Near the tree was a large building of prideful people pointing at them with scorn. In the dream the spirit told Joseph Sr. that the fruit was the love of God and that the building was Babylon. While detractors would claim the translated account was "influenced" by his father's dream, supporters maintain the same instruction can be given to different men in different generations from the same heavenly source.

The Smith parents were concerned about bringing up their children right, setting examples of honesty, thrift, and sobriety. Certainly their debt-payment sacrifices were a highlight. Believing that hymns were a form of music combined with prayer sung to God, the children were taught to sing hymns on their knees. They also heard their parents pray for their offspring to be protected from sin. The prayers were lengthy, and while at least William, who would later rebel against Joseph's teachings, did not care for the large amount of parental instruction, Lucy claimed she taught her children to walk "in the love of God," and that "never was there a more obedient family."

Meanwhile, in 1817 when Joseph was 11, a new neighbor moved nearby—just one mile away from Belcher, Massachusetts. As their nearest neighbor now, the family of Orin (spelled with one r) and Sarah Rockwell became close friends with the Smiths. Their four-year-old son, Orrin Porter Rockwell (who would generally go by just "Porter") attached himself to young Joseph. They likely fished, played, and performed chores together, with Porter considering Joseph his closest friend the rest of his life.

Despite the hope the Eerie Canal brought, a depression hit. And it was tied to the nation's struggle to recover after the War of 1812. In 1819 when Joseph Jr. was 13, farmers began selling their lands, and many had to just walk away from all they owned. Joseph later writes, "It required the exertions of all that were able to render any assistance for the support of the Family therefore we were deprived of the benefit of an education suffice it to say I was mearly instructed in reading writing and the ground rules of Arithmatic." But they continued reading the Bible and learning from their parents in a home school, struggling through intense poverty and barely surviving.

Lucy and Joseph Sr. were both socially conscious and obviously felt the pains of ostracism from the more well-to-do, especially for their children. Nevertheless, they were looked upon as reliable hard workers. Their reputation was that none could outwork them, and they consistently showed their Christian charity. A neighbor, Orlando Saunders, claims, "They were the best family in the neighborhood in case of sickness; one was at my house nearly all the time when my father died." He also considered them honest.

Dr. John Stofford says of Joseph Jr. that he was "a real clever, jovial boy. . . . The old woman [Lucy] had a great deal of faith that their children were going to do something great." He also says that Joseph's father learned a great deal from the home schooling that the children had, joining in with them, apparently after his workday.

Lucy states that young Joseph was not as fond of reading as the other children, and less inclined to read the Bible, although he would think deeply about things and meditate.

Joseph himself states that between ages 12 and 15 he became "seriously imprest with regard to the all important concerns for the welfare of my immortal soul." This led him to begin reading the Bible. He became concerned about the situation of the world with its "wickedness" and "contentions," along with his own sins and mistakes. This was written in a ledger book on six pages during the second half of 1832, his first account of his own religious experiences.

Then, at age 14, he lifted his concerns to a different plane—he became simultaneously intrigued and bothered by the contentions among the local religions. He writes that there was "an unusual excitement" on the subject of religion. He adds that priest and convert alike contended with one another. Lucy meanwhile in Vermont had attempted to persuade her husband to join the Methodists, but Joseph Sr.'s father and brother had dissuaded him from it. Now, in Palmyra, the contention caused her to doubt all the churches, but she hoped to find the true, authoritative church. She decided to join the Presbyterians, with three of her children joining her—Hyrum, Samuel, and Sophronia. One issue may have been convenience—it was the only church with a meetinghouse.

But the contentions continued to bother Joseph. *The Palmyra Register* reports revivals spreading throughout the state in 1820. The Philadelphia General Assembly of 1820 for the Presbyterian Church states that six extremely active areas for revivals were in New York alone, of the eight areas in the United States they cited.

Some of these revivals were all-day events, attended by a couple hundred or even several thousand participants coming from miles away, bringing their families and goods in wagons. They cooked out in the open and often stayed several days. They socialized and listened to music. Markets were set up and produce would be sold, and even alcohol, which may have had some effect on the revivals. Traveling ministers would take turns preaching, sometimes three at a time in different parts of the camp. Traveling ministers were in fact the norm of the day even when there were no revivals, and they would preach in cabins and schools and under the stars.

Joseph may have attended out of curiosity, out of respect for his mother, or out of the desire to sell pies, as the family did attempt selling wherever there were crowds gathered, as did some other families imbued with an entrepreneurial nature. Joseph may have told an acquaintance later that he wanted to feel what his mother, his sister, and his brother experienced at a revival meeting, and even shout like some others did, but that he could not. An 1851 writer of local history in the nearby town of Phelps says that Joseph caught "a spark" of Methodism in a camp meeting and was an "exhorter" in the evening meetings, which may or may not be true. This would have taken place "down in the woods" on the road to Vienna (later called Phelps). Nevertheless, Joseph felt he could not find any church as set forth in the New Testament.

When he was 14, in the spring of 1820, he had the following feelings and this resulting experience, which would astonish the world:

"In the midst of this war of words, and tumult of opinions, I often said to myself, what is to be done? Who of all these parties are right . . . . I was one day reading the Epistle of James, first chapter and fifth verse which reads, 'If any of you lack wisdom, let him ask of God. . . .' Never did any passage of scripture come with more power to the heart of man than this did at this time to mine. It seemed to enter with great force into every feeling of my heart. I reflected on it again and again . . . . At length I came to the conclusion that I must either remain in darkness and confusion or else I must do as James directs . . . . I retired to the woods to make the attempt. It was on the morning of a beautiful, clear day, early in the spring . . . . It was the first time in my life that I had made such an attempt, for amidst all my anxieties I had never as yet made the attempt to pray vocally.

"After I had retired to the place where I had previously designed to go, having looked around me, and finding myself alone, I kneeled down and began to offer up the desires of my heart to God. I had scarcely done so, when immediately I was seized upon by some power which entirely overcame me, and had such astonishing influence over me as to bind my tongue so that I could not speak. Thick darkness gathered around me, and it seemed to me for a time as if I were doomed to sudden destruction.

"But, exerting all my powers to call upon God to deliver me out of the power of this enemy which had seized upon me, and at the very moment when I was ready to sink into despair and abandon myself to destruction—not to an imaginary ruin, but to the power of some actual being from the unseen world, who had such marvelous power as I had never before felt in any being—just at this moment of great alarm, I saw a pillar of light exactly over my head, above the brightness of the sun, which descended gradually until it fell upon me.

"It no sooner appeared than I found myself delivered from the enemy which held me bound. When the light rested upon me I saw two personages, whose brightness and glory defy all description, standing above me in the air. One of them spake unto me calling me by name and said—pointing to the other—"This is my beloved Son, hear him."

C H A P T E R 3

J OSEPH continues his narrative . . .

"My object in going to inquire of the Lord was to know which of all the sects was right, that I might know which to join. No sooner, therefore, did I get possession of myself, so as to be able to speak, than I asked the personages who stood above me in the light, which of all the sects was right (for at this time it had never entered into my heart that all were wrong)—and which I should join.

"I was answered that I must join none of them, for they were all wrong, and the personage who addressed me said that all their creeds were an abomination in his sight; that those professors were all corrupt, that 'they draw near to me with their lips but their hearts are far from me; they teach for doctrines the commandments of me: having a form of godliness but they deny the power thereof.'"

". . . And many other things did he say unto me, which I cannot write at this time. When I came to myself again, I found myself lying on my back, looking up into heaven. When the light had departed, I had no strength; but soon recovering in some degree, I went home. And as I leaned up to the fireplace, mother inquired what the matter was. I replied, 'Never mind, all is well—I am well enough off. . . .'

"It seems as though the adversary was aware, at a very early period of my life, that I was destined to prove a disturber and an annoyer of his kingdom; else why should the powers of darkness combine against me? Why the opposition and persecution that arose against me, almost in my infancy?

"Some few days after I had this vision, I happened to be in company with one of the Methodist preachers, who was very active in the before mentioned religious excitement; and, conversing with him on the subject of religion, I took occasion to give him an account of the vision which I had had. I was greatly surprised at his behavior; he treated my communication not only lightly, but with great contempt, saying it was all of the devil, that there were no such things as visions or revelations in these days; that all such things had ceased with the Apostles, and that there should never be any more of them.

"I soon found, however, that my telling the story had excited a great deal of prejudice against me among professors of religion, and was the cause of great persecution, which continued to increase; and though I was an obscure boy, only between fourteen and fifteen years of age, and my circumstances in life such as to make a boy of no consequence in the world, yet men of high standing would take notice sufficient to excite the public mind against me, and create a bitter persecution; and this was common along all the sects—all united to persecute me.

"It caused me serious reflection then, and often has since, how very strange it was that an obscure boy, of a little over fourteen years of age, and one, too, who was doomed to the necessity of obtaining a scanty maintenance by his daily labor, should be thought a character of sufficient importance to attract the attention of the great ones of the most popular sects of the day, and in a manner to create in them a spirit of the most bitter persecution and reviling. But strange or not, so it was, and it was often the cause of great sorrow to myself.

"However, it was nevertheless a fact that I had beheld a vision. I have thought since, that I felt much like Paul, when he made his defense before King Agrippa, and related the account of the vision he had when he saw a light, and heard a voice; but still there were but few who believed him; some said he was dishonest, others said he was mad; and he was ridiculed and reviled. But all this did not destroy the reality of his vision. He had seen a vision, he knew he had, and all the persecution under heaven could not make it otherwise; and though they should persecute him unto death, yet he knew, and would know to his latest breath, that he had both seen a light and heard a voice speaking unto him, and all the world could not make him think or believe otherwise.

"So it was with me. I had actually seen a light, and in the midst of that light I saw two personages, and they did in reality speak to me; and though I was hated and persecuted for saying that I had seen a vision, yet it was true . . . . I was led to say in my heart: Why persecute me for telling the truth? I have actually seen a vision; and who am I that I can withstand God, or why does the world think to make me deny what I have actually seen? For I had seen a vision; I knew it, and I knew that God knew it, and I could not deny it, neither dared I do it; at least I knew that by so doing I would offend God, and come under condemnation.

"I had now got my mind satisfied so far as the sectarian world was concerned—that it was not my duty to join with any of them, but to continue as I was until further directed."

Over the years Joseph would write about his experience on six different occasions. All six accounts reflect consistency on the major facts. One truly interesting additional fact in one of his accounts is that he saw many angels in addition to the Father and the Son.

Because of the ridicule and reviling that resulted from opening up to one minister, Joseph was obviously deeply pained and embarrassed and therefore would tell very few in the future of his account—his family and only the closest of friends—for many years, and even then reveal only partial details in some of the accounts. Years later, in 1832, he would write his first account; then in 1838 he would write the fullest account, which would be published in 1842 and presented to the public, being the opening pages to his own history. This history he decided to publish after numerous critics had reported distortions about him. It was only then that missionaries began including the First Vision as part of their presentation. Another reason for not focusing on the First Vision may be that The Book of Mormon was his focal point as the key to people's conversion, and he wished to present that as his only tool, but with time and reflection and, as Latter-day Saints believe, inspiration, it came to be included in the cornerstone of people's conversions.

After Joseph made public his claims, many in the community would not associate with his family, and later the noted anti-Mormons of the day would claim the family members were of such low class that no one would associate with them. Joseph's brother William states, "We never knew we were bad folks until Joseph told his vision. We were considered respectable till then, but at once people began to circulate falsehoods and stories in wonderful ways." Thomas H. Taylor, a local attorney, states, "There was something about him they could not understand; some way he knew more than they did, and it made them mad . . . . I can take you to a great many old settlers here who will substantiate what I say." He also states, "I knew them very well; they were very nice men, too." The man who set the type for The Book of Mormon, John H. Gilbert, reports succinctly, "Oh, I don't think the Smiths were as bad as people let on for."

But why the opposition? Latter-day Saints believe that with the Restored Gospel of Jesus Christ on the earth, there is an adversarial being, literally Satan, the devil, who opposes the work of the Restored Gospel—which all began with the First Vision.

So why was Joseph, of all people, chosen to be heaven's mouthpiece? Some have rejected his message because the restoration did not occur through established ministers of religion. As Eliza R. Snow, who was very close to him, analyzes, "He was a mere boy, honest, full of integrity, unacquainted with the trickery, cunning and sophistry employed by politicians and religious hypocrites to accomplish their ends. Like Moses of old, he felt incompetent and unqualified for the task—to stand forth as a religious reformer in a position the most unpopular."

Perhaps a deeper analysis comes from Brigham Young, who states Joseph "was foreordained in eternity to preside over this last dispensation," specifically, "long before the foundations of the earth were laid."

Joseph's family embraced his report of the First Vision, but his mother, a sister, and at least one brother continued active in the Presbyterian faith another seven years, until about October 1827. (Presbyterian records indicate their memberships were suspended on March 2, 1830, after 18 months of inactivity.)

Immediately after his experience in the Sacred Grove behind the Smith home, Joseph told his mother, "I have learned for myself that Presbyterianism is not true," but added that he would not try to prevent her from going to any church she wished to attend.

No more visions were forthcoming for several years. Meanwhile, Joseph grew and became an even harder worker and, along with his brothers, sisters, and parents, barely stayed above the line of starvation, struggling to make a living. But now he faced the ridicule, disdain, and open hostility of neighbors scoffing at his story—all because the minister in whom he had confided broadcasted the news.

His mother adds in her *History of Joseph Smith by His Mother: the Unabridged, Original Version* that Joseph was once crossing his yard, coming home from an errand, when a gunshot fired past him. His family ran outside and searched, but the ambusher was gone, leaving (as they found the next morning when they could see more clearly) only an imprint in the mud where he had lain under a wagon. But the missed shots had killed their cow, hitting it in the head and neck.

Over the next two years, the family built a new house in the winters and farmed in the summers. According to Lucy, the house was first framed and, finally, at the end of two years, they had all the necessary materials to build it.

Joseph writes of his teenage years that he was not involved in any church, "having been forbidden [by Deity] to join any of the religious sects of the day," adding that he was persecuted by those who should have been his friends. Thus, "I was left to all kinds of temptation; and mingling with all kinds of society, I frequently fell into many foolish errors, and displayed the weakness of youth, and the foibles of human nature." He clarifies that he was not guilty of "any great or malignant sins. . . . But I was guilty of levity, and sometimes associated with jovial company, etc." His enemies never claimed he was involved in vandalism, sexual promiscuity, or dishonesty, but his friends claimed he drank "socially, like everybody else," as reported by Ezra Pierce.

He also apparently fought to some extent, perhaps defending himself against persecution, and later he states it gave him a sense of shame, especially since his parents had taught him that fighting and quarreling were "beastly" sins. Later, when he was almost 29, he would write that his vices were of a "light" and "vain" mind, wherein he exhibited "a foolish and trifling conversation." This, he states, was the worst that his accusers could substantiate against his moral character. He was feeling weighed down by his imperfections, believing his behavior was "not consistent with that character which ought to be maintained by one who was called of God as I had been." Thus, on one Sunday night in 1823, when he was 17—in fact, the night of September 21, 1822—he felt a tremendous concern about how he stood in the eyes of God, and prayed from his bedside. In supplicating the Lord, he felt confident he would receive an answer, and soon a light appeared in his room, which increased until it was "brighter than the noonday sun."

He declares, "A personage appeared at my bedside, standing in the air, for his feet did not touch the floor. He had on a loose robe of most exquisite whiteness. . . . His whole person was glorious beyond description.

"I was afraid; but the fear soon left me. He called me by name, and said unto me that he was a messenger sent from the presence of God to me and that his name was Moroni; that God had a work for me to do; and that my name should be had for good and evil among all nations, kindreds, and tongues . . . . He said there was a book deposited, written upon gold plates, giving an account of the former inhabitants of this continent, and the sources from whence they sprang. He also said that the fullness of the everlasting Gospel was contained in it, as delivered by the Savior to the ancient inhabitants; also that there were two stones in silver bows—and these stones, fastened to a breastplate, constituted what is called the Urim and Thummim—deposited with the plates; and the possession and use of these stones were what constituted 'Seers' in ancient or former times; and that God had prepared them for the purpose of translating the book."

Joseph further states that Moroni instructed him to show the plates, breastplate, and the Urim and Thummim to no one without permission, or he would be destroyed. Joseph said he could see in vision the location of the plates, as Moroni further spoke. The light then gathered around the angel until the room was dark, except for the pillar of light that rose skyward. Moroni ascended within the pillar until he was gone. Joseph, lying there and thinking about what he had just seen, saw the previous conduit of light grow bright again. Moroni reappeared and stated the same things as before. This time, however, he added that the sword, famine, and pestilence would be coming in Joseph's generation. Moroni disappeared as before, then came a third time and repeated again what he had said, this time adding that Satan would try to tempt him to obtain the plates for money, due to his family's extreme poverty.

Joseph writes that the next morning he arose exhausted, and went to work in the fields but was too exhausted to be of any use. Joseph's father told him to return home to be doctored, while Lucy recalls that Alvin, his oldest brother, asked him to keep up with the work.

While climbing the fence to return home, Joseph collapsed to the ground and lay unconscious.

C H A P T E R

4

THE next thing Joseph realized, he was being called by Moroni, who stood in the air again surrounded by light—even though they were in the sunlight. Moroni repeated the same messages as before and this time also said he should tell it all to his father. Lucy adds that Moroni asked him why he had not told his father already—Joseph's response was that he feared his father would not believe him. Moroni then stated, "He will believe every word you say to him." That soon proved to be true. Joseph went directly to his father and told him. Joseph's father heard him out, believed his son, and told him it was from God. He also told Joseph to do everything as he was commanded.

Joseph then went directly to the Hill Cumorah—so named, he would learn later, from the plates he would translate. It was a hill almost four miles south of Palmyra on the road from Palmyra to Canandaigua, just south of Manchester. The hill was on the east side of the road. He climbed the high hill and, nearly at the top, found the place he had been shown in vision. There he saw a large stone partly buried. After brushing the dirt from the edges with his hands, he lifted the stone with a lever. There, lying in a box cemented together with a sort of plaster, he saw the plates, the breastplate, and the Urim and Thummim. When he tried to remove the objects, he had another appearance of—or heard the voice of—Moroni, who told him not to take them yet. He would have to wait till the next year at the very same time to try again. He was also told why he could not take the plates—because his heart was not right yet, as he sought to use them "to obtain riches." Later, his friend Oliver Cowdery would state that the plates could "relieve his family from want" and that he was further tempted to use the riches to "raise him above a level with the common earthly fortunes of his fellow man"—in other words—the plates could make him rich.

A year later Joseph tried obtaining them again—he returned to the hill and went right to the spot. But Moroni was concerned about Joseph's attitude. Lucy indicates that it was at this time that Joseph hoped to find something within the box to profit from. She further states that Joseph thought he had kept the commandments sufficiently to receive the plates and was fully expecting them at the end of the first year. Instead, Joseph was surprised that Moroni was not pleased with him, says Lucy, and caused the plates to disappear. Joseph was told to come back a year later.

He did so, and was given instructions by Moroni once again. As before, he was told he was still not ready to receive them. Joseph finally knew, obviously, he would have to cleanse his heart completely of any iota of hope of using the plates for financial gain. Finally, the fourth year, on September 22, 1827, he was told by Moroni he was ready to take the plates.

Lucy reflects on the four-year period and its effect on her family: On the first night Joseph had seen the plates, he told his family about them and requested them to not tell anyone else. They grew closer. Lucy says the result was that 'the sweetest union and happiness pervaded our house, and tranquility reigned in our midst." She says the family would sit and listen to Joseph in the evenings, expecting to soon receive additional important information.

The Smiths' trusted neighbors, the Rockwells, also were enraptured by young Joseph's stories of the angel Moroni. In both families' homes Joseph would tell them of seeing the gold plates. According to Elizabeth Roundy, to whom Porter later related his childhood experience, he "begged his mother to allow him to sit up and keep the pine torch burning, their only source of light in the evening."

Although eight years younger, it was during this several-year period in which the boys grew up together that Porter and Joseph developed a lifelong friendship—one of undeviating loyalty to one another and one that would serve Joseph well in later years. Their camaraderie also increased when Porter broke his leg at age 10, in 1823. A Palmyra doctor tried straightening it but managed to leave Porter with one leg shorter than the other, giving both boys a tell-tale limp that would last a lifetime, and which probably gave their neighbors a chuckle or two—seeing the two lads often coming into town together walking the same odd way.

Meanwhile, each winter during this period the family worked on their house. Alvin was in charge of construction, selflessly wanting a place for his parents to feel settled. But only two months after Joseph's first visit to the Hill Cumorah, Alvin became severely ill. With their own doctor away, another, named Greenwood, prescribed for him, giving him calomel. Alvin at first turned it down, but finally gave in. He soon realized the substance was stuck in his stomach. He knew he would shortly die. He called in each member of his family to say goodbye, and asked the next two oldest, Hyrum and Sophronia, to make certain the house was finished for their parents and to take care of them in their old age. He called Joseph in alone and requested him to follow through as commanded by Moroni and make certain he obtained the buried plates. Four days later he was dead. The autopsy showed the calomel was stuck in his upper bowel, surrounded by gangrene.

The hardship on the family could not be measured. One neighbor stated that Alvin was the main worker of the family farm. Lucy adds that because of his innate goodness that the entire neighborhood mourned his death. Joseph states that Alvin was the "noblest" of the family and that he had "no guile." He was also an example of justice to Joseph. Once he and Joseph had attended a fighting match between two Irishmen. One was winning and decided to gouge out the eyes of the other, until Alvin jumped in, "took him by his collar and breeches and threw him over the ring." Young Joseph would later say, "I remember well the pangs of sorrow that swelled my youthful bosom and almost burst my tender heart when he died."

According to brother William, a Reverend Benjamin Stockton (presiding elder of the Presbyterian church to which Lucy belonged) indicated that because Alvin would not attend church he was going to hell. This did not sit particularly well with Joseph Sr., who was already antagonistic toward religious organizations. And then another public obstacle came their way.

Rumormongers claimed Alvin's buried body had been mutilated. Gossip spread like a rainstorm and it was the talk of the town. To find out if this was true, Joseph Sr. and a group of friends realized the grizzly necessity of digging up the grave and inspecting the corpse, now 10 months old—which they did—and found the rumors false. To set the record straight, they advertised in the *Wayne Sentinel* for two weeks, beginning with that day—September 25, 1824—stating that no one had touched the body and asking the rumors to cease.

The family continued to receive harassment, however, which would even step up in intensity . . .

The Eerie Canal was being completed and was the most important economic event in the growing, young United States for development westward. The middle part had been completed first—actually as early as 1820—and the eastern part was finished in 1823. The final section, the western third, was completed in 1825, whereupon the governor, DeWitt Clinton, just reelected, celebrated his seven years of work by taking a barrel of water from Lake Erie to the Atlantic, where it was dumped on November 4, 1825, after a nine-day journey of 363 miles.

Meanwhile, Palmyra had mushroomed from a few cabins and a couple stores to a regular little town of brick homes, a hotel and a tavern, plus 10 gristmills, 17 sawmills, 6 distilleries, and an ironworks. Manchester also had a wool mill dating back to 1813, but which now could produce finer wool for finer clothes. By late 1825, after the canal had been opened a short time,

Palmyra boasted of having dry good stores, a dancing school, and two millinery shops. Right along the canal is where commerce boomed and farmers brought their produce for shipment. A bugle would announce the arrival of a barge, which could carry up to 75 tons, far superior and faster than here-to-fore used wagons. Thus, shipping costs were reduced to a fraction and the area's economy boomed. It was much easier now for people to move west and develop the country as well, with a way to sell their goods all the way back on the east coast.

The Smiths, meanwhile, were a poor and struggling family and not part of Palmyra's developing society. They were, in fact, struggling to keep their newly built house. It had been finished in 1823 when Joseph was 18. In 1825 they were putting the finishing touches on it with a hired carpenter named Stoddard. Lucy states they were just months away from their last payment on the farm when Stoddard suddenly offered them $1,500 for the house. Lucy and Joseph Sr. refused to sell. So Stoddard decided to outsmart them. He and two friends went to the Smiths' sales agent a few miles south in Canandaigua and lied, saying Joseph Sr. and Joseph Jr. had deserted the family and that Hyrum was destroying the farm—ruining the land by chopping down the maple trees. The agent believed them and gave Stoddard the deed to the property upon receipt of the last month's payment.

Then Stoddard turned around and told the Smiths they needed to pay him $1,000 for the deed. With no options but to comply or lose the farm altogether, and being practically broke, still saving money to make the final payment some months away, they were forced to look for a new landlord. They found a Quaker gentleman named Lemuel Durfee who bought the farm for $1,135 from the con artist Stoddard. He showed sympathy, allowing the Smiths to lease the farm from him, which they did for another three years, until December 30, 1828. Then they decided to move to a larger house just south of them and across the road. Lucy was especially attached to the first house because of Alvin's work on it, he wanting to settle his parents there, so she viewed losing the house a tragedy.

Ever since Joseph's report to the one minister about his First Vision, the entire family had become the target of harassment. And enemies would find other angles on which to attack him . . .

*Richard Lloyd Dewey* | JOSEPH SMITH: A BIOGRAPHY

C H A 5 T E R

W

HEN Joseph was 20 he was approached by a wealthy farmer in South Bainbridge, New York, Josiah Stowell, to find a lost silver mine in the Susquehanna Valley. Stowell had already paid to have some excavation activities take place at the mine, based upon a document that described the mine and its location, and which he believed had been discovered and explored by Spaniards. He heard Joseph possessed a certain talent for finding ancient treasure, so he made him an offer. Joseph at first refused to go, but finally acquiesced when Stowell offered him high wages, which turned out to be not much at all—$14 per month—but Joseph thought he would be paid more when offered the job. He accepted the offer.

Joseph, his father, and several neighbors began the journey with Stowell to the site of the buried treasure. Noteworthy is the fact that numerous wealthy people were swept up by the excitement of buried treasure and of finding it, and many in the country were engaged in treasure hunting.

Stowell's group arrived in Pennsylvania just below the state line of New York, where he boarded with the Hale family of Harmony, Pennsylvania, near the "silver" mine. The Hales were unusually charitable people, opening their home to traveling ministers and leaving food on the doorsteps of needy families, generally after hunting trips by the father, Isaac Hale, who would salt the meat and give much of it away.

The Hales had nine children. Their seventh youngest was Emma. Born July 10, 1804, she taught school, had dark hair, and charmed people with her large hazel eyes. Joseph was smitten by her.

He was a handsome and intriguing lad—tall and muscular, with a "large full chest," broad shoulders, blue eyes, and auburn hair. He had a steady, serene penetrating gaze, according to Parley P. Pratt, while Governor Thomas Ford would say he was "uncommonly well muscled." He had long legs, was described as quite handsome, and had a voice that was "low and soft" but could project well to large groups of people. While common belief is that he stood six feet tall (the standard even-number expression for tall people of the day), and which was reported by one of his uncles, he apparently grew to between 6'2" and 6'3", according to those who saw him in adulthood. By 1842, at age 36, he would weigh 212 pounds, but when he courted Emma at age 19 he was likely well under 200 and rather lean. He also had an attractive smile, and he smiled often, according to a later writer for the *St. Louis Weekly Gazette*. David Whitmer says, "He was a very humble and meek man," and Eliza R. Snow says, "He was humble as a little child." His expression was "mild and almost childlike," according to Emmeline B. Wells. He bore "an unconscious smile," reports Parley P. Pratt, who would later play a significant role in his life, and was "affable, beaming with intelligence and benevolence, mingled with a look of interest." He "had a very pleasant disposition and always seemed to be happy," said Elias Cox, and Joseph described himself as a "playful and cheerful" person. He was a practical joker with his "most familiar friends." Later, for example, his friend Benjamin Johnson held nine silver dollars in his hand. Joseph hit his friend's hand from underneath and the coins scattered everywhere. The two men then playfully wrestled. He also could "crack a joke," said Jacob Jones. He was considerate of others and, according to the future first governor of California, Peter Burnett, he "would not oppose you abruptly, but had due deference to your feelings." According to John Hess, "there was something heavenly and angelic in his looks that I never witnessed in the countenance of any other person." He may have looked young for his age at 19 when he met and showed interest in Emma, which perhaps may have been somewhat embarrassing for her, because when he was in his thirties he was described as "young looking" for his age." Yet it may have bothered Emma even more that he was a year and a half younger than she. But the interest he took in other people, his warmth, charm, cheery disposition, and smile, no doubt melted her, and soon they were courting.

Her parents "bitterly opposed" their relationship, Emma would write, mainly because of his reported First Vision. Emma's father Isaac also became opposed to the digging project, losing faith in it, and thereafter looked down on the boarders. Isaac further claimed Joseph was not educated and was careless and also rude to his father, although Smith family records never claimed that. Joseph's wealthy boss, Mr. Stowell, however, always looked upon young Joseph with respect, and would until his dying day, even later believing in Joseph's church and seeing him as a prophet. (This despite the fact they never found any treasure.) Stowell had hoped Joseph possessed a gift for "divining"—using a rod or some other means to search for treasure by holding it over the ground until it would "dip" where the treasure was supposed to be buried. But Joseph's method was different. Isaac claims Joseph would look into a stone in a hat, covering his face with it, and he further recalls that Joseph stated a large treasure was near them, but as they became closer to it he could no longer see it. Lucy and Joseph report that it was Joseph himself who told Stowell to give up. In mid-November, perhaps November 17, 1825, after a month of searching, they all did give up. But repercussions came from this event that would haunt the Smith family for decades.

According to both young Joseph and his mother Lucy, his enemies would declare that Joseph was a "money digger" and could not be trusted. Certain people looked down on diviners of treasure or water, despite the fact water divining was a respected and standard method for finding wells by America's early settlers, and some people reportedly had a remarkable ability to find wells.

Joseph's father and neighbors who were part of the project returned home, but Joseph stayed on Stowell's farm. He worked for Stowell as a farmhand and attended Emma's school when he could to study reading, writing, and more about Emma. And despite Isaac's opposition, he courted her, riding to nearby Harmony as often as he could. Fortunately for him, Joseph's own family did not need his services on their farm as much now because they had a good crop and produce prices had increased. Furthermore, the Eerie Canal was being built, and the local economy, including the population, was booming. So Joseph was free to stay and work and primarily court Emma.

With all the ridicule and harassment over the reported First Vision he had received in Palmyra, he had never made an avowed enemy in his life. Until now. Nor had he ever appeared in court, nor had most young men his age. But he was about to—because of a self-declared enemy he soon encountered.

A member of his boss's family named Peter Bridgeman decided to make life hard for Joseph. He claimed Joseph was an imposter and a disorderly person. Joseph went to trial in Bainbridge, New York, on March 20, 1826, at age 20, and was tried by Albert Neely, a justice of the peace. Joseph was charged with a misdemeanor as a "glass looker" and possibly only had to pay the judge's trial costs of $2.68. In at least three of the several trial reports still in existence, Joseph actually testified against himself.

Because Peter Bridgeman had pushed the trial forward, the justice of the peace likely saw the events as rather harmless, or something somewhat on the absurd side to pursue in court, since so many respectable citizens utilized the services of diviners, as stated, for both treasure hunting and water searching. Perhaps the judge saw the irony of Joseph being one of the few, if not the only, to ever have any charges brought against him for it. Hence the misdemeanor charge. Furthermore, Joseph apparently had given up his divining activities before the trial anyway, so it is likely that Bridgeman was out to get him for some other reason.

Five years after the event, in 1831, A. W. Benton published
a religious periodical (typically anti-Joseph) that stated "the
public had him arrested (in truth it was one person) as a
disorderly person, tried and condemned before a court of
justice (absurdly strong language, since he was immediately
released with no reported fine or sentence), but because he
was a minor, because they hoped he might reform, he was
designedly allowed to escape." He was simply released, and
even "honorably acquitted," according to Oliver Cowdery, who
would become Joseph's scribe and who, just nine years after the
trial, would state it was an "officious person" who had charged
Joseph as disorderly, and that no action was required.

The possibility exists that Joseph did see other treasure,
as well, but likewise could not obtain it. In 1878 Brigham Young
wrote that Porter Rockwell was "an eyewitness to some powers
of removing the treasures of the earth. He was with certain
parties who lived nearby the site where the plates that contain
the records of The Book of Mormon were found. There were a
great many treasures hid up by the Nephites. Porter was with
them one night where there were treasures, and they could
find them easy enough, but could not obtain them."

Similarly, Martin Harris, another early convert, later reported
he accompanied two acquaintances, all taking "some tools to go
to the hill and hunt for some more boxes, or gold or something,
and indeed we found a stone box. We got excited about it and
dug quite carefully around it, and we were ready to take it up,
but behold, by some unseen power, it slipped back into the
hill."

Many influential people and men of wealth, besides Josiah
Stowell, were "money diggers" and rodsmen. It was practiced
among many respected Christians and community leaders.
Stowell had actually been taught "in the spirit of orthodox
Puritanism" and was an active Presbyterian with the reputation
of "a very industrious, exemplary man."

Nevertheless, enemies to Joseph, years later, would try to
emphasize Joseph's money digging in order to discredit his later
work in translating The Book of Mormon, which would come from

the gold plates. Because he also used a seer stone in translating most of that book and in presenting a number of his revelations later used in the *Doctrine and Covenants*, enemies for years tried to tie him into the myths that unfortunately surrounded the activities of many rodsmen and money diggers. (See Appendix A for more on "Money diggers and rodsmen.")

Joseph likely was subject to superstitions as well as misunderstood Bible doctrines that he held until the restored gospel was given to him several years later.

While Latter-day Saints believe the adversary can counterfeit true spiritual gifts, there is some evidence that there were indeed "diving rods" that were "divine." Oliver Cowdery possessed a "rod of nature" that Joseph stated in the *Book of Commandments* was "the work of God."

After his court appearance, Joseph continued working and living on Josiah Stowell's farm while courting Emma for several months. At her home her brother Alva, especially, and other brothers pestered Joseph constantly, perhaps about the First Vision or glass looking or both. During a fishing excursion, the brothers so hassled Joseph that he tossed away his coat and challenged them to a fight, an example of his quick temper when harassed.

The next thing Joseph did was ask his parents for permission to marry Emma, which they readily granted. In November 1826 he left the farm of Josiah Stowell to work for the old family friend Joseph Knight Sr. Thereupon he saved as much money as possible for the wedding. Knight lent him a horse whenever he needed it, and another local, Martin Harris, who had hired Joseph as a boy, now gave Joseph a fine gift—a new suit.

Much better dressed now, he approached Emma's father and asked for her hand in marriage . . .

C H A P T E R 6

EMMA's father refused. The reason—Emma's father and mother did not know him well enough and did not approve of his business. Joseph believed, however, it was because of his own unusual religious experience, while Isaac was a dyed-in-the-wool Methodist.

Thus, a plan was formulated. Joseph and Emma decided to elope. One Sunday morning on January 18, 1827, the 21-year-old Joseph took off riding with the 22-year-old Emma while Isaac was at church. Neighbors saw them tearing past on an old horse, Emma riding behind Joseph, just like the storybooks. They galloped to South Bainbridge and were married by Squire Tarbill at his home.

After the ceremony they left for Joseph's homestead in Manchester. There, Joseph's parents welcomed her as their own daughter, and they lived with them while young Joseph farmed through the next season.

Some months later, Emma decided she wanted her belongings, since she had taken off with Joseph to Manchester with only the clothes on her back. She wrote her father, asking for her other clothes and property, and he complied.

In August 1827 Joseph rode to get her belongings, and the Hales greeted him more kindly. Isaac claims Joseph at that time said he would give up "glass looking" (which he had sometime before anyway), would move back with Emma to Harmony, and would work there, with Isaac helping him find new employment. Alva also shook hands with Joseph, agreeing to bury their differences, and Alva's change of heart was apparently sincere—he later committed to helping Joseph move from Palmyra to Harmony, a daunting, several-day task on rough roads.

Joseph then returned to Manchester. On the 21st of the next month, September 1827, according to Lucy, he went to the shopping district in behalf of his father and did not return. Anxious, his parents waited and wondered. Finally Joseph arrived and collapsed into a chair. Joseph Sr. questioned why he was late and what was wrong. Joseph responded that the angel Moroni had appeared to him again as he had passed the Hill Cumorah. It was, as Joseph explained, a bittersweet experience—Moroni had confronted him about neglecting the work of God, but the sweet message was that Joseph could now retrieve the gold plates! His heart was ready. He no longer looked upon the gold plates as treasure, but as a gift from God to assist mankind.

However, the story is a bit different from Joseph Knight Sr., who had been staying at his parents' as a guest.

Knight reports that Joseph said he still did not know if he would get the plates. In this more dramatic version, Joseph told him the angel said if he would do what was right, he would obtain the plates the following September 22nd, "and if not he never would have them." He was speaking of the next day! Joseph apparently felt the pressure, wondering if he was worthy enough to obtain the plates this time, knowing it was now or never. That night they all went to bed, and in the morning when Knight awakened, his horse and wagon were gone. Then Joseph came into the house for breakfast but over the meal did not say anything. After breakfast Joseph called Knight into the other room "and he set his foot on the bed and leaned his head and said, 'Well, I am disappointed.'"

Knight writes that he replied to Joseph, "Well, I am sorry."

"Well," said Joseph (writes Knight), "I am greatly disappointed; it is ten times better than what I expected."

"Then he went on to tell the length and width and thickness of the plates, and said he [thought] they appear to be gold. But he seemed to think more of the glasses or the Urim and Thummim then he did of the plates, for, says he, 'I can see anything; they are marvelous.'"

Joseph adds that he was to have the plates, etc., until the messenger came for them again.

In Lucy's *original* biography of her son, she states Joseph handed her the Urim and Thummim, saying "See here, I have got a key." She says it consisted of two smooth diamonds of three corners, both placed in glass with the glass set in silver bows, like old-fashioned glasses. Later she says Joseph showed her the breastplate covered in a muslin handkerchief. Because of its thinness, the metal could be felt and seen. She described it as concave, with metal straps for fastening the object to one's hips and shoulders, and that it was quite large, obviously made for a large-statured man.

When Joseph brought home the plates, his father evidently asked him, "What, Joseph, can we not see them?" Joseph responded, "No. I was disobedient the first time, but I intend to be faithful this time, for I was forbidden to show them until they are translated." Through the cloth his family did handle them, and his brother William said they were thin metal sheets that could be turned like book pages. He also said they were an alloy of gold and copper, much heavier than stone. He figured they weighted about 60 pounds.

Joseph Sr. did tell their family friend Martin Harris about the plates, ordering him to tell no one. Nevertheless it was likely that through Martin—from Martin telling his wife—that the community at large learned of the plates, and rumors spread like wildfire. While some neighbors of course looked upon the plates as a hoax, others believed their existence because of the honesty of the Smith family. Among those was longtime Palmyra resident Thomas H. Taylor, who said he knew the Smiths very well and figured Joseph did receive plates out of the hill. "Why not he find something as well as anybody else. Right over here, in Illinois and Ohio, in mounds there, they have

discovered copper plates since." He confessed he never saw
The Book of Mormon after it was published and did not know
anything about it, nor care, but believed Joseph did receive the
plates. He says the Smiths "were good, honest men." Artifacts
made of copper were also discovered in the western region of
New York, as close as nearby Canandaigua.

With the word out, certain neighbors harassed the Smiths
with incessant questions, demanding to see the plates, sneaking
around the property, and even attempting to steal them. Joseph
Knight Sr. says people came to see the plates, but Joseph told
them he could not show them. "But many insisted and offered
money and property to see them. But, for keeping them from
the people, they persecuted and abused them." He says Joseph's
family had to finally hide them.

Once when he brought the plates out of a hiding place into
the house, he was attacked by three men and beaten with
guns. In the attack he dislocated his thumb when he hit the
third attacker.

One neighbor named Alva Beaman actually helped Joseph
hide them once when a mob invaded the Smith home searching
for them.

Martin Harris states that certain money diggers were also
among the harassers.

On one occasion, a glass looker named Sallie Chase directed
a small mob of ten men to search the Smiths' property while she
used a piece of green glass that she employed to see unusual
things. Her brother Willard obtained the services of a conjurer
from 60 miles away—either his sister or another—to learn where
the plates were located. In their search they tore up the Smiths'
property, including the floor of their cooper shop.

Before the translation was complete and the book was
published, word did get out that the plates contained more
than their intrinsic worth—that they actually had been
discovered "through superhuman means," and that it was "an
ancient record, of a religious and divine nature and origin" (as
published in the June 26, 1829, issue of the *Wayne Sentinel*).
Rochester newspapers published similar statements.

Soon it was obvious there was no way for Joseph to translate the plates in peace—unless he and Emma moved. Martin Harris, as much as he had created problems for Joseph by leaking word out about the plates, also became a blessing for him. Perhaps the first time he helped him (other than giving him money for his suit) was when he came up to Joseph in town and presented him with fifty silver dollars, saying he wanted Joseph to use it for the Lord's work. This allowed Joseph to move to a safe place to begin translation. Joseph had worked for Harris at age 10, when his pay was 50 cents a day—a fair wage for the time.

Martin Harris had joined at least five religions and knew the Bible backward and forward. His wife was a Quaker and at one time he had been as well. He sported a distinguished look with side whiskers. He owned 240 acres, grew wheat, and owned a factory for making flannel cloth, as well as other businesses. Civically, he was the overseer of highways, a school commissioner, and was known to be honorable. And slowly he became more and more involved with Joseph.

Joseph also received assistance from young Porter Rockwell. Although his own family was practically destitute, Porter was so convinced of Joseph's account that he worked daily, after farm chores, picking berries and chopping firewood by moonlight, "giving the money to the Prophet to help print The Book of Mormon," he would later say. However, the printing costs would actually be financed elsewhere later. So his modest financial assistance was likely to help Joseph move so he could translate—or, during the translation phase that soon occurred, so that Joseph could devote more time to the plates.

The next assistance Joseph likely received was from Alva Hale, Emma's brother, who, as mentioned, came from Harmony to help them move.

At that point Joseph placed the metal plates in a box, which he then put in the bottom of a 40-gallon barrel of beans, concealed among their household goods in the wagon, in case they were waylaid. Then they set off on their four-day journey, 128 miles south to Harmony, Pennsylvania. The journey was not without hardships—they faced freezing winter cold and Emma was pregnant.

When they arrived at Harmony, Pennsylvania, the Hale family helped them unload. The Hales immediately discovered the small box in the bean barrel but did not believe it held gold plates. Isaac said the box was the size of those used for window glass—which was 10 by 12 inches. He felt its weight but was not allowed to look inside. This angered him, so he ordered the box taken out of the house.

Joseph and Emma took up residence on her family's property. Over two years later her parents transferred this section of the property over to Joseph for $200. Emma also owned six acres somewhere on their property, perhaps next to where they lived. Their first house was her oldest brother Jesse's old house before Jesse had moved to Illinois. It was a three-bedroom frame house on 13 ½ acres on the Susquehanna River, 450 feet from her parents. The upstairs was partitioned off and made into a room with an east-facing window. Here, apparently, Joseph translated many of the plates. Downstairs was a combined living room and kitchen, a fireplace and, around the corner from the third room, a bedroom. In that upstairs room, immediately after settling in, Joseph began translating.

The initial period he translated was from December 1829 until February 1830—two months. Emma was his first scribe, and then her brother Reuben assisted. Joseph's first translation tool was the Urim and Thummim, which he used for the first part of the book; then he used a small, dark-colored stone, which Emma described as not quite black.

Emma wrote hour after hour as Joseph translated, his face inside the hat with the stone in it. Emma details: "No man could have dictated the writing of the manuscript unless he was inspired. . . . When returning after meals, or after interruptions, he would at once begin where he had left off, without either seeing the manuscript or having any portion of it read to him. This was a usual thing for him to do. It would have been improbable that a learned man could do this; and for one so ignorant and unlearned as he was, it was simply impossible."

Joseph testified that he translated the record "by the gift and power of God."

They struggled to survive their first married winter. Joseph Knight Sr. states that Joseph could not translate much because he was poor and had no other means to live but to work, and he had no one to write for him because his wife was busy with housework, even though she did transcribe when she could, which was comparatively seldom. Emma's family, though now civil, were all against Joseph and would not help him.

Thus, he and Emma came up to see Knight and plead his case. But Knight was at that time not in "easy circumstances" and could not commit to help him. Knight's wife and family were also all against him helping Joseph. "But," says Knight, "I let him have some little provisions and some few things out of the store—a pair of shoes and three dollars in money to help him a little."

In January 1830 Knight took Joseph Sr. and Lucy and Joseph's brother Samuel from Manchester to visit Joseph and Emma in Harmony. There, Knight gave them some money to purchase paper for transcribing. Two months later Knight took a sleigh to see them again, and this time brought his wife Polly along. Joseph persuaded her to the validity of his revelations, and she switched from enemy to convert, staying active in the faith till her death.

Martin Harris then helped Joseph again. Earlier, when Joseph and Emma had the plates in Manchester, Martin's wife Dolly demanded to see the plates, but Joseph refused. She was hard of hearing, and whenever someone said something, she could not completely hear, and because of that she became suspicious of them.

After Joseph and Emma moved to Harmony, Martin received a vision he knew was from the Lord, stating that because he had helped Joseph move to Harmony and because of his faith, he was now allowed to see in vision some of the Lord's work that Joseph was about to do. Martin immediately planned to go to Harmony to obtain transcribed characters from the plates. Dolly learned of Martin's plan to get the characters, so she made up her mind to go with him. But he knew her ability to make problems and gave her the slip. He then headed south to Harmony with Hyrum.

When Martin arrived at Harmony, he announced to Joseph that the Lord had shown him a vision to go to New York City with some of the transcription characters. Says Joseph: "So we proceeded to copy some of them, and he took his journey to the eastern cities and to the learned."

Feeling Joseph's work was true and possessing a certain pride wherein he viewed his own reputation on the line, Harris worked hard to get the transcription validated. He may have had a third motive for getting involved with the plates. He went to the home of John A. Clark, a reverend in Palmyra. Clark perceived that Martin was driven by a two-fold mission—to clarify religious doctrine and to make money from the venture. Clark says he visited him "in earnest."

Next Martin went to Luther Bradish, an assemblyman in Albany, the capital of New York State. Bradish had visited Egypt and studied antiquities to some extent.

Martin wished to visit one of the five noted scholars of the day who had some knowledge of Egyptian characters. To do so he needed a "letter of introduction," a popular formality of the times, and to obtain one he went to a man named Mitchell, likely Samuel L. Mitchill, a doctor, professor, congressman, and classicist, in the hopes of gaining his assistance in meeting one of those five scholars, who included one from Columbia, two from Harvard, and two from Yale. Of the five, only one was available at the time—Charles Anthon of Columbia College. Mitchill granted Martin Harris his "letter of introduction," so off to New York City went Martin. Anthon had taught Greek and Latin for eight years, had never married, and was 41. He lived on campus in lower Manhattan. After the two men visited, Martin came back with this report, as published by Joseph in the *History of the Church*:

He showed the characters and the translation to Anthon, who declared the translation correct, "more so than any he had before seen translated from the Egyptian," reports Joseph.

Martin showed him additional characters that had not yet been translated. Anthon said they were "Egyptian, Chaldaic, Assyric, and Arabic," and wrote him a certificate verifying that. But as Harris was walking away, Anthon asked where he had found the characters. Harris told him they were from plates that an angel of God had revealed. Anthon asked to see the certificate back, then tore it in pieces, declaring that there was no such thing now as angels ministering to people. He then offered to translate the plates—and in his supreme arrogance—added that he would only do so if they were brought to him. Martin told him that he could not, that part of the plates were sealed, and that in any case he was forbidden to bring them. Anthon responded, "I cannot read a sealed book."

Martin Harris then went back to Dr. Mitchell, whom Martin says agreed with Anthon's verification.

Anthon may have been overstepping his bounds, as Egyptian translation could not take place until Jean Francois Champollion would discover how to decipher hieroglyphics with the Rosetta stone, publishing his Egyptian grammar in 1836, eight years *after* Harris visited Anthon. And his Egyptian dictionary would not come out for 13 years, in 1841.

Six years after their visit, Anthon wrote the first of two letters describing their visit, but another 13 years after their visit he refuted most of what Martin Harris claimed. People who knew Martin vouched for his honesty and integrity, and Joseph readily accepted his report. Anthon began by denigrating Harris's character, calling him "a plain and apparently simple-hearted farmer." Anthon then *claimed* that Martin said he had been asked to contribute toward publishing the book, and planned to sell his farm, so he had come to New York for a second opinion. However, in 1828 when Martin visited Anthon, Martin had not even been approached by Joseph about the book's printing, and probably had not even considered selling his farm to get the plates published at that time. Anthon also describes the characters in one of his letters, but they do not even come close to the characters that Martin took to Anthon, as Anthon says they came from Greek and Hebrew alphabets and were in a circle, similar to the Mexican calendar and "that the paper contained any thing else but 'Egyptian Hieroglyphics.'" Anthon could not have translated hieroglyphics as early as 1828, as stated, but he should have known what they looked like. Either Anthon's selective memory came into play, or he felt jilted when Martin declined to let him translate, and wished to condemn that which he could not become a part of.

In the second letter 13 years later, Anthon wrote an Episcopalian priest, saying he had told Martin Harris that the characters were a conglomeration imitating various alphabets. Anthon adds—possibly still feeling Martin had slapped him in the face—that "the countryman," Martin, later came back and tried to give him a printed copy of the "golden Bible."

Probably the most accurate statement that Anthon made was when he told Martin Harris that the characters looked "very remarkable, but he could not decide what language they belonged to."

John H. Gilbert stated that Martin returned feeling "Joseph was a little smarter than Professor Anthon."

The Saints felt that Martin Harris took a part in fulfilling a prophecy of thousands of years earlier when Isaiah, the Old Testament prophet, wrote, "And the vision of all is become unto you as the words of a book that is sealed, which men deliver to one that is learned, saying, read this, I pray thee, and he saith, I cannot; for it is sealed."

As for whatever became of the transcript that Martin Harris took to Charles Anthon, it may have ended up in the possession of David Whitmer. In any case, the copy he had was later given to the Reorganized Church of Jesus Christ of Latter Day Saints by his descendants in 1903. Lucy, meanwhile, claimed that Martin Harris's wife Dolly made a copy of it but nothing else has been reported of that purported copy.

Sixteen years after the visit—of Martin to Anthon—a small unofficial Latter-day Saint newspaper in New York City, titled *The Prophet*, published three lines of characters that it claims to be from Martin's transcript. Dated December 21, 1844, it states, "The following is a correct copy of the characters taken from the plates which The Book of Mormon was translated from: the same that was taken to Professor Mitchell, and afterwards to Professor Anthon of New York, by Martin Harris." The source, not given, was likely from a black and gold placard of that same year, which has the same characters and nearly the same description. The publisher of that placard is not known. No definite determination has been made to determine whether or not the characters are Egyptian. The Book of Mormon is, of course, not written in true Egyptian, but a "reformed" Egyptian.

Martin's desire to help Joseph did not go without opposition. Joseph's mother Lucy reports that Dolly came to her and indicated she was opposed to her husband helping Joseph financially.

When Martin returned from New York City, he conducted business until about April 1828, then struck out for Harmony to help Joseph as his scribe. Dolly demanded to go with him, which he undoubtedly opposed, but she wore him down and won.

Then, once at Joseph and Emma's home, Dolly proclaimed she would see the plates or not leave.

CHAPTER 7

BRAZENLY, Polly Harris searched all through Joseph and Emma's house, but could not find the plates. So she went out in the snow and began digging up the ground.

No luck.

So over the next two weeks she played the role of "busybody"—going to the neighbors and telling them Joseph was out to get her property. She also claimed he was a "grand imposter." Meanwhile, Martin kept acting as Joseph's scribe, putting up with Dolly's shenanigans. Even Joseph and Emma tolerated her.

Martin, hearing her incessant complaining and doubts, likely was influenced at one point. One day, just to prove to himself that Joseph was not a fraud, he substituted another stone for the seer stone, wondering if Joseph would continue "translating." Joseph immediately announced he could not translate—everything appeared dark.

A great relief came to them all when Dolly headed home, but the damage had been done—the neighbors were now alerted, fully suspicious, and antagonistic toward Joseph. Martin stayed 10 more weeks with Joseph, helping him from April through June of 1828—the second phase of Joseph's translating.

When Dolly returned to Palmyra, she stirred even more fires—hounding all the neighbors to let her store her belongings and household items, supposedly fearing Joseph would steal them.

On June 14, 1828, Martin completed his work as scribe, finishing 116 pages on foolscap paper, and left for Palmyra. He had plead with Joseph that he might show the 116 pages to several of his family members—his wife, his wife's sister, his brother, and his parents—but when Joseph inquired of the Lord, he was told no. Martin was incessant and plead with Joseph to ask again. Again the answer was no. Martin prevailed upon him to ask one more time. When Joseph did so, the Lord, says Joseph, told him to go ahead. But as part of the deal, Martin was told he could show them to only four parties, and he had to covenant with the Lord to obey this counsel. Elated, Martin left with the 116 pages.

The next day Joseph and Emma's first child was born—but lived only a few hours. The baby boy's grave site was visible from Joseph's translation room.

Emma then lay in bed for two weeks, close to death. Joseph cared for her and apparently thought only of her, ceasing translation work. After two weeks Emma recovered and became concerned about the 116-page manuscript. She requested Joseph to return to Palmyra and recover it.

Suddenly consumed with concern, he struck out on the long four-day journey. So overwhelmed with worry was he now that he walked the last 20 miles through woods, arriving at his parents' early one morning, exhausted.

They sent for Martin and waited impatiently for him to arrive. The hours passed slowly. Finally Martin trudged onto their property, head down, lingering a long time at the fence. Hyrum thought he was ill and so commented to him. Martin, still at the fence, finally replied, "Oh, I have lost my soul!" He explained that the manuscript was lost.

Martin had shown the 116 pages to his wife Dolly, then had locked it in her bureau at her request. When his wife was gone one day, Martin had dived into a discussion with a friend who expressed great doubt about the 116 pages, so Martin disregarded his covenant and decided to show them to him.

Not finding the key, he broke open his wife's bureau, grabbed the manuscript, and waved it in front of his friend's face. Dolly returned, saw her bureau broken into and partially damaged, and became even more resentful of her husband.

Martin had then begun showing the manuscript around indiscriminately to friends. He evidently then took it for granted, not bothering to show it to anyone. At that point, the Smiths came calling. The gravity of the situation apparently dawned on him when he opened the bureau—and it was gone. Suddenly realizing the importance of his earlier directive, he tore apart the house, but no manuscript. Additionally, he now felt guilty about his neglect and unauthorized showings.

At the Smith home Joseph reacted, according to his mother, by exclaiming, "Oh, my God! All is lost. . . . What shall I do? I have sinned—it is I who tempted the wrath of God." He paced the floor crying. He turned to Martin and demanded he look again, but Martin informed him that he had searched everywhere, even ripping open the bedding looking for it. Joseph replied, "Then must I return to my wife with such a tale as this? I dare not do it, lest I should kill her at once. And how shall I appear before the Lord? Of what rebuke am I not worthy?"

While Dolly claimed she did not take it, the Smiths and Martins disbelieved her, figuring she had given it away in order to make Joseph's work look foolish. One Palmyra citizen says Polly stole it while Martin slept, then burned it, not telling anyone of her deed until several years after the plates were published. Emma's family knew another person, Mrs. McKune, who reported to them that Dolly burned part of the manuscript but kept part of it to discredit Joseph. The manner in which she could discredit Joseph is simple—if he published the book, she would bring to light the original copy and point out any possible wording discrepancies. Latter-day Saints believe the concepts would have been the same, but since Joseph used his own vocabulary to express those concepts, there likely would have been changes in the wording of a second draft, which enemies would have jumped on to discredit the work, understanding neither how translation works nor the intent of the scriptures, which have never been word-perfect, Latter-day Saints also believe, including the Bible (especially the Bible, with its translation procedure consisting of manuscripts making the rounds among committees of English scholars appointed by King James, where points were actually debated and wording was not consistently agreed upon). But with the 116-page manuscript, the Lord had a back-up plan, Latter-day Saints further believe, by outwitting her—Joseph was not to again translate the stolen parts, but rather translate *other* plates he had—which was an account written by Nephi of *the same events*, but from a different perspective, one of both religious and secular history rather than mere secular history (which the lost manuscript contained) making the new beginning of the translated work even more valuable, Latter-day Saints maintain.

When Joseph returned to Harmony, he was so wrought with grief, taking blame for the lost manuscript, that all he did was work on the farm.

A few months later, in the fall of 1828, Joseph Sr. wrote his father and brothers that his son Joseph was receiving visions. Joseph Sr.'s brothers all scoffed at the news, but their father Asael believed it, feeling a branch of the family would someday be raised up to greatly affect mankind for the better. In the excellent work by George Q. Cannon, *Life of Joseph Smith the Prophet*, the only biography of Joseph written from interviews with Joseph's personal friends, Cannon states that Joseph's grandfather Asael in fact believed that one of his seed would "promulgate a work to revolutionize the world of religious faith." The younger Joseph then wrote a letter to at least one of his father's brothers, including a warning to the wicked of the earth, and that uncle (and at least one of his sons) had a change of heart and believed it, saying, "Joseph wrote like a Prophet."

Joseph continued farm work under the strain of renewed criticism from Emma's father, who felt Joseph had wasted his time with the seer stone and the Urim and Thummim. Ironically, Joseph was in large part dependent on his father-in-law, and no doubt lived under that emotional burden while his wife recovered from ill health. Joseph's other turmoil, of course, and a much greater one, was dealing with the loss of the manuscript and feeling guilty. He did not write to his parents for two months.

Worried, they set out to visit him. Lucy writes that when they saw Joseph he still had his pleasant expression, and they were grateful to hear that the plates and translating tools were on Emma's bureau in a red morocco trunk.

Lucy and Joseph Sr. now met Emma's parents for the first time. Lucy details them as very respectable and highly intelligent, having a good lifestyle.

Finally, after 10 months of no translating, in February 1829 Joseph received a revelation stating he should begin translating again. He also received a revelation for his father stating that "a marvelous work" was about to come forth to the world, and if his father desired to be a part of it, he was now called.

Emma, somewhat recovered from the physical and emotional strains of the past 10 months, now again began acting as scribe for Joseph, whenever she could break away from the all-consuming household chores that engulfed every family—making soap, preparing meals, repairing possessions, sewing torn clothes, making new clothes, and laundering by hand. Lucy states Joseph wanted the work to progress faster than what Emma was able to contribute, so he began praying to the Lord to send him a scribe.

Martin meanwhile thought he should perhaps help financially and unfortunately shared that idea with his wife, who began hounding him incessantly, calling him crazy, predicting he would ruin his family and himself if he financed the "golden Bible." Therefore, Martin was not sure if he should get involved, but was intrigued by the thought of further helping Joseph and his work.

The following month, March 1829, Martin took a trip to Harmony. When he saw Joseph he requested that someone be permitted to see the plates, as he would feel more secure if there was a witness. Later that month Joseph reported that the Lord gave him a revelation stating there would be not just one, but three witnesses, and if Martin would humble himself and admit his mistakes *he would be one of them.* Furthermore, Martin would be able to declare to the world that *he* had actually seen the plates. Because of Martin's propensity for needling Joseph, the revelation added, "You shall say unto him that he shall do no more, nor trouble me any more concerning this matter." The revelation then declares to Joseph to cease translating for a time, until "I will provide means whereby thou mayest accomplish the thing which I have commanded thee."

That revelation was soon fulfilled when Oliver Cowdery came knocking at his door. He was a year younger than Joseph, born in Vermont, and the son of a follower of Nathaniel Woods, a rodsman and religious leader from Oliver's hometown of Wells. Oliver had moved to New York City and then to Palmyra as a school teacher, had heard of Joseph's work, and had made the trip south to Harmony to help him. Specifically in Palmyra, Oliver had heard of Joseph through his friend David Whitmer, age 24. Oliver boarded with various families, the tradition of school teachers, and when he finally boarded with the Smiths, he asked Joseph Sr. about his son. Joseph Sr. was at first hesitant, but gradually unfolded the full story of the plates. Oliver, intrigued, decided to head to Harmony.

On Oliver's journey south, he went to Fayette, New York, and visited David Whitmer. He told him he would write him as soon as he got to know Joseph and could come up with an opinion.

On April 5, 1829, he arrived in Harmony. He and Joseph visited for two days, and Joseph convinced him it was "the will of heaven" that Oliver should be his scribe. They began translation together on April 7.

While obviously grateful for this new help, Joseph still suffered from poverty. Within a few weeks Joseph Knight Sr. heard of his hardships and once more came to his rescue. He took Joseph, Emma, and Oliver some lined writing paper, nine or ten bushels of grain, five or six bushels of potatoes, and a pound of tea. When Knight arrived, Joseph and Oliver were gone, looking for a place to work, but they found none. Upon returning and seeing the food and goods, they rejoiced (and certainly Emma along with them). Knight reports, "and they were glad, for they were out." Knight adds that their "family" consisted of Joseph and Emma, Oliver, and Joseph's brother Samuel.

Oliver then wrote David Whitmer, who was waiting for his opinion about Joseph and his revolutionary religious ideas. Oliver told him that Joseph did have the record of an ancient people, containing their revealed truths. That same month, still April 1829, Joseph received for Oliver a revelation through the Urim and Thummim. In it Oliver is directed to "stand by" Joseph "faithfully, in whatsoever difficult circumstances he be for the words sake." Also to "admonish him in his faults" and "receive admonition of him," to "be patient, be sober, be temperate." Then comes the clincher that convinced Oliver: "Behold I am Jesus Christ, the Son of God. . . . If you desire a further witness, cast your mind upon the night that you cried unto me in your heart, that you might know concerning the truth of these things. Did I not speak peace to your mind concerning the matter? What greater witness can you have than from God?"

Oliver then confided in Joseph that he actually had "cried" unto God in his heart while in the Smiths' Palmyra home one night in bed, praying to know the truth about the plates. The Lord had given him the witness he so described in the revelation through Joseph—of speaking peace to his mind concerning the matter—and Oliver had told no one of it. Thus, Oliver was convinced.

In an earlier revelation for Oliver—his first—Joseph had told him the Lord was granting unto Oliver a gift to translate, if Oliver so desired. Joseph also could have used the help. But when Oliver sat down to translate, nothing happened. Joseph then received another revelation explaining why: "You have not understood; you have supposed that I would give it unto you, when you took no thought save it was to ask me. But behold, I say unto you, that you must study it out in your mind; then you must ask me if it be right, and if it is right I will cause that your bosom shall burn within you." This would be used by Latter-day Saints as a guide to understanding how prayers are answered.

Oliver had evidently thought God would simply give him the translated words—but it required mental effort. Joseph then informed him the Lord was releasing him from translating, but he should continue to act as Joseph's scribe.

Over the next few weeks, both Joseph and Oliver discussed the "authority" of baptism, feeling no one could just go out and baptize someone without divine authorization. Their concern grew, and they finally, on May 15, 1829, went into the woods to pray about it. To their surprise a heavenly messenger came to them in a conduit of light.

CHAPTER 8

THE angel laid his hands on both young men and said, "Upon you my fellow servants, in the name of Messiah I confer the Priesthood of Aaron, which holds the keys of ministering of angels, and of the Gospel of repentance, and of baptism by immersion for the remission of sins."

This messenger announced himself as John the Baptist. He said he was sent to the two young men by Jesus' earthly Apostles, Peter, James, and John, who held the higher—the Melchizedek—priesthood, which Joseph and Oliver would later receive from those Apostles themselves, who were now resurrected beings. John the Baptist then told Joseph to baptize Oliver and vice versa. Then he conferred the lesser—or Aaronic—priesthood on each man. He also said this priesthood should remain on the earth as long as the earth would stand. After their baptisms they came out of the water "filled with the Holy Ghost," wherein they not only rejoiced, but prophesied many things to come. Oliver excitedly exclaimed, "What joy! What wonder! What amazement!" He says of John the Baptist: "His voice, though mild, pierced to the center, and his words, 'I am thy fellow servant' dispelled every fear. . . . What joy filled our hearts. . . . The assurance that we were in the presence of an angel . . . and the truth unsullied as it flowed from a pure personage, dictated by the will of God is to me past description."

As for the higher priesthood, there is no actual record of the ordination, but references to it exist, and it likely occurred in the next year or so. Oliver would later say that the Apostle Peter was the one who conferred the Melchizedek Priesthood on them and that both men were allowed to "look down through time, and witness the effects these two [priesthoods] must produce."

Joseph and Oliver kept the experience to themselves, except perhaps to Joseph's trusted family, because of their past experience of letting out information about the First Vision and the metallic plates. Those trustworthy family members included Joseph's younger brother Samuel, who was at first doubtful, but on Joseph's advice he went to the woods to pray. There, he was convinced of the truth. He was soon baptized and would remain faithful for the remainder of his life. He would live only a few more years, during which he would become one of the first missionaries, one of the eight witnesses to The Book of Mormon, and would actually die for the restored gospel.

Joseph's oldest living brother Hyrum then came to Harmony for a visit. Joseph told him that the Lord had just given him a revelation declaring that "a great and marvelous work" was about to come into the world and that he should help with the work. He accepted the future call.

Things continued looking up. Joseph Knight Sr. came upon several occasions during this time with more wagonloads of provisions, bringing his son, Joseph Knight Jr., from their home in Colesville, New York. Joseph Knight Jr. later declared that his father had stated that Joseph Smith Jr. was the best farmhand he ever had, and "a boy of truth." Joseph Knight Jr. had also worked with young Joseph Smith on the farm in their younger years. Before Joseph's move to Harmony, both Joseph Knight Sr. and Jr. had believed Joseph Smith when he told them of his First Vision, but two of the older Knight brothers did not.

Joseph then received a revelation for the elder Knight to keep the Lord's commandments and to help establish Zion.

Needing assistance to survive while he continued the work, the David Whitmer family came to the rescue . . .

It was now June 1829. David Whitmer, Oliver's old friend, suddenly felt impressed to help Joseph. He came to Harmony and finally met Joseph for the first time. He then persuaded Joseph to move to his father's home in Fayette, New York, 135 miles away, where Joseph would have free food and a room, along with David's brothers to act as scribes. David also said the people in his neighborhood were anxious to hear Joseph's message. Seeking to end the incredible loneliness he had endured since a boy of 14—having few believers in his work—Joseph wished to gain momentum by widening his circle of believers. So Joseph accepted young David Whitmer's offer.

Joseph and Oliver climbed aboard the Whitmer wagon and rolled northward to their new home, leaving Emma, who wished to remain behind on their homestead in Harmony with—or at least next to—her parents.

David Whitmer's parents had moved to Fayette from Pennsylvania in the early 1800s. Of their eight children, three helped Joseph immensely—David Jr., John, and Peter.

Now in Fayette, Joseph translated fairly quickly, but not without obstacles. The main problem, he admitted to David Jr., was his own mind being too concerned with things of this world, keeping him from translating until he would go out to pray. Just as David had claimed, many Fayette citizens showed interest in Joseph's work. They even invited him to speak in their homes. And they also invited their friends to listen. Many believed what Joseph said. And some of these were willing to embrace his teachings.

Now in Fayette, Oliver Cowdery continued helping Joseph as his scribe, along with the Whitmer brothers. Then, no sooner had Martin Harris arrived in June 1829 from Palmyra, than he began asking Joseph for a revelation about seeing the gold plates. Joining him were Oliver and David Whitmer—all three trying to convince Joseph to let them see the plates. Martin had learned three months earlier, of course, that he was to be one of them, but now he was pressuring Joseph again.

Several mornings later, after the daily Whitmer family meeting of singing, Bible reading, and prayer, Joseph announced to Martin that if he would humble himself and seek forgiveness for his mistakes over the missing manuscript, he would that very day see the plates, along with Oliver and David.

The four men walked into the woods, sat on a log, and discussed things for a while, then began to pray—first Joseph, then the others. Nothing happened. They prayed once more. Again nothing. Martin then arose, feeling it was his fault that nothing was happening, because he lacked the proper faith. He left the group and the others each prayed as before.

"All at once," says David Whitmer, "a light came down from above us and encircled us for quite a little distance around; and the angel stood before us. He was dressed in white and spoke and called me by name and said, 'Blessed is he that keepeth His commandments.'. . . A table was set before us and on it the records were placed. . . . While we were viewing them, the voice of God spoke out of heaven saying that the Book was true and the translation correct."

Joseph then went into the woods searching for Martin, and found him not too far away praying. Martin asked him to pray in his behalf, that he might behold the plates. Martin then received his vision. Finally he exclaimed, "'Tis enough; mine eyes have beheld." He jumped up, rejoicing.

Joseph's parents were visiting the Whitmers when the four men in the woods returned to the Whitmer home. Lucy says it was between 3 and 4 o'clock in the afternoon and that Joseph threw himself down beside her and said, "You do not know how happy I am." He explained that since his friends had now seen the plates—with an angel testifying of them—he was no longer "alone" and felt relieved of the heavy burden.

When Martin, David, and Oliver came into the house, they signed an affidavit stating what they had seen, "wherefore we know of a surety that the work is true." Lucy records that Martin was still reeling, almost overcome with joy.

Soon afterward Joseph returned to Manchester to his parents' residence. Several other men came with them, and they were the next—and last—to see the plates: the Eight Witnesses. They were the David Whitmer sons—Peter Whitmer Jr., Jacob, John,

and Christian—as well as their sister's husband, Hiram Page;
and Joseph's brothers, Hyrum and Samuel. Joseph took them
into the woods near his family home, possibly near or in the
Sacred Grove itself, where Joseph had his First Vision, and there
Joseph—rather than the angel who showed them to the first
Three Witnesses—showed the plates to the Eight: "And we also
saw the engravings thereon, all of which has the appearance of
ancient work. And . . . we have seen and hefted. . . . And we lie
not, God bearing witness of it." This was the signed statement
of the Eight Witnesses. An additional testimony of the "Three
Witnesses" was included in the initial edition of The Book of
Mormon. Every edition since has included the testimony of
both the Three and the Eight Witnesses.

Later John Whitmer wrote his own testimony that "I have
most assuredly seen the plates from whence The Book of
Mormon is translated and that I have handled these plates,
and know of a surety that Joseph Smith Jr. has translated the
book of Mormon by the gift and power of God."

Hiram Page also wrote another: "To say that a man of Joseph's
ability, who at that time did not know how to pronounce the
word Nephi, could write a book of six hundred pages, as correct
as the book of Mormon without supernatural power . . . it would
be treating the God of heaven with contempt to deny these
testimonies."

After 1837 all the original three witnesses left the church,
but none ever retracted nor denied their testimony of seeing
the plates. (See Appendix C about what eventually happened
to these 11 witnesses.)

It was now March 1830, the manuscript was finished, and
Joseph knew he immediately had to get it published. The first
step was to find a printer. He checked out several and chose
Egbert B. Grandin, the publisher of Palmyra's *Wayne Sentinel*.
There was one catch. Grandin demanded a guarantee—before
he would even start setting type—of $3,000.

Martin Harris was the man Joseph needed to put up the
guarantee. Joseph knew it and soon Martin realized it. Dolly

CHAPTER 8                                          59

fought all the way, of course, but Martin's conscience came
through and he mortgaged his farm.

When it was time to put up the cash, Dolly fought so
vehemently that Martin backed away from his promise. Instead he
sought to get a loan to pay Grandin. So he went to a Geneva, New
York, bank. The banker was impressed with Martin's business
reputation and with the fact that the Presbyterian minister in
Palmyra had recommended him, but when he learned what the
loan was for, he turned Martin down flat.

Hyrum Smith was so thoroughly disgusted with Martin's
cowardice to sell his farm, that he told Joseph to simply find
another source. One option, Hyrum heard, was selling the
Canadian copyright to raise money. Whereupon Joseph sent
Oliver Cowdery and Hiram Page to Toronto to sell the Canadian
copyright.

Joseph had felt that sending the small delegation was the
result of revelation, but the two men could find no one interested
in the Canadian copyright. They returned to Manchester, New
York, empty-handed. They went straight to the Whitmer
homestead and found Joseph. They and the Whitmer brothers
were dumbfounded. All they could do was stare at Joseph,
waiting for a response as to why the trip had failed. Joseph,
apparently humble enough to admit he did not know, left the
group. He pulled out the seer stone and inquired. His answer,
which he immediately reported to the group, was that some
revelations were from God, others are "of man," and others
are "of the devil."

David Whitmer believed and reported later that a man can
be deceived because his "own carnal desires" take precedence,
even if he asks the Lord for an answer. On those occasions he
will receive an answer "according to his erring heart," but it
will not be a revelation from God. David summarizes that the
Toronto experience is a case in point, and "they all should
have profited." David Whitmer and Hiram Page eventually felt
the reason the revelation had failed was because Joseph was
pressured to seek the revelation in the first place, essentially

"demanding" an answer, when such an answer was not naturally forthcoming.

Meanwhile, the Smith family fully supported Joseph. The future governor of Utah, Stephen Harding, graduated from college and came home to Palmyra. He went straight to Joseph at the print shop to learn more about the book that he heard was being printed and, although Harding was perceived as just another young man in the town, Joseph graciously invited him to his home. There, Oliver read portions of the manuscript to him, and he was generously fed with fresh raspberries, bread, and milk by Lucy Mack Smith, who stayed up late with him to talk further, after all had gone to bed—a typical display of the family's warmth to strangers and support of Joseph.

Martin Harris finally decided to pull through. On August 5, 1829, he mortgaged his farm for $3,000 and committed to pay Grandin the entire amount within a year and a half. Grandin could now sell Martin's farm if Martin defaulted, so with that backup, Grandin began production on The Book of Mormon.

One good thing came from Martin's lost 116 page manuscript. Joseph had learned to always make a backup copy and not trust so much in his fellowman. He assigned Oliver to make a copy for the printer, keeping the original himself, which Joseph locked away and kept guarded 24 hours a day by his family. Meanwhile, Oliver and others delivered only a few pages at a time to the printer, as needed, with all such deliveries accompanied by a bodyguard.

The manuscript copy itself was kept by Oliver for the rest of his life. On his deathbed he gave it to David Whitmer. This copy was the one with the printer's marks—including lines close together, written in ink on both sides of each page. It was written on unruled foolscap paper—about 400 pages (250 sheets total).

With all their precautions, an enemy still managed to get ahold of the manuscript. Writing under the name of Obadiah Dogberry, one Abner Cole somehow acquired a few pages, possibly with Grandin's help, possibly not, and proceeded to set type on the press he rented from Grandin on off hours. Cole was a former justice of the peace, was known as a town "busybody," and had decidedly anti-Joseph views. He determined to print pages of The Book of Mormon in such a way as to make the book look bad—by printing a few pages, then making derogatory remarks. It so happens that Hyrum Smith chanced onto the scene and saw some activity in the print shop on a Sunday. He went upstairs, found Cole, and asked what in the world he was doing there where their all-important project was being printed. Suspicious, Hyrum looked around and discovered something startling— a prospectus of Cole's small weekly newspaper, including an ad that announced that parts of The Book of Mormon would be printed in his next issue! The reason, Cole stated, was to allow subscribers access to the book without having to buy it.

H YRUM confronted Abner Cole on the spot, demanding he stop printing parts of The Book of Mormon. Cole all but laughed in his face—he blatantly refused Hyrum's demands and kept right on printing, completely unintimidated by Hyrum's gentle demeanor. Soon his paper, the *Palmyra Reflector*, went on the streets, shockingly including some pages of The Book of Mormon, while editorializing that "priestcraft is short-lived."

Joseph, despite his generally mild manner, always looked upon his own not-backing-down nature that, upon occasion, could quickly degenerate into fisticuffs as being a fault. Nevertheless, he was the man meant for the job. When Hyrum told him of Cole's shenanigans, Joseph made the long haul from Harmony to get in his face and convince him to stop. He threatened Cole with a copyright lawsuit, and that did the trick.

In Palmyra, strangely, groups of people were becoming upset that the book was being printed. Local newspapers harangued against it. A large meeting was held, and people promised not to buy the book and even to convince others not to buy it. Even Grandin was pressured to stop. And he did. He told Martin Harris he would need full payment before he could continue, breaking his contract that allowed another year for full payment.

Harmony was an ironic name for the town in which Joseph lived. Once again he mounted up and rode off to Palmyra to settle the printing conflict. He first went to Martin to urge him to simply pay off the debt in full. But Dolly would have no part of it. And it was Dolly who Martin had to live with and listen to day by day, hour by hour—not Joseph.

To Martin's credit, he had the faith to accept Joseph's calling as a prophet, so when Joseph told him of a revelation from the Lord stating that he should get out of the bondage of debt, to pay off the printer, and to "not covet thine own property, but impart it freely to the printing of The Book of Mormon," he acquiesced.

Martin sold part of his farmland to a neighbor and paid off the printer—over shrieks from his wife echoing across the meadows.

Finally, after all the work, the persecutions, the attacks by strangers to grab the manuscript, the shenanigans of "Obadiah Dogberry," the mob meetings, the slander by Dolly, the gossip by neighbors, and the financial nightmare that Joseph had faced trying to get the book published while also struggling to survive—he smiled broadly as the first copies rolled off the press and were boxed up in March 1830. On March 26 it was first advertised for sale—and probably came off the press that same day. All 5,000 copies were bound in beautiful brown leather, perhaps of varying types.

Martin, panicking that the book was not selling because of the neighborhood boycott, found himself each day on a street corner, wearing a gray suit and a huge stiff hat, hawking the book to neighbors. Whether he was tossed out there on his ear by Dolly to get his money back, or whether he was simply there on his own accord to promote the amazing historical and spiritual contents of the book, or both, he met with little success. At least at first. He sold only a few copies—each for $1.25. A trickle toward his $3,000 investment. But eventually he did get all his money back—repaid by Joseph himself.

The first edition contained just under 600 pages. The book follows three groups of people to America, mostly from 600 B.C.

to A.D. 421. As with the Bible, it is divided into books—15 in all, named after the main author of each. They are taken from three plates—engraved records by the authors. The first set is the Plates of Nephi—consisting of two sections of records—a non-religious history in one and a religious record in the other (the first one large, the second one small). The second set is the Plates of Mormon—on which the ancient prophet Mormon abridged the Plates of Nephi and added a commentary—hence the name of the overall book—followed by his son Moroni who continued the commentary. This was the same Moroni who later appeared to Joseph Smith. Third and finally is the Plates of Ether, which Moroni abridged. This is a chronicle of the Jaredite people, who came to America many generations before the Nephite people, at the time the Tower of Babel was destroyed.

The story of Lehi begins The Book of Mormon, where a man leads his family in a boat to the new world. They are divided by contention. The descendants of two of the sons become the Lamanites, who became the darker skinned Native American people, while the descendants of the other sons and their friends become the more righteous Nephites, who retain a "fair" skin. Through all their battles and contentions, intrigues and conflict, assassinations and all-out war, are the teachings of the Nephite prophets, who admonish the people to keep the commandments in order to be protected from the ever-attacking Lamanites.

Ten key points in The Book of Mormon are:

1. The book is a second witness of Jesus Christ. The title page in fact states the purpose of the book is to convince "Jew and Gentile that Jesus is the Christ, the Eternal God."

2. America, the promised land, is choice above all other lands.

3. The people will not be protected unless they keep the commandments of God.

4. Churches will become man-made and contentious with one another (which many of Joseph's converts would find a true doctrine, wanting to be free from the verbal attacks of pastor versus pastor).

5. The Nephites would in their pride build up churches that would deny the miracles of God and rely on their own wisdom.

6. The hand of God the Father was paramount to establishing the United States—a prophecy that a new country would break away from its mother country and be set up as a free people by the hand of God the Father himself, in order that the true, restored church could later be established and thrive there. (George Washington himself wrote of miracle after miracle that his small rag-tag army received from heaven in defeating the greatest army in the world—the highly financed, well-trained, seemingly invincible and innumerable forces of the British.)

7. Government should be established by law—not men, and be determined by the voice of the people and their representatives—which is the outline of a republic, which took place among the Nephites after overthrowing a monarchy.

8. Christ appeared to the Nephites, his "other sheep" who are referred to in the New Testament of the King James Bible.

9. A utopian society existed for 200 years after Christ visited the Americas. The Nephites and Lamanites lived in peace, in which there was one harmonious church with no poor among them. As 4 Nephi 16 states, "surely there could not be a happier people among all the people who had been created by the hand of God."

10. Materialism and pride crept in among the ancient Americans, then class distinction arose, and finally warfare. The Lamanites and Nephites were separated into tribes again after the government broke down. The Lamanites swept over the unrighteous Nephites, and the only survivor among them was Moroni, who made his way to the Hill Cumorah and buried the metal plates.

Despite organized opposition to the book, believers in it became missionaries and took the book through nearby states and Canada, finding hundreds of people who would read and pray about it. Numerous converts would attest in their recorded journals to a common thread leading to their conversions—that they had asked God if the book was true, after first reading it, and that they had received manifestations, through strong feelings in their hearts, that it was indeed true. This, Joseph asserted, was the Holy Ghost testifying to them. These conversions took place despite attempts by ministers to dissuade their congregations from reading it. Many others were converted because they refused to have anything to do with the existing churches that were slandering each other. Still others were amazingly "prepared" for Joseph—they were waiting for the primitive church to be restored, complete with the gifts of healing, etc.

Pastors in particular attacked the book. One interesting case, however, was that of Alexander Campbell, founder of the large and growing Campbellite church, who, seemingly somewhat impressed, found 20 specific religious issues addressed by the book—still, he denounced it (although in less vitriolic terms than other church leaders, until his co-founder, the charismatic Sidney Rigdon, deserted him for Joseph's fold, following which Campbell went through the roof).

Another well-known convert story is that of Parley P. Pratt, later one of the first twelve Apostles under Joseph. (See his amazing and beautifully written first-hand account—including conflicts with enemies, battles, and missionary experiences, both humorous and inspiring—in *The Autobiography of Parley P. Pratt* (newest edition in modern typeface, Stratford Books, 2005). He read the book with such excitement that he could not sleep or eat. He testified, "As I read, the spirit of the Lord was upon me, and I knew and comprehended that the book was true as plainly and manifestly as a man comprehends and knows that he exists."

Others studied the missionaries' messages long and hard—Brigham Young for two years and Anson Call for six months (determined, actually, to prove the book *false*). But after months of prayer and study, they became convinced it was true.

Newel Knight believed from reading the Bible that there had been a great apostasy from the true church many centuries earlier. When he heard Joseph speak, he felt he was honest, and determined to read the book. He became convinced the church was true and was a *restoration* of the earlier church and gospel from the time of Christ—not a *reformation* or breakaway church from the Roman Catholic Church that Lutherans, Anglicans, Methodists, and other churches were—and that The Book of Mormon was a completion of the word of God which, *with* the Bible, made a more complete set of scriptures.

Enemies would criticize the book, and for decades their various theories were popular, but in time were disproved. (See Appendix B for a brief review of some of the most popular ones.)

Eleven days after The Book of Mormon came off the press, "a marvelous work and a wonder" was launched—the most significant event since the Atonement and Resurrection of Jesus Christ, claim Latter-day Saints—it was time for the church of Christ to be restored to the earth . . .

AND it happened at the Peter Whitmer home. Neighbors, friends, and the few who had previously been baptized joined together for a church service of prayer, blessings, confirmations, and the sacrament; they organized America's newest church, under the laws of the land, the Church of Christ (later, in April 1838, renamed the Church of Jesus Christ of Latter-day Saints). The term "saints" meant mere disciples or members, which, Joseph defined, was used in New Testament times, rather than a revered saintly status.

Six men were ordained the first elders—Joseph, Hyrum and Samuel Smith, David and Peter Whitmer Jr., and Oliver Cowdery.

Those baptized at this first meeting included, among others, Porter Rockwell and four of Porter's family—his mother, a brother and two sisters—and Martin Harris. Joseph's parents were also baptized. Joseph's father had refused to join any church, and his mother had always been wanting to belong somewhere— so they were finally united in a faith. From the shore of Seneca Lake, Joseph watched his father be baptized, then broke into tears of joy. "Oh, my God! Have I lived to see my own father baptized into the true church of Jesus Christ!" Joseph Knight Sr. wrote that Joseph "seemed as though the world could not hold him. He went out into the lot and appeared to want to get out of sight of everybody and would sob and cry and seemed to be so full that he could not live. Oliver and I went after him and came to him, and after a while he came in. But he was the most wrought upon that I ever saw any man. But his joy seemed to be full. I think he saw the great work he had begun and was desirous to carry it out."

Before the meeting began, some members expressed that they needed a leader. They asked Joseph to inquire of the Lord concerning the matter. When the meeting ended, Joseph received a revelation that told them that Joseph should be called "a seer, a translator, a prophet, an Apostle of Jesus Christ, an elder of the church through the will of God the Father, and the grace of your Lord Jesus Christ." They also learned they should keep a "record."

Joseph's goal was now all-consuming—to carry the gospel as quickly as possible to all the world, as time was relatively short before the Second Coming of Jesus Christ.

Five days later Cowdery gave the first "church talk"—a public address in church—at the Whitmers. A large crowd heard him, and five more were baptized, including Hiram Page. Days later Oliver baptized another seven.

Soon, Joseph's father and brothers went out on missions to teach and baptize. They went literally without purse or scrip—poor as church mice—to begin with. Sixteen went the first year, and over triple that—58—the next.

In August 1830 Joseph's father and brother Don Carlos, age 14, were sent on one of the first missions—to northern New York state and Canada. On their journey they stopped at Joseph Sr.'s parents' siblings' homes in St. Lawrence County. All accepted the gospel except one sister, Susanna, and one brother, Jesse, who threatened to throw Joseph Sr. out of his parents' house, backing up his threat with an ax. At another brother's home, Joseph Sr. was teaching them when Jesse stormed in and told him off—"shut up your head," he declared. But another brother, Silas, sent Jesse away. Joseph Sr.'s father was not baptized, but firmly believed.

As in the mission field, there was also success—along with opposition—at home. Soon there were three branches of the fledgling, little church—in Manchester where Joseph lived, Colesville, and Fayette, all small New York towns. Because of the unusual message, those who did not gravitate toward it were finding excuses to oppose it. Mobs began to gather at church meetings and would throw mud and sticks at them, according to Joseph's brother William. Joseph's sister Katherine says people would throw rocks and sticks at their home. The teachings of the church were opposed by the clergy, and roughnecks would gossip at the taverns about the Saints, just as much as the area's women would at tea parties. But all this did was stir interest in the group, and Joseph was confident the honest in heart would accept the message once they heard it.

To make that happen he worked harder than ever to spread his message. On one trip he went to Colesville to visit the Knight family. There, an extremely unusual incident occurred. After holding several meetings in the village, Joseph saw the first miracle of the church performed. Newel Knight and his wife Sally were attending a meeting when Joseph asked Newel to pray. Newel declined, saying he would rather pray alone. Afterward he went into the woods, feeling bad about the incident, and had to practically drag himself home. After arriving he sent Sally for Joseph, who came straightaway. By then, Newel's body was thrashing about, his arms, legs, and face distorted. Eight or nine neighbors and relatives watched, astonished and saddened. Then Newel begged Joseph to help him—to cast out the devil. Joseph took him by the hand and, using the newly restored priesthood, commanded, in the name of Jesus Christ, the devil to leave. Newel stated that he actually saw the devil immediately leave him and disappear. He then had heavenly visions. Most of the company at the scene were so convinced that they were baptized. Needless to say, word of this event spread like a forest fire. The next month Newel was baptized.

The month after that, June 1830, the first general conference (in today's terminology) of the church was held, and all church members attended. Members now numbered 27, five of which were the Rockwell family, although Porter's father would hold off another two years. At this conference were also many visitors.

During the meeting Newel Knight had a vision. Later he records he saw Jesus Christ on the right side of God the Father during the meeting and understood that he would someday return to their presence—which is the doctrine of one's "calling and election made sure."

Soon afterward, another incident occurred in Colesville. A local Presbyterian minister, John Sherer, the pastor of the largest of the local churches, went to Newel and Sally Knight to visit Sally's sister Emily. He figured her to be a member of his church and was there to dissuade her from becoming interested in the new church. But Emily would not budge, so the reverend resorted to stratagem—he thought he could change her mind if he could just get her out of the Knight home where there was such a "bad influence" on her. So he told her a little white lie—that a brother of hers was waiting outside to take her home. When she went outside, the good reverend grabbed her by the arm and tried to force her to leave with him, but he was soon overwhelmed by not only Emily but her older sister Sally, who came flying out of the house. The reverend was not yet finished and would try another trick later that week.

The next unusual incident also occurred in Colesville. A party of five came from Manchester—Joseph, Emma, and three others—where Joseph Knight had a number of villagers ready for baptism. On Saturday several of them built a dam across a stream to allow for baptizing the next day. But Saturday night a mob demolished the dam, prompted by several preachers, including, very possibly, Reverend Sherer.

The Sunday meeting continued nevertheless, with several visitors, including those who had torn down the dam. When the church service ended, they complained against the new church and started a loud commotion. Suddenly Reverend Sherer appeared, this time with a letter from Emily's father giving him power of attorney. Either he was truly concerned for her soul, or unable to lose a battle, or possibly he was just a bit obsessive. In any case, with his newfound authority he forced Emily to go with him. The church members watched in dismay as he took her away from their meeting. Despite his high drama, Emily soon got out of his grasp and was eventually baptized into the new church.

Sherer did not remain voiceless over this defeat. He wrote to the leaders of the American Home Missionary Society, complaining about her loss and stating that about 20 had joined the Saints in Colesville alone. Pastors were now losing members of their flocks left and right and were becoming incensed.

But the drama of the broken dam was not over. The next day, early Monday morning, the Saints repaired the dam and began baptizing—13 in all. Concerned neighbors received word of it, which spread quickly through the village. Soon a mob gathered and heckled the Saints, laughing and asking them if they were washing sheep.

After the service a mob of 50 men followed Joseph and his party to Joseph Knight's home, yelling threats all the way. Joseph's group then left for Newel's house, and the mob followed, continuing their shouts.

Monday night Joseph was hit with a new form of persecution that would characterize the rest of his life. When the 13 new members awaited their confirming ordinance at a meeting, a sheriff arrived, grabbed Joseph, and arrested him. Using the law and arrests, enemies of Joseph would hound him, wasting not only his time, but most of the money he would ever have. He would face about 48 lawsuits and later spend literally all his money on attorneys. On this occasion the sheriff claimed Joseph had been "disorderly" because of preaching The Book of Mormon. He then hauled Joseph away to trial at South Bainbridge.

On their journey the constable informed Joseph that the mobbers who had sought the warrant were planning to ambush him. The constable then said he was dead set against it because he was discovering that Joseph was not the kind of person that he had been led to believe. Their wagon was soon swarmed by a taunting mob, who expected the sheriff to give up his prisoner to them. To their surprise, the sheriff bolted away from them and escaped with Joseph.

Arriving in South Bainbridge, the sheriff secured a room above the tavern. He had Joseph sleep on the bed, while he slept on the floor with his feet propped against the door and a loaded musket beside him.

At trial Joseph was furnished legal assistance by his friend Joseph Knight. This consisted of two farmers who knew the law but were not lawyers—John Reid and James Davidson—who helped Joseph prepare for the court. Reid would remain Joseph's friend for life, although never accepting the faith.

Joseph Knight would pay the consequences for helping Joseph—that very night the mob attacked his farm, overturning some wagons, sinking others in the stream, and blockading his home. Before this night he had been well respected and even beloved by fellow villagers as honest and helpful.

At 10 A.M. Joseph Smith's trial began. Joseph Chamberlain served as justice of the peace and heard two prosecutors— Burch and Seymour—before a huge gathering of spectators. Many spoke up against Joseph, repeating the rumors they had heard. Many witnesses were called, including Josiah Stowell, who had sold Joseph his horse on credit. Stowell said the credit note he had with Joseph was as good as gold, and he would sell another to Joseph on credit that very day if asked. The prosecutor then tried to coerce Stowell into agreeing with a popular story in which Joseph had claimed an angel told Stowell to give one of his horses to him. Stowell flatly denied it. Stowell's two daughters were then called. They had known Joseph before he was married, when Joseph had lived in their home. The prosecution hoped the girls would dampen Joseph's character—but they crushed the prosecution by speaking of Joseph in only the highest terms regarding both public and private behavior.

The trial was essentially over. The mob sat there with long faces. Joseph seemed above reproach. But then the prosecution figured they had worked too hard to let Joseph go that easily— so they conjured up a way for the trial to continue under false pretenses, hoping to buy time for another warrant from a different county to be brought against him. While senseless and wandering testimony continued past midnight, Joseph was not allowed to eat or drink all day. Finally Joseph was acquitted. But immediately upon stepping outside, he was grabbed and arrested again.

CHAPTER 11

HE man who now arrested Joseph was a new constable, who threw insults and abuse at Joseph. He knew Joseph was thirsty and exhausted, but drove him on a hard wagon ride 15 miles to Broome County.

This constable took him to a tavern, where a mob awaited and spat upon Joseph. They yelled, "Prophesy, prophesy!" Joseph asked for food and was given bread crusts and water. In their room the constable forced Joseph to lie next to the wall, while he lay beside Joseph with one arm over him so he would not escape.

The constable then hauled Joseph to Colesville, the site of his next trial. Joseph's two new farmer friends would defend him again. The same prosecutors then came riding into town. At court they presented their case before three justices who were prejudiced against Joseph. The same witnesses as before were called, and their lies and contradictions were so obvious that even these justices had to reject most of their testimonies.

One of the prosecutors, a determined Presbyterian, Seymour, summoned Newel Knight to testify. Seymour asked him if Joseph had cast the devil out of him. Knight said no, it had been the Lord who had, although Joseph had had a hand in it. The prosecution then demanded to know what the devil looked like, obviously taunting him. Newel was told he did not need to reply to that, but he volunteered to if Seymour would agree to answer a certain question. Seymour agreed. Newel asked, "Do you, Mr. Seymour, understand the things of the spirit?"

"No, I do not pretend to such big things."

"Well then, it would be of no use to tell you what the devil looked like, for it was a spiritual sight . . . and of course you would not understand it."

Newel got him on that one, and the spectators all laughed at the prosecutor.

The prosecution, not to be outdone, then sent out for all the drunks they could find whom they could talk into testifying against Joseph. These new "witnesses" filled the stands with more hours of gossip than they had already heard—until 2 A.M. Then the prosecutors presented two more hours of argument in court. Seymour spent a long time in his summation, also bringing up the old money digging incidents. Joseph's new friends, however, debated the points ably and pointed out that the intent of the prosecution was to hound Joseph, not to serve justice. The three judges, though opposed to Joseph, had to acquit him, but attempted to please the audience and the prosecution by directing a long, hounding lecture at Joseph.

One Presbyterian who helped instigate the trial, Cyrus McMaster, told Joseph that he considered him guilty "without judge or jury." This fairly well summarizes the intent of the prosecutors as well. Another man, A.W. Benton, who had obtained the first warrant for Joseph's arrest, admitted that he had done so to awaken Joseph's followers to his supposed delusion, which had no basis in law.

When Joseph was released, a mob gathered and went searching for him, planning to tar and feather him.

The second constable who had given Joseph grief now changed his mind about him and apologized. He even led him to safety on a relatively unused path so he would not be caught by the mob. Taking this path, Joseph escaped.

Joseph rode until dawn without stopping at the house of his wife's sister. Emma was there waiting for him, relieved when he arrived unharmed. From there they went on to Harmony "in good spirits," reports Joseph.

Two months passed. It was now July 1830.

Emma had endured trials as well, especially the loss of their son and no steady income from her husband, but seemed to be persevering. Nevertheless, she was evidently complaining to some extent, as Joseph then received a revelation, which she accepted, admonishing her not to murmur (complain), but to be a comfort to him, to console him in the spirit of meekness, to continue as his scribe. In this capacity, it must have been for other documents with which Joseph needed assistance, since The Book of Mormon was finished. She was also commanded to expound scriptures and exhort the church, as well as to select hymns for use in meetings. She was further told that Joseph would support her from the church and that she was an elect lady. She apparently accepted the revelation, as she was confirmed not much later in her home in the presence of several friends, one of them being John Whitmer, who was living with them and assisting Joseph in copying and sorting his revelations. The other friends present were Newel and Sally Knight.

Joseph next received an unusual warning. As he went out to find wine for the sacrament, he was stopped by an angel. He was told not to buy wine from their enemies anymore, apparently for their protection so they would not be poisoned, and he was told they were to only use wine freshly made by themselves—apparently as juice before it fermented.

So the group made their own "wine" and partook of the sacrament, after which both Emma and Sally were confirmed in their new callings.

Joseph probably intended to farm again as that very month he paid $200 for 13 acres right there in Harmony. But then animosity from his father-in-law reared its ugly head once again. Issac Hale, Emma's father, had generally gotten along with Joseph since they had lived on his land, but when a Methodist minister spread malicious lies about Joseph to Isaac, Emma's father became angry at his son-in-law and would not allow his teachings nor defend his name among the villagers anymore.

Joseph was also harassed. A preacher named Nathaniel G. Lewis inquired if the seer stone could be used by any person to translate. Joseph's answer was yes, and Lewis asked to borrow it, apparently in mockery, which bothered Joseph. Others also apparently ridiculed him there in Harmony.

In late August 1830 Joseph traveled with Hyrum, as well as David and John Whitmer, to Colesville, New York, again. Joseph felt it was their duty to visit the members there, despite the open hostilities against them. So they had a prayer for protection. They were so specific in their supplication that they actually asked God to "blind the eyes" of their enemies so they would not recognize them and therefore not attack them. As they approached Newel Knight's home, they came upon a large number of road workers, several of whom were their enemies. Joseph records, "They looked in earnest at us, but not knowing us, we passed on without interruption." They held their meeting that night, having the sacrament and a "happy meeting." Joseph felt they had "much reason to rejoice in the God of our salvation and sing hosannas to His holy name."

It was now September 1830. Back in Waterloo Joseph would face a new form of opposition. Oliver decided Joseph had made an error in one of his revelations, claiming that Joseph was saying he could forgive sins—which Joseph never claimed, as only the Lord could, he said. But Joseph was already being taken to task by one close to him, and this was just a foreshadowing of the problems that would haunt him all his days—talented, capable, but very proud close associates would question him, would think they could lead better than he, and would eventually oppose him. On this occasion Oliver had sent a letter to Joseph from the Whitmer farm in Fayette where he was staying, so it was clear to Joseph that Oliver could be—and was—stirring up the pot there, creating trouble. Joseph was incredulous and challenged Oliver on how he suddenly had the authority to change wording to a revelation.

Joseph was the shepherd of the new flock and, as such, received inspiration, he stated, to protect it. He next received a revelation stating that his brother Hyrum and his father were in danger. So he told Hyrum to go to Colesville and his father to go to Waterloo, ahead of his family. Joseph's mother says he also received a revelation to move to Waterloo himself. Since Joseph had not even a horse and wagon to his name, Newell Knight came to the rescue once again and helped them move away, leaving their furniture locked in their home. It was the last time they would ever live with Emma's family.

On the way to Waterloo, they stopped at the Whitmer home in Fayette, likely to quell the doctrinal uprising Oliver was attempting.

When Joseph arrived there he saw the Whitmers had, as he feared, sided with Oliver. Joseph reasoned with them and finally persuaded Christian Whitmer to see things his way and, with Christian's help, finally persuaded the rest of the Whitmers—and Oliver himself—to his viewpoint.

This problem settled, David Whitmer led several others in another dissension—they felt Joseph should not have given up using the seer stone after The Book of Mormon was translated. Joseph explained that from then on they should rely instead on the Holy Ghost. At that point David believed some of Joseph's revelations were wrong and that Joseph should instead rely on the seer stone. Most of the new members, however, did not find anything wrong with Joseph giving up the stone. Still, this was the first seed of "apostasy" from David that would later lead him down deeper paths.

Joseph then got more disturbing news: Hiram Page had been receiving and presenting revelations to the members about church government through a stone *he* had. He had in fact collected a large number of these "revelations" and some of the members were beginning to believe them.

Something had to be done about it, felt Joseph, who was disturbed over the ordeal, not knowing what to make of it, much less what to do about it. When Newel Knight came to see Joseph in September for the second general conference and found Joseph deeply concerned over the stone, they both knelt and prayed most of the evening for help.

Just before conference, which was held a few days later, Joseph received a revelation saying that no one was to receive revelations for the entire church except Joseph "until I shall appoint unto them another in his stead," quotes Joseph of the Lord in this revelation. He also learned that Hiram Page had been deceived by Satan in using the stone and that the material he had written with the stone's help was not from God.

Joseph received another revelation that week stating that it was time to begin gathering the Saints.

But increasing drama ensued when the conference started on September 26, 1830. With 62 members now in their ranks, Joseph found himself at the center of a verbal firestorm. Oliver stood and proclaimed that Joseph could not receive commandments for the entire church, and that others, like Page, had a place in the church because their revelations for the church were just as valid. But Joseph showed his authority by standing and announcing that Hiram Page's revelations were, quite simply, false. Page and his followers were stubborn and would not back down. Joseph brilliantly avoided argument and contention—he immediately and simply asked for a vote of confidence from the church.

Calmness overtook the congregation, and even Hiram Page agreed the stone's revelations were false; then he also sustained Joseph as leader and prophet. The remainder of the three-day conference went peacefully. Newel Knight states that God gave Joseph great power, and "none who saw him administer righteousness under such trying circumstance could doubt that the Lord was with him." At the conference three other revelations came forth, calling certain men as missionaries; members were confirmed; men were given the priesthood; and church business was conducted.

Joseph then received a revelation for Hyrum which stated that after the conference he and his family should move to Colesville, which they did, moving in with Newel and Sally Knight. Hyrum proclaimed the gospel almost full time by teaching in nearby villages, where he made several converts. Joseph also received a revelation for his father to leave, but his father procrastinated to act on it, and from that came a dire consequence . . .

A man came knocking at the door demanding $14, saying he had bought a note from Joseph Sr.'s creditor. Joseph Sr. offered him all the money he possessed, $6, with a promise to pay the rest later, and Lucy even offered to pitch in her gold jewelry—but the man refused, saying that unless Joseph paid the entire sum immediately, he would go to debtor's prison. He did give Joseph Sr. one way to get out of it. He would have to renounce The Book of Mormon and burn his copies—then he would forgive the debt. Joseph Sr. refused, and the constable standing in the shadows was given the go-ahead to haul Joseph Sr. off to jail.

There he languished for a month, with Lucy left alone to tend their nine-year-old girl. Horrific for Lucy, a mob attacked them that night. They began stealing their supply of corn, which the Smiths had stored to get them through the winter, and then they threatened to wreck the house. Suddenly her son William, a powerfully built, towering lad of 19, entered holding a large spike and shouted at them, "I'll be the death of every one of you!" Terrified, they all ran out of the house.

J

OSEPH Sr. was confined four days in a cell, then spent the remainder of the month in the cooper's shop of the prison yard. Each Sunday he taught his fellow prisoners, converting two men whom he afterward baptized.

One concern some of the men had expressed during the recent September conference was their desire to teach the Lamanites in the West, since it had been stated in The Book of Mormon that they would someday again be taught the pure gospel. Missionaries of other faiths had attempted with varying degrees of success, but the Latter-day Saints felt the harvest was ripe for them because they had the gospel in its fullness and The Book of Mormon that detailed the spiritual history of the Native American's ancestors.

That month four missionaries immediately went westward, hopeful they would convert many, but managed to only convince a few. However, on their journey, they converted a major figure for their fold, one Sidney Rigdon. The four who went westward consisted of Parley P. Pratt (baptized only a month earlier by Oliver), plus Oliver himself, Ziba Peterson, and Peter Whitmer Jr.

Parley had been converted recently to another church— before meeting Oliver. He had been convinced and converted by Sidney Rigdon to the Campbellites in Ohio and was in fact heading to New York on a mission for that faith when he heard about The Book of Mormon. As a result of reading the book, he realized he had found the true religion. He sent his wife ahead to her parents in New York, then visited his only relatives to convert them to the Mormons, not knowing a great deal yet himself. The only convert he made there was his brother Orson, later another significant figure in Joseph's group. The two brothers had then attended the September 1830 general conference and met Joseph, whom they immediately believed to be a prophet. Parley was then assigned as a missionary to the Native Americans.

Emma and several women had made the men's clothes for the journey to the Lamanites, and the four then embarked with great hopes. They planned to not only make Lamanite converts but to spearhead the way west for the entire church to Zion, which they figured would be somewhere in the West.

In their first attempt they taught the Lamanites in Buffalo among the Cattaraugus tribe. They left two books, since some could read English.

They continued west, teaching Lamanites and whites alike at hamlets along the journey.

It was their next stop, in Ohio, where they converted Sidney Rigdon. He was 37 and very charismatic. He had studied under a Baptist minister, obtained a license to preach, and was known for his public speaking ability. He left preaching for a while to become a tanner for his wife Phebe's brother, and there met Alexander Campbell, who converted him to the Campbellite faith. He became a pastor for them and set up congregations in Bainbridge, Mentor, and Kirtland, Ohio, establishing a large gathering in the latter township. Rigdon refused to charge for his services, just, he stated, as the Apostles of old had not, but the people so respected and loved him that they built him and his wife a house at the edge of town.

Rigdon then decided to start a communal society, so he split with the Campbellites, since Alexander could not accept such a lifestyle and, in August 1830 at their Campbellite conference, Sidney took out on his own, maintaining his congregation in Mentor, Ohio.

He was now free from all associations when the four Mormon missionaries found him in Mentor, Ohio, at his home. He told them he had the Bible and felt that was enough, but was willing to at least read The Book of Mormon. "When you come again, I will tell you what I think about it."

Then the missionaries asked to preach to his congregation, a bold move that took him back, but he hesitantly consented. Parley and Oliver spoke to the group, and finally invited Sidney to respond. He thoughtfully shuffled to the podium, looked out over his flock, and told them, "Brethren, we have listened to strange doctrines tonight, but we are commanded to prove all things and to hold fast to that which is good." He asked the missionaries to spend the night. They left him a book to read while they went to Kirtland, just five miles away, for two or three weeks.

His son John reports that his father Sidney could hardly eat, so taken was he by reading the book. "He read it both day and night. At last he had read it through and pondered and thought over it."

At Kirtland, Ohio, meanwhile, the four Mormon missionaries created quite a stir—many listened to them and were moved by their words. The town was a rough one. It survived by trading with trappers and had a population of 2,000 residents.

Whether or not they were truly this optimistic, the local newspaper reported that the four expected to convert and gather the Indians, and that miracles would be manifest. All four missionaries were not only new converts, they were in their early thirties and, obviously, were zealous, upbeat, charismatic personalities who at times were more hopeful than realistic.

When they returned to Sidney, they found he had studied the book for two weeks. He felt the book went hand in hand with his own convictions of a gathering and a nearing millennium. Sidney asked about Joseph Smith and learned he was only 24, with no real education. That was the clincher. He was completely convinced the book was of God. The missionaries invited Sidney and his wife to attend a baptism service. Several converts in

Kirtland were joining the church the next week, and the Rigdons agreed to attend and watch. But the power they felt at the service convinced them it was something worth more than just watching—they decided to be baptized themselves.

When Sidney returned to Mentor, his congregation was buzzing like hornets. They demanded to know where he stood. He boldly declared from his pulpit that he knew the Mormon doctrines were true, and that he was going to teach them— no matter what. So they took a stand: They not only disallowed him to preach at his church, they refused to allow him and his family to move into the new house they had built for them.

So Sidney's next step was to move to Hiram, Ohio, with his wife and form a branch of Joseph's group with about 20 others. Then in December 1830 Sidney went with Edward Partridge to visit Joseph Smith.

As for Edward Partridge, in Ohio, he had doubted the missionaries at first, and had even told Oliver they were imposters. But Oliver had countered by saying he was grateful that a God in heaven knew the hearts of all men, intimating that Edward did not. Edward may have been intrigued by that, as he then read The Book of Mormon. He finally decided to go with Sidney to visit Joseph Smith in person.

Joseph baptized Edward himself on December 11, 1830, in Seneca Lake. Joseph immediately received revelations for both men, saying that Edward, a quiet man, would teach the gospel powerfully and that Sidney would perform great things.

Meanwhile, the four missionaries in Ohio continued teaching and converting. One convert was a medical doctor, Frederick G. Williams, who left his practice and joined them on their mission.

Their next stop: The Wyandot tribe near Sandusky, Ohio. That tribe was expected to be forced to move soon, under orders of the U.S. Government, so they were too busy to even listen to the group of now five missionaries.

By January 1831 it was time for the missionaries to head into the huge prairies alone without even so much as taking mules. Thus, there was no food for them in the desolate winter. They trekked 1,500 miles across snow and hard winds, carrying heavy packs, having no fire, eating frozen corn bread and raw pork, and seeing no other people until their final stop—Independence, Missouri—the far western outpost of America.

Two missionaries stayed in town to work for a wage so they could all survive. The other three went to see Chief Anderson, leader of 10 tribes of the Delawares, who said he never allowed his people to be visited by missionaries. But he was so impressed with their message—that The Book of Mormon was for them and their people—that he changed his mind. He called a council of 40 tribal leaders to listen to Oliver Cowdery. He also agreed to have copies of the book left for those who could read. Finally, he agreed to his people hearing more. He himself was convinced. Oliver wrote Joseph, "He believes every word of the book, and there are many now in the Nation who believe, and we understand there are many among the Shawnees who also believe." Chief Anderson would have been influential in numerous Lamanites accepting the restored gospel, but certain whites stepped in and stopped everything cold—missionaries from other churches, combined with U.S. Government Indian agents.

Parley P. Pratt says the tribe was becoming excited about their message when these opponents—who were evidently envious of their success—made certain that the Mormons were blocked from seeing the tribes again, claiming them to be "disturbers of the peace."

Oliver, Parley, and the other missionary returned to Independence to join the remaining two, and there they could only teach the white settlers. The Mormons had had high hopes for the Lamanites, but it would have to be in a future time.

Meanwhile in New York, Sidney Rigdon quickly became Joseph's closest friend and counselor. Joseph was ecstatic that the Lord had sent him "this great and mighty man" to help with the work.

But when Sidney encouraged Joseph to go with him to Kirtland, some of the members became concerned. Especially when—without so much as Joseph even visiting Ohio—on

January 2, 1831, he announced he had a revelation stating that the whole church was to move to Ohio. Most followed willingly, seeing the news as an adventure and unquestionably the will of the Lord. Others of less faith, including (at times) David Whitmer, despite his earlier miraculous experience, thought the idea of moving *en masse* was not wise. In Whitmer's case it may have been inspired by the difficulty of leaving his property, being the son of a well-to-do farmer.

Some actually accused Joseph of inventing the revelation in order to accomplish his own desire to move, so it took Joseph a few weeks to convince them it was the will of the Lord and that it was now time.

So in late January 1831 Joseph, Emma (now pregnant and experiencing her eighth move in four years of marriage), Edward Partridge, and Sidney Rigdon left on the 300-mile journey for Kirtland, Ohio, in Joseph Knight's sleigh. The Ohio frontier would be their newest home . . .

CHAPTER

# 13

I n the spring the main flock in New York would be coming, first having to sell their properties and goods, some at a loss. But they would soon learn that sacrifice was the order of the day, and would be for decades while establishing the Kingdom of God on the earth, as their leaders taught.

In early February 1831 Joseph's group reached Kirtland, Ohio. First they went to Sidney Gilbert's home to stay, but Emma did not like the look of the rooms, so they went to the home of Gilbert's partner, Newel K. Whitney. Both men ran the same general store on Main Street. The Whitneys were gracious hosts and loved having the prophet and his wife stay with them for several weeks.

The Whitneys, when still not members, had prayed the previous autumn asking to receive the Holy Ghost. They heard a voice instructing them that the word of God was on its way. Parley P. Pratt and the other three missionaries had then arrived and converted them. So Joseph and his flock had a bit of a stronghold in Kirtland from which to work—about 100 members, in addition to the 60 in New York.

In Ohio Joseph set out to organize and present church doctrine, mainly by publishing his revelations so they all could have access to them. But the challenge of the Ohio Saints was living up to the standards that Joseph taught. While having the truth, they still had to battle human weaknesses and were guilty of struggling with envy, pride, and disobedience to what many felt were the commandments of God.

While the New York Saints had struggled with some degree of rebellion, Joseph had thrown himself into Ohio—from the frying pan into the fire. First off was more "counterfeit" revelations to contend with, similar to Hiram Page's stone in New York—but this time in the form of a member of the church known as Sister Hubble who believed not only she was a prophetess but began issuing commandments and revelations, and even gaining followers. Joseph believed the Lord set things straight with a revelation to him: "This ye shall know assuredly—that there is none other appointed unto you to receive commandments and revelations."

Joseph was further disconcerted by the strange behavior in his meetings—of some members going into fits and trances. He pronounced the behavior was not of the Lord, was not a manifestation of the Holy Ghost, but rather was a sign of the adversary. He then appointed Parley P. Pratt, when Pratt returned from his Lamanite mission in the West, to rout out the evil spirits in the branches of the church. This he did by using the restored priesthood powers that Joseph had used to exorcize the evil spirit from Newel Knight when he was overtaken in New York.

Despite the setbacks, Joseph saw tremendous potential in Ohio. Isaac Morley generously had a cabin built for Joseph and his family, in answer to a revelation on February 4, 1831, that stated a house would be built for him. As for Joseph's own view on living well while helping others, he believed in the finer things of living—did not want to live as a Spartan—but also was generous to a fault and believed in absolute sharing. He often shared or outright gave whatever he had to others. Possessing the heart for it himself, Joseph received a revelation on February 9 stating that they should divide their property and live the Law of Consecration. They divided up the various jobs, while the temporal leader among them, Edward Partridge, was chosen by the Lord, said Joseph, as a special "bishop" to oversee all their worldly concerns—buildings, cattle, crops, lands, and all their goods—also including helping the sick and aged, supervising new businesses, and building schools and churches. This task included the redistribution of all goods and food according to each family's stewardship, while all surplus would be used to expand the kingdom as the bishop saw fit. While in the sectarian tradition it could be considered an early form of communism, it was in Joseph's view the Lord's way of economic prosperity. While Latter-day Saint observers since that time have viewed Marxist communism as an economic and political system advanced by the adversary as a "counterfeit" system vastly different than the Lord's where the principles of force and uninspired judgements of men oversee that system— the Lord's "united order" utilizes voluntary compliance with heavenly inspiration. The only condition for the Lord's law of consecration to work, as Joseph pointed out, was for the Saints to be humble in their attitude, giving of their substance, and hardworking.

Their bishop, Edward Partridge, was known for his honesty, humility, and perseverance when the Saints' imperfections later set in, and it was his task to settle their squabbles and problems. All this was appointed by God, as Joseph proclaimed, to alleviate their poverty, rid themselves of materialism, share equally among one another, and allow Joseph to be free to work on spiritual matters—including revising the King James Bible. In this task he set out to find certain verses which, The Book of Mormon explains, had through the centuries been tampered with, having their "plain and precious parts" removed. Thus, Joseph was able to clarify some of the verses that had been muddied. (The version used today by the Church of Jesus Christ of Latter-day Saints is the original King James Version—with Joseph's corrections in footnotes, perhaps to have a certain common ground with outside Christians and in order to promote missionary work—while the Missouri-based Community of Christ uses only Joseph's revised version. Parenthetically, the revisions are far fewer than other well-known revisions of the King James Version.)

Of equal importance to Joseph was his family. On April 30, 1831, Emma gave birth to twins—a boy and a girl—but she had been weakened by her midwinter ordeal traveling to Ohio, and after only three hours the babies died. The Morleys' daughters kindly nursed her back to health, but Emma was now childless after three births. However, a neighbor, the wife of John Murdock, died nine days later, leaving twins born the same day as Emma's. Emma and Joseph took in the two babes to raise, and named them Julia and Joseph Murdock Smith.

In New York the main body of Saints prepared themselves to leave, but were continually hounded by neighbors. Newel Knight did his utmost to help the Colesville members emigrate as a group.

The Fayette group met a different fate. Neighbors not of their faith kindly saw them off, waving good-bys, praying for their safe journey, and one man even gave them $17—a generous sum in their day. The Fayette group finally set forth, led by Lucy Mack Smith, Joseph's mother, who received a unanimous vote to not only lead them, but to dispense food among the needy, taking 80 members on a five-day barge journey through the Erie Canal. While disconcerted by the human frailties among them, she saw some members spending their last money on clothes and then expecting others to give them food. She stamped out bickering and complaining, disciplined the overenthusiastic children, assisted with sick children and babies, and counseled the teenage girls to not flirt with strangers. She led them through songs and prayers—all of which pleased the captain and the other passengers. At one point, with their barge caked in by ice, the strong-willed teenager, Porter Rockwell, left the boat to visit his uncle, whereupon Porter's mother tried to stop him, but he paid no attention to her. She called upon Lucy to get him back on the boat. "Mother Smith, do get Porter back, for he won't mind anybody but you." But Porter would not even obey Lucy this time. However, other teens disembarking with young Porter were reprimanded and cajoled by Mother Smith, and they all returned to the barge. Porter would meet up with the group in Kirtland later, much to the temporary consternation of his parents.

The Colesville and Fayette Saints soon rendezvoused in Buffalo. But bad weather iced them in at the harbor on Lake Erie, and the trip to Ohio was delayed for two weeks. More stormy weather hit them on their journey across Lake Erie, and all the Saints got seasick. Finally they arrived in Fairport, Ohio.

They all disembarked and made their way to Kirtland, 10 miles further overland. And there, they rejoiced.

PART II


# Ohio and Missouri

C H A P T E R

# 14

At Kirtland the Morleys took in Joseph's family for the first two weeks. The New York Saints, meanwhile, settled together outside Kirtland in the village of Thompson, Ohio. Newel Knight was their leader, and they became the first group to live the Law of Consecration since the time of the Nephites in ancient America, 1,400 years earlier, said Joseph. They even kept their New York name—the Colesville Branch. Two local converts, Leman Copley and Ezra Thayre, shared 1,000 acres of their land with the Colesville Branch, purchased by the church on contract.

The first Ohio general conference was held in June 1831 at Kirtland.

Joseph attracted visitors far and wide across the state. He improved his speaking ability and, according to witnesses, could hold audiences in the palm of his hand, able to speak hours at a time and mesmerize those listening to him. Some visitors came to scoff at him, others to hear with a sincere heart.

The next recorded miracle by Joseph was when a Mrs. Johnson came to visit him. Accompanying her was her husband, John Johnson, a wealthy farmer in Hiram, Ohio, and their Methodist minister, Pastor Booth. They were simply talking about religion when one asked if there was any man on earth that God had given the power to heal. Mrs. Johnson suffered so badly from rheumatism that she could not lift her arm above her head. After they began discussing other subjects, Joseph took her hand and calmly pronounced, "Woman, in the name of the Lord Jesus Christ I command thee to be whole." She immediately raised her arm, shocking the others, and the very next day did her chores with no pain.

Pastor Booth and the entire Johnson family joined the church. While it is church policy to not seek converts through miracles, occasionally there have been conversions as a result of miracles, but Latter-day Saints believe such conversions often do not last because little or no faith was exercised, and when trials of faith later arise, they are too weak to pass the tests, and generally fall away. Latter-day Saint diaries indicate conversions had a far greater chance of lasting when people sought and received a witness of the truth from the Holy Ghost.

Then a bizarre conversion took place when a popular Campbellite pastor named Simonds Ryder heard a Mormon girl predict an earthquake in Peking, China. The prediction came to pass six weeks later.

Many Saints waited anxiously to learn where Zion would be. While Ohio was to be the settlement for some, others were anxious to be assigned to live in the new Zion. Then came a revelation disclosing Zion's location—Missouri. In June 1831 Joseph was instructed in revelation to go there. A dozen men were told to travel with him. While Joseph and Sidney Rigdon would soon leave with Edward Partridge and Martin Harris, eight others were commanded to go in pairs and take different routes, seeking converts along the way.

Meanwhile, the Ohio Saints were already having problems. Before Joseph left, Newel Knight came to him telling of their troubles—Leman Copley (who had been excommunicated for unbecoming conduct) and Ezra Thayre wanted out of the covenant of consecration and wished to relinquish the deal wherein the Colesville Saints could purchase their land at half price. They also demanded the Saints to leave, despite the written contract they had with them. Copley also wanted to level a fine of $60 per family for "damaging" his property because they had altered his houses and planted crops on the land—in others words, they had vastly improved it, and now he wanted money for that. Joseph then received a revelation for the Colesville group—that they should pack up at once and leave for Missouri. Because they had been displaced by the two landowners, they were more than willing to travel to the new land of Zion. With Newel Knight leading them, they would soon set out on a journey three times longer than the trip from New York had been—it would be 900 miles to Missouri.

Joseph hoped God would bring him able-bodied men to help the Saints with needed skills once they settled there. He knew not all were going there, as the church would retain its headquarters in Ohio. He was therefore pleased that, just before leaving for Missouri, another talented man converted to the fold. William W. Phelps had moved with his family to be with Joseph in Ohio, wanting to do the will of God, he said. Once there, he received a revelation through Joseph that he should be baptized and given the priesthood, then go to Missouri and print books with Oliver Cowdery. Phelps had edited a political party newspaper in New York and had even run for lieutenant governor of New York.

Joseph and his friends set out for Missouri as soon as they could, leaving June 19, 1831.

His group traveled by wagon, canal boat, and stagecoach to Cincinnati, Ohio, then took a steamer to Louisville, Kentucky, and another steamer to St. Louis, Missouri. Finally they headed over the desolate land on foot, walking 250 miles in the now intolerable midsummer heat and humidity.

Arriving at the far western outpost of the United States known as Independence, Missouri, in July, Joseph was saddened by the locals he encountered—"lean in intellect and degraded," living on dirt floors, no glass for windows, cooking wild game on campfires right outside cabin doors, boys up to age 10 running about with no pants in the summer, one school, three stores, and a brick courthouse. Only 2,823 white settlers had been counted there in Jackson County the year before in the 1830 census. And everyone wore skins—no homespun cloth for clothes—and had practically no cash for purchasing items. They were, in effect, wilderness people.

On the first Sunday there, W. W. Phelps taught and converted two people. And Joseph, ever optimistic despite the general condition of the people, saw the place as beautiful, with rolling prairies filled with flowers, and tall hardwood trees lining the streams and rivers. He told the Saints the soil would produce plentiful crops—food and cotton. The Saints could live well on the wild game and they could create industry. But not without facing their most difficult problems to date . . .

CHAPTER 15

I n Thompson, Ohio, meanwhile, the Saints were taking their time leaving. The two landowners who had apostatized wanted them off immediately, so Newel Knight urged the Saints to get going. Finally they did, arriving the same month at Independence. Joseph placed them in the Kaw township, 12 miles west of Independence, closer to the Native American border. Emily Austin records, "We now resorted to flatboats to take us up the river to the mouth of Big Blue, in Jackson county, and to the ferry landing, and here we disembarked and our journey was ended, except a few miles by land into the country."

Young Porter Rockwell was now age 17. He helped his parents, brothers, and sisters build their farm there. But taking the ferry for the first time lit a fire under him, and he fell in love with river life and decided to own his own river barge.

He soon would, and would immensely enjoy ferrying members and non-members alike across the Big Blue. His first winter there he met Luana Beebe. He was so taken by her that, after farm chores each day, he would trek 15 miles into the city to court her. His tenacity paid off, as seven months later they would be married.

Within a year there would be 900 Saints in western Missouri. Porter's home was host to church leadership meetings for elders and high priests. One day a church conference was actually held on his barge, which made him extremely proud. In late

July 1831, the same month they arrived there, Joseph received a revelation stating this was the land of promise. Independence would be the center of Zion and the home of the temple. For the first time, the Saints were given the go-ahead to buy land—and in fact were commanded to do so. Sidney Gilbert was to set up a store, and a printing press would be brought in from Cincinnati.

Sidney Rigdon offered a prayer that consecrated the area for the gathering. Joseph assisted by laying the first log of the first home in the promised land, and the Saints immediately began constructing homes with fury, all with freshly hewn logs and smooth corners—in contrast to the thrown-together, messy-looking wilderness homes of the locals. Then the Saints built a schoolhouse. Despite their general optimism Sidney wanted to return to Ohio, and Edward Partridge thought the soil was poor. Not outright dissension, but complaints.

On August 8 they held the first funeral since the organization of the church—that of Polly Knight, wife of Joseph Knight Sr., who had contracted an illness coming west from Ohio. Showing her faith, she had refused to remain behind, and asked God only one thing—to allow her to live long enough to reach the promised land. Her husband was additionally distressed when he discovered wild hogs trying to dig at the spot where she was buried. Despite being quite sick, he took his ax "and went and built a pen around it. It was the last I done for her."

On the same day as the funeral, Joseph received a revelation that sent him and a few others back to Kirtland. Having been there less than a month, they immediately left. Edward Partridge was the mainstay assigned to remain in Missouri as bishop of Zion.

Joseph would stay in Ohio and direct two settlements from there—Kirtland and Independence. Some in Missouri, of course, wished Joseph would stay with them, but Bishop Partridge functioned courageously and efficiently as the Saints practiced the Law of Consecration in Missouri.

Partridge's family meanwhile remained in Kirtland, suffering from disease. He had the painful duty of asking his wife to make her way with their sick children to Missouri, and to leave the house he had bought in Ohio, which he had never lived in. He wrote her on August 5, 1831, feeling he had such a heavy responsibility for the floundering kingdom in Missouri—with so many destitute families depending on him—that he could not return to help her. But he was torn, knowing she would have no help. Fortunately his children were recovering from the measles by now, but the oldest was still suffering from lung congestion and a fever. They sold their property at a great sacrifice—his friends even thought him crazy for it—and his family set out on the journey a few months later with W. W. Phelps and Sidney Gilbert.

His family finally arrived in Independence. He rented a house from Lilburn W. Boggs, later the governor of Missouri and avowed enemy of the Saints. Showing their magnanimity, the Partridges took in a widow with four children for the winter, and later Edward built a tiny cabin just a half mile from Independence.

In their new community, school and life in general was frightening for the children. One day a crowd of Native Americans poked their faces in the doorways and windows to watch and intimidate the teacher, who bravely proceeded to march out to the chief to have a word with him. The kids stared, petrified.

While the Saints lived the Law of Consecration fairly well at first in Missouri, many in Ohio were less committed. Those with more goods were not inclined to share with the less fortunate, even with Joseph there to teach and chastise them.

One positive thing that happened to Joseph in Ohio was being relieved of dealing with the temporal and financial affairs of the Saints. He received a revelation on December 4, 1831, that named Newel K. Whitney as bishop in Kirtland. This assigned him as the overseer of the storehouse and the Ohio Saints' funds, as well as the well-being of the members there—similar to what Edward Partridge was doing in Missouri. Whitney was also assigned to "administer to their wants" by having them pay for whatever they received from the storehouse. But if they lacked money to pay for goods or food, they would be placed on an "account" that would be handed over to the Missouri bishop—Edward Partridge, "the bishop of Zion"—who had the added burden to pay the Ohio storehouse debts out of whatever surplus he had. Evidently, the Ohio Saints were suffering even more than the Missouri members. So Edward Partridge in Missouri was stretched even more in his calling, being ultimately responsible for the debts of both groups of Saints, almost 900 miles apart.

Joseph and Emma now moved with their small family—the two adopted twins—to Hiram, Ohio, 30 miles southeast of Kirtland, to live with the John Johnson family. Being a wealthy man, John sustained Joseph in his revising of the Bible, with Sidney Rigdon as scribe. Both men also revised the compilation of revelations, which would be printed in Missouri at their own press and titled *Book of Commandments*, the precursor to *The Doctrine and Covenants*. Meanwhile a special series of four conferences took place November 1–12, 1831, in which the Saints sustained the motion to publish the book. There they ratified it as "the foundation of the church in these last days."

The book would contain all 49 revelations Joseph had received during the first two years in Ohio (there were apparently others but they were not recorded). These revelations gave instructions on how the Lord wanted to run his church, with specific admonitions to members, from which all could learn. The revelations generally had one thing in common—they were received when Joseph went to the Lord with a question on an item of concern, and many would begin with, "I inquired of the Lord and received for answer the following."

Since Joseph was uneducated and his scribe Rigdon was educated, some have suggested Sidney wrote or had a hand in the contents of the revelations but, if one compares their writing styles, it is obvious Sidney had no hand in them except as taking dictation, because his writing style was very broad, general, and not organized, whereas Joseph's revelations were forceful, specific, and to the point, say analysts.

Anson Call witnessed Joseph receiving a revelation on more than one occasion. He reports that Joseph's face would actually light up and shine with a brilliant whiteness. Others said his

CHAPTER 15                                        103

face would become illuminated and "transparent" when he was
being inspired.

Parley P. Pratt adds that when Joseph received revelations,
he would state each phrase clearly and slowly, and add a long
pause to allow the scribe to write the words. He never hesitated,
backtracked, or even had them read back to him.

Zebedee Coltrin writes that some elders once tried to
correct the grammar, but Joseph declared that every word of
that revelation had been dictated by Jesus Christ. However,
Joseph did later, for the sake of publication, allow the revelations
to be slightly improved and corrected for clarification. Joseph
oversaw this process, not changing the meaning of the contents,
receiving help from Oliver and Sidney.

There was always someone to offer an opinion or criticize
Joseph, which would prove a major trial in his life. Even on
this issue of revising, William McLellin and others disagreed
with the prophet. However, Joseph always followed his
heart and obviously felt such corrections were in harmony
with the will of God and would not detract from the intent
of any information, while making them more readable and
grammatically correct.

Ever to have critics in his midst, Joseph saw several members
attempt to write revelations themselves, perhaps not thinking
Joseph's were adequate, but when they sat down to attempt the
task, they failed miserably. It seems some suffered from rather
sizeable egos—they thought they were entitled to revelations for
the church since they were on the "ground floor" of its beginning,
and also saw themselves as more talented than Joseph, and
certainly more educated. William McLellin attempted to write
a revelation in November 1831, but failed. He then humbled
himself and added his name to a list of 10 elders who bore
testimony of the book of Joseph's revelations, saying that God
had "borne witness to our souls, through the Holy Ghost . . . that
these commandments were given by inspiration of God." Later,
despite their support, McLellin and others would apostatize
from the church, ever falling under the spell of criticism and
seeing things they would do differently.

JOSEPH SMITH: A BIOGRAPHY | *Richard Lloyd Dewey*

Joseph and company finished correcting the revelations on November 15, 1831. Then Oliver and John Whitmer set out for Independence on the 900-mile journey to get the book published at the church press.

Upon arriving, Oliver, John Whitmer, and W. W. Phelps, who was the printer, further prepared the book for publication. However, Joseph warned Oliver through a letter on July 31, 1832, "not to alter the sense of any of them," or he could come under condemnation.

While the *Book of Commandments* was being delivered to and prepared for publication in Missouri, Joseph worked feverishly revising the New Testament, a project that would never be as significant as his other dictated works nor as extensive as he probably had hoped it would be, due to lack of time to work on it, which was the result of interruptions and persecutions that began while living at the John Johnson farm. It was during this time, in fact, that his worst persecution to date began to occur.

CHAPTER 16

JOSEPH's new wave of persecution began on three major
fronts. First, certain members apostatized and outright lied
to the locals about him. Second, some locals understandably
became upset over what they mistakenly assumed about the
Law of Consecration, thinking that converts were having their
property appropriated by Joseph, who would reign as a despot
over them, along with Sidney Rigdon. Third, they began hearing
that Joseph had initiated the practice of polygamy, which likely
did occur in late 1831. But they did not understand or accept
that it was due to a private revelation Joseph had that instructed
him to practice it as the ancient prophets of God in the Old
Testament had, Joseph would explain. When the locals got word
of it they took it upon themselves to attack Joseph physically.
Further regarding polygamy, Joseph asserted that God himself
had instituted the practice in Old Testament times, as he would
in modern times. But for now, only Joseph, and soon a few others
in church leadership, were instructed to practice it.

Lyman Johnson later told his missionary companion, Orson
Pratt, that Joseph had shared with him in 1831, while Joseph was
living on his father's farm, that God had revealed to him that
plural marriage was to be practiced, but the time was not yet.
Joseph B. Noble said that Joseph told him that polygamy was
revealed to him during the time he was translating the scriptures,
which would have been the New Testament that he revised in

1831. (The practice would end in 1890 due to compliance with federal law, and even be outlawed by the church, so strictly in fact that members who continued the practice would be summarily excommunicated, as they are also today. This has given rise to certain splinter or "apostate" groups from the church that outsiders view as Mormons, but who the Saints themselves see as far distanced from the church.)

Just before the three-fold prongs of attack began against Joseph, he had a revelation—an actual vision—along with Sidney Rigdon, that established Latter-day Saints' doctrine of the hereafter and even explained the reason for and understanding of the rewards for keeping the commandments of God. They reported they literally saw into the heavens. And they described it vividly—what it was like, what was there, and the feelings they had. This remarkable vision occurred in the presence of about 12 elders on February 16, 1832, in Hiram, Ohio.

It began when Joseph was revising a portion of St. John's Gospel. Sidney Rigdon was taking dictation. With 12 witnesses watching the two men, they were suddenly enveloped in a vision. The heavens opened to them and, as they sat for about an hour, Joseph and Sidney spoke throughout the event. Joseph would describe what he saw, then Sidney would say, "I see the same." They would take turns, as Sidney would report what he was seeing and Joseph would respond, "I see the same." Neither moved about the entire time, but when it was over, Sidney was exhausted and white, whereas Joseph was robust and at ease. Joseph smiled, "Sidney is not used to it as I am," reports Philo Dibble, one in the room who "saw the glory and felt the power, but did not see the vision."

They bore testimony afterward of what they saw: "And we beheld the glory of the Son, on the right hand of the Father, and received his fullness; and saw the holy angels and them who are sanctified before his throne, worshiping God, and the Lamb . . . and . . . this is the testimony last of all, which we give of him: that he lives!"

In the next revelation, Joseph announced that in heaven there are three degrees of glory, a description that is similar to but more detailed than Paul's first letter to the Corinthians (I Cor. 15:31) in the New Testament, which states, "There is one glory of the sun, and another glory of the moon, and another glory of the stars; for one star differeth from another star in glory. So also is the resurrection of the dead." Joseph then elaborated that the highest glory is the celestial—like the sun, for those who receive the testimony of Jesus, are baptized, and are valiant in keeping God's commandments. The next highest glory is the terrestrial—like the moon in its brightness, for those who are honorable but not "valiant," whether they are baptized or not. The third is the telestial glory—like the brightness of the stars, for those who had lived dishonorable lives on the earth, including liars, adulterers, others who are immoral, and murderers. The rewards for faithfulness on this earth, no matter the trials, explained Joseph, "was beyond the narrow-mindedness of men."

In March 1832, the very next month, Joseph received another revelation concerning the church storehouse helping the poor, "That you may be equal in the bonds of heavenly things, yea, and earthly things also. . . . For if ye are not equal in earthly things ye cannot be equal in obtaining heavenly things." Later, the Law of Consecration would be revoked, but the principle of sharing, giving, and helping the poor was made abundantly clear and is still an integral part of church doctrine and practice.

Joseph admonished the Saints to keep God's commandments in order that they may return to live in his presence in the Celestial Kingdom. "Ye have not as yet understood how great blessings the Father hath in his own hands and prepared for you. . . . The kingdom is yours and the blessings thereof are yours, and the riches of eternity are yours." The revelation compares the Saints to small children, stating they do not understand what awaits them if they will but obey.

Meanwhile in Missouri, W. W. Phelps published the prospectus to his newspaper, *The Evening and the Morning Star*, stating it was to publish the revelations of God, announce the return of Israel, and provide news of the church.

As Joseph would teach, whenever ground was made in the Kingdom on earth, the adversary would try to thwart it, but would in the end fail. With the newest February and March revelations of 1832 providing the clearest path yet for the Saints regarding where their God wanted them to go—indeed laying out the very purpose of earth life and providing a veritable road map to get there—the greatest opposition to date would now be launched.

The aforementioned three-pronged persecution began. John Johnson's four sons, despite seeing their mother's arm miraculously healed by Joseph Smith, turned against him viciously. They got it in their minds and discussed it among themselves until they became bitter over it, that Joseph was trying to take over their father's farm. Three of them left the church and riled up a number of locals against Joseph. The fourth son, although not leaving the church, was chastised by Joseph for his rebelliousness.

Meanwhile, an amazingly shallow—if not downright silly— reason for apostatizing came to light when Simonds Ryder left the church because he received a letter from Joseph and Sidney stating that he had been called to preach, and that the will of the Lord was made known to them by the spirit. But the mission call letter misspelled his last name with an *i* instead of a *y*. Ryder was so offended that doubts began creeping in, fearing that the Spirit of the Lord had made a mistake in his mission call, since Joseph had made a mistake in spelling his name.

Then he and Ezra Booth began negative discussions about Joseph and the church, talking themselves into all-out apostasy.

At the church's general conference on September 6, 1831, the elders voted that Ezra Booth not preach the gospel anymore, due to reasons of apostasy. He then became the first apostate to publish against the church. Since he was educated and could write well, he became the most influential dissident of the area. And all nine of his letters were printed in the *Ohio Star* at Ravenna, Ohio.

First, Palmyra newspapers had criticized the coming forth of The Book of Mormon, then Ohio papers had begun the tirade, but now the first national press began slamming the church.

On August 31 and September 1, 1831, the first national articles appeared. A reporter named James Gordon Bennett had gone to upstate New York, after the Saints had left that state, and interviewed enough church critics that he wrote an article for the *Morning Courier and New York Enquirer,* which made the Saints look not only ridiculous, but downright nonreligious. This article helped shape public opinion, as it was published by other papers, and even had an effect on how historians for over a hundred years looked upon the church.

But the attacks on the church that gave them the most immediate grief were the nine letters by Ezra Booth in the local Ohio paper, which riled up the heretofore tolerant Ohio citizens. Booth had become bitter over his trials in Missouri and, as a former Methodist minister who hoped to have increased power, had become furious when the Savior would not grant him "power to smite men and make them believe"! Booth's letters made some fairly outrageous claims—a dozen main ones in all, but three that seemed the most incendiary—that Joseph and Sidney planned to rule as dictators in Missouri, that the Saints were inciting the Indians to warfare against the whites, and (in a truthful but out-of-context claim) that Joseph said the Bible was defective in its present state. (Joseph maintained that through the centuries the "plain and precious parts" of the Bible, as referred to in The Book of Mormon, had been taken out, which contradicted the teachings of *men* in the major churches, especially those who had held possession of the Bible manuscripts, making it necessary to revise certain passages in the Bible. Furthermore, there were some mistakes made in earlier translations.)

In response to Booth's nine letters published in the newspaper, Joseph and Sidney left their revising work at Hiram, Ohio, in December 1831 and held meetings in the villages to counter Booth's letters. They finished in mid-January 1832 and went back to revising in Hiram, believing they had assuaged most of the bad feelings against them.

But just two months later, on March 24, 1832, the worst attacks yet came against Joseph and Sidney.

Joseph and Emma were exhausted from caring for the sick twins, Julia and Joseph Murdock, now 11 months old. Joseph fell asleep while holding his son. Outside, Simonds Ryder snuck up to the house with 40 or 50 men who were half drunk; whiskey had been given them by Ryder and two or three of John Johnson's sons. The men were all from Hiram, Garrettsville, and Shalersville. Inside, Emma heard tapping on the window, then saw the door burst open. She screamed.

C H A P T E R 17

J OSEPH was awakened by Emma's scream, then was grabbed and carried out of the house by a dozen men who grasped him by his clothes and hair. He kicked one man loose from him, then the others swore they would kill him if he did not allow them to have their way with him. They choked him into unconsciousness and carried him further away from the house. In a meadow they ripped off his clothes, leaving him with only his collar, and they beat him mercilessly. One scratched him until blood poured down his body, yelling at him, "G – – d – – – ye, that's how the Holy Ghost falls on folks!" (The quote is given precisely as recorded in Joseph's journal.)

Then a man tried forcing a vial of acid in his mouth to pour down his throat, but Joseph clenched his teeth. The man broke his tooth, causing him to speak with a slight whistle for years, until his tooth was repaired in Nauvoo.

They had planned to castrate him, and had even brought a Dr. Dennison along to perform the operation. They placed Joseph on a wooden plank to be used as their operating table. But when the doctor saw him helplessly stretched out on it, he changed his mind and refused.

The men next poured hot tar over Joseph. This was a torture in and of itself, as tar has to reach a high temperature to melt; then it soaks into the pores of the skin and is very painful to have removed—but it has to be removed because it stops the skin from breathing, which can be fatal. The mob then poured pillow feathers over their victim to humiliate Joseph, which was part of the evil ritual.

They left him in his misery. He struggled to stand and pull the tar away from his mouth so he could breathe, another painful ordeal, and then he staggered home.

When Emma saw him in the darkness of the doorway, she thought he was covered with blood, and she fainted. Friends had gathered at the house by now and immediately covered his nakedness with a blanket at the doorway and took him inside. Mrs. Johnson, who had been healed by him, covered him with lard to make the operation of removing the tar easier. That lasted all night, with Mrs. Johnson and others scraping and peeling the tar from his skin. His body was now lacerated. His baby twin boy, Joseph Murdock, already weak from the measles, was made sicker from exposure by the open door when the mob had attacked, and died a few days later.

The same mob then went to find Sidney Rigdon. They grabbed his heels, dragged him outside over the frozen ground, and injured his head severely, knocking him unconscious. They also poured tar and feathers over him and left him for dead. Later he arose and wandered about, delirious. His wife found him staggering about and brought him in. For days he was out of his mind, asking for a razor to kill both his wife and Joseph.

Later one of the mob commented that Joseph had fought ferociously, while Sidney had attempted to calm them, calling them gentlemen. These men, according to Simonds Ryder, were not fighting Joseph over religion, as had been the case in New York; rather, Ryder claims they had found papers that they interpreted as showing church members' property would be taken away and controlled by Joseph—a warped interpretation of the Law of Consecration.

It is possible that John Johnson's daughter, Nancy Marinda Johnson, was by now a plural wife of Joseph, and that her brother Eli, who had apostatized from the church, was angry because he was under the impression Joseph had been promiscuous with her, not knowing of the actual marriage. It had been Eli who had called for the castration. Only one person other than Eli made the allegation that Joseph had more than one woman in his life—Ezra Booth, who also assumed Joseph was married only to Emma, and therefore accused Joseph of being immoral.

The next day after the attack, amazingly, Simonds Ryder and Felatiah Allen, instigators who had provided whiskey for the mob, went to church with other mob members. They were surprised when Joseph got up to speak. He never made mention of the assault. Neighbors who had assisted him spoke in church after his sermon and told of the events the night before. His graciousness served as an example and touched some of the mobbers. That day three new members were baptized, and tradition has it they had been part of the mob.

Because of the mob attack, Sidney Rigdon was now in fear of future attacks. He moved with his family to Kirtland, then to Chardon. But he would soon take another trip with Joseph, along with Newel K. Whitney and Peter Whitmer, to Missouri on April 1, 1832, just a week after the attack, in order to quell unhappy feelings in Missouri.

Emma and baby Julia meanwhile went to live with Newel Whitney's family in Kirtland.

There, Emma had a humiliating experience. But through it she remained remarkably gracious. She had been invited to live in the home by Newel, but Newel had made the indelicate mistake of forgetting to inform his wife. So when Emma and little Julia showed up at Newel's doorstep, Newel's sister-in-law confronted her and said she would move out if Emma moved in. Newel's daughter, Elizabeth Ann, was therefore forced into a corner and, wishing to make peace in the family, asked Emma to leave.

Because of Emma's desire for order and maintaining peace in the kingdom, she told no one of her experience till years later. Finding herself homeless now, she moved in with other church members, including Lucy Mack Smith, who said Emma worked faithfully "for the interest of those with whom she stayed, cheering them by her lively and spirited conversation," which gives an insightful glimpse into Emma's character.

Joseph, finally arriving in Missouri, was able to tackle problems there first hand. The members were complaining that they were having to assume the debts of the Ohio Saints, whom they thought were wealthier, although they were actually having to struggle on the frontier like overworked oxen. They were living the Law of Consecration well, however, in all other respects, and they had survived the first winter in the wilderness community too impoverished to buy much of anything at the stores, but were basically happy and comfortable. Church activity was high and they got along well.

On April 26, 1832, they held a council of the church, and Joseph was sustained as president. That same day, Joseph received a revelation for Newel Whitney, Sidney, Oliver, Martin Harris, and himself, saying they were to help the poor, both there and in Ohio, and that they were to be equal. Minutes of the meeting maintained that they were all "united together in love," and all differences were settled.

Two and three days later Joseph visited the Colesville branch in Kaw, Missouri, where his friend Porter Rockwell lived. Old friends were reunited, and the Saints rejoiced seeing their old New York friend and prophet.

With harmony restored, a week later, on May 6, 1832, Joseph, Sidney, and Newel Whitney began their return trip to Ohio. When they reached New Albany, Ohio, their stagecoach horses panicked. Newel jumped out for safety, but his foot caught in the stagecoach wheel and was broken, along with his leg, in several places. Joseph jumped out without harm.

While Sidney went ahead to Kirtland, Joseph cared for Newel in a public house at Greenville, Indiana, for four weeks. Joseph set bones and cared for him, and when a doctor finally arrived and saw what a proficient medical job Joseph had done, he said he wished a Mormon could stay in his town, thinking all had the skills of Joseph.

Soon afterward Joseph contracted a stomach sickness and vomited so hard that his jaw dislocated. Newel laid his hands on him and, through the power of the priesthood, said Joseph, he was healed from that very moment. On June 6, 1832,

Joseph wrote Emma, saying he had gone almost every day to a small grove of trees to pray and meditate and had cried "for my folly" for allowing the adversary to have power over him in the past—but felt he had been forgiven. He was apparently to some degree a perfectionist, and along with that had likely chastised himself for what he saw as a weakness—being forcible and highly energetic toward others to get things done.

Afterward, with Newel still in bed nursing his injury, Joseph prophesied to him that if he would start the next morning, they would take a wagon to the river and quickly catch a ferry to take them across, where a wagon would be waiting. The wagon would take them to a boat landing, and they could immediately board a boat and be heading upriver before 10 o'clock. Though still recovering from his horrific accident, but with terrific faith, Newel agreed, and found every detail to happen just as Joseph said it would.

They soon found themselves home.

Later that same month of June 1832, the first edition of *The Evening and the Morning Star* was published in Missouri as the westernmost newspaper in the United States.

New converts and move-ins from Ohio began pouring in daily, and there were now 300 Saints in Independence.

No sooner had Joseph quelled the problems there and returned to Ohio, than a new problem arose—only half the incoming new members were embracing the Law of Consecration. And those who were belonged to the poorer class. Another problem was that even though members entering the Law of Consecration agreed to give up their property if they apostatized, the courts were upholding their desire to get it back, so the laws of the church were being defied and ripped to shreds.

In their Missouri newspaper W. W. Phelps criticized those who made more money by working for non-church members. The Law of Consecration would not work unless they fully lived it and worked solely within their own community. He also let his feelings be known about the lazy. Joseph backed him up and informed them of a new rule—no one could be baptized who would not enter the Law of Consecration.

The Saints' next problem came simply from growing pains. W. W. Phelps stated in the July issue of his newspaper that the land they had plowed and prepared would only provide enough crops for those already living there. New move-ins were causing a shortage of food, and there was just not enough to go around. They would have to split their food among more members than they had counted on, but they would survive.

But then a new problem arose—this one from non-Mormon neighbors. The older settlers were now beginning to see the Saints as a threat, not just growing in numbers but befriending the Native Americans and even spreading their beliefs that the "Indian migrations" were part of the gathering tribes of Israel. Ironically, the Saints were thrilled by the very sight that horrified the old settlers—seeing the "savages" passing their town by the thousands. Unfortunately for these Native Americans, they had been displaced and sent from their own lands by the U.S. government, so now they were camping outside town on their way west to their new "Indian territory." The Indian migration was, of course, a tragic occurrence The Saints were feeling compassion for the Indians, having experienced exile themselves. Still, the Saints rejoiced to see them gathering in the West, hoping they could someday have access to teaching the restored gospel to them, hopefully away from others—the competing, jealous missionaries and incompetent Indian agents who had earlier combined to stop the Saints from converting many.

In his newspaper Phelps took liberty with official church positions—not only inaccurately publishing his views that the Indian displacements were part of the Second Coming of Christ—but also predicting that the Second Coming would take place by 1841. Most importantly, however, were his newspaper articles that would in effect light a spark that would send a prairie fire through their community—he accidently angered the old settlers. And he did so with a single newspaper article. But it was an incendiary article that would set the stage for an explosion.

MEANWHILE, back in Ohio, Joseph decided it was time to open a general store. He left his wife and daughter Julia in a house that was formerly a general store owned by Newel K. Whitney and Algernon Gilbert, and asked his brother Hyrum to keep an eye on them. Then Joseph and Newel shot up to Albany, New York City, and Boston to secure loans and goods for the store they hoped to open.

In New York City Joseph explored Manhattan Island several hours each day, while Newel inspected and ordered merchandise. Newel had experience as a successful businessman, so was fit for the job.

Joseph had time to walk among the crowds in New York City and ponder. Because of that, he wrote Emma on October 13, 1832, describing the magnificent buildings, stating, "The language of my heart is like this." He then detailed to her that he liked the works that made man more comfortable and happy. And that the Lord was not displeased with that. But "only against man is the anger of the Lord kindled because they give not the glory; therefore their iniquities shall be visited upon their heads and their works shall be burned up with unquenchable fire." He saw transgressions of God's commandments in people's faces and stated that only their dress made them look beautiful. He felt sad for the people of the city. "Oh, how long, oh Lord shall this order of things exist." He would become so consumed in his sadness, meditating while exploring the city and studying its people, that he would retire to his room at night to think about his wife and Julia. He encouraged Emma, stating he felt for her and hoped God would soften the hearts of those around her to be kind to her. He reminded her that God is her friend and that "you have one true and living friend on earth—your husband." Meanwhile, Emma was about to again give birth.

There in New York City, Joseph stayed with a hundred boarders from all parts of the globe. He befriended in particular one young man from Jersey, who spoke with him long into the night. So attached did they become that they did not want to part from each other when the man's boat left the next day.

Joseph and Newel ordered $20,000 worth of goods and returned to Ohio. They arrived home November 6, 1832, just after Emma delivered their first biological son who would live, Joseph III. Not just the parents rejoiced, but all the church joined in who had followed their child-related travails.

The store that Joseph opened was his first commercial enterprise for the church. It was poorly furnished and had one major flaw—Joseph's heart. His heart was too big to turn people away who could not afford to pay, so he would extend credit to just about everyone. But the disaster came sooner than expected. Soon they were out of goods, and Joseph was in his deepest financial straits yet. He then attempted to run a sawmill and a leather tannery—but those failed also, probably because of his "unreasonable" generosity.

On November 8, 1832, two days after returning from New York, Joseph was working in the woods with his brothers near his parents' house, chopping wood, when three new converts arrived. They hailed from Mendon, New York, near Rochester. Their journey had begun two months earlier, but they had stopped and taught friends their newly accepted gospel. One had studied it, in fact, through The Book of Mormon for three years before finally accepting it.

His name was Brigham Young. The others were his brother Joseph and his friend Heber C. Kimball—all of tremendous importance later to the church.

Later to become the best known (perhaps other than Joseph) of all Latter-day Saints, Brigham was 31, a painter, glazier, and carpenter. He was solidly built, charismatic, and powerful. At the age of 28 he had moved to Mendon where he had read The Book of Mormon, left there at his brother Phineas's home by Joseph Smith's brother Samuel. He was later converted by elders traveling through; then he went to Canada to convert his own brother, Joseph Young, a Methodist minister. Brigham's wife had died just two months before he met Joseph Smith, leaving him with two little girls. Brigham rejoiced when he met Joseph, saying, "My joy was full at the privilege of shaking the hand of the Prophet of God and receiving the spirit of prophecy, that he was all that any man could believe him to be as a true prophet."

That same first day, they walked back to Joseph's parents' house and, at a meeting that night, Joseph asked Brigham to teach the group. Then a new type of miracle occurred—the first one of its category in well over a thousand years—Brigham got up and spoke in an unknown language, one in fact he did not even know. Joseph stood and said, "Brethren, this tongue that we have heard is the gift of God." Then Joseph began to speak in an unknown tongue and afterward said, "Brethren, this is the language of our father Adam while he dwelt in Eden; and the time will again come, that when the Lord brings again Zion, the Zion of Enoch, this people will then all speak the language which I have just spoken." This was the "gift of tongues," which was also *practiced* by early church members in New Testament times. Joseph actually spoke in tongues several different times. Zebedee Coltrin says he also heard Joseph sing in tongues.

As with so many other manifestations of the Holy Ghost, including healing and using seer stones, for every such gift that God gave members of his church, Joseph believed, so did the adversary have power to bestow counterfeit gifts. Healings from outside the restored priesthood, for example, were generally accompanied in pentecostal assemblies where people shouted and became very dramatic, whereas in the Lord's way, said Joseph, such gifts were bestowed quietly, reverently, and with dignity. Speaking in tongues could be from the Lord, Joseph taught, if someone was there to understand and interpret what was being said, while the adversary's counterfeit form had people blathering about in gibberish that no one else could understand, even, it has been reported, blaspheming and swearing against God in foreign languages, which the person speaking has no understanding of, but of which they are convinced is a manifestation of "speaking in tongues," which they believe is from God.

Because Joseph had found occasion to rebuke members of the church in Ohio for manifesting counterfeit spiritual gifts, some at this meeting where Brigham spoke in tongues thought Joseph was going to rebuke him as well. While it was Joseph's first time to witness that gift, it had been manifested by other church members, perhaps Brigham himself, in Mendon, New York, and in Pennsylvania. From that point, this manifestation became common among the members in Ohio.

Brigham took an immediate liking to Joseph and his teachings, and states that he "treasured them up in my heart."

Meanwhile, events were shaping in other parts of the country that caused Joseph reflection. John Calhoun, in South Carolina, vehemently opposed tariffs imposed by Congress in 1828, and now another one imposed in 1832. Fed up, he threatened to secede his state, South Carolina, from the union, but President Andrew Jackson called up the army and navy to attack them. South Carolina backed down and it seemed the country was united again.

But on Christmas Day, 1832, Joseph had a revelation predicting the great Civil War that would begin in South Carolina. He predicted the South would seek other countries to come to its aid and that even slaves would rise up. A most important aspect of the prophecy was that the war would be extremely bloody, including "the death and misery of many souls." He also predicted "fierce and vivid lightning and the thunder of heaven," referring to artillery and cannons that would be witnessed by the millions who would fight when the prophecy came to pass in 1860. The call to positive action by the Saints was to "stand . . . in holy places, and be not moved," which one might interpret as continuing the missionary effort and other programs of the church.

(Joseph also prophesied events other than the coming of the Civil War. Later, in 1844, for example, he would speak from a woodland grove as a violent storm approached. He told the congregation to remain seated and the storm would not bother them. "The storm divided over the grove," reports May Westover. "I well remember how it was storming on all sides of the grove, yet it was as calm around us as if there was no sign of a storm so nearby.")

Two days after the Civil War prophecy Joseph received a revelation known as the Olive Leaf, which revealed functions of the school of the prophets, information about the Lord's Second Coming, and how the Holy Ghost helps people.

A month later, on January 23, 1833, Joseph announced a new ordinance—the "washing of feet," as in New Testament times. He washed and dried the feet of men in the group, then gave a warning—that after receiving this "higher ordinance," if any should willfully break the commandments, they would be delivered to "the buffetings of Satan until the day of redemption."

Joseph had worked hard whenever he could for almost two years at revising the New Testament, and finally completed it in January 1833. On February 2 he boxed up the manuscript and announced it must not be opened until it reached Missouri and could be published. He hoped to have this revision of the Bible published in one volume with The Book of Mormon, but the press would be destroyed before that could take place, and his revised Bible would never be published during his lifetime. And thus the church would never utilize it, as stated earlier.

The next month, February 1833, came the revelation known as "The Word of Wisdom." Strong drinks and hot drinks—which church prophets have since interpreted as alcoholic drinks, tea, and coffee—along with tobacco, were discouraged from use by the Saints, but not by commandment; that would take place two decades later under Brigham Young, when it would become designated a commandment (and in later years was expanded to include illegal drugs and the misuse of prescription drugs). On the positive side of the commandment, all grains, and especially wheat, were recommended for use, along with herbs, but the flesh of beasts and fowls was to be used sparingly. "And all Saints who remember to keep and do these sayings, walking in obedience to the commandments, shall receive health in their navel and marrow to their bones. . . . And shall run and not be weary, and shall walk and not faint." (A year later Joseph did put some teeth into the admonition by stating that disobedience to it was grounds for being released from church office.)

The following month, March 1833, Joseph had the church buy three farms in Kirtland. The French farm was acquired for brickmaking, with Frederick G. Williams in charge.

Despite the church store's problems, Joseph's 140-acre farm was doing well and, even with frequent problems, the Law of Consecration was working overall, helping the poor especially. Missionaries were also finding great success, bringing in new people daily, all gathering to Ohio and Missouri.

Two months later, on May 25, 1833, his uncle John Smith arrived, being the first of his father's relatives to join, and at once his uncle began teaching the gospel. John's sons were John and George Albert Smith—George later becoming a president of the church. When Joseph's uncle John spoke near his home in New England, ministers would follow him and degrade the church, so he sold his farm and set out for Kirtland with two covered wagons carrying his wife, two sons, and daughter Clarissa. Five hundred miles later he arrived and bought a farm of 27 acres. And hired Brigham Young to lay his cabin floor.

A week later, on June 1, 1833, Joseph received a detailed revelation about the upcoming Kirtland Temple, even about its construction and size—55 by 65 feet. All three of the First Presidency saw in vision the pattern for building it. Frederick G. Williams writes, "The building appeared within viewing distance: I being the first to discover it. . . . After we had taken a good look at the exterior, the building seemed to come right over us."

After it was built, he said it looked exactly as he had seen it in vision. He would then teach that sacrifice brings forth blessings. Three men would go out with flyers to publicize it and to raise money for building it—his brother Hyrum and two others, Reynolds Cahoon (who would play a major role in an all-important decision in his life later in Nauvoo), and Jared Carter. Joseph himself would labor hard at the building, working in the stone quarry two miles south of the temple to gather and cut stone for it and also cutting timber for it.

On June 5 George Albert Smith, only 15 years old at the time, hauled the first load of stone for the temple. Even the fund-raisers—Hyrum and Reynolds—began digging a trench for the walls and actually finished the task themselves. The cornerstone was laid only seven weeks later, on July 23, 1833. Joseph had admonished the Saints to build the best building that hands could build to be the Lord's temple. "Shall we, brethren, build a house for our God of logs?"

It would take three more years of hard work and sacrifice for the struggling but growing community to complete the temple. Joseph was continually the primary force behind it, often providing pep talks.

About this time Joseph designed a city. He had seen the chaotic townships of most communities, especially in the western wilderness, where huts, lean-tos, and poorly built cabins had been thrown up facing odd directions, not even along streets, while sometimes placed in the middle of what should have been streets. So he envisioned a highly organized, well-conceived plan for a township: It had wide streets, public squares for civic and church buildings, a storehouse, schools, houses of stone and brick amidst groves of trees and gardens and, finally, farms on the outside of the city—all similar to the future Nauvoo. However, in the city of Zion he pictured half-acre lots for residences, while in Nauvoo they would have beautifully laid out full-acre lots. The plat for this envisioned city had each square mile divided into 10-acre blocks. He hoped that, after the first town of 20,000 inhabitants would fill it, a second town of the same size and design would be built, and so on.

He also visualized the temple in Independence, Missouri, as bigger than the one in Kirtland. It would be 65 by 87 feet.

But just as he was hoping to realize his dreams—especially with able and skilled craftsmen such as Brigham Young and his own uncle John coming into the fold—new attacks from enemies began and, as was always the case, they involved either the press, pastors, or apostates.

The first attack came from an apostate. Philastus Hurlbut, described earlier, had joined the church and then left it, first being disfellowshipped (while serving in the East a missionary) for "unChristian conduct with women," later detailed as using obscene language to a young female member. He had earlier been sent away from his previous faith by the Methodists for immorality. But in March 1833 he visited Joseph in his home and became converted, then ordained five days later by Sidney.

Hurlbut had hoped to marry into a prominent church leadership family and had been given the title "doctor" by his parents, in the old tradition that the seventh son would have supernatural powers. Capitalizing on this, Hurlbut had claimed in Kirtland he was a "physician." He was handsome and ambitious, but pompous and poorly educated, according to Joseph E. Johnson, who had lived with him when Hurlbut had boarded with his family for a year.

Although initially disfellowshipped for those obscenities to a young woman, he was later excommunicated when he openly criticized the church. He wished to stay aboard, so he appealed it, saying he had been absent from the church court. He requested a hearing. There, he confessed his mistakes and was granted his membership back. Apparently within hours, however, he bragged to the people that he had deceived "Joseph Smith's God." The church court called him in for another meeting and this time excommunicated him for good. He was infuriated and took the stance of an enemy to the church from thenceforth.

He went to Solomon Spaulding's brother, wife, and neighbors (as detailed in Appendix B), then made it his life's goal to discredit Joseph. For two months he attempted to prove The Book of Mormon was tied to Spaulding's manuscript, but failed. Then he interviewed about 100 locals in Palmyra who were willing to make negative comments about the Smith family and sign an affidavit. One interesting note that may or may not be true has to do with the source of the seer stone Joseph used to search for treasure—before he received the one with the ancient plates. A Willard Chase claims that Joseph and his brother Alvin Smith had helped Willard dig a well in 1822, where they found the interesting stone, which Joseph claimed afterward had special powers.

Hurlbut then took the written comments on tour back to Ohio and spoke against the Saints. Brazenly, he even took them into Kirtland. The non-Mormons he spoke to believed him lock, stock, and barrel and became incensed at the Mormons. Threats were hurled at the Saints.

To defend their lives and property, the Latter-day Saints had to stand guard day and night, even sleeping in their work clothes. George Albert Smith guarded Sidney Rigdon's house. Joseph also had guards at his home every night. Most of the elders kept guns at their sides, and this angered some of the other elders into leaving the church, as they were committed pacifists, not believing in fighting, even in self defense.

Then some of the Saints began believing Hurlbut's papers. So, to counteract his attacks, Joseph actually read them at meetings and labeled them the work of the devil.

Sidney Rigdon, ever since his head injury, would never be the same. From then on he would make all matters dealing with apostates worse by unjustifiably fanning the flames. In Hurlbut's case, Sidney made unproven claims that angered Hurlbut so intensely that he took it out on Joseph and made a public threat to kill him.

C H A P T E R

# 19

BECAUSE of the threat on his life, Joseph filed a legal complaint. Hurlbut was hauled before court on April 12, 1834, and convicted. He was also ordered to "keep the peace" for six months or he would lose a $200 bond.

Thereafter, because of the outrageous death threat against Joseph, Hurlbut lost most of his credibility among members and non-members alike, but nevertheless found a willing audience in a newspaper editor.

Eber D. Howe of the *Painsville Telegraph* paid $500 to Hurlbut for the rights to his work and published them later that year in the first well-known, if not the first ever, anti-Mormon book, *Mormonism Unveiled*. This book, which the Saints decried as completely erroneous, did nevertheless influence writers, opinion makers, and historians for generations.

To combat the negativity, William H. Kelly of the Reorganized Church years later went to Palmyra to interview some of the same people Hurlbut had spoken with, plus he spoke with numerous others. In contrast to Hurlbut, Kelly found an even split in Palmyra among those who knew the Smiths—those who spoke favorably versus those who did not. A disclosure that both Hurlbut and Kelly did not make was that many opinions had come from mere rumor and gossip, rather than from those who actually knew the Smiths. The results were published in *The Saints Herald* on June 1, 1881. Hurlbut, it seems, had edited out

50% of his interviewees—the ones who had spoken favorably of the Smiths.

In Missouri, meanwhile, the seeds were being sown for the onslaught of an all-out war.

The lower-life element had become disenchanted with the religious beliefs of the Saints, then started becoming jealous of their industriousness. Some anti-Mormon religious leaders organized a band of vigilantes to purge the countryside of these undesirables.

Heretofore, it was the rabble-rousing poorer class who were antagonistic toward the Saints, but with the onslaught of pastors, a new group of enemies appeared at Independence—the more respectable middle class.

The local ministry had now accomplished the first stage of their design, so they held a large gathering to whip the mob into a frenzy to start the second stage. As the meeting progressed, however, an unplanned cog hit the works—someone starting passing bottles around—and the carefully orchestrated gathering soon degenerated into a whiskeyfest, whereupon most of the mob staggered away, stoned.

Porter's closest neighbor, David Pettegrew, explains the reason behind the growing opposition:

"The gathering of the Saints continued, brethren came in daily from all parts of the United States, and this began to raise some excitement amongst the people opposed to our church. The gift of tongues, I think, was the cause or means of the excitement. When they heard little children speaking tongues that they did not themselves understand, and knew also that those children could not have acquired the different tongues by learning, a Mr. Pool, of Independence . . . observed that he understood the tongue that they spoke. It was the Delaware tongue, and he believed that this Book of Mormon was true because these children had never learnt these different tongues that we now hear them speak. Some of the local, anti-Mormon lawyers observed that if we did not put a stop to such things and suffer it to go on, all Independence will believe."

There were now actually a total of 10 concerns the old settlers had:

First, they began to feel crowded. They had moved there to begin with because it was wide open territory, and they wanted to be away from civilization. So when the U.S. Government redefined the borders and decided that all areas west of them were "Indian lands" only, and off limits for whites, they began to feel hemmed in. Therefore, when the Saints moved in, and in even greater numbers, the old settlers felt even more hemmed in. (By mid-1833 over 1,000 Saints had emigrated there.)

Second, the old settlers saw the Mormons befriending the Indians, whom the settlers saw as their enemies.

Third, the Saints were declaring in their newspaper and in meetings that the Indians would be restored to their rights and former strength, which the settlers saw as practically inviting the Indians to declare war against them.

Fourth, the Saints were inviting envy. They were taking care of their own poor, building better houses than they, establishing larger farms, and setting up mills.

Fifth, the old settlers feared the Saints' growing power base. It was bad enough that they were growing in population, but soon they would be able to elect county officials.

Sixth, they disliked their strange religious beliefs—seeing angels, believing in a gold bible, and performing miracles, when the popular Protestant notion was that miracles had ceased since the time of Christ.

Seventh, they misinterpreted the Saints' doctrine that the area was the land of their inheritance, so they thought the Saints would actually oust them from their own property.

Eighth, was the same old outcry by "rival" churches who saw the Saints as their enemy. In mid-1833 Reverend Pixley from the Missionary Society and Reverend Finis Ewing of the Cumberland Presbyterians took up the torch of public outcry against the Saints. Pixley wrote to newspapers all over the state. He also spoke publicly against them in speeches to both Indians and whites, and finally he published a pamphlet against them, which he carried to the homes of the locals. In it Ewing wrote, "The Mormons are the common enemies of mankind and ought to be destroyed."

Ninth, was the miracle of seeing children speak in tongues, which could not be explained away.

The tenth and final "straw" was Phelps' newspaper article, mentioned earlier. Most of the Saints were New Englanders and abolitionists, and certainly did not own slaves, which was enough fuel of its own to incite the locals against them, but when Phelps published his newspaper article entitled "Free People of Color"—the locals were enraged. The background to the article is this . . .

Earlier that year several free African-American members of the church had attempted to emigrate to Missouri along with the whites. However, they found Missouri laws prevented them from entering without a letter that proved they had citizenship in another state. In order to communicate to them, Phelps reprinted the laws in his newspaper in July 1833, and added an editorial that on the one hand tried to remain neutral: "As to slaves, we have nothing to say," but he then turned around and exposed his and the Saints' true feelings in general on the subject: "In connection with the wonderful events of this age, much is doing toward abolishing slavery." And that was the line that lit the fuse.

That one article declared all-out war on the old settlers without even knowing it. And it now set the fuse for those settlers into an armed uprising against the Saints . . .

CHAPTER *20*

A mob of 500 met. And its leaders this time made certain whiskey would not be passed around. The settlers frothed at the courthouse and made up a manifesto of grievances, specifying two of the ten issues above—the fact that they believed the Saints were "deluded fanatics" by believing in revelations, and also wanting their homeland as their inheritance. They stated they had put up with this until now, but Phelps' article inviting free people of color from outside Missouri to join the church and move to Missouri could not be tolerated. They feared that by having free people of color among them, it "would corrupt our blacks and instigate them to bloodshed." Therefore, "we believe it a duty we owe to ourselves, our wives, and children, to the cause of public morals, to remove them [the Saints] from among us."

The manifesto gave them a short time to move out, and declared the Saints would be compensated for all property they could not take. On the surface this was semi-generous, but there was a catch—if they refused to leave the land in peace "as they had found it," then the settlers would do whatever it took to get rid of them, even "forcibly if we must." The biggest catch of all was that the manifesto left the locals an "out" to not pay for the farmlands of the Saints, since they were highly cultivated by now and could not be left "as they had found it." Hundreds of men signed it, including Judge Samuel Lucas.

It also announced a mass meeting at the courthouse on July 20, 1833, to determine the next step.

Scuffling about to avoid catastrophe, Phelps printed a special edition, backtracking and not even presenting the truth. He claimed his article had been misunderstood and that the Saints wanted to stop free African-Americans from emigrating to the state and even prevent them from coming into the church. One statement was truthful—he admitted his article was not church policy but was his own attempt to soften the escalating situation.

The mob saw through his attempt and held its next meeting. Pettegrew records:

"This first mob part I saw were going by my house on their way to Independence to a great council held there. . . . They had a solemn and determined look. I saw several women in their company who seemed to be more interested in mobbing than their husbands. I remember very well that for 2 or 3 days of their appointed meeting that it rained in torrents and I never heard in all my life such terrible thundering—the earth fairly shook, and during these heavy rains and storm I saw women returning home with their husbands from the mob meeting seeming perfectly satisfied with their day's labor. Although the lightning would flash so vividly as almost to blind, the thunder rolling over their heads and it looked as if heaven had opened its fury upon the earth, yet these persons went on regardless of all."

At their July 20 meeting, a mob of several hundred met and decided no more Saints would be allowed into the county. They also decided that those already there must leave, and that their press, storehouse, and shops must close immediately. Finally, with cruel sarcasm, they demanded that those who refused to leave should ask those among them who had the gift of prophecy what would happen if they didn't leave.

A dozen Missourians delivered the ultimatum to six local Latter-day Saint officials. The reply was that the six would have to consult with church leaders in Kirtland and that it would take three months to receive an answer.

When the dozen Missourians galloped back to the townspeople with this report, the mob went into a rampage. They galloped into the woods searching for Mormon property. Discovering the home of W. W. Phelps, they thoroughly vandalized it, throwing his furniture into the street. Then they galloped about the woods, searching for the Mormon newspaper press in a separate building. They finally discovered it and "piled" his press, dumping it out the second story window. Then they searched about for the *Book of Commandments* that was then being printed, and destroyed all they could find.

They grabbed some of the elders, tied them up, and whipped them. Women and children ran in horror into the woods to hide. The mob went searching for Bishop Partridge. Three of the mob charged right into his house and found him sitting with his weakened wife who was recovering from childbirth. His little girls, who were coming home, watched all this from the creek—they saw the mob surrounding their house, then taking their father away. They heard the mob say they were going to kill their father.

Partridge was taken to the public square by 50 men. Among them was Judge Samuel D. Lucas. Another, Russell Hicks, told Partridge that since he was the Mormon's leader, he must agree to leave. Partridge told them he had not hurt anyone and would not leave, and that if he had to suffer for his religion, it was no more than others had done. The mob yelled, "Call upon your Jesus!" Then threw him on the ground and beat and kicked him. Hicks began tearing off his clothes, but Edward asked that he be not made naked in public, so some of the mob stepped in and let him keep his clothes on, but they torturously tarred and feathered him, applying tar that was mixed with acid, which burned into his flesh.

Edward took his abuse quietly. Some of the mob felt sorry for him and their anger dwindled. Many became sober and silent, then let him get up and start for home, with the help of one young Latter-day Saint who came to assist him.

When he arrived home, his daughter thought he was an Indian covered in feathers. Neighbors made an upstairs room more private for him by putting up blankets to block sight of him as they pulled the tar and feathers off. During the ordeal he said he was proud to have suffered for the truth.

Charles Allen also had his clothes ripped off. He was told to either deny The Book of Mormon or leave the county, but he refused both. So they tarred and feathered him as well, surrounded by hundreds of the mob.

Porter, meanwhile, had been peaceably operating his ferry, when this same evening a dozen Missourian passengers whirled on him and warned him to deny the church or they would tar and feather him too. Porter said nothing. Once ashore they left without paying their share and laughing at him.

This was Porter's first brush with the Missourians. Its psychological impact affected his complex personality. In his short life he had demonstrated a tendency for defiance, but one can only guess at the rancor brewing within him now as he watched the Missourians galloping away from his ferry, still laughing. The prophet of his boyhood had taught him to "love thy enemies," and Porter now faced Joseph's doctrine head on.

As the next day dawned, the Saints sought redress from the government. State officials told them they would "look into it." Riding out to inspect the damage done to the Phelps' home, the Lieutenant Governor of Missouri, Lilburn W. Boggs, surveyed the scene, shook his head, and uttered a remark that quaked the Saints—it would probably be best if the Mormons simply left the territory.

Boggs, age 42, was a native Kentuckian. He had moved from Kentucky to Missouri in 1816 at age 24, had worked in St. Louis as a bank cashier, and next as a traveling merchant. He had moved to Independence and served as a state senator before his current position. As a speculator, he had *competed with the Saints for land in Jackson County* and saw them as competitors. He was also pro-slavery, and now more emphatically told the Saints, "You now know what our Jackson boys can do, and you must leave the country."

Less subtle caveats came from night-riding mobocrats— armies of Missourians who now rode through the streets of

Independence, warning Latter-day Saints to leave the county or be flogged.

But the Saints would not budge.

To intimidate them, the mob gathered in the streets by the hundreds, sporting rifles and a red flag in the "token of blood." And they gave the Saints an ultimatum . . . They had to leave. Otherwise they would whip Mormon leaders to death and turn their slaves loose on Mormon villages to burn crops and tear down houses. Six Latter-day Saint leaders offered themselves as ransom, even unto death, if they would allow the rest to stay in peace. The Mormon offer was turned down, so the mob hit them with another demand—half the Saints would have to leave by January 1 and the other half by April 1; furthermore, they reiterated their demand that their newspaper and store would have to be discontinued and no more Saints would be allowed to enter the region. To that, the Mormons agreed.

When Joseph Smith received word of the Missouri persecutions from Oliver Cowdery, he cried aloud, saying he wished he were with his people to share their distress. (Not much later, Joseph would reveal his tremendous respect for the power of the press and an informed people—on October 1, 1833, he would send Oliver to New York to buy another printing press for $800. This would be set up in Kirtland where *The Evening and the Morning Star* would have its name changed to simply *The Evening and Morning Star,* with plans to move it to Missouri.)

As for how to handle their persecutions in Missouri, on August 6, 1833, Joseph received a revelation. It counseled the Missouri Saints to patiently endure their persecution and support the law of the land. He sent messengers with this revelation, along with his own suggestion that the most distressed should leave, and the rest should bear it until all violence ceased. He also stated that God would allow them to stand in their own self-defense. He sent his messages through Orson Hyde and John Gould, asking them to add their own advice.

The Saints in September then sent a signed petition to Governor Daniel Dunklin of Missouri, explaining the situation and requesting that troops protect their rights. Taking the message was W. W. Phelps and Orson Hyde.

But Dunklin refused to protect them. In a letter to a friend, Dunklin confesses, "I have no regard for the Mormons as a separate people; and have an utter contempt for them as a religious sect."

Joseph and Sidney were in Canada on October 5, 1833, when Governor Dunklin replied to Missouri church officials, offering a feigned sympathy and telling them to sue in the local courts. So the Saints went to a top Missouri law partnership, Alexander Doniphan and David Atchison, who were secured for $1,000, a higher-than-normal amount, but for a reason—the attorneys were afraid they would lose business by taking their case. The Saints agreed and signed a note for that amount. They were now standing up for their rights in the courts.

Immediately, word went out to the Missourians of their action. A mob formed the next night, October 31, 1833. This day of the year would be brought to the U.S. as "Halloween" a decade later, but for the Saints, it would hold some significance beginning this year. Nearly 50 mobbers attacked the small village of the "Whitmer Settlement" on the Big Blue River—the homes of Porter Rockwell and his parents, along with 10 other cabins. They pulled off roofs, broke up furniture and beds, and smashed pillows, leaving thousands of feathers floating over the homes' interiors. They tied Porter's brother-in-law, George Beebe, and his neighbor, Hiram Page, to a tree and whipped them. Others were also flogged senseless while their wives looked on. At the home of David Whitmer, mobocrats could not find Whitmer, but grabbed his wife by the hair and pulled her out screaming, then demolished her cabin. They beat up and threw stones at some of the men, but the Rockwells were spared. Women and children ran into the woods, exposed to the freezing cold all night. The mob rode off, ecstatic, screaming victory chants into the chilled evening air.

The next day the Saints were in a panic, knowing what had happened the night before could be merely a foretaste. Now, throughout the country, each Saint wondered if his property would be hit next. They were also in a scattered situation, their settlements extending east 10 or 12 miles. "What to do for safety they knew not," reports the *Times and Seasons* in 1839. "To resist large bodies of the mob . . . appeared useless, and to gather together into one body immediately was impracticable. . . . It was concluded to obtain peace warrants if possible against some of the principal leaders of the mob. . . . They then went to a magistrate and applied for a warrant but he refused to grant one."

Nightfall was closing in. The Saints knew Missourians would attack . . . but the question was where. Meanwhile, "the streets were filled with mobbers passing and re-passing, threatening the Saints in different directions with destruction."

That night, as expected, the mobocrats gathered in droves. The plan was to attack a small Mormon community called Colesville and make it such an example of their ferocity that all the Saints of Missouri would *want* to leave.

At Colesville, however, the Mormons were prepared—much to the Missourian's surprise. Two Missouri spies preceding the mob had been sent to the village where Parley P. Pratt caught sight of them and shouted a warning to the village. Pratt was then clubbed by the two Missourians—until other Mormons came to his rescue—and the two spies were apprehended. When the mob abandoned their attack, the two prisoners were released.

JOSEPH SMITH: A BIOGRAPHY | *Richard Lloyd Dewey*

Back at Independence, the Mormons were not so well prepared. Mobocrats moved on the town, attacking, plundering, and demolishing Mormon homes. David Pettegrew details the scene: "They threw down some houses and shot at Sister Shurwood and several other sisters as they were running in a cornfield. I distinctly heard the reports of their guns." Men were whipped. Sidney Gilbert's house was partly demolished, and Orson Pratt was rifle-butted in the head. (He would live through the injury, however.) Women and children were chased out of their homes. The store was broken into and goods were scattered in the street.

Meanwhile, at the Big Blue River, Missouri horsemen converged on another Mormon settlement. Porter was busy manning the ferry when the mobocrats reigned in at his father's cabin. Stripped to the waist and smeared in war paint, they terrorized Porter's mother and eldest sister.

The mobbers then found a Mormon octogenarian, David Bennett, ill and unable to move. They beat him up, then shot him in the head. Miraculously he lived.

In the onslaught of destruction, several Mormons decided to defend themselves . . .

They gathered in a cluster and galloped off toward the disturbance. The mob saw them coming and fired—but missed. And the Mormons fired back. One Missourian was shot in the thigh and, because of his screams, the mobbers panicked and galloped away, frenzied, frustrated, and frothing.

With fury they retaliated and went on a pillaging spree. They discovered Porter's home where, neighbor Pettegrew reports, "They threw his house down, or all they could, cut open feather beds, destroyed all of his furniture and all they could lay hands on."

The Missourians galloped away into the night.

Not knowing what else to do, the next day two Latter-day Saint committees appealed to circuit judges. All they could obtain, however, were arrest warrants, "but it was too late to do anything with them," reports the *Times and Seasons*.

One mob member who broke into the store was grabbed by several Mormons and taken to a justice of the peace who refused to even issue an arrest warrant. Later, ironically, the arrested man obtained a warrant for false arrest against the several Saints who had caught him—Sidney Gilbert and three others—and the Saints were arrested and tossed into jail. (No evidence was ever presented that the Saints broke any laws.) The judge, Samuel Weston, it turns out, had been a signer of the manifesto against the Saints.

Now, certain Missourians friendly to the Saints advised them "to leave the State immediately, as the wounding of the young man on Saturday night had enraged the whole county" against them. They also said it was a common expression among the mob that Monday, in two days, the 4th of November, "would be a bloody day."

Next day, November 3, 1833, the mobbers somehow secured a cannon. Then, November 4, the inevitable happened. "A large mob collected at Wilson's store, about a mile west of the Big Blue," continues the *Times and Seasons*. They rode to the Big Blue River and took siege of Porter's ferry and drove him and his family away with threats. While his ferry was kept under siege, others rode back to Wilson's store. There, two children informed the mobocrats that 19 Mormons were marching on the Big Blue Village to defend fellow Mormons against the Missourians.

From Wilson's grocery a combined army of 50 mobocrats charged off to ambush the 19 Saints.

Spotting the coming army, the 19 defenders slipped into cornfields. The Missourians searched the fields, strong-arming Mormon women and children into helping with the hunt.

Then came a twist the Missourians had not expected . . . 30 other Mormons suddenly appeared. Because of their frenzied search, the Missourians had not seen this second Saint force approaching behind them and had left themselves wide open.

A number of the arriving Mormons had seen their homes unroofed in recent days and were hot for revenge. As the mobbers realized their predicament, they panicked and opened fire—but the Mormons would not flee. They simply stood there, taking the gunfire, and none would drop. Then they began advancing on the Missourians . . . slowly at first . . . and then breaking into a charge.

O F the 30 Saints, only 17 had guns, but they charged with such intensity that they frightened the Missourians into a panic. One of the mobbers, a local attorney named Hugh L. Brazeale, claimed with bravado, "With ten fellows, I will wade to my knees in blood, but what I will drive the Mormons from Jackson County." But the Saints shot Brazeale dead. They also killed Thomas Linville and wounded five or six other Missourians. A number of horses were also killed in the battle—a common occurrence in skirmishes.

Meanwhile, only two Mormons dropped from Missourians' lead balls. Philo Dibble was shot in the abdomen, but following a priesthood blessing he recovered immediately. Andrew Barber was also shot but died the next day. He was the first Mormon to ever die in battle.

The Missourians were humiliated, having been scattered by a smaller Mormon force. They now held meetings and formulated another plan. This time they would fight back in an altogether different manner—one the Saints had seen before, but never with such destructive intensity as would now be unleashed . . .

Through rumors. Wild rumors. Mobocrats now sent messengers to inform all of Missouri that the Mormons had ransacked Wilson's store, had shot his son, had attacked Independence, had allied themselves with Indians, and were presently about to launch, as a combined force, a complete massacre on the entire state of Missouri. The defeated mobocrats hoped the rumors would reach the governor's ear and that he would actually call the state militia against the Mormons.

When stories of the joined Saint and Indian insurrection reached Lieutenant Governor Boggs, he believed them. Immediately, he sent the Jackson County militia to "rescue" Independence: Colonel Thomas Pitcher, another signer of the Missourians' manifesto, was placed in command of the Missouri force and now drove his troops forward to engage the Mormons head on.

But this time the Saints were prepared and armed. They had just received news of the three jailed Mormons, and their reaction was furious. Two hundred Saints now mounted up and rode forth to Independence to free their brethren from jail.

Unknowingly, they rode directly toward the Missouri militia—who were now coming down the same road, straight toward them.

The face-to-face, man-to-man confrontation would occur just around a woodland bend—and at their forefront rode Porter Rockwell, who had had enough of the Missourians' abuse.

The two forces halted and faced each other. The Saints now learned that the three jailed prisoners had been released by the mob and their own leaders had made a momentous decision—to evacuate the county. So when Lyman Wight faced the militia, the militia's commander, Colonel Pitcher, realized the Saints now had the wind knocked out of their sails and felt no desire to fight, so he decided to play upon their naiveté. He shrewdly confessed that he and fellow Missourians had been at fault for all their prejudice, and suggested that the Mormons, as an act of good faith, deliver their arms to the militia.

Boggs himself suddenly rode up and urged them to cooperate, promising the Mormons that the mob would be required to surrender their guns as well. However, certain Saints on horseback spotted some of the mob members within the militia force, facing them just yards away, and were suspicious. But their leader, Lyman Wight, was overly optimistic, if not gullible, and decided to show good faith—he agreed to the terms and ordered his men to give up their weapons. But only if the militia would disarm the mobocrats as well. Of course Colonel Pitcher agreed. So the Mormon force complied and threw down their arms. The militia gathered them up and rode gleefully back to Independence. There, they spread the word quickly that the Saints were now disarmed.

Seeing them defenseless, the mob immediately launched an unabashed orgy of destruction.

Many Saints were caught, tied, and flogged. Others, ill and aged, died from the cold. Families were scattered in the confusion. Children were lost from their parents.

Lyman Wight, the once proud leader of the potentially powerful Mormon army, was not only disarmed now but personally hunted. He reports, "I was chased by one of these gangs across an open prairie five miles, without being overtaken, and lay there for [several weeks] in the woods, and was three days and nights without food."

At this point David Pettegrew adds:

"The mob now started towards my house and I made all haste for home and when I arrived I found the mob had driven my family into the streets, and were driving the brethren out of their houses and homes, placed them in the public road and told them to leave. 'If you do not flee for your lives,' said they, 'your God-damned noses will smell hell.' . . .

"I now saw my family in the streets houseless, we must go or die. I bid them to march on as well as they could. I then returned to my house, endeavoring to take what I possibly could with me. No one can tell, or imagine, the feelings of my heart upon re-entering, in that once . . . cherished home. I looked around to see what I could take with me. The Book of Mormon, my Bible, a razor and a decanter of composition which my wife had requested me to bring were all I took. After leaving everything I bid farewell to my home and hastened to overtake my family. I found them placed in wagons as they were still sick. My wagons and animals were not home and, of course, they had to be left. . . .

". . . We travelled south, nothing but the canopies of Heaven for our covering, the earth for our beds, and in a large open prairie we saw daily companies of armed men as we passed along. . . . The third day we came to a cave, where we found shelter. . . . This cave was fifty feet long. . . . The mouth of this cave fronted towards the northwest, and the cold winds had a fair chance at us. We experienced a very severe storm while in this cave and the sick suffered dreadfully."

Lyman Wight adds that he caught up to 190 women and children who had walked 30 miles across a prairie that was "thinly crusted with sleet, and I could easily follow on their trail by the blood that flowed from their lacerated feet on the stubble of the burnt prairie."

The *Times and Seasons* continues, "Two of these Missouri companies were headed by Baptist preachers. The Reverend Isaac McCoy headed one [of] about seventy. . . . They broke open houses and plundered them."

Four old Mormons sought to stay until the spring thaw. "These veterans," reports the *Times and Seasons*, "the youngest of the four being 94 years of age, were assailed by a mob party, who broke in their doors and windows, hurling large stones into their homes . . . and thus they were driven from their homes, in the winter season. Some of these have toiled and bled in the defence of their country; one of them (Mr. Jones) served as lifeguard to General Washington in the revolutionary war."

In short, that night mobbers attacked every village, wrecking or burning over 200 Mormon homes, scattering farm animals, whipping men, and ripping from their homes the old and the sick. Over 1,200 Saints were forced into the cold November storm.

The Mormons then fled to the shore of the Missouri River, and there they waited for churning waters to clam.

On Thursday, November 7, 1833, the Missouri River was lined with the Saints and whatever few items of property they could bring with them, including a few chests and a little food. Makeshift tents, lean-tos, and tepees were constructed, and campfires were drowned by the pouring rain. People wandered about aimlessly, still looking for missing family members.

On a good note, the Mormon prisoners who were to be executed escaped.

Since the ferry was inoperative, over a thousand Saints were stranded at the shore. Most of them stood day and night beside campfires, seeking to survive on what food they could find. They waited day after day for freezing rains to cease and for the river to calm. Finally, after a week of escalating hopelessness, a small miracle occurred and their spirits were lifted. A gigantic meteor shower rained from the heavens.

On November 13 at 2 A.M., tens of thousands of meteors showered the earth, lighting up the sky in a dazzling display of heavenly fireworks, the brightest ever recorded in history. The heavenly bodies left large, long green trails as they passed into the earth's atmosphere—the meteors continued to increase in number until dawn—and the Saints took it as a sign that the heavens were aware of their sufferings for Christ. Parley P. Pratt, in his own mesmerizing writing style, records what he witnessed:

"All the firmament seemed enveloped in splendid fireworks, as if every star in the broad expanse had been hurled from its course and sent lawless through the wilds of ether. Thousands of bright meteors were shooting through space in every direction, with long trains of light following in their course. This lasted for several hours, and was closed only by the dawn of the rising sun. Every heart was filled with joy at this majestic display of signs and wonders."

When the river calmed enough, they crossed the waters into Clay County. Barges took them across the river 24 hours a day. But the going was slow, especially with windy weather still whipping the water.

Emily M. Austin records their arrival: "[We] had already arrived and more were on their way. . . . We lived in tents until winter set in, and did our cooking in the wind and storms." She reports children were crying and people were begging for cold water.

Some found barns, shacks, and toolsheds to live in, sometimes with 15 people sharing a room, as in the case of the John Corrill family when they finally found a stable.

While most of the Saints had fled directly to Clay County, some fled first to the counties of Van Buren, Ray, and Lafayette, and others even remained in Jackson until joining the main group at Clay. David Pettegrew reports the problems facing one such smaller group:

"We remained in Van Buren County until the last of February. Our sufferings were to that extent that my pen cannot describe them. While residing in Van Buren County a mob made its appearance for the purpose of still driving us on. . . . Mr. [John] Cornet told me if I did not leave this place immediately he would spill my blood. I told them of the property I had left in Jackson County and that I was very determined not to dispose of my farm; that I left the country, although I was destitute of means, provisions and all the necessities of life, and that the weather was extremely cold, the snow deep and my family barefooted. My wife told them that we had been robbed of everything. . . . 'You wish us to turn out in this cold and deep snow, that we may freeze.' . . . They then accused us of being British Tories. . . . We had given them no cause to believe anything of the kind, and their imagination had gone far beyond their reason. I told them that they could bring no charges against me, and why they should still continue that persecution I would be pleased to know, but it was all to no purpose; they were enraged and told us to leave immediately. . . .

"My wife and myself had gone over to Mr. Hartely, who was a [non-Mormon] friend of ours. As we came near the house we saw a large company of horsemen at his house, and on coming up we found them to be a mob party on their way to tear down our houses. Mrs. Hartely was quarreling with them in our behalf. She was a noble-hearted woman, kind and generous almost to a fault. She told Mr. Langly that if he unroofed our house that she would accommodate us in her house, and Mr. Langly told her if she did so he would tear the roof off her house. 'Mr. Langly,' said she, 'poor dog that you are, talking about pulling the roof off my house, you poor miserable wretch, the only thing you possess in this world is a little sugar tail filly. You can't raise corn enough to feed your chickens. Go home, and attend to your own business and you will do a great deal better, and if you ever put your foot in my house again I will be the death of you.' She struck several over the head with her broom. . . .

"I was obliged to leave my family in care of Mr. Hartely, who promised me he would do all in his power to care of them.

"I then made my escape across the Missouri River and there waited for the arrival of my family. They were a long time coming as the mob did everything in their power to prevent my family from joining me, but my wife managed to get away unobserved, and I rented a farm in Clay County."

After the Saints fled Jackson County, two other counties also chased them away.

Nearly all the Saints were now in Clay County, including the Parley P. Pratt and Edward Partridge families. Porter Rockwell's former neighbor, Pettegrew, details his experience there:

"The majority of the people looked upon us as a poor deluded people, and thought many of us were Christians and honest. When any of them were sick they would send for us to sit up and nurse them, and they thought a great deal of the Mormons. When the cholera made its appearance amongst them, they would invariably call upon us to take care of the sick and would shed tears when we would leave them and beg us to remain, as though we could save their lives. . . .

"At the time the cholera was raging in the county, Judge Cameron would spend a great deal of his time with me. He had resigned the gambling table and now wished to instruct himself upon religious matters, and he was very much afraid to die. He told some of the brethren that he believed I was a good Christian, but when the cholera subsided I did not see him so often, though he was still very friendly to me and my family and did many favors."

The people of Clay County received the Saints warmly, and the Saints sought the peace of a simple farm life. Yet within three years local religious leaders would once again, as in Jackson County, stir up the local populace.

Slavery flourished in Clay County, and because of the Saints' criticisms of slavery, David Pettegrew records: "The old feelings and excitement of Jackson County now began to show itself in Clay. It was first started by the ministers of the gospel such as Edwards and Balden, Baptist ministers, and others soon followed. They soon had the people to arms and . . . we were now forced to take up arms in self defense. The excitement had got to its highest pitch and their head men such as Judge Cameron, Judge Birch and others made several speeches to the people, which seemed to allay somewhat their excitement. They came to the conclusion to give us Caldwell County and that we should live there by ourselves, and thither we moved. The land we had purchased we had to leave unsold."

C H A P T E R  23

M

EANWHILE at Kirtland, Joseph had predicted that stars would fall from the sky within 40 days. One disbeliever wrote down the prediction in order to prove Joseph a false prophet. When 39 days had passed, a church member, Josiah Hancock, and his friend were out hunting and came upon the disbeliever's house. The man showed his notes to Hancock, then taunted him, asking what he thought now that the prophesy had not been fulfilled. Hancock said there was still one day left and that if Joseph had said it would come to pass, it would. That night as Hancock and his friend stayed at his house, a tremendous meteor shower began and lasted until dawn. Hancock reports studying the face of the disbeliever and finally records that he "turned pale as death, and spoke not a word."

Now back in Kirtland after his brief mission to Canada, Joseph Smith saw the meteor shower as well. He was awakened at 4 A.M. by a man who wanted him to see the dramatic display. Joseph was keeping a hand-sized, personal journal at the time, and recorded the wonderment of it by saying, "O how marvelous are thy works, O Lord."

It was another month, however, before he heard the news of Missouri. On December 5, 1833, he received a letter from W. W. Phelps detailing the atrocities. He also received a report that Orson Hyde had written in the *Missouri Republican* contradicting Phelps' facts, so Joseph was not certain which report was accurate; thus, he was not immediately able to advise the Saints on what to do, but he did assure them they were being watched by heaven, and stated that those who live for Christ Jesus are and would be persecuted and that "it is to be expected." Realizing his advice would be incomplete until he had all the facts, he urged those who still had their arms to stay on their lands and defend it to the end. He also counseled them to itemize all their grievances of loss of property and abuse, and to seek legal compensation. He said that Kirtland had no means of supporting or helping them. Days later he wrote them again, stating how concerned he was for them and, after pondering the situation, added an insight—that some in Missouri had become disobedient and broken the covenant, implying that was one reason for their persecution.

On December 15, 1833, W. W. Phelps concurred with Joseph, having been among the Saints in Missouri: "I know it was right that we should be driven out of the land of Zion, that the rebellious might be sent away." However, he raises the age old question: "But, brethren, if the Lord will, I should like to know what the honest in heart shall do?" He says their clothes are worn out and they are depleted of the necessities of life. He asks if they should buy or rent land where they are. "Such is the common language of the honest, for they want to do the will of God . . . for there are those among us that would rather earn eternal life on such conditions than lose it." He then says, "We hope for better things and shall wait patiently for the word of the Lord." The Saints awaited Joseph's word on what to do next.

On December 16, 1833, Joseph received another revelation, which answered probably the most pressing question of the day—"why the persecutions?"

"I, the Lord, have suffered the affliction to come upon them . . . in consequence of their transgressions. . . . There were jarrings, and contentions, and envying and strifes and lustful and covetous desires among them. . . . Notwithstanding their sins, my bowels are filled with compassion towards them." The promise is then made that . . .

1. The Lord's indignation is soon to be poured out (which most of the Saints may have interpreted as immediately, but which referred to the Civil War tribulation that would occur in just over 25 years, bringing misery to many souls).

2. That those who have been scattered shall be gathered. (That would take place soon, but not immediately, as the Saints would be spread through several counties—although mainly would be together in Clay—for two more years, then temporarily gather in northwestern Missouri for only two years, then in western Illinois for eight years, and eventually would gather more permanently in the western U.S., beginning in another 13 years from the time this revelation was given.)

3. That they would return to Jackson County and "come to their inheritances," which is a prophecy Latter-day Saints believe is yet to be fulfilled, as they believe a significant number of Saints will yet return to and inhabit that county in Missouri. Others have surmised that it could be just before the Second Coming of Christ that this second gathering to Missouri takes place, or perhaps even afterward.

4. That no other place will be the permanent gathering spot of the Saints for the true or final gathering. Thus, all gatherings that have taken place before now have only been temporary, and the true gathering, which is prophesied to include the lost tribes of Israel, will take place when the Saints return again to Jackson County, Missouri.

But of course the Saints in 1834 thought the gathering was imminent. They thought it would be time to return to their homes soon. Thus it was with chagrin that W. W. Phelps wrote to Joseph on February 27, 1834, that the Missourians were not enforcing the law to help the Saints.

W. W. Phelps charged Judge Samuel Lucas and others for the loss of his press and other damaged property, but the defense prevailed, saying the press was merely "moved" (two stories down, to a crashing blow in the street, scattering all the parts), that no other "unnecessary" damage was done, and that the house belonged to an old settler anyway, James H. Flournoy.

Edward Partridge also charged Samuel Lucas and others with assault for "greatly" hurting him. Court was held in Independence on February 24, 1834, and the defendants claimed their attack on Partridge was in "self-defense." John M. Walker ludicrously defended himself by saying he did "necessarily and unavoidably" beat Partridge and tear his clothes, "and unavoidably did besmear the said Edward with a little pitch, tar and feathers."

Three days later about a dozen Saints, led by Edward Partridge, returned again to court, subpoenaed as witnesses by the state and escorted by a "mob" militia—50 former mobbers under Captain Atchison, for the ostensible purpose of prosecuting some mob members who had driven the Saints from the county.

But once at trial the courthouse was surrounded by hundreds more, which so intimidated the "militia" that the court dismissed the witnesses and the militia. The militia, likely with smiles on their faces, now returned into the ranks of the mob, while the dozen Saints rode as quickly as possible out of the county, probably being followed by the freshly dismissed militia troops who now blended into the mob.

The Saints never received any reimbursement or redress from their treatment in Jackson County. Some tried to return to their homes but were turned away with burned houses and beatings with clubs. The Saints told the governor about their guns being taken away by Colonel Pitcher, and he responded, perhaps sincerely, by ordering Colonel Pitcher to return the guns. But in an inept military procedure, Pitcher had not secured the Mormons' weapons, letting the mob members among them steal the guns for themselves. And there was no record of who got what guns from the Saints. When the colonel demanded their return, the militia members defied him and refused to surrender the stolen weapons. Pitcher, perhaps not caring, siding with them, or being intimidated by them, dropped the matter. The guns were never retrieved.

The governor reacted well. He investigated the mob action and arrested Colonel Pitcher for disarming the Saints. He even offered to send the state militia—likely from other quarters of the state—to guard them en route to their homes in Jackson County, and he recommended that the Mormons request weapons from the state and even organize themselves. Then he added this clincher—that he could not leave a force to guard them once they were back in their homes.

The Saints realized that even if armed again, they would be so outnumbered that they could not stay in Jackson County without assistance from the state militia. Thus, the governor, though helpful in some respects, did not live up to his office by promising them a full return to their land, complete with protection, as he should have and was his duty to. His earlier-mentioned prejudices that were revealed in the letter to his friend were rising to the surface.

Later in February 1834, Parley P. Pratt and Lyman Wight arrived in Kirtland and talked Joseph into taking action. They asked for an army to help reinstate them in their homes, thinking they were saving Zion, not realizing that the timing and methods of prophecy are not always for the immediate here and now, as some Saints have since analyzed.

So an event next occurred which, in hindsight, some Latter-day Saints believe was a way that God would teach the Saints a lesson and eventually also save them. On February 24, 1834, Joseph received a revelation saying, "The redemption of Zion must needs come by power; Therefore I will raise up unto my people a man, who shall lead them like as Moses led the children of Israel." They thought the Lord was referring to Joseph Smith, but the fine print reads "will raise up"—indicating it would be in a future day.

If, on the other hand, the language of the Lord did mean for that day, and if Joseph was to be the one, he would soon be curtailed by rebellion within the ranks, just as Moses was, which the revelation also uses as a comparison. (In consequence of the rebelliousness of the children of Israel, it took Moses 40 years to lead them to a place that could have taken only months otherwise.)

In any case, the army led by Joseph would soon launch toward Missouri, with the supposed mission of redeeming Zion. Yet, knowing of their weaknesses, Latter-day Saints later believed the Lord had other plans for this army that Joseph called "Zion's Camp." With years since to reflect on it, Saints believe God knew the rebelliousness that would occur in the ranks and that the little army would actually serve two other purposes—but neither being to return the Saints to Jackson County. Perhaps had there been no rebelliousness, this might still have occurred, but in heaven's wisdom these two tasks were accomplished:

1. Zion's Camp would prove as a testing ground for the Ohio Saints, showing who would follow Joseph without complaining, thus qualifying those who would be placed in leadership positions to help lead the church for generations. (Future prophets and presidents would be among this crop, and the future Quorum of the Twelve would also be chosen from Zion's Camp—those who most faithfully served and endured.)

2. It would prepare the Saints for the far more arduous task of migrating over 12,000 Saints to the Rocky Mountains 15 years later. Hence, Zion's Camp would teach them how to traverse difficult terrain, how to survive with only basic necessities when traveling and dealing with elements of bad weather, and how to feed and care for large groups of people and animals when migrating, many of whom would be old or sick.

For the immediate task at hand, the Saints thought they were recruiting an army to reclaim their Missouri lands by force, and they thought the prophecy was for the immediate future, and that Jackson County was theirs for the taking right now. What a rude awakening they would soon behold . . .

I N Kirtland, Ohio, the Saints spent two months recruiting brethren for the Zion's Camp army to head to Missouri. They also disbanded the Law of Consecration. On April 10, 1834, the Kirtland council realized most of the men would be joining the army and leaving Ohio soon, so there was no way to run the Law of Consecration—no leaders and practically no male followers would be around to earn money to be divided, so the whole plan was abandoned. Another reason the Law was abandoned was that the Saints possibly were not ready to live it—so it was put aside for another time.

Two weeks later Joseph received a revelation, on April 23, which divided up church property as stewardships to be overseen by various leaders. (Oliver Cowdery and Frederick G. Williams would oversee the print shop, Newel K. Whitney the store, Joseph the temple lot, and Sidney Rigdon the tannery.)

While the Lord had always commanded the Saints to stay out of debt, Joseph was directed in the same revelation that for one time only they could mortgage the church properties so they could be free from bondage.

Meanwhile, they still wanted justice for the Missouri Saints. They wrote the President of the United States, Andrew Jackson, on April 10, outlining their grievances, asking him to call out federal troops, since local Missouri judges were among the mobbers, and they reminded him that Independence was within 30 miles of federal troops at Ft. Leavenworth.

Then they wrote Governor Dunklin of Missouri again, telling him of the letter to the President and asking once more for his help, but only in the form of one simple task—to write Andrew Jackson and back up their request. But Dunklin refused. His excuse was that he (Dunklin) would have to see the Saints' petition before he could endorse it. He also said he thought they were asking for more than what the President had power to accomplish. The country was at that time extremely states'-rights oriented, yet supporters of the Constitution would have seen to it that the Saints' lives and property were protected—which in fact was the most important intent of the Constitution.

On May 2, 1834, the War Department replied in behalf of the President. They turned down the Saints' request, passing the buck to the State of Missouri, saying it was not a matter for the federal government because the violations were "not of the laws of the United States."

For the expedition, Zion's Camp raised $200 from Kirtland members and $251.60 from Saints in the East. Obviously, the Missouri Saints were depleted of funds and could donate nothing. This new army even had a small recruiting poster written on May 10 by Sidney Rigdon and Oliver Cowdery. The poster stated that the greater the numbers they had, the less likely the mob would be to fight them, and the more likely they would be to stop the acts of aggression. But if the Saints did not fight back then, they would not be safe anywhere else in the country.

On April 19, 1834, Sidney was set apart to lead the church, while Joseph prepared to leave with the army. A few other men would stay in Kirtland with Sidney, including Oliver and some workers to build the temple, as well the sick and older men. Half the men comprising Zion's Camp were leaving from Kirtland and the other half from Pontiac, Michigan. Hyrum Smith and Lyman Wight would lead this second group.

In Kirtland Joseph gave another prophecy that would be fulfilled: On May 4, 1834, he told the soldiers that those who lived properly would return, but those who did not would be visited by the wrath of God.

Indeed, there would be those who would be out and out rebellious, some actually apostatizing on the trip, while others would be out for blood, not having the right spirit. Others, said William McLellin, wanted "distinction and glory." And, in his opinion, most men did lose sight of delivering Zion, and instead put their faith in "their own all powerful arms." He summarized, "A different spirit had seized almost the whole ranks of the church, from what had hitherto propelled them onward." What had "hitherto propelled them onward" had been the desire to provide a service to others, thinking they were really going to redeem their fellow Saints' property in Jackson County

On Sunday night they packed their gear. The next morning, May 5, 1834, Joseph's army of about 200 men commenced their long march toward Missouri. Only a few rode horseback, taking 20 wagons filled with provisions and clothing to help the Missouri Saints. The best rifle shooters flanked the expedition on both sides as they traveled.

Joseph's chief assistant was apparently young George Albert Smith, his cousin. Also joining them was another cousin Jesse Smith, the son of Joseph's uncle, John Smith, the relative so antagonistic toward The Book of Mormon. Lucy Mack Smith tried talking Joseph out of taking his young cousin with them, knowing his father would not approve, but young Jesse insisted on going. Joseph would feel particular travail when his young cousin would die on the journey, feeling not only sad for him, but for the increased schism that it would cause within the family.

As the march began, Joseph was not at their forefront. They knew spies might be on the lookout to take potshots at him, so he marched within different groups and traveled under the name of Squire Cook. For protection he was also given a ferocious bulldog by Samuel Baker, a rifle, and two brass-barreled horse pistols captured from a British officer in the War of 1812. During the journey he worked right alongside with and just as hard as the other men. When wagons got stuck in the bogs, he was the first one to pull on the ropes to haul the wagons out.

Eleven wives and seven children joined the march, and all the men were assigned chores—cooking, tending horses and wagons, and setting up tents. Unlike any army known in history, the men chose their own captains. Companies of 12 men were grouped together. One captain was Brigham Young, who carried a gun, an ax, and even farm tools in readiness for battle. The chief recruiter on the journey, when they came upon small branches of the church, was Parley P. Pratt, who was also assigned to procure more arms and provisions along the way.

The first day they traveled 27 miles. Joseph gave his young cousin George Albert Smith a pair of his own boots when the young man developed blistered feet from his new boots. Joseph chose him as his chief aide and even had him sleep in his tent. Each day he would fetch water, perform errands, and build a fire for the camp's cook, Zebedee Coltrin. The food was considered good but sometimes there was not enough.

On May 6 they arrived at New Portage and gathered all their money into one pot, living their own Law of Consecration.

When they approached villages they would split up and even travel solo in order to avoid suspicion, but the fact that so few women and children were traveling caused curiosity. At some towns people would swarm upon them, inundating them with questions. But they answered so vaguely that all it did was invite numerous other questions. Still, people did not know who they were or what they were doing. Sometimes in their answers they would say they were "coming from the east and going west" and had no leader. Other times people found the site of so many men with no families so odd that they would follow a long way asking questions to not just a few but to many of the men, demanding answers, but getting none, which only piqued their curiosity more.

At Dayton, Ohio, on May 16, 1834, a large representation of officials came out to question them. George Albert was the most ragged, youthful, and unsophisticated-looking member of the group. Joseph appointed him as the one to answer all the questions. And it worked. He fell back to the rear of the march, looking pathetic in his beaten-looking straw hat. The curiosity seekers pounced on him for answers, figuring him too tired and perhaps even too stupid not to answer directly. He reports he was courteous but so vague that the townspeople returned completely befuddled, in fact literally scratching their heads. He says he had many comical conversations in which people learned absolutely nothing.

Guards were posted at night and, once or twice, thieves attempted stealing their horses but did not succeed.

A trumpet sounded every night, and mornings at 4 A.M., and the men immediately had prayer in their tents.

On Sundays, if strangers showed up at their meetings, they would teach Protestant doctrine as a cover, each man teaching what he had known before he was converted. The hodgepodge of doctrine must have confused the curiosity seekers even greater.

In Indiana on May 18, 1834, after church, Joseph wrote Emma, saying that his younger brother William and cousins Jesse and George were humble and determined to be faithful.

Because they were trying to not attract much attention, their journey went slower than otherwise. But they succeeded for the most part. They took muddy side roads, passed through heavy forests, and walked around villages.

But the treachery of the trek began to take its toll. Over the course of the 40-day, 1,000-mile journey, men began separating themselves into camps of complainers and non-complainers, obedient versus rebellious. Some began murmuring about the heat and weariness of the march, saying that God did not expect this much of them.

One day Sylvester Smith decided he would not share his bread, so Parley P. Pratt went hungry. Joseph warned Sylvester to watch out for God's wrath. The next morning every horse in camp was ill, and Joseph warned the entire camp that it was a sign of God's warning them that they should humble themselves, which the men did, for the most part. The only horse that did not recover was Sylvester Smith's.

On May 26 the men came upon Paris, Indiana, and passed through a 16-mile prairie. Its expansiveness deceived the Eastern Saints, who thought they could catch a deer before they realized it was farther away than their eyesight perceived. The heat increased, and the water was so infested with bugs that they had to strain it. They also had to avoid rattlers.

At Decatur, Indiana, Zion's Camp stopped while one brother bought a horse. To keep their spirits up during this lull, Joseph organized them into three divisions for a war game. Two of the groups went into the woods and attacked the third group in camp. Many of his captains proved more militarily skillful than they had expected, and the entire army had its spirits raised. One man was wounded, however. In his exuberance, Heber C. Kimball grabbed the sword blade of his "enemy" and cut his hand.

Somehow, their enemies got wind of who they were and gathered in large numbers near the Illinois River. When Zion's Camp left Jacksonville, Illinois, their enemies planned to not let them cross the river. On the eastern shore of the river, the ferryman counted 500 Mormon soldiers, when in fact there were less than 200. When the enemy asked the ferryman how many he saw, he told them exactly the number he had counted—500. They immediately gave up on stopping Joseph's army. In response to this apparent miracle Joseph told his men that angels were going before them and they need not fear. The official record of the camp declares that they were in "the presence of angels while on the march to Missouri, for we saw them." Evidently, so did the ferryman.

On their journey Joseph taught them numerous times to conserve natural resources and not to hunt unless necessary. One afternoon, while they pitched their tents, they found three rattlesnakes. The men were ready to kill them when Joseph said, "Let them alone—don't hurt them! How will the serpent ever lose his venom, while the servants of God possess the same disposition, and continue to make war upon it? Men must become harmless." In his journal, Joseph adds, "I exhorted the brethren not to kill a serpent, bird, or animal of any kind during our journey unless it became necessary in order to preserve ourselves from hunger." He had the snakes carried on sticks across a creek and let go.

On June 3, when they were on the opposite shore, Joseph and several others ascended a mound beside the water, several hundred feet high. George A. Smith records: "And from the summit . . . we could overlook the tops of the trees and the meadow or prairie on each side of the river as far as our eyes could extend, which was one of the most pleasant scenes I ever beheld. Atop the highest mound were three altars, one above another." Joseph told them they had been built "according to the ancient order." They saw human bones on the ground. "This caused in us very peculiar feelings, to see the bones of our fellow creatures scattered in this manner—fellow creatures who had been slain in ages past," continues George Albert Smith. "We felt prompted to dig down into the mound and, sending for a shovel and hoe, we proceeded to move away the earth." After they dug a foot down, they found almost the entire skeleton of a man with an arrow between two of his ribs. As they left the hill, Joseph enquired of the Lord and learned in a vision that the remains were those of a man named Zelph, "a white Lamanite, a large thick-set man, and a man of God," says Joseph. "He was a warrior and chieftain under the great prophet Onandagus, who was known from the Hill Cumorah, or eastern sea to the Rocky Mountains. . . . One of his thigh bones was broken by a stone flung from a sling while in battle years before his death. He was killed in battle by the arrow found among his ribs, during a great struggle with the Lamanites."

While some felt inspired by Joseph's teaching along the journey, others complained. The murmurings and rebellions returned and even increased when wagons got stuck in mud and had to be pulled away with ropes. The food supply dwindled; the water ran out; the weather got hotter; bread, cheese, and bacon spoiled; blistered and bleeding feet increased; stomachaches became common; and horses became bloated from the prairie grass. For the horses they created a concoction of cayenne peppers, tobacco, and copperas mixed in whiskey, called "18 × 24," which cured a few and killed a few—or perhaps they just died anyway. Bickering began to arise.

Some stayed faithful and never complained, including the 80-year-old man who gave Joseph his bulldog—Baker. Samuel Baker refused to tire out the horses and demanded to walk the entire way. Others got lazy and would ride in the luggage wagon a couple miles when they had the chance. But according to George Albert Smith, Joseph was the single most shining example of humility. As his special aide, George watched as Joseph never complained the entire trip, even while suffering with bloody feet, right along with his men. He said some men murmured to Joseph about everything. He would also serve and provide for the men before himself, setting an example of Christian service and admonishing those in his company of 12 to follow suit.

Joseph at one point bought 12 cured hams and 25 gallons of honey. The hams did not feed the entire troop, so Joseph and his company sacrificed and ate mush and honey. When they finished dinner, some of the ungrateful men outside tossed six hams at their tent door, complaining that they did not like them—part of them had been damaged. So Joseph had his cook fry them up, and his company got enough to eat for the first time in 48 hours.

Joseph had to deal with the troop's bad attitudes. On June 3, 1834, he held a meeting with them all and announced that the Lord had revealed to him that a scourge would come upon them unless they straightened up.

They reached the Mississippi River the next day and found the river, at this spot, a mile and a half wide. Just one ferry worked there, so it took two days to get everyone across. Meanwhile, some fished and hunted for the whole group. One man made a fife and gave it to his commander, Sylvester Smith, who marched his men into camp to the tune of the instrument, but Joseph's new bulldog got excited and barked ferociously at them. Sylvester yelled in a rage over the dog.

The next morning Joseph heard more grumbling about the dog, and told them that the spirit of division and the shedding of blood across the world resulted from the attitude of saying that "if a dog bites me I will kill him," and "if any man insults me I will kill him," and "if any man injures me I will injure him." Then Sylvester marched up to Joseph and told him, "If that dog bites me I will kill him."

Joseph immediately prophesied in the name of the Lord that if he did not rid himself of his wicked spirit, the day would come when a dog would gnaw his flesh. Sylvester retorted, "You are prophesying lies in the name of the Lord!" Joseph got heated and would have fought him, which was a characteristic (as stated earlier) of Joseph's—to want to settle things with his fists—but several others jumped in and stopped the fight. Joseph then asked them if they were ashamed of such a spirit and answered rhetorically, "I am."

From June 7–12, 1834, the camp stayed in the woods near Salt River, Missouri, where a small branch of the church aided them, washing, baking, mending clothes, shoeing horses, and repairing their guns. On June 8 Hyrum and Lyman Wight joined Joseph with the other portion of Saints who had marched from Michigan. The total group now numbered 205 men with 25 wagons. Among the group were 12 older gents called the Silver Greys, who ate with Joseph. He said he was delighted to see them, as well as the younger men, joining their army.

Joseph then chose 20 men as his lifeguard—as most military and political leaders throughout history have had—and he was designated the commander in chief of the camp. Hyrum was chosen captain over the newly organized lifeguard, and young cousin George Albert was chosen their armor-bearer. His young cousin liked this promotion, which took him everywhere with Joseph and allowed him to keep Joseph's weapons clean and loaded. It also gave George Albert the chance to actually carry them—something a young man of his temperament enjoyed, especially since it allowed him to stay away from performing duties for the cook.

Lyman Wight was made second in command after Joseph. He marched the camp to the prairie, inspected their guns, oversaw target practice, and drilled the men half of one day that week. There, a convert from Ireland, who had served over 20 years in the British dragoons, trained the men in swordsmanship. They were being honed into a more effective combat team.

On June 7 a leak hit the newspaper in Independence, Missouri, warning the citizens that a Mormon army was coming with 200 to 600 armed men. It also stated that a dissenter had told a spy that they were attempting to recruit the help of Indians in their "holy war" against the county. Such reports by dissenters, while typically inaccurate (regarding not only the Saints taking the offense and waging war against the locals, but actually recruiting Native Americans in their cause), were proving themselves once again as Joseph's greatest problem. While typical of the distortions dissenters would spread, it created its desired effect—it riled up the locals.

And because of it, the locals suddenly raised the cry, "The Mormons are coming!"

OMEN and children hid in the woods while 200 to 300 Missouri men set up guard at ferry landings. They also set fire to abandoned Mormon-owned houses. Rumors spread that the Mormon army planned to slay the women and children. One local wrote that 500 well-armed young men were with Joseph, ready to attack just a mile away! Other counties began coming to Jackson County's aid.

The same newspaper that had reported the spy's warning, the *Missouri Intelligencer and Boon's Lick Advertiser,* printed on June 21, 1834, that the locals were about to reap the bitter fruits of their lawless acts. And that since the courts had been closed to the Mormons, they were doing the only thing they could. The editorial suggested it was doubtful that the Jackson County citizens had the sympathies "or even the respect" of a large portion of the state.

Nevertheless, enough allies were coming to their rescue from other counties that the Mormon army would be insured of a heated battle against overwhelming odds.

The Saints in Clay County, where most of the expelled Saints were still living, learned that most of western Missouri was gathering to fight the oncoming Ohio Mormon army—Zion's Camp. So the Missouri Mormons decided to pitch in and produce swords, knives, pistols, and rifle stocks, while the women molded lead balls.

Joseph's army was expecting Governor Dunklin to keep his word—to safely escort the Missouri Saints back to their Missouri homes when they gave him the word, and then, as he had said, to leave them alone once they resettled. This in fact was the reason Zion's Camp was there—to *replace* the Missouri militia in order to just keep the peace.

But the governor *opposed* the coming of the Ohio Mormon army. On June 6 he reveals why in a letter to Colonel J. Thornton: "A more clear and indisputable right does not exist, than that of the Mormon people, who were expelled from their homes in Jackson County, to return and live on their lands." But he continues by saying: "The Mormon's have no right to march to Jackson county in arms. . . . Men must not 'levy war' in taking possession of their rights." Either through ignorance or misinformation he believed they were coming to give battle and take back their lands by force, so he was now suddenly opposed to the Saints.

Joseph sent Parley P. Pratt and Orson Hyde to the governor to ask him to keep his earlier promise. They merely wanted the *Missouri* militia to get the Missouri Saints back in their homes. But by the time Pratt and Hyde arrived, the governor had made up his mind that the Mormons were going to be the aggressors and attack the locals, so he decided against helping them at all. (He determined, however, to do his part as a "statesman" and ask for a federal fort to be placed there, one which could protect the Saints with federal troops. He also pondered the idea of dividing the county into Mormon and non-Mormon lands so they could live more peaceably.)

Pratt and Hyde galloped back to Joseph and told him the governor's decision. While deeply saddened, Joseph apparently made this decree—that since the governor of Missouri had abandoned them, they were left unto themselves and perhaps would become a reclaiming force to take back their lands by battle if necessary; however, Joseph's disposition was inclined to show military force only to obtain peace. So he marched the men ahead 12 miles and crossed the Charlton River, coming ever closer to the hotbed awaiting them in Independence. There he was met by Bishop Edward Partridge, who had good news, for a change—that the Saints had for the most part gathered together again, no longer scattered across several counties as they had been when they fled Jackson County—and were now back as a group in Clay County, and in good spirits, despite their hardships.

The show of force by the Mormons did, to some extent, work. The next day, June 16, 1834, the locals decided to meet with them to see if they could work out a peaceful solution. Delegates from the Mormons in Clay County (with numerous local residents of Clay there to add their two cents worth) met at the county courthouse at Liberty township. There, delegates from Jackson County came with an offer. The meeting had 800 attending. Figuring both parties could not live together, the Jackson County delegates offered to buy the Mormons' property or sell their own, at double value, as determined by a committee from both sides. Once again, this was an offer that looked good on the surface, but the Saints quickly saw through the sham—most of their property had been destroyed, so it was worth only a few cents on the dollar. As for purchasing the Missourians' land, the Saints were now so broke that they could in no way purchase the old settlers' property.

Meanwhile, the citizens from Clay County let it be known that they wanted the Mormons out of their county as well. A Reverend Riley said they had been there long enough. But he was countered by the meeting's moderator, Turnham, who said they should not disgrace themselves like the Jackson County residents had. "For God's sake don't disfranchise or drive away the Mormons. They are better citizens than many of the old inhabitants." The Saints said they would talk to their leaders, that all they desired was peace, and that they would attempt to keep the Zion's Camp army out of Jackson County until an answer was given. Thus, the Mormon delegates were using Joseph's show of force to their advantage at the negotiating table.

Despite the Mormons being able to put teeth into their words, one of the Jackson County delegates, Samuel C. Owens, decided to make an anti-Mormon speech. Judge John Ryland countered him—perhaps out of principle, perhaps out of respect for Joseph's large well-trained force waiting just outside of town. Judge Ryland said he had called the meeting to create understanding and solutions, and then told the non-Mormon delegates from Jackson and Clay Counties to obey the laws. Finally, he told the Mormons that all of the area were against them now, and that if they should retake Independence, numerous hosts from adjacent counties would attack them. Alexander Doniphan concurred, "That's a fact."

However, Doniphan vocally *supported* the idea of Joseph's soldiers coming to the Missouri Mormons' assistance. He found it valiant that some Mormons would be willing to sacrifice their lives for their friends. But those comments did not set well with the Mormon-bashers, and shouting began. Some wanted to end the meeting, others to continue, but no solutions were reached. The meeting officially ended right then, however, as someone at the door yelled, "A man stabbed!" Some of the Missourians said, loud enough for all to hear, that they hoped it was a Saint, but when they went outside to investigate the problem, they found instead that one Missourian had merely punched another, so the crowd dispersed—all 800.

The Jackson County delegation left the meeting, angered that there was no resolution. Twelve days later *The Missouri Intelligencer and Boon's Lick Advertiser* would report the meeting unsuccessful and state that the next action taken would likely be war. Then came a self-fulfilling prophecy. Samuel C. Owens, James Campbell, and 15 others headed for Independence to raise troops against Joseph Smith. Campbell promised that *turkey buzzards would eat his own flesh before two days passed* if he did not "fix Joe Smith and his army."

On June 17 at sunset, Campbell, Owens, and 10 of their party crossed the Missouri River at Everett's Ferry, and their boat capsized in the middle of the river. Three weeks later Campbell was found on a pile of driftwood five miles downriver. His flesh had been eaten by turkey buzzards. Five others also drowned.

Samuel Owens was washed ashore on an island four miles downstream, naked. He blamed the Mormons for tampering with the boat. Joseph denied it. He said that what had occurred was not the work of man, but was heaven-sent.

On the same day as the capsizing, June 17, 1834, Zion's Camp crossed the Wakenda River. Arriving at the opposite shore, Joseph was told that the mob was ready to attack them. He knew his men were prepared. But he despised bloodshed, so he had to devise a plan that he hoped would prevent the spilling of blood. Fearing an enemy ambush near the woods, he sent his army into a prairie, carrying wood for fires and water for drink.

During this "retreat," Lyman Wight complained. Sylvester Smith sided with Wight, trying to mutiny the men against Joseph. He succeeded. Twenty men stayed with Sylvester Smith and Lyman Wight as they camped near the river. The men following Joseph had to endure bad water, not enough wood for cooking, and a difficult night. The next morning Lyman Wight and his men came marching into Joseph's camp, with Wight apologizing, but Sylvester angrily told Joseph off, claiming he was lying again in the name of God.

With the enemy gone for now, they marched forward, determined to see the Missouri Saints gathered in Clay County. Two days later, passing through Ray County, they were told that the enemy was waiting ahead, near Clay County, ready to attack them. But they kept marching anyway and arrived at Clay County ready to face the enemy head on in battle if necessary, so determined were they to meet with their comrades, the Missouri Saints. That night they strategically camped on an elevation between two rivers—the Little Fishing and Big Fishing.

The enemy meanwhile learned or figured out that the Ohio Mormon army was heading toward the Missouri Mormons in Clay County. So they planned to attack them above the mouth of Fishing River in Clay County. Two hundred anti-Mormons decided to meet sixty more from Richmond and march on Zion's Camp.

But just before the battle would take place, Joseph would see the hand of God intervene once more. He went to the woods and prayed, reporting afterward that he received an answer—they would be spared.

The next night five enemy soldiers rode the camp of the Ohio Mormon army and told them they would "see hell before morning."

# CHAPTER 26

THE enemy then began their advance. Forty armed men crossed the river on a barge—likely Porter Rockwell's old ferry that had been stolen from him, damaged, and then repaired for the Missourians' own use. The barge took them from Jackson County to Clay. After the 40 mobbers left the barge, the barge again crossed the river to get another load of men. But before it arrived there, a harsh wind came, and the barge barely made it back to the Jackson County shore.

Night quickly came and a thunderstorm blew in with fierce lightning. Then came cold, heavy rain and huge hailstones the size of eggs. The hail came so hard in fact that it smashed all their crops and cut tree branches in half. The mobbers on the Jackson County shore dove for cover under wagons. The 40 men who had been let off across the river had no cover and were bombarded, bruising many and even breaking their rifle stocks in half.

The hail left Joseph's army alone, but tents were blown over and their blankets were soaked. To escape the downpour of rain, they entered a Baptist church, sleeping there overnight.

The next morning the 40 enemy on the shore nearby retreated back across the river—their horses having panicked and run away from the hail and lightning, and their ammunition too wet to even shoot. One Missourian had been killed by a lightning bolt. Another was recorded saying that if that was the way God fought for the Mormons, they should just go ahead and surrender. The 40 mobbers returned to their homes at Independence.

Joseph's army moved five miles out to the prairie the next day.

The Clay County sheriff came to see him June 22, 1834, to give him the views of the residents of Clay and Jackson Counties again and to learn what the Saints planned to do. What he told Joseph was the same plan that the residents had told the Missouri Mormons at the June 16 assembly at Liberty, Missouri—either the Mormons would have to sell their land in Jackson County or purchase the settlers' property, and in either case their Zion's Camp army had to stay away from Jackson County while they negotiated.

Joseph told the sheriff that he did not plan to attack anyone and that their guns were only used in self-defense. He then made a fair counter offer—that they would buy the settlers' property at an amount to be agreed upon by both sides, but *after* the damages caused by the mob were subtracted. The Missouri Saints, he said, would pay within a year and would stay out of Jackson County until they paid the debt in full.

A revelation then came to Joseph after his meeting with the sheriff. He read it to his army, reporting that the Saints had not shared with the poor and afflicted as they should have and that Zion (in Missouri) could not be built unless it was based on principles (such as sharing) of the celestial kingdom. The members would be chastened and would have to wait for the redemption of Zion. Interestingly, and surprisingly disappointing to many in Zion's Camp, Joseph reported that the Lord revealed he did not require at their hands to fight the battles of Zion, but "I will fight your battles." He said the Lord would send "the destroyer" to lay waste to their enemies in "not many years hence," to clear the way for moving back to Zion. The revelation then stated that the Lord had heard the prayers of the obedient among those in Zion's Camp, and that he had prepared a blessing for them if they would continue faithful. Joseph reported also that God said they had been led on this march "for a trial of their faith." Also, they were told to seek peace with the settlers, buy all the land they could in Jackson

County (a directive, possibly, to future generations some Saints now believe), and wait until their army could "become great" (again, likely a directive to the Saints in the distant future) before they regained their lost property. Those of the present army who had families with them would stay in Missouri only a while longer, while the rest should go back to Ohio and receive their "endowment" in the Kirtland temple, "which I have commanded to be built unto my name in the land of Kirtland."

The rebellious among them wanted to stay and fight. Lyman Wight thought they were giving in too easily. Others said they would actually rather die than leave without fighting. Gnashing in anger and showing their bravado, they pulled out their swords and mauled a patch of brush. Several more men announced they would leave the church.

Joseph's journal records, "While we were refreshing ourselves and teams about the middle of the day, I got up on a wagon wheel, called the people together, and said that I would deliver a prophecy. . . . I said the Lord had revealed to me that a scourge would come upon the camp in consequence of the fractious and unruly spirits that appeared among them, and they should die like sheep with the rot; still, if they would repent and humble themselves before the Lord, the scourge, in a great measure, might be turned away; but, as the Lord lives, the members of this camp will suffer for giving way to their unruly temper."

On June 23, the army went to Liberty, Missouri. Five miles outside of town they were met by Missouri Mormons who recommended to Joseph's army that they not continue into Liberty. The reason—the settlers there were angry and ready to fight. So Zion's Camp changed course and went to Rush Creek, where they camped out in a field belonging to a church member. Joseph, William, and his two young cousins went to the nearby house of Sidney Gilbert, just three quarters of a mile away.

The day after they arrived at their new spot, June 24, the chastisement that Joseph had predicted hit them—a violent attack of cholera. Those standing guard were smitten so suddenly that they still had their weapons in their hands, crashing to the ground, struck with severe pain. Then they filled the air with howls and moans.

The next day the healthy among them were separated into small groups and sent to the homes of members in the vicinity. That day Joseph wrote Thornton, Atchison, and Doniphan and told them they would disband Zion's Camp and use every measure to assure peace.

Because of rebellion, says Joseph in his journal, Zion's camp was struck with cholera—one third in all, 68 men—and it happened in less than a week. Flour and whiskey were mixed as medicine, and patients were dipped in cold water to fight the vomiting and cramping. Joseph kept in touch with Missouri church leaders in Liberty via an early version of the pony express. The rider was James Henry Rollins, who took messages back and forth, giving updates on the sick and how the Missouri Saints could assist by providing shelter and obtaining medicine. Of their army, 14 died.

Due to their inability to obtain coffins, the dead were carried off each day, wrapped in blankets, on a horse sled to a half mile away, where they were buried near a stream. Seven months later Joseph told Brigham and Joseph Young: "Brethren, I have seen those men who died of the cholera in our camp; and the Lord knows, if I get a mansion as bright as theirs, I ask no more." Joseph Young recorded, "At his relation he wept, and for some time could not speak." Despite the rebellion and complaining that brought on the curse, Joseph saw the mercy of God extended to the Zion's Camp members who died due to their overall sacrifice for others—the Missouri Saints—in their attempt to restore them to their homes.

Joseph, Hyrum, and William all came down with cholera. Sidney Gilbert was among the 14 who died, passing away on June 29, 1834, along with four others. In the Gilbert home Joseph had massaged him and given him medicines, but to no avail. His body was buried with others during a thunderstorm, in the mud, in a shallow grave. Pony message rider Rollins, along with Joseph's two young cousins, George Albert and Jess, were all struck by the disease. Jesse became ill when he and George

Albert were burying one of the dead. George Albert cared for him for 30 hours, then George Albert was struck with it. Jesse died on July 1.

George Albert Smith lamented Jesse's loss and wished he had instead been taken, because he felt Jesse was more educated, had better eyesight, and possessed other qualities—which George lacked—that made him more fit to be of service to the church. Little did the young man know he would someday lead the church in its highest position. He expressed his shortcomings to Joseph, who replied, "You do not know the mind of the Lord in these things." An understatement in "notable quotes since the Restoration," if ever there was one. And George's humility was typical of the church presidents who preceded him.

On July 3, 1834, Joseph disbanded Zion's Camp. Lyman Wight stood before the group and told them they were dismissed and should return home. They divided all the money left among them equally—each receiving $1.14. Joseph that day helped Missouri's bishop by putting together a high council in Zion, with David Whitmer as president, W. W. Phelps and John Whitmer his assistants, and 12 councilors. It is possible that four days later, when they were set apart in their callings, that Joseph ordained David Whitmer to take his place in the church if Joseph should die, but that, believe Latter-day Saints, like all promises, was conditional—based on David's future faithfulness.

Joseph, Hyrum, and a few others began their journey back to Ohio on July 7 and, after a month in the sweltering, humid heat, they arrived at Kirtland the first week of August 1834. The Saints were thrilled to see them coming into town—especially because of a major false report they had received—one Roger Orton had ridden from Missouri to Ohio in 15 days when cholera broke out, and told the Ohio Saints that all the men in Zion's Camp were dying.

Joseph had the sad task of reporting the 14 deaths to family members himself.

The remaining members of Zion's Camp returned in small groups or alone over the next few days and weeks, most of them weak, suffering from more sickness and exposure.

A few had apostatized on the trip to Missouri, a few others had left the church upon reaching Missouri and not getting their way—of fighting—and a few more defected from the faith on the way back to Ohio. This was disheartening news to Joseph, ever sorrowful for those who once had the light of the restored gospel and then left its ranks. Those who defected on the way home complained that the journey had wasted their time, and some even sued Joseph in December for back pay. Sylvester Smith, true to form, went to other church leaders in Ohio and demanded that Joseph be brought before them, which they did. He accused Joseph of usurping power, being a false prophet, taking money, and prophesying lies. Joseph said Sylvester's complaints were lies themselves.

For six hours Joseph had to explain to his high priests and elders in a meeting on August 11 why he had rebuked Sylvester. He explained how the Camp money was spent, and he convinced them he was innocent. Sylvester himself then asked for forgiveness for accusing him of prophesying lies, thus taking back one of his accusations. But when asked to publish a statement that cleared Joseph of his charges, Sylvester refused. So he was voted guilty of a misdemeanor. However, two months later he did send a retraction to the *Messenger and Advocate* newspaper.

Sylvester's case was an example of forgiveness by those offended. Joseph not only forgave him but later actually called him to be his scribe. Latter-day Saints believe he repented of his mistakes and that the Lord must have forgiven him also, as he was soon appointed to a high church office.

The Saints now prospered—building farms, commerce, and the temple. Their peace would only prevail a few months, but in those months they would make tremendous progress. *The Evening and Morning Star* newspaper published only a few issues in Kirtland, and then was replaced with the *Latter-day Saints' Messenger and Advocate*. In the winter that closed 1834, they built a structure to house the newspaper and other printing work and to provide a school for elders (the first office of the

Melchizedek priesthood), which would school them on how to better serve as missionaries.

As 1834 came to a close, the people continued to build and prosper. In early 1835 they took major steps forward as a result of revelations Joseph received. For example, the three witnesses chose the Twelve Apostles that winter—all from Zion's Camp volunteers. The Apostles also received their endowments—special ordinations and classes in the temple—and they left Kirtland for a long mission overseas. Chosen were Brigham Young, Heber C. Kimball, Parley and Orson Pratt, John F. Boynton, Thomas B. Marsh, William Smith, Lyman E. and Luke S. Johnson, Orson Hyde, William E. McLellin, and David W. Patten. On March 12, 1835, Joseph recommended that they go to the eastern states, and in early May they left and began by holding conferences in the few branches of the church spread across Maine, Massachusetts, New Hampshire, Vermont, and Canada—including eastern Canada. Joseph's title changed from "first elder" to "president," and Oliver Cowdery's to "assistant president." Oliver had to first acknowledge he had been "second elder" all the while, a gentle rebuke, as he had aspired to be the church's leader much of the time, and in his own mind likely had been.

During this period the first Quorum of Seventy was chosen from Zion's Camp as well. Seven groups of 10 were divided, each under a president. Two of the presidents were Sylvester Smith and Brigham's brother, Joseph Young. Within the first quorum was George Albert Smith, Joseph's loyal, young assistant during Zion's Camp. There were now five equally authoritative quorums—the Presidency, the Twelve Apostles, the Seventies, and two high councils—one in Zion (Missouri) and the other in Ohio. The Twelve began acting as the premier quorum, a move that some members of other quorums criticized. So on March 28, 1835, the president was directed to be the main leader over the church—prophet, seer, revelator, and translator. The Apostles were to travel under the church president's operatives.

Significantly for the growing kingdom, Joseph's father was chosen as church-wide patriarch. In that capacity he would give patriarchal blessings, which are guides for members to use their entire lives, and which would be recorded and saved in church archives while a copy would be given to the members to hold and review often throughout their lives. Also that spring, Sidney Rigdon was chosen as first counselor and Hyrum as second counselor to Joseph. Don Carlos Smith was chosen as president over the high council in Ohio—the high priests.

In July 1835 a most unusual visitor came to Kirtland. A man named Michael H. Chandler brought four mummies and a few papyrus scrolls that had been discovered four years earlier by his uncle, a French explorer named Antonio Sebolo. His uncle had not left him any Egyptian treasures, so Chandler hoped to make money off the artifacts—therefore he was anxious to sell them to the Saints. He had heard in New York that no one could translate the scrolls, but someone at the U.S. Customs House had told him of Joseph translating ancient plates. This was still one year before the Egyptian grammar would be published and six years before the Egyptian dictionary would be printed. Jean Francois Champollion had discovered how to *decipher* hieroglyphics with the Rosetta stone and had previously published works on it, but mankind was still in the dark when it came to *translating* hieroglyphics. The timing was perfect for Joseph and the Saints because, had Champollion's Egyptian grammar and dictionary been published just a tad earlier, Joseph likely would never have received them. As it turns out, the scrolls were of monumental importance. Joseph writes in July 1835: "With W. W. Phelps and Oliver Cowdery as scribes, I commenced the translation of some of the characters or hieroglyphics, and much to our joy found that one of the rolls contained the writing of Abraham, another the writings of Joseph of Egypt."

Joseph then leased a room at the inn of John Johnson and there exhibited the scrolls and mummies. Afterward they were shown in a top room of the temple. Enemies immediately generated rumors, lying that Joseph claimed they were the bodies of Joseph and Abraham in Egypt.

For the remainder of July, he translated an alphabet for the *Book of Abraham* and compiled a grammar of the ancient Egyptian language. But he did not use them; rather, he translated by revelation.

Joseph did talk with Professor Joshua Seixas about the written scroll, who examined it "and pronounced it to be the original beyond doubt." Seven years later it was published as *The Book of Abraham* in a third scriptural volume (as a companion for the Bible and The Book of Mormon) entitled *The Pearl of Great Price; a Selection from the revelations, translations, and narrations of Joseph Smith.* (Also within the latter was *The Book of Moses,* which was revealed to Joseph in June 1830, two months after the church was organized.)

It is quite possible that Joseph did not need the scrolls to produce *The Book of Abraham*, but that they stimulated his mind and, coupled with the spiritual communication with the heavens that Latter-day Saints believe he possessed, he received the book through "revelation" rather than "translation." The scrolls disappeared years after Joseph's death, and until recently it was thought they were burned in the Great Chicago Fire of 1871, which it is possible most or all were. However, in 1968 a professor from Utah discovered what may have been part of them at the Metropolitan Museum of New York. The church bought the artifact in 1969. Some Egyptologists gave a preliminary report that the portion obtained in 1969 was of other material not related to Abraham, which gives credence to the theory that he did not translate it but rather received a revelation as he studied the scrolls, as concepts and words came to him comprising the entire *Book of Abraham* while he had other material in front of him. Another possibility exists—that the portion obtained in 1969 was not a substantial enough segment for those Egyptologists to determine if it was part of the scrolls Joseph used. In any case, the Church of Jesus Christ of Latter-day Saints views the book—and all *The Pearl of Great Price*—as scripture, while the other break-off churches do not.

Peace existed in Kirtland during the spring of 1835. But mild contention began to rear its ugly head that summer, when Joseph received confirmation from the Lord, he said, that the ancient practice of polygamy should be restored.

C H A **27** E R

T

HE practice of polygamy, however, was not yet for the entire church, which would come later. Joseph was the first who was told through revelation, he stated, to practice it, and soon there would be others among the church leaders who would follow.

While he may have first learned of and practiced the doctrine four years earlier, Joseph took his first plural wife known by most historians just before or during the summer of 1835, and her name was Fannie Alger. (Benjamin F. Johnson believed he married her the next year, 1836, at Kirtland.) She was well liked by all and was considered lovely and of a pleasant disposition. She lived in Joseph's home. This marriage was later confirmed by Heber C. Kimball in the St. George Temple, according to Benjamin F. Johnson, who was an active church member all his life. (One of the presidents of the first Quorum of Seventy, Lyman R. Sherman, also evidently told Benjamin Johnson, his brother-in-law, that Joseph had confided in him that the ancient practice would be restored to the church.)

Oliver Cowdery and Warren Parrish both knew of Fannie, according to Johnson. And both men, along with Jared Carter, began criticizing Joseph for the marriage. Benjamin Johnson said Oliver and Warren became "a law unto themselves" and were "left in darkness." He believed, as Saints did then and now, that when members become unjustifiably critical of church leaders, they lose the companionship of the Holy Ghost and are "left in darkness." Jared Carter in fact decided that since Joseph was practicing polygamy that he should as well, but Joseph would not allow it, according to Benjamin Johnson. Oliver wrote his brother three years later, criticizing Joseph. Joseph tried to convince him to retract his criticisms but Oliver would not.

One year later, according to a not entirely reliable source, a certain number left the church over another issue—Joseph told a congregation in the temple, according to this report, that members had no right to question him. Benjamin Winchester, who left the church later and may not have understood the doctrine, stated also that two or three families were involved in some controversy with Joseph, likely meaning that Joseph had taken two or three other plural wives from families who objected, although the women themselves had consented.

On still another matter entirely unrelated to the above two, Joseph received subtle persecution by the county in which they lived, Geauga, because they would not recognize marriages performed by the Saints. So Joseph circumvented them by performing others' marriages and sending the certificates to an adjoining county, Medina, where they were recognized.

The first marriage he performed was between Newel Knight and Lydia Goldthwait on November 25, 1835. Knight was a bachelor, but enemies would make controversy of it because, although they loved each other, Lydia was already married. She wanted out of the marriage and felt "stuck" because her husband would not release her from marriage. (Parenthetically, her husband also had no interest in her religion.) Joseph stepped in and essentially recognized her wishes for a divorce, and then he married Newel to Lydia. He told them in the ceremony that marriage was instituted of heaven in the Garden of Eden and should be performed by the priesthood. (The policy of the church—especially since, and to an extent at that time—has been to encourage spouses to remain together even if one of them does not convert. In the case of Lydia Goldthwait, the divorce was based on other issues anyway.)

His next ceremonies to perform were in December 1835, then three more on January 17, 1836, and another on January 20, 1836. On March 20, 1836, Joseph printed a number of certificates at the print shop with blanks to be filled in. These could be used by elders who had the authority to marry couples, so that Joseph would simply have to add his signature as presiding officer.

As for polygamy, Joseph would announce it as a revelation eight years later, but it would be denied by church leaders and labeled merely a "tenet" of what they practiced until after they later arrived in Utah.

That winter Joseph attended numerous parties and feasts and enjoyed sleighing. The snows came hard and he enjoyed the white winterland beauty. He officiated at some weddings and simply attended others. He loved visiting with friends and family. He enjoyed hosting the numerous guests to his home and his town, which included curious visitors to see the mummies, some traveling from as far away as New York.

His personality was also mellowing. About seven months later Lorenzo Snow would see Joseph for a second time, having met him only once in 1832. This time "he seemed to have changed considerably in his appearance. . . . He was very ready in conversation, and had apparently lost that reserve and diffident feeling that he seemed to have before. He was free and easy in his conversation with me, making me feel perfectly at home in his presence. In fact, I felt as free with him as if we had been special friends for years."

Joseph meanwhile had not lost his propensity for hard work, for which he was so well known as a youth in Palmyra. Here, as in his early days, Wilford Woodruff reports, "He was a laboring man, and gained his bread by the sweat of his brow." William H. Walker writes that he and Joseph worked together in the hay field at "mowing grass, with a scythe many a day, putting in 10 hours' good hard work. Very few, if any, were his superior in that kind of work." As for Joseph's orderliness, Jesse W. Crosby says Joseph always kept his property clear of rubbish. "His wood yard was an example of order. Logs were neatly piled and all trash cleared away. If he did not finish the log on which he was chopping, the remnant was laid back on the pile and not left on the ground for a stumbling block. The chips he made he picked up himself into a basket and put them in a wood box which stood in the wood yard." He adds that Joseph "always left his fence clear of everything that might gather fire. . . . He was orderly."

Joseph personally worked on building houses for the widows. In his own house he built kitchen fires, carried out ashes, hauled in wood and water, and assisted in "the care of the children," observed Jesse W. Crosby firsthand. John Bernhisel, a boarder with the family, labels Joseph "a tender and affectionate husband and parent." He played checkers with friends and other games with the children—significantly, *"their games."* He would match couplets in rhyme and present riddles to others. He loved music and dancing, and could sing well. Two of his favorite church hymns were "The Spirit of God" and "Redeemer of Israel." "He would become so inspired with the spirit of the music that he would clap his hands and shout hosanna to the Lord," says Eunice Snow, a childlike trait that enamored him to the hearts of others.

On November 2, 1835, Joseph, Oliver, and others visited Willoughby College near Kirtland. The dean was John C. Bennett, who would later be a major player in their future settlement of Nauvoo. The purpose of their visit was to hear a physics lecture by the Jewish academician Daniel Peixotto. Joseph liked him and invited him to teach Hebrew in Kirtland, but the professor turned him down. Nevertheless, this single lecture is what possibly sparked Joseph's keen interest in Hebrew.

Joseph pushed for education in Kirtland and persuaded children and adults alike to go to school. After much planning, the school bell rang for its opening the day after the Hebrew lecture, on November 3, 1835. Known as the Kirtland School of the Elders, it was a public school. He dedicated it with a prayer. In the same prayer he called upon the members to prepare for their endowment in the temple.

The school was for studying academic subjects and religion. Academic subjects were taught to 100 adults and children, under

William McLellin's supervision, in the areas of English grammar, penmanship, math, and geography. McLellin was a member of the Twelve and would later give Joseph tremendous grief. But for now he was of great service to the Saints. Joseph would also organize several Schools of the Prophets and Schools of the Elders—in both Kirtland and Jackson County.

At Kirtland, Joseph presided over them and also served as one of the teachers. One reason for their education, Joseph said from a revelation, was that the missionaries would better relate with those they contacted. Joseph also attended a music class by Gustavus Hills.

Then a remarkable spiritual incident occurred at the School of the Prophets in Kirtland. Zebedee Coltrin reports that Joseph had been teaching the group about prayer, and then, while praying, they saw someone walk through the room. After Joseph asked the others if they had seen him, he told them it was Jesus Christ, the Son of God. Joseph told them to resume praying, and then another visitor appeared—this one in a bright light. The power they felt pierced the marrow of their bones, Coltrin declares, adding, "I saw him." Joseph announced this second being was God the Father. This remarkable incident reportedly occurred on the second floor of the Newel K. Whitney Store.

Another time, Coltrin reports seeing Adam and Eve sitting on a golden throne. He states that Joseph and Oliver witnessed the vision with him.

Because of Joseph's interest in Hebrew, he and his close friends launched into a serious study of the language the day after the school was opened. Meanwhile, he attended school with the other adults and made fast progress in his education.

During this time, Oliver took a trip to New York to buy a book bindery. He returned with many Hebrew books for the Kirtland School and gave Joseph a Hebrew Bible, a grammar lexicon, an English dictionary, and a Greek lexicon. When Oliver returned, Joseph spent the day looking through the books and studying the Hebrew alphabet—which he evidently relished. At night he met with his Hebrew class, which decided to hire a Jew as their teacher.

To accomplish that Joseph found a young professor teaching at the Hudson, Ohio, seminary. Joshua Seixas, who had reviewed *The Book of Abraham*, came from a well-known family and had studied Aramaic, Arabic, and Syriac to help him teach Hebrew. He had worked years on a Hebrew manual to help promote the Bible, then had taught briefly at Oberlin College, where one of his students had been Lorenzo Snow (later to arrive on the Mormon scene and years later to become the fifth president of the church).

Joseph and his friends studied earnestly before Seixas came and, when Joseph wasn't consumed with church duties, he would pull out his Hebrew studies and dive in—whether with friends, alone, at the office, or in council meetings. He even studied when he had a very bad cold that kept him from work.

Seixas arrived on January 26, 1836, and taught two one-hour classes per day, five days a week. Classes started immediately, and Joseph recorded he was extremely pleased with the first lesson. He would in fact continue enjoying every lesson from him. Seixas was paid $320 for teaching a seven-week course. By late February 1836 he found an overflow crowd of students wanting to learn from him, so he began teaching four classes each day. His pupils even had to split apart a Bible in order to share it, such was the shortage of materials. Joseph actually began reading from the Hebrew Bible in less than three weeks. Seixas said of them that they were "the most forward class" he had ever instructed for the same length of time.

Joseph records that he "delighted in reading the word of the Lord in the original." And, "It seems as if the Lord opens our minds in a marvelous manner, to understand His word in the original language." Joseph also hoped God would "endow us with a knowledge of all languages and tongues that His servants may go forth." That hope would come to pass as The Book of Mormon was later translated into dozens of languages, and missionaries would learn even dozens more to teach throughout the world.

One day Joseph invited Seixas to his home to teach him the gospel, but he records that even though the Lord was striving with the professor, he did not accept the gospel. Nevertheless, Joseph saw him as a "chosen vessel unto the Lord to do His people good." Seixas indicated he was genuinely impressed with his students because he chose his top nine, Joseph among them, to have special classes.

The seven-week contract was extended. After seven he went home for his goods and his wife. He had agreed to ten weeks, but for some unknown reason left after nine. The last day of class was March 29, 1836. Orson Hyde wrote a thank you letter two days later. Joseph and his friends put so much importance into their study of Hebrew that they actually continued with classes right up through the week of dedicating the Kirtland Temple.

Meanwhile, in addition to studying Hebrew, during that same time span Joseph worked hard at learning Egyptian.

The most powerful event in moving the church forward took place at the completion of the Kirtland Temple. The Saints sacrificed by donating jewelry, valuable china, and glassware that was broken up and used on the walls, and even gold rings to give it a unique glow. The outside had been finished January 8, 1836, and in February the lower room was painted, with Brigham Young supervising, leaving his Hebrew classes to make sure it was done right. Women sewed white canvas curtains to separate the large room into several smaller ones. It was all finished and dedicated on March 27, 1836, two days before the last day of Hebrew classes.

The dedication lasted seven hours. It started at 9 A.M., but the Saints gathered by 7 A.M., so anxious were they for a seat. A thousand were personally seated by Joseph, Oliver, and Sidney, and another thousand were turned away until the next session the following day. Some, however, went to an overflow crowd of a separate meeting in the schoolhouse. The dedication ceremony began with Sidney reading psalms from the Bible. A choir sang. Prayers and hymns ascended to heaven. Sidney spoke for two and a half hours in one of the greatest sermons of his life. He said this was the only large house of worship on earth built by heavenly revelation. He had the quorums and the congregation sustain Joseph as prophet by rising from their seats. More hymns followed. Joseph stood and asked the same quorums and congregation to sustain the other church leaders and the presidency; then he gave the dedicatory prayer. Following that, his brother Don Carlos Smith blessed the sacrament, whereupon the bread and wine were then passed to the congregation by the elders.

Then the miracles began . . .

As people shared their testimonies, angels were seen amidst the congregation. Brigham Young spoke in tongues. Joseph blessed the Saints and they returned to their homes.

But that night when Joseph met with the quorums, other miracles—even greater ones—occurred. Some members prophesied, others saw visions, many spoke in tongues. A loud, mighty rushing of wind filled the temple when George Albert Smith stood to bear his testimony, and the entire congregation immediately stood. Joseph saw numerous angels filling the building. Outside, people rushed to the temple, hearing the noises coming from inside and seeing a pillar of fire rest upon the top of the building.

Two nights later Joseph met with the quorum presidents and their counselors in the temple, and they stayed together all night. The next day at 8 A.M., 300 men had their feet washed in a sacred temple ordinance. They fasted all that day, received other temple ordinances, and that night at 7 o'clock partook of the sacrament. Joseph announced that all the ordinances were now performed and they were ready to go out to build the kingdom of God. At 9 P.M. he left the temple in order to rest for another service the next morning. However, the other men there remained all night.

The following day, March 31, 1836, another service was held with a full house. After the sacrament, Joseph and Oliver received an amazing revelation. First they went behind the white curtains, called veils, and bowed in silent prayer. Then a vision opened to them. Joseph writes:

"We saw the Lord standing upon the breastwork of the pulpit, before us; and under his feet was a paved work of pure gold, in color like amber. His eyes were as a flame of fire; the hair of his head was white like pure snow; his countenance shone above the brightness of the sun; and his voice was as the sound of the rushing of great waters, even the voice of Jehovah, saying: I am the first and the last; I am he who liveth, I am he who was slain; I am your advocate with the Father. Behold, your sins are forgiven you; you are clean before me; therefore, lift up your heads and rejoice. Let the hearts of your brethren rejoice, and let the hearts of all my people rejoice, who have, with their might, built this house to my name. . . . Yea the hearts of thousands and tens of thousands shall greatly rejoice in consequence of the blessings which shall be poured out."

Those blessings to be poured out would apparently be the fruits of missionary work—by those who attended these meetings. In the same revelation the Saints reported that Moses, Elias, and Elijah, all known from the Old Testament, came to them and gave them the keys of their dispensations. Moses gave the keys of the gathering of Israel, Elias the dispensation of the gospel of Abraham, and Elijah the keys to salvation for the dead—those living in the spirit world after they leave this earth.

The next Monday, April 4, 1836, the missionaries began leaving the town in droves to spread missionary work. And the Lord's promises, stated Joseph, would be fulfilled.

For Joseph personally, the month of May was spectacularly fulfilling. His uncle Silas and others of the Smith family moved to Kirtland. He learned his 93-year-old grandmother, the widow of Asael, Mary Duty Smith, was on her way and, after a 500-mile journey to see her descendants one final time, had stopped at Fairport, Ohio.

So Joseph and Hyrum jumped on a carriage and rode off in a flash to get her. Hugs were in order as they welcomed her and brought her to Kirtland. Interestingly, she recognized all her descendants when she saw them. She was especially pleased to see her grandchildren for the first time. Joseph had a special place in her heart, as she told him she knew he was the prophet whom her husband Asael had predicted years earlier would be raised up in the family. She also said that when Asael had heard about Joseph's work, he knew Joseph was "the very prophet that he had long known would come in his family." Her visit was extremely happy but brief, as she died days later on May 27 at sunset, peacefully in her sleep. Wishing to keep family conflict at a minimum, Joseph did not seek to have her baptized because of her oldest son's opposition; nevertheless, she died strong in the faith, Lucy said.

June also was a happy month for Joseph. On June 25, 1836, his and Emma's second son was born, Frederick.

The Saints in Missouri, however, were struggling, which caused Joseph great concern. On December 10, 1835, he had mailed to Governor Dunklin of Missouri the petitions he had gathered. The parcel was so large that it cost $5—a substantial sum for the day.

On January 22, 1836, the governor responded. He sympathized with them, but still felt their only recourse was through the courts. Dunklin's request to build a fort nearby had evidently been turned down by the War Department. The fort could have protected the Saints if they returned. So Joseph knew his cause in Jackson County was sunk.

Things grew even darker when the hospitality of the old settlers in Clay County dried up, and they began demanding the Saints leave. They had for a while been helpful to the refugee Jackson County Saints, but then problems erupted. It had not taken long before the old settlers in Jackson had incited the Clay residents—so the old settlers of Clay now also believed the Saints looked at Clay as theirs to take, and that they planned to institute anti-slavery political policies, befriend and join forces with the Native Americans, and inflate land prices.

A common practice of the day was for citizens in a county to band together and work on public projects such as roads.

But on June 24, 1836, the old settlers in Clay County who were working on a road began mumbling—why should they "bust their rears on the county road," since the Mormons were going to "take over" the county anyway?

So when a group of Mormons showed up to pitch in, the old settlers not only walked off the job, they sent word out to hold a protest meeting. And they held it four nights later. A large crowd attended, and the more they talked, the more excited they became. Almost immediately they passed resolutions to get rid of the Saints altogether. But it didn't stop there. That very night they organized a mob and attacked the Saints—six mobbers grabbed a Mormon and whipped him with 100 lashes, nearly killing him. Other Saints were attacked in various ways.

The next day, not knowing they were under attack, 300 Mormons came rolling down the county road with 35 wagons. The old settlers had gotten wind of their approach the night before and excitedly got 100 armed mobbers to go out to turn them back. When the old settlers found them, they told them they were not welcome, then insulted them by following the Saints as they turned around and headed back. True to their directives from church leaders, the Saints simply wanted to avoid conflict, and complied.

On June 29, 1836, the old settlers met in Liberty. There, a committee of nine men drafted a letter for the Saints. Among them were the Saints' friend Alexander Doniphan and fellow attorney David R. Atchison. They reminded the Mormons that their leaders had earlier stated that if ever they were asked to leave, they would, and now was the time to do so. They also complained that the Saints were from the East and were thus not compatible with their Clay neighbors, having different speech and customs. They candidly confessed that they were not certain as to the truthfulness of their own allegations, but that the community was excited nonetheless. So they recommended that the Saints move to Wisconsin, a territory of abolitionists and Easterners. They then asked the Saints, "in a spirit of frank and friendly kindness," to leave them after "their crops are gathered, their business settled, and they have made every suitable preparation to remove." Their letter also said those Mormons with 40 acres could stay for years if it took that long to dispose of it without loss. They also included a false allegation based on misinformation—they said the Saints planned to take over the local country there.

On July 1, 1836, W. W. Phelps and the Saints replied, saying how grateful they were that the settlers had helped them when they were booted out of Jackson County, but they denied the false allegation. Nevertheless, they agreed, for the sake of peace and friendship, to leave.

The old settlers then did a magnanimous thing—they appointed representatives from each town to raise money to help the poor Saints to leave.

But the magnanimity was replaced with insults. On July 1 and 2, 1836, companies of old settlers, numbering 500, formed, ready to drive the Saints out by force if they were not willing to move as they had agreed.

On July 25 Joseph wrote the Saints in Clay County telling them that the fault was not with them. He also counseled them to not be the "first aggressors." Then he added: "Give no occasion, and if the people will let you, dispose of our property, settle your affairs, and go in peace. You have thus far had an asylum and now seek another, as God may direct." He concluded that they should stand by the U.S. Constitution and observe its principles, be prudent, preserve peace with all men, "and above all, show yourselves men of God, worthy citizens."

He then wrote the Clay County settlers, via Doniphan, Atchison, and the other seven delegates of the committee at Liberty, diplomatically stating that he respected their desire to avoid bloodshed and that he admired their candor, but that he must for the sake of justice defend the Saints from the "foul" charge against them, and that their constitutional rights were being deprived. He clarified that it was not true and not just to claim that the Saints planned to take over the country but, rather, their religion demanded strict obedience to the law—and to prove it, they had given up their rights in Jackson County rather than fight, always waiting for legal redress.

Joseph appealed to Governor Dunklin again. But on July 18 the governor wrote back saying that while he disagreed with what the citizens had done, he still felt they had *their* rights. He said in effect that the majority rules, and that the voice of the people was all that mattered, thus completely overlooking the fact that the Constitution was established in large part to *preserve property*, including that of the minority. (Otherwise, other minority religious groups, such as the Amish and Quakers, could likewise have their rights trampled upon, along with any minority race that immigrated to the United States, and thus have their rights subjugated to the whim of the majority. In an amazing display of ignorance, Dunklin seemed to think that the United States was a democracy—a pure mobocracy—and not a republic, as he then reveals his political philosophy to Joseph, "In this republic the *vox populi* is the *vox Dei.*" (The voice of the people is the voice of God.)

In June W. W. Phelps and Edward Partridge made a scouting expedition to the northwest part of the state—actually two trips—where they found a new home for the Saints. Unlike anywhere else they had settled, it was mostly a prairie devoid of trees. The only trees were along riverbanks. Nevertheless, Phelps thought the old settlers there were generous and friendly. So in July they began their next exodus. They bought up or laid claim to large sections of land and began farming at once. They made the unfortunate mistake, however, of spreading themselves over 20 miles, in numerous small communities, but their central city became known as the town of Far West. By October they also had a good-sized township in Shoal Creek. In December they requested to incorporate their new county, known as Caldwell.

Their ally, Alexander Doniphan, was in the state legislature, and he supported their request. However, the state now had a new governor, as Daniel Dunklin had stepped down a bit early, in September 1836.

This new governor was their old enemy from Jackson County, Lilburn W. Boggs. Still considering himself their nemesis, he denied the Saints' petition for the county incorporation at

Caldwell. However, he was overridden by the state legislature. And he now obviously looked upon Doniphan—as he especially would later—as his enemy. Doniphan did sadly report to the Saints that because of Boggs they would have less area to settle than he had hoped or expected.

While the Saints would settle Caldwell County, the county north of them was known as Daviess County, where non-Mormons were expected to settle.

The old settlers in the area, particularly in Daviess County, had only been there two and a half years before the Saints—since early 1834. They were pleasant folk who would become bitter enemies. One of the Saints' main future enemies was Robert P. Peniston, the cornmeal miller.

Before he set up his mill, the old settlers in three counties had to either mill their own corn or travel all the way to Liberty in Clay County. The corn mill in Daviess paved the way for a general store, although crude and ill supplied. Before that they would have to travel to a town on the Mississippi River for supplies, or to Independence in Jackson County. Next they opened a grocery store, and then a blacksmith shop. Gallatin also developed. Native Americans in the area got along well with the whites, receiving a means to obtain goods to trade with the whites.

At Far West, which became the county seat as well as the principle town in Caldwell County, the Saints built up the town at break-neck speed—adding not only log but frame houses, shops, and schools. The Saints' community spread out 20 miles in all directions from the city. Only a handful of non-Saints were in Caldwell County, and did not mind seeing the gathering taking place. Nor did they mind seeing them controlling the elections and most of the county offices and judgeships. The town quickly began to prosper.

But back in Ohio, Joseph's main concern was not having enough money. Payments were due for the store merchandise he had received from New York, Cleveland, and Pittsburgh on credit, and there were debts associated with the defunct Law of Consecration, with the temple, with buying land in Kirtland,

and with helping the poor among them. Joseph also owed money in Ohio on the printing press shop, the tannery, and the sawmill—everything they had tried to be industrious with. Now a new need was added — having to come up with the cash to buy land in Caldwell County for the Missouri Saints. (Adding to his difficulties, Joseph was personally poor all during the Kirtland years, making sacrifices for the temple and trying to support his family.)

It was now the fall of 1836 and Joseph came up with a plan. They would build a bank and combine their resources, print their own money in order to make payments among themselves easier, and keep money in their city so that their economy would boom, rather than buying items elsewhere with money printed elsewhere.

The name of their bank was the Kirtland Safety Society Bank, and with all his efforts to help his people financially, Joseph was about to take their finances from bad to worse, and literally spark an insurrection among them.

A prophet he was to his people, but not an economist. Still, Joseph's plan may have worked had the national economy allowed it. Those who had the facts would rightly blame the national economy that would soon sink into a major recession, which had nothing to do with their own abilities or inabilities as bankers. However, some were so incensed from losing their money that they blamed him anyway. And it was from this group that a new wave of apostasy began. It all officially started when they drew up their agreement for the bank on November 2, 1836.

Oliver Cowdery shot off to Philadelphia to get plates manufactured for printing their local bank money. (All bank-printed money was known as "notes," as designated herein.) Meanwhile, Orson Hyde rode off to Columbus, Ohio, to ask the state legislature for a charter.

They were hopeful that they would get the bank charter from the state—and were shocked when they were turned down. They thought the reason was religious discrimination, but it was possibly due to the fact that most requests were being turned down by the legislature. And the reason for that was—too many banks were starting up around the country—especially in Ohio. Also, inflation was rising fast, and more printed money by yet another bank would only make that matter worse. But, being determined to move forward with a new bank, the Saints did what the law allowed them to.

The backdrop for being turned down goes back to a decision President Andrew Jackson made four years previously when he turned down the charter of the Bank of the United States. This allowed for government deposits to be made into state banks. Because of that, there was a huge surge in start-up state banks who wanted in on the action. To make matters worse, a gargantuan number of private banks were launched so they could jump into the fray.

So, with the hoped-for state charter being turned down, the Saints decided to start yet another private bank.

However, with "plan B" in effect, Joseph felt tremendous financial pressure—he could not pay off the debts he owed on store goods obtained from New York, Cleveland, and Pittsburgh, as he had planned by owning the state-chartered bank. So he was left to issue notes only from his private bank, and his creditors would not accept notes from a private bank such as his. Nevertheless, the private bank would still help the local economy by keeping money at home. Or so they hoped.

One other important factor occurred on the national scene—the national government would sell public lands for bank notes. This allowed land sellers and buyers to go wild with speculation—buying land left and right with whatever bank notes they could come up with.

Then, with bank regulations taken away, there came not only the flurry of private banks, but banks started by people who knew nothing about banking—especially on the frontier. At those unsophisticated, private, frontier banks, only a little security was given by individuals for loans, which put those banks especially in danger.

Some banks were started just so the owners could get out of debt or give themselves a quick, easy profit. A group of such people would sometimes print their own money and pay off their debts. In these cases they would open their banks deep in the wilderness, so that if anyone wanted to redeem their notes, it was practically impossible. The term "wildcat banks" came into being—where banks existed so far in the wilderness that only wild animals could access them. But other private banks were honest and attempted to help their local economy, as was the case with the Kirtland bank.

Sidney Rigdon did not want to establish the bank, but Joseph persuaded him. Others in leadership, such as William McLellin, were not persuaded either, but the bank moved forward.

Because they had optimistically moved forward with what they thought would be a state-chartered bank, they had drawn up an agreement among themselves. So now this agreement had to be canceled. On January 2, 1837, they adopted a new agreement for the private bank. They wrote an introduction to the agreement, stating the purpose of the bank—to improve merchandising, mechanical arts, and agriculture. To launch it, 188 people "subscribed" to it, and the bank would have 32 managers. Sidney Rigdon was president and Joseph Smith treasurer.

The basis of the bank's operation would be to issue notes for mortgages on private property. From that, more notes would be issued. This was a common method of banking then. People bought stock in the banking company by trading their lots.

One small catch to all this was their name. Only a state-chartered bank could use the word "bank" or "banking company" in its name. Private banks such as theirs were not allowed to use those terms.

So when Oliver returned with the highly expensive, very handsome printing plates for making money, they could not be used. The name on the plates was "Kirtland Safety Society Banking Company," and that name was off limits, since they had been turned down as a state-chartered bank.

Therefore, they came up with an ingenious little plan. They changed the name on their paper money. They accomplished this by first printing the bills on the new plates, then reprinting or stamping the bills on another plate, which they made locally. That local plate had the word *Anti-* installed just before the word *Bank*. Then they printed the bills on a third plate, also made locally, with the letters *ing* to be used after the word *Bank*, thus making the new name on the paper money, the "Kirtland Safety Society *Anti-*Banking Company."

This private bank was a "stock association" with limited power to issue only notes. They promptly printed $200,000 in bills.

But the true cash that the bank had was eaten up quickly because, although they adopted a strategy that made sense, it was misused by the people of Kirtland: The bank officials wanted to get rid of other banks' money in the city; so they honored other banks' bills by redeeming them with cash specie whenever such bills, which were issued from other banks, were brought to their bank. Once the Kirtland bank had these bills from other banks, they would keep them out of circulation in their town by holding them in their vaults. This way only Kirtland's bank bills would be in local circulation.

Their private bank began on October 18, 1836. Four men held 3,000 shares, Sidney and Joseph among them, and most of the rest were owned by 30 people, eight of whom were Joseph's relatives, all believing the bank would be a success. In all, 69,636 shares were issued. The face value of shares was $50, but they paid only a fraction of that to own a share—over 95% paid just 26 ¼ *cents* per share. That could have been meant as a down payment, but most never paid more than that. Joseph Smith and several others paid more, and some less. Later when things went sour, shareholders (at least those with bad attitudes and especially those who would apostatize) claimed they lost 99% of their investment, but in reality they lost about 50%, because the stock only dropped to 12 ½ cents per share.

But hopes for material gain were high for a while. People were cheerful and the local economy was booming. There were now 2,000 Saints living there, but in reality the construction quality of the buildings left a bit to be desired. Joseph's house was small, and most people lived in cheaply put together homes of board or clapboard. Only the temple was solidly built.

Perhaps because of their poor living conditions, people were hungry for a change. Unfortunately, writes John Whitmer, it was not coupled with sharing, sacrifice, and humility. He writes that the "whole church" became enamored with materialism, partaking of the "spirit of speculation," and was "lifted up in pride." Many Saints thought they were now rich. Fifty-dollar bills had been bought for only a quarter, so some, according to Oliver, began to buy merchandise in the thousands of dollars, running up tremendous debts for store goods and clothes. Some took advantage of Joseph's desire to make things right with people. Those who took advantage of him were generally those who wanted to make a quick buck at others' expense. They would go to him and demand full payment of their notes at face value. Since Joseph always wanted to keep everyone happy, he would pay them off, which quickly depleted the cash in their bank. When Joseph had run the general store, he had manifested this same tendency—of placing other people's needs first by giving out store merchandise. And unfortunately he ran the bank the same way—not requiring immediate payment from customers.

So when he paid out the last true cash the bank had, in late January 1837, it was depleted of funds. Thus on January 27, 1837, the *Painsville Telegraph* notified everyone in the area that the Kirtland bank would not pay cash for any more notes, and would instead pay with land. Immediately there was a rush to get rid of the Kirtland bills—by Saints and non-Saints alike.

Aside from Joseph's lack of a firm hand in holding onto the bank's cash when people came to him to redeem their notes, a national bank crash was in full sway, and millions around the country were affected the same way.

The reason, to a large extent, was another political decision by President Andrew Jackson—he had decreed in July 1836 that the U.S. Government would no longer accept notes from state and private banks for the sale of public land, because the new bank bills had overwhelmed the U.S. Treasury. Therefore, he made only gold and silver acceptable means of payment when selling public lands. Because of that, the public grabbed up all the gold and silver coins then in circulation and hid them at home. With bank notes no longer useful even for public land, the notes began going for a discount, and some became completely useless as any kind of legal tender.

Beginning November 1, 1836, just four months after Andrew Jackson's decree, 83 of the 89 state banks in the U.S. would go out of business within 12 months. Numerous private banks would join them, including the Kirtland bank. There would in fact be a national financial crash. So in 1837, the year of the Kirtland bank's demise, every bank in Ohio closed except one.

Nevertheless, Joseph was blamed by some in church leadership who did not have the power they wanted, and by many of the rank-and-file Saints whose dreams of material wealth did not materialize. Even non-Mormons, who could and would blame Joseph for the bank's demise instead of the general economy and questionable political factors, decided to single him out as their scapegoat.

So in February 1837 Joseph had a writ served against him for illegal banking. On March 24 he logically pointed out in court that the state law he was accused of breaking had not yet been activated when his bank was established. He lost the case anyway and was fined $1,000 plus court costs. He appealed later but there was no ruling made on it.

In February 1837 the Kirtland bank officially went under, yet continued to limp along until July 2, 1837, when it finally closed its doors. In general, it was a short-lived, four-month failure that filtered out more of the Saints, many of whom lost a substantial portion of their money—but at most, as stated, 50%. (The Jackson County Saints, and later two other communities, would lose basically everything.) Unfortunately, the Kirtland bank had obtained investments from church members away from Kirtland, including those in Canada, and non-Saints as well. Joseph had apparently believed in the bank all the way into the third month, because he placed a notice in their newspaper, the January *Messenger and Advocate*, requesting those abroad to buy stock. Joseph did place a stipulation on its success, however, often overlooked by historians—Wilford Woodruff writes that Joseph told him he had received a revelation from God the morning of January 6, 1837, stating that if the Saints would keep the Lord's commandments, the Kirtland Safety Society would be successful. And with that stipulation in place, the bank had begun to fail. Too many Saints had in fact backslid. Many, including leaders, were overly critical all through the bank's operation and judgmental of Joseph and Sidney. The apparent weaknesses of pride and love of money took precedence over obedience and humility, some felt, and in general the Saints did not live up to the Lord's admonitions.

Even with the financial problems overwhelming the entire country, Joseph stood, on April 6, 1837, and proclaimed his dream for Kirtland's success. It was during the church's general conference. He had seen in vision the city as it could be—and which he still thought and hoped it would be—not realizing the extent of the apostates' work among them, which would soon make life so unsafe for him that he would have to flee for his life. Joseph's vision had included steamboats entering the city and their goods being exported on railroads to many places, probably even to Missouri. Chapels would be built, "beautiful streets" would be constructed, and the notable of the earth would come visit them. All would have come true if the Saints had been obedient, not materialistic, and not critical, he would soon come to believe.

Sidney Rigdon also spoke, requesting the Saints not to demand payment from the church, but to let those debts go.

The following Sunday Joseph proclaimed in the name of God that "severe judgment awaited those characters that professed to be his friends & friends to humanity & the Kirtland Safety Society but had turned traitors," writes Wilford Woodruff in rough penmanship, adding that Joseph is to the gentiles (non-Saints) like a "bed of gold concealed from human view; they know not his principle, his spirit, his wisdom, virtue, philanthropy, nor his calling. His mind, like Enoch's, swells wide as eternity. Nothing short of a God can comprehend his soul."

By the next month, people were talking against him in the streets, and even those in high places of the church were plotting his demise.

Parley P. Pratt returned from Canada the summer of 1837 and also fell into the trap of material concern and quarreling with Joseph. He disliked what had happened to real estate he had bought—he decided he had earlier paid too much for it—and now threatened to sue Joseph over it. The high council met to decide if action should be taken against him, since he was one of the Twelve, but they could not reach an agreement, so nothing was decided. Parley soon went to him in tears and "with a broken and contrite spirit." He confessed he had "erred in spirit, murmured, or done or said amiss." Parley adds, "He frankly forgave me." Soon he asked Joseph if he could go east on a mission, and was granted it.

But Joseph's enemies prevailed. He writes that the apostates and non-Mormons who were against him united "in their schemes . . . and many became disaffected toward me as though I were the sole cause of those very evils I was most strenuously striving against, and which were actually brought upon us by the brethren not giving heed to my counsel." Joseph felt that despite the national collapse, their bank still would have succeeded had the members stayed united and not made a run on the bank.

On May 28, 1837, he defended himself, while speaking in the temple, convincing many, says Wilford Woodruff, but not enough.

With disaster imminent and Kirtland ready to fall—along with many of its members on the brink of leaving and others already gone—Joseph was greatly distraught.

C H A P T E R 30

WITH everything about to collapse about him, Joseph writes, "In this state of things . . . God revealed to me that something new must be done for the salvation of His church." And the first big step in that direction occurred days later when, on June 4, 1837, Joseph visited Heber C. Kimball in the temple, a man who stuttered, and said to him, "Brother Heber, the Spirit of the Lord has whispered to me: Let my servant Heber go to England and proclaim my Gospel, and open the door of salvation to that nation."

And open the door it did. In fact it opened the flood gates. Thousands of British citizens would be converted and pour into the church, then emigrate to America to—not only add strength, craftsmanship, trade skills, and loyalty, but—practically save the church.

At first Heber was stunned to receive the mission call. Because of his speech impediment he thought: "The idea of being appointed to such an important mission was almost more than I could bear up under. I felt my weakness and was nearly ready to sink under it, but the moment I understood the will of my heavenly Father, I felt a determination to go at all hazards, believing that he would support me by his almighty power, and although my family were dear to me, and I should have to leave them almost destitute, I felt that the cause of truth, the gospel of Christ, outweighed every other consideration. At this time many faltered in their faith, some of the twelve were in rebellion against the prophet of God."

Wishing to accompany Heber were Orson Hyde, Willard Richards, and some from Canada who desired to take the message to their family and friends in England. Joseph gave them one admonishment—keep it simple and stick to the "first principles" of the gospel, avoiding more complex or deeper doctrines.

Heber's wife Vilate endured the separation along with the other wives of the departing missionaries. Most were destitute, finding it a tremendous trial of their faith. The only way they could keep themselves and their small children alive was to sew, clean, wash, and cook for others. The church helped where it could but it was not enough. They barely survived, and their sacrifice was paramount to their husbands'—and the church's—success, which would soon be poured upon them.

On June 13, 1837, their husbands left for England, taking no money of their own, living only on the generosity of people along the way. Making their way to New York, they would set sail on July 1, 1837.

Meanwhile, still in June 1837 at Kirtland, Joseph and Sidney were again attacked by their local enemies—apostates and those not of their faith. Sidney was summoned before the court for manufacturing "spurious money." Joseph was also charged with conspiracy to take the life of one Grandison Newel, a charge filed out of spite.

Joseph and other church leaders went to court in Painsville, 18 miles away, with word spreading all through the area about the trial. Joseph was convinced the charges were not only absurd but were generated to make the church look bad.

On June 17, 1837, Oliver officially joined the opposition as a judge. Despite his former closeness to Joseph, he ruled that the local bank money was "not lawful," and even ruled against someone who used Kirtland money to pay a tradesman.

In July Joseph was arrested three times, possibly more. He was acquitted all three times that are recorded. Despite the disobedience of the Saints to Joseph's admonition not to "run on the bank" and not to seek full cash value for the bills, Joseph was still blamed—hence, his court appearances. While overlooking that fact, the following editorial in the Kirtland *Messenger and Advocate* nevertheless defended him by saying that a man may be a "celebrated divine, and be no mechanic, and no financier, and be as liable to fail in the management of a bank as he would in constructing a balloon."

Joseph and Sidney completely separated themselves from the bank in early July 1837. Taking their places were two men who would by design make matters even worse. Although Joseph did not know it while it happened, the two were soon engaged in activities to incite the people even further against the church. And to Joseph's surprise they were . . .

His own scribes, Warren Parish and Frederick G. Williams.

Creating incredible damage, they apparently withdrew thousands of dollars in useless notes from the vault and sent representatives among the local citizens to buy livestock, wagons, and farms, according to George Albert Smith. Benjamin Johnson said that Parrish and Williams signed and sent many banknotes out with runners to cheat people. He says people blamed Joseph for the fraud—and Parrish and Williams meant for that to happen—then they unofficially slipped out of the church. (Parrish, during this time, had an affair with a Mrs. Zerah. He soon became a clergyman in Mendon, New York, and went insane by 1870. Williams, however, was rebaptized a year later.) They may have also printed $25,000 in notes after Joseph had ordered the printing of money stopped. Joseph claims Parrish took off with over $25,000, presumably in specie, but if that is what Joseph meant, he might have been misinformed, as the stock ledger shows only just over $20,000 was paid into the bank. Possibly what Joseph meant was that the $25,000 that Parrish took was in the bank's own useless notes, or it is possible Joseph was merely somewhat off in his math, if he was correct in the form of money that was taken.

Joseph left during the middle of July 1837 for a mission to Canada and returned five weeks later in late August. While he was gone, Parrish had a field day destroying Joseph's image.

He issued numerous bank notes at 25 cents on the dollar, which the bank could not redeem. Not knowing an apostate was now in charge of the bank, Nathan Tanner and others still had faith in it and sold everything they owned to help the bank redeem the notes that people were now trying to cash in. Tanner sold his wagon and last team of horses, along with his watch and his last cow, to help the bank cover the notes.

Parrish and Williams, meanwhile, were methodically destroying the Saints' economic system even further, breaking the finances of other individual members and running Joseph's reputation even further into the ground in the process—simply because most members were believing there must be some hope in the bank if it was still selling notes at this late date, even if Joseph was no longer in charge, since he had appointed these two men.

In August 1837 Joseph had to put a stop to the shenanigans—he notified the public through their newspaper that the bills were no longer valid in Kirtland.

When some people lost property, the price of everything else dropped drastically. Criticism of Joseph came in barrages from in and out of the church, and still more members apostatized. Warren Parrish resigned from the bank, having accomplished his mission of sabotage, and of course now joined in the throng of throwing barbs at Joseph, even in the *Messenger and Advocate*, which he edited.

And then the three witnesses to The Book of Mormon surprisingly joined in—Oliver Cowdery, Martin Harris, and David Whitmer. Secret meetings were held every Thursday at Whitmer's house, and they even published a flyer to gain more followers. Many in town supported this "new party," as Lucy labeled them.

When push came to shove, on September 3, 1837, during general conference, Sidney asked the members to sustain Joseph, which they actually, surprisingly, unanimously did.

On September 17, 1837, Newel K. Whitney, bishop of Kirtland, with Joseph's blessing, sent a proclamation to the members, requesting them to "gather up your gold and your silver and all the means you have and send on to the Saints who are engaged in this great work of building the Zion of God," thus wanting to help the members in Missouri. Joseph likely saw the writing on the wall and knew he and the faithful in Ohio would have to leave soon for Missouri.

Also in August 1837 Sidney proclaimed in the *Messenger and Advocate* that it was time for the newspaper to come to an end. Warren Parrish's days as editor (and bank manager) were over. (Parrish actually wanted out anyway.) The newspaper would be replaced by the *Elders' Journal.*

Two months later, October 1837, the new newspaper began with Thomas B. Marsh as "publisher" and Joseph as editorial chief.

In mid-October 1837 Joseph and Sidney took the long journey across three states to Far West, Missouri. Joseph greeted his friends with hugs, and then they got down to business. He met with them about the church being reorganized in Kirtland, and they all voted in agreement. Soon he took another trip—he returned to Kirtland in mid-December 1837 and found his city ready to crumble.

WARREN Parrish had united with two members of the Twelve who had apostatized—Luke Johnson and John Boynton—and started their own church, the Church of Christ. Not only that, they now claimed Joseph and his followers were heretics.

Joseph took action. He called all the quorums to the temple and firmly testified in behalf of his calling. Sidney then spoke, revealing his claim that the apostates were guilty of counterfeiting, adultery, and stealing. When Sidney left, thoroughly exhausted from his own ailments and the exertion he had made in behalf of Joseph and himself, the assembly began shouting and accusing Joseph.

Joseph was left with no alternative but to excommunicate the leaders of the apostates. So there were now two main groups—Joseph, Sidney, and what was left of the church leadership on the one side, and on the other, John and David Whitmer and the Cowdery brothers, who still accused Joseph and Sidney of printing worthless money. Joseph and Sidney then leveled the same charge against the apostates.

Mob action took over. Just before Christmas Brigham Young boldly defended Joseph as a prophet and declared he was not in error or transgression. Three days before Christmas the mob went after him. Brigham hid in the back of a wagon and barely escaped Kirtland alive.

# CHAPTER 31

The next week Joseph's parents and family also fled. Enduring hardships and sickness they walked in the cold weather. Joseph's niece was actually born in a hut on the way to Far West. But Joseph stayed in Kirtland, hoping against hope to save his city.

The last week of December 1837 saw a number of apostates cut off from the church—28 in all, including Martin Harris, Luke Johnson, John Boynton, Warren Parrish, and Cyrus Smalling. Another 10 to 20 had been excommunicated during the previous two months.

With Joseph the final straw broke when he heard yet another warrant was out for his arrest. Grandison Newell charged him with fraud. Joseph decided to finally give up on Kirtland and to escape mob violence, "which was about to burst upon us under the color of legal process," summarizes Joseph.

On January 12, 1838, he escaped. According to one account, a repentant apostate warned Joseph of a plot to kill him. Before Joseph could escape, a mob appeared. Friends helped him into a box that was nailed onto an oxcart. Then he was driven away from Kirtland to safety, where he and Sidney rode off on the two fastest horses they could find. They galloped off at 10 P.M., reportedly predicting before they left that Kirtland would be destroyed.

Joseph and Sidney finally reached Norton, Ohio, where they practically fell off their horses, exhausted, and joined their families.

Five days later they continued the 900-mile journey to Far West. Traveling through several Ohio towns was dangerous for them because Parrish and Williams' runners had recently unloaded worthless Kirtland bills in these towns. Thus, Joseph was attacked by angry locals. In other towns he was spotted and served with writs. He became an escape artist, often hiding in the back of his wagon.

At Dublin, Ohio, Joseph ran into Brigham and others. He volunteered to chop wood to earn money, but Brigham counseled him to just rest, feeling money would come his way. Presently, a member by the name of Tomlinson gave him $300, having just sold his farm after many failed attempts.

Joseph and Sidney split up to lead two different groups along separate routes. The traveling was hard, cooking was difficult, and the coldness was unbearable. Emma was pregnant.

They finally arrived March 14, 1838. At Far West the townspeople greeted them in a somewhat different spirit than the Ohio Saints, who were giving him problems—they cheered and cried when they saw him. Greeting him was a large group, led by Porter Rockwell, who hugged him. The group then sang for him. The prophet and his wife afterward retired to the home of George and Lucinda Harris.

Three weeks later Sidney's group arrived, having fought through a blizzard. When Joseph heard they were coming, he ran out to greet them, tears flooding down his face. He immediately asked Sidney to speak the next Sunday.

Sidney spoke for two hours on Sunday in a large schoolhouse they had built near town.

Back in Ohio, when money became practically impossible to obtain and business slammed to a standstill, the remaining faithful Saints began leaving for Far West. As an example of sacrifice to help his people, Nathan Tanner, who, as mentioned, had given all his livestock, wagons, and farms to keep the bank going, was left penniless, so he placed what belongings he could on an old cart led by an aged stagecoach horse. On his way to Far West, the cart broke into pieces, killing his daughter. He buried her on the roadside.

In Kirtland the printing press office was taken from the church by the court and sold at an auction. Those who won it—Grandison Newell and another apostate—actually cheered when they won but, after taking the press to their office, they got drunk and their office caught fire and burned down. Along with the press. Meanwhile, Joseph would secure another press in Far West and resume his station as editor of the *Elders' Journal*—a 10-month service that had begun the previous October and would continue until August of that year, 1838.

When one dissenter told George Albert Smith that "the prophets were Tyrants, Jesus Christ a Despot," Warren Parrish agreed. But some apostates stayed committed to certain tenants—Martin Harris and the other witnesses, as discussed previously, would, through the remainder of their lives, testify to the truth of The Book of Mormon.

Significantly, it was mainly the poorer Saints, not so attached to property, who followed Joseph west. They sold what property they had, worked long hours to pay off their debts, and obtained wagon teams to make the arduous journey to Far West. Their wagon train began its trek on July 6, 1838, being over a mile long. Amazing to some of the Saints was the fact that some of the apostate leaders—specifically Oliver and the Whitmers— decided to follow Joseph to Far West to continue haranguing him and possibly to attempt wrestling the church away. They apparently saw themselves as rightful heirs to a kingdom.

Kirtland meanwhile became headquarters to several splinter groups, including the Church of Christ, led by William McLellin, who would soon leave for Far West himself. Yet some of Joseph's loyal followers remained in Kirtland as well, continuing with church meetings and even missionary work. It is unknown why they did not take the journey to Far West, but there were similarly numerous other branches of the church in towns and villages throughout the East, Midwest, South, and Canada who also did not "gather" with the Saints, yet remained active in the faith. The Kirtland temple, however, was destroyed, and as the years went on, the city was engulfed by nearby Cleveland.

Of interest to his followers and enemies alike, Joseph never walked away from his debts. Even though Joseph now lived in Far West, he appointed Oliver Granger as his agent to settle the official church debts in Ohio held by the First Presidency, and admitted his concern, "for until they are [paid] I have to labor under a load that is intolerable to bear." Meanwhile, the Kirtland store and his house were held in judgement by the court until he could pay off the debt on the Kirtland bank money plates. Joseph directed Granger to not only pay off that debt, but also the judgment that was attached to the temple mortgage. Even though it was not in use, he wanted the temple free and clear.

Life in Far West would now have its joys, as Joseph appreciated the beauty of the wide-open spaces along the rolling prairies, but he would also here receive new trials on a new level.

C H A P T E R **32**

B

Y the spring of 1838 Joseph and the Saints were again flourishing. They had established themselves in the western section of the county, in a land parcel far away from outsiders and the trouble outsiders had always brought. Within one year the town would have 150 log cabins (although slapped together crudely with boards), six stores, and a farm for practically every family, laid out the way Joseph liked towns to be—with large lots and wide streets. Part of the main square had been excavated, where the foundation for the temple had been laid. Sidney's house also stood in the square and was temporarily used to perform temple endowments. His house was better built than other structures in town, using double logs. On June 2, 1838, Joseph and Emma's third son, Alexander Hale Smith, was born into this town of now 1,500 inhabitants, which was comprised mostly of women and children. But everything was now prepared. And the town was ready for immigrants.

The Saints' reputation was favorable throughout the neighboring counties because their leaders showed integrity and honesty in business, for which the locals gave them credit.

Joseph wanted to expand to the upper Missouri River area, but when he sent agents to buy government land there in March 1838, he was turned down because of the new gold-for-payment-only policy. And the Saints simply did not have any gold—they were too poor.

So he went to the wilderness. He personally surveyed and laid claim to thousands of acres outside Far West. On one of his expeditions to Daviess County, he discovered (along with others in his party) a spot of most unusual high ground looking out over the prairies and the Grand River. There he found an ancient altar. He declared the place Adam-ondi-Ahman, where Adam and Eve had dwelt in the Garden of Eden. He also said Adam would someday come to visit his people there and sit, "as spoken of by Daniel the Prophet." The Saints now established a village there by the same name.

While the local settlers admired the Saints' business practices, they soon became disenchanted with them. Three problems arose, the same as at Jackson County: their anti-slavery views, non-traditional religious beliefs, and expansion—seeing more Mormons moving into the area weekly. Just the previous year, in 1837, the old settlers had chased a newspaper editor, Elijah Lovejoy, out of town for editorializing against their court refusing to rule against a lynch mob that had killed African-Americans. They had even burned one man to death who was merely accused of murder. When Lovejoy fled for his life to Illinois, he was chased down and murdered.

Thus, the Saints found themselves in this type of hornet's nest of suspicion, bigotry, narrow-mindedness, and potential mob violence.

But some Saints viewed their real enemy as the dissenters. Joseph found it necessary to now excommunicate several once-close associates who had apparently been overtaken by what he saw as greed and lust for power. John Whitmer was one of the first, then W. W. Phelps was cut off for misuse of church funds, and finally Oliver Cowdery was excommunicated for "urging vexatious law suits against the brethren" and for an apparent attempt at counterfeiting. Two days later Joseph disfellowshipped David Whitmer and Lyman E. Johnson.

A small number of the apostates—Oliver Cowdery, John and David Whitmer, and Lyman Johnson—moved 25 miles outside of town to the home of another apostate who had now arrived in Caldwell County, William McLellin.

Soon they would be igniting the locals into a rage, but the chief instigator was not one of the main Ohio apostates—it was, surprisingly, Joseph's right-hand man, Sidney Rigdon.

The problem Sidney gave Joseph, however, was not due to apostasy—it came from an act of folly.

Perhaps still suffering from the Kirtland night of being dragged over rough ground by a mob, receiving head injuries, and wandering about in a delirium for hours wanting to kill Joseph and his own wife, he made a spectacular blunder, even though it was years after the injuries. On the next Sunday after the dissenters moved just out of town, Sidney preached that they had the right to get rid of the troublemakers. On June 17, 1838, he stood before a large congregation for one hour and preached his now infamous "Salt Sermon." He quoted Matthew 5:13, "Ye are the salt of the earth," but if you lose your savor, you will be "trodden under foot of man." He apparently equated that to the dissenters, saying they had lost their savor and therefore should be trodden down by the rest of them. When he accused them of being liars, swindlers, and counterfeiters, he was in fact accurate, but he took the solution to the absurd extreme when he called for them to be "trampled" down.

It is unknown how much Joseph went along with or opposed Sidney on this tirade, but he was likely taken by surprise. Dissenters claimed Joseph went along with it, but in the unlikely event he did, certainly he was ill advised by Sidney or another associate or even Emma. Some in the congregation, such as Reed Peck, thought it was all just a farce to scare the dissenters away and to stop them from opposing the church leaders. But the dissenters didn't leave.

Sidney then wrote a letter. He accused them of several crimes and of trying to rouse up mobs in Clay and Ray counties. He then collected signatures from 84 men, which he sent to the apostates, demanding they leave in three days under penalty of a "more fatal calamity" if they refused to depart. Of these signatures, B. H. Roberts reports: "If these accusations were true, they constituted crimes which lay open to the law, and should have been punished by the law. Those eighty-four citizens of Caldwell county were not justified in taking the law into their own hands." But the men signing the letter hoped the dissenters would just leave.

Instead, it had the opposite effect. Oliver, the Whitmers, and Lyman Johnson took the letter to a Clay County attorney. Then they complained to the Missourians that on their way home from visiting the county attorney, they had been ejected from their houses, as writs of attachment had been sworn against their property (but their claim is highly doubtful because the dissenters still were not leaving). Others who sided with the dissenters, such as W. W. Phelps, John Corrill, and others, heaped on more lies and told the Missourians that when they complained to church leaders of the writs, they also became grouped with the dissenters. The effect was to fan the flames of hatred against the Mormons even higher.

Because of that, several Latter-day Saints then formed a secret band to retaliate against the apostates. This band of Saints determined to fight local Missourians and even assassinate church members whom they found in disagreement. The leader of the group was a new convert on the scene—Sampson Avard. A rough-and-tumble type of fellow, he wanted to gain power for himself by starting a secret group called the Danites (also known as the Brothers of Gideon, the Sons of Dan, and the Daughters of Zion), complete with passwords. His plan: to coerce and even kill dissenters and, as Joseph reports, to raid the Gentiles and steal their property. John Corrill says many of the Danites did not know Avard's purpose, soon calling him a grand "villain." Lyman Wight said Avard actually planned to take control of the church.

Avard organized his band into companies of 10 and 50, cloning the church's self-preservation groups that harvested crops for the poor and chopped their firewood, but some people would begin to confuse the two organizations, thinking they were one and the same (which was Avard's intent). Joseph thus quickly clarified that misconception.

Joseph writes of the twisted thinking of Avard by quoting his words to his several captains: "And thus you will waste away the Gentiles by robbing and plundering them of their property, and in this way we will build up the kingdom of God. . . . If any of us should be recognized, who can harm us? For we will stand by each other and defend one another in all things. If our enemies swear against us, we can swear also." Joseph says the Danite captains were surprised at Avard's words, at which Avard continued: "Why do you startle at this, brethren? . . . If any one of this Danite society reveals any of these things, I will put him where the dogs cannot bite him." Joseph continues that his captains then pointed out to Avard that his plans were against the law and the doctrines of Christ and the church. Avard replied that he cared nothing for the law and that God's laws would prevail.

Lorenzo Dow Young has left the most telling account of this episode:

"In the latter part of the summer, I found he was in Far West among the Saints holding secret meetings attended by a few who were especially invited. I was one of the favored few. I found the gathering to be a meeting of a secret organization of which, so far as I could learn by diligent inquiry, he was the originator and over which he presided. At one of these meetings he stated that the title by which the members of the society were known, 'Danites,' interpreted meant 'Destroying Angels,' and also that the object of the organization was to take vengeance on their enemies. Avard considered it the duty of the members to pursue them to the death, even to their homes and bedrooms. At different times new members were sworn in by taking the oath of secrecy and affiliations. The teachings and proceedings appeared to be wicked, bloodthirsty, and in direct antagonism to the principles taught by the leaders of the church and the elders generally. I felt a curious interest in these proceedings and determined to hold my peace and see what would develop. . . .

"From the meeting I went direct to Brother Brigham and related the whole history of the affair. He said he had long suspicioned [sic] that something wrong was going on but had seen no direct development. He added, 'I will go at once to

Brother Joseph, who has suspicioned [sic] that some secret wickedness was being carried on by Dr. Avard.' Dr. Avard was at once cited before the authorities of the church and cut off for his wickedness. He turned a bitter enemy to the Saints."

Meanwhile, several dozen good Saints had been duped into joining the Danites, including Porter Rockwell. But when Joseph explained to Porter and others what Sampson's group was all about, they ashamedly withdrew. Enemies of the church would claim for over a hundred years that Porter and others kept the Danites going and working in behalf of Joseph and later Brigham, but their claims were the result of an overactive imagination. Later Brigham did refer to them tongue in cheek as he joked that the Danites would clean out Utah territory, but no evidence of the group beyond Avard's day has ever existed, and Joseph was adamant that no one should be involved in Avard's or any such "secret combination," claiming such groups are defined clearly in The Book of Mormon as being of the devil.

An amusing angle to the distortion was the willingness with which the Saints "used" the rumors. Oliver Boardman Huntington jokingly confides in his journal: "This society of Danites was condemned by the public like the rest of Mormonism; and there was a great [concern] about the Danites, all over the county and among the army; but who and what they were no one was any wiser for anything they heard; and as many stories were in circulation, the most horrid and awfully distorted opinions their minds could imagine, and they all thought that every depridation [sic] was committed by the Danites; Danites, awful Danites; every mobber was afraid of the thoughts of one of them awful men.

"And if they [the Latter-day Saints] were to see a man of their own [the mobbers'] acquaintance, and were told in confidence [by a Latter-day Saint] he [a mobber] was a Danite, they would even shun his company and conversation. Such being their opinion and belief of the Danites, and we knowing it, concluded to make the best of it."

Joseph writes in his diary: "The Danite system alluded to by Norton never had any existence. [Avard had only tried to get it initiated, but it was stopped by Joseph before it got going.] It was a term made use of by some of the brethren in Far West, and grew out of an expression I made use of when the brethren were preparing to defend themselves from the Missouri mob, in reference to the stealing of Macaiah's images (Judges chapter 18)—If the enemy comes, the Danites will be after them, meaning the brethren in self-defense." This single reference had been so twisted and magnified out of both context and proportion that church enemies made a crusade of it against the Saints and felt "Danites" were behind every mysterious occurrence for decades afterward.

According to dissenters Reed Peck and John Cleminson, Joseph had attended one of their meetings, had spoken to them, and basically knew what they were up to, but the testimonies of these two men before the Missourians were typical of those attempting to discredit Joseph and tie him to Avard's band.

Other enemies of the church, of course, claimed Mormon leaders had actually *organized* the Danites. Many of the enemies, but not all, were embittered ex-Mormons who, then and later, produced some widely accepted published works whose incessant hue and cry of the Danites over the decades influenced even many Latter-day Saints into believing in their existence beyond Avard's day, and that in Joseph's day they were sanctioned.

The fact is, when Joseph learned of the Danites, he quickly cut off Avard.

Riled up that his plan went awry, Avard himself became a dissenter, left the church, went to the locals at a hearing in Richmond, Missouri and, according to Joseph, lied to them. Avard claimed Joseph himself was the Danite leader, and that Joseph wanted the dissenters put away and the local settlers robbed. Before the Fifth Circuit Court of Missouri, he claimed, "I consider Joseph Smith Sr., as the prime mover and organizer of this Danite band." That was the first rock thrown into the hornet's nest.

Joseph excommunicated him three months later in March 1839. Avard had been the Danite leader from June to November

1838, right up to the time he went to the Richmond hearing in November 1838.

Another challenge for Joseph would soon arise. On July 8, 1838, he received and announced a revelation that the Law of Consecration should be revived. In this, the Saints would give their surplus property to the bishop and pay a 10% tithe on their annual income. That income would be used for the temple, supporting the three-man First Presidency, and for building up Zion as determined by the bishop.

Reed Peck, who was in the process of dissenting (so his view of the whole affair could be somewhat tainted), says Sidney threatened those who would not enter the Law of Consecration. If true, he was still apparently not acting in his right mind as he tossed another barb at the dissenters—he even used the old threat, according to Peck, of calling out the now-defunct "Danites."

CHAPTER 33

NOT caving to his threats, the dissenters refused to participate in the newly revised Law of Consecration. And when Oliver threatened that he would take the matter to the courts, Sidney talked Joseph into giving up the idea, fearing the dissenters would win. As a result, the second attempt at the Law of Consecration failed.

As for W. W. Phelps, David Whitmer, and Oliver Cowdery, they had sold their Jackson County land in January 1838, six months earlier, for their own gain, seeing the prospects of living there useless. But in so doing they had defied Joseph's decree. Next, they defiantly claimed that if they could not have the freedom to do so without being censured, they would also sell their property in Far West and move out. They said they utterly refused to be controlled by ecclesiastical power in matters they saw as temporal. Again, the issue of property and material gain versus obedience, as Joseph saw it. They also may have been challenged by their pride—they saw Joseph as less capable, less educated, and they felt it an insult to follow him. Similarly, as cited earlier, Joseph had found detractors in his earlier years in New York, when several thought they could write better revelations (at which they had admittedly failed; Oliver himself thought he could translate part of The Book of Mormon, but likewise failed). Meanwhile, although receiving writs against their properties, they would not leave the area, determined to stay close to Joseph to dog him.

As for the Law of Consecration, since Joseph feared the dissenters would win in court if he instituted it again, and since the rank and file members were slow to agree to it anyway, he presented a new plan. While being short of true consecration, he proposed the church would rent property from members so they would still retain ownership (which apparently seemed so important to them) while the church would have use of it from 10 to 99 years, without interest. Four corporations would be formed of shopkeepers, mechanics, laborers, and farmers. They could use the machinery, land, and help of other Saints to benefit themselves and others. This plan would pay $1 per day to each worker and take care of the needs of all families. Every able-bodied male of age would thus receive guaranteed employment, apparently in an area of his choice.

But only some of the church members approved. And among those who did, it was slow to take effect. Joseph, though disappointed, was more concerned over how the Lord might again chastise his people for not complying with their hearts. But in the meantime, the dissenters continued chanting their opposition to Joseph—even against this revised, milder plan.

In one dramatic showdown, John Corrill announced he did not believe the revelation. Reed Peck claims Joseph took that challenge personally and, as was a weakness that Joseph never specifically admitted to but which apparently was the greatest of all his personal challenges, he became angry and wished to start a fight.

By their disobedience, the stage was being set, according to some, for their destruction once again.

At the July 4 celebration of 1838, the Saints held a gigantic party and laid the cornerstone of the temple in the main square of the city. Mormon and non-Mormon dignitaries from the state sat on a newly built stand beside a newly built flag pole that sported an eagle and the American flag. A company of local

Mormon militia marched through, a small drum corps leading the procession around the square.

Then Sidney stood and, evidently still not of right mind, began to speak to the crowd, first giving a good, standard patriotic speech, then veering into something along the lines of: "It shall be between us and them a war of extermination . . . for we will carry the seat of war to their own houses and their own families, and one party or the other shall be utterly destroyed." While that quote is from an unreliable source, no less than Sampson Avard, it is likely accurate. The rank-and-file church members were mortified by Sidney's speech, and now glanced at their non-Mormon guests, wondering just how much Sidney could sabotage everything they had worked for.

Further rocks were thrown by Sidney when he made the next statement—that they would no longer indulge "vexatious lawsuits."

From that, the populace perceived—and likely accurately so—that Mormon judges and constables would begin to neglect their duties in lawsuits, putting out only half-hearted efforts to enforce the law when Saints were sued or when outsiders attempted to collect debts (which did in fact happen).

What happened next was the direct result of Sidney's speech. The populace, statewide, became completely riled up, fueled by newspapers.

More rocks were thrown when the Saints filled up all liveable space in Caldwell County and then broke the unwritten agreement the original settlers thought the Mormons had made—that the Saints would only live in Caldwell. (After the Saints had begun moving in, it had taken only 18 months before Caldwell County was filled to the brim, so the incoming Saints now began colonizing adjacent counties—Daviess, Carroll, and Ray.) There was more buzzing from the locals.

Especially from some who had, until now, actually admired the Saints and had decided the rumors about their bad character were false. But at this point they were becoming resentful when they saw additional rocks coming their way . . . in the form of the Saints becoming *active in politics*.

Despite the slander from dissenters, the Saints were enjoying serenity for a time, but this calm turned out to be just another lull before a storm . . .

Only this one was political.

As a voting bloc the Saints were now hot property. And just before elections the Missourians began lobbying for their vote. This much longed for attention came to the Saints, despite a reported incident by enemies that 20 Mormons had driven Missourians from Mormon-owned land. (The story went that Missourians had attempted to settle the Mormons' property, and in anger the Mormons had reacted; 20 gathered themselves into a vigilante-style posse and rode forth, snapping whips at the Missourians' feet and driving them away.)

From this rumor alone some Missourians were fused and ready to explode, but their public servants kept them at bay, desperately seeking the Mormon vote.

Except for one candidate.

The corn mill owner in Millport decided to run for the state legislature. William P. Peniston, running on the Whig ticket, was a militia colonel for Daviess County. Determined to win, he held a rather non-traditional political campaign—rather than canvassing the settlements to gain non-Mormon votes, he threatened the Mormons to leave the county. Joining him was candidate for justice of the peace, Adam Black.

As election day loomed, other candidates came to the Saints with a bit brighter strategy—they were *nice* to them. They made promises that appealed to the Saints, and Peniston saw it as a better method than his. So he changed his strategy. He tried flattering the Saints, saying he had been wrong about them, and he told Lyman Wight they were "first-rate citizens." He even went to church meetings with the Saints. But it didn't take much for him to change his methods once again. When he learned they were going to vote for his opponent, Judge Warren, he turned *against them* again. (The reason the Saints preferred Warren was because Warren was a Democrat, and so were the Mormons. Furthermore, Warren had been kind to them from the beginning and had even helped the poor among them with food.)

Seeing the election slipping away, Peniston adopted still another strategy—he decided to *keep them from voting.*

Then the storm broke.

Taking the Saints completely by surprise, the Missourians' hostility burst forth on—of all days—election day, August 6, 1838. That morning candidate William Peniston made an inflammatory speech against the Saints, saying they would not vote if they came to the polls. (In Daviess County only a comparatively few Saints were even eligible to vote, but Peniston went to great pains to see that they didn't.) He gathered about 50 locals to the main street in Gallatin where the voting was taking place.

After his speech whiskey was passed around, and the scene was ripe for action.

As the first group of Mormons rode up to the Gallatin polls, Peniston stood on a whiskey barrel, which had been emptied into the 50 settlers, and shouted taunts to the Saints. He claimed they were counterfeiters, liars, and thieves.

A drunken Missourian named Dick Weldon swaggered up to a Mormon. the ensuing melee set in motion events that would sweep the Mormons and Missourians into a virtual war . . .

CHAPTER 34

INFLAMED by Peniston's speech, the drunken Weldon told the Mormon, named Samuel Brown, "The Saints are not allowed to vote in Clay County no more than the damned Negroes." Weldon then reared back his fist while another Saint, named Perry Durfee, caught Weldon's arm. Durfee was knocked down and several Missourians pounced on him with boards and clubs. Durfee shouted for help.

Five infuriated Mormons ran into the mob, knocking and punching their way toward Durfee, sending a dozen Missourians sprawling.

But then one of the Saints became isolated in the mob. Twenty mobbers turned on him and pulled out knives—he took off running, dodging them, and escaped without being touched. In anger, the mob immediately attacked all 10 Saints. Four to 12 locals were on top of each Mormon, cursing them, when Mormon John Butler grabbed a stick from a pile of lumber and lit into the mob. Ironically, almost comically, Butler "commenced to call out loud for peace," but, as he says, "at the same time making my stick move to my own utter astonishment." He tried hitting them "light," but they fell all about the street.

In awe the mob stared as he whacked away at the locals, purportedly sending all 20 to the earth.

In summary, a handful of Mormons had rescued Durfee from a glut of soused Missourians. One of the Mormons later confided: "I felt the power of God nerve my arm for the fray. It helps a man a great deal in a fight to know that God is on his side."

The Saints walked away from the unconscious, drunk locals and voted, then strode to their horses and rode off defiantly.

Those Missourians who were still conscious were struck with amazement. Less then 10 Saints had stayed off 50 to 100 Missourians who, after realizing other Saints might be showing up to vote, panicked and broke into a run.

But news of the event ran even faster than the Missourians . . .

Rumors spread that the Mormons had routed them (which they had) and left two dead in the street (which they had not).

Stories of the incident roared through the state like prairie fire, and the anger of the Missourians now began billowing toward a darkening sky.

Meanwhile, news of the episode spread with equal speed to Joseph at headquarters—an express rider galloped in the report to him and, because of expected reprisals, he organized 20 horsemen. He then personally led his platoon down the road to Daviess County and rendezvoused with another Mormon group. From there they galloped to the home of the local justice of the peace, Adam Black, the anti-Mormon candidate just recently elected.

There, one of two things occurred, according to conflicting sources. Joseph either politely asked Black to sign a promise to not harm the Saints, or Black himself volunteered to sign it (which is what John Taylor reports). In any case, he quickly composed a statement and added his signature, saying he was "not attached to any mob" and would not attach himself to any and would not "molest" the Saints if they would not molest him. He also claimed he would support the Constitution.

After Joseph rode away, Black mounted up and galloped off to the Missourians, telling them he had just been forced to sign a pledge, and then he wrote up a warrant for the arrest of Joseph for "harassment."

Peniston immediately thudered off to Judge Austin A. King and told him that Joseph had forced Adam Black to sign the promise, had threatened his life, and now planned to drive all the locals out of the county and steal their land. When Peniston wrote an affidavit of these claims, a sheriff charged off to Far West to arrest Joseph and Lyman Wight.

But when the sheriff arrived, Wight refused to be arrested. He shouted in his face that the whole of Missouri could not take him. The sheriff left, riled up like a wolverine.

Newspapers throughout the state reported Wight's defiance, and mobs gathered in mass meetings from Daviess to Carroll Counties. They sent runners to other counties for help to fight and kill the "belligerent" Mormons.

Then, even worse for the Saints, word of Black's story of being "harassed by Joseph" shot through the settlements and made its way to the governor of Missouri, Lilburn W. Boggs, also recently elected. Boggs would not stand for a judge in his state to be terrorized by a local religious zealot, so immediately sent 400 militia to capture the prophet. Additionally, word was spread that recruits were needed. As a result, mobocrats from 11 counties joined forces and galloped off to support Justice Black. Boggs supposedly feared Joseph would resist arrest, but he likely cared less about Joseph's arrest and more about frightening the Saints into leaving the state of Missouri.

But Joseph countered his move. As mobocrats waited for arms to arrive, the Saints ambushed a supply wagon filled with guns intended for the mob.

The strategy backfired, as this only aggravated their mania.

Boggs was now out for blood.

In a frenzy he ordered the militia to destroy all Mormon resistance.

And he sent the militia general, David R. Atchison, Joseph's former co-attorney, to quell the "uprising."

When Atchison arrived with 400 militiamen, Joseph asked him what the Saints could do to stop the Missouri onslaught. Atchison advised him to do just one thing. Go to trial.

So Joseph went to Judge Austin A. King on September 7, 1838, and requested a trial. In the trial the judge realized Adam Black had lied about the Mormons' intentions, so Joseph was released on a bond of $500, if he would keep the peace.

The locals were beside themselves with anger. They did not get the verdict they expected or hoped for, and began joining the militia. The *Jeffersonian Republican* reports, "The Mormon War is the all-engrossing topic of conversation."

The conversation turned to war. The more they talked, the more they convinced themselves to kill the blasted Mormons.

CHAPTER 35

A T the isolated village of DeWitt on the Missouri River in Carroll County, there was a sizable Latter-day Saint population from move-ins the previous year. The Saints had seen DeWitt as an economic boomtown, being the river port village for Far West, through which they would receive both goods and people.

They had not expected to be the first community attacked by the mobs. So when they saw the mobs advancing, they hurriedly set up a barricade of wagons. Gunshots rang out from both sides. The Saints, seeing themselves hopelessly outnumbered, held firm nonetheless. The mob then demanded they leave town. A runner from the Saints galloped off to Joseph.

At Far West the runner stormed in to see Joseph and told him of the siege on DeWitt. Joseph, in his typically courageous manner, called for a group of volunteers, which he would lead. They took off for the impending battle, making their way carefully along back roads, where they outsmarted the mob and snuck around them into the village.

There, Joseph found the Saints low on supplies. He realized they could not fight or hold the city much longer. So he sent another runner out of the city—this time to the governor himself. His message: a request for the state militia to protect them. Joseph either believed in the proper legal recourse until the bitter end, or he did not realize the dedicated anti-

Mormon position of both the state militia commanders and the governor himself. At the same time, the militia commander at Boonville, General Samuel Lucas, wrote Governor Boggs about the situation at DeWitt, not knowing Joseph was about to request the militia's assistance, and said that if a fight was to take place at DeWitt, "those base and degraded beings [the Saints] will be exterminated from the face of the earth." He added that four or five thousand locals had volunteered for the state militia to annihilate the entire Latter-day Saint community. Ironically, it apparently did not even enter his mind that the state militia should legally *protect* the Saints, rather than *attack* them.

So the governor sent a message back to Joseph—that "the quarrel was between the Mormons and the mob." Therefore, the governor implied, the Mormons would have to fight the mob on their own.

The mob militia swarmed down on Far West. Surrounding it. Laying siege to it. So no one could leave the city or go help those at DeWitt. Their plan was to isolate DeWitt from the greater Mormon population and simply take apart the villagers at DeWitt.

At DeWitt the Saints realized their helplessness, and surrendered. They deserted their village. On October 12, 1838, they walked away from their homes, leaving everything to the mob, trudging about five days to Far West, many without food, some dying of exposure and hunger and being buried on the "roadside," as they called it in their journals.

At Far West the refugees arrived from DeWitt. They lived in tents and wagons, some with only a blanket to protect them, and this was their condition for several weeks. All they had to eat was cornmeal and pumpkins, which gave them diarrhea.

Fed up, Joseph called a meeting on the Far West town square on October 15, 1838. His now famous speech declared: "We have applied to the governor and he will do nothing for us. The militia of the county will do nothing. All are mob; the governor is mob, the militia is mob, and the whole state is mob." He then declared war.

C H A P T E R **36**

MEANWHILE, across the county at the village of Adam-ondi-Ahman, Mormon men were hitched to trees and flogged, then left tied and bleeding for their wives to cut down.

In Far West Joseph made plans to defend the village, not knowing it had already been attacked. Soon he himself marched out with a detachment led by George Hinkle. And on the way there they joined Lyman Wight's men heading for the village.

But when they got there, they found the community literally destroyed. Cattle had been scattered, farms burned, and two Mormons taken prisoner and ridden out of town on a cannon. They now wished only to protect the Saints in outlying areas.

But the mob beat them to it. At those outlying areas the mobbers attacked farms, chased off livestock, and burned several houses. The families then fled into the village, which the mob had left in shambles.

At 11 P.M. Agnes Smith, Don Carlos's wife, entered the village with two babies. She had walked three miles in the snow, as it had stormed for two days, and then she had waded up to her waist in the shallow but freezing waters of the Grand River. She arrived at the feet of Lyman Wight and told him her house had been burned and her property taken by the mob. Her husband, meanwhile, was on a mission to Canada, filled with fear for his family's welfare.

Lyman Wight galloped off to the Ray County militia and charged into the office of General H. G. Parks. He yelled at him to stop the mob violence. Parks seemed sympathetic and gave him permission to send a company of Mormon militia to break up the mobs around Adam-ondi-Ahman.

Wight and David Patten gathered 40 Mormon militiamen together and marched them to Gallatin. There, according to Reed Peck, who at this point was apostatizing and whose reports are likely not only inaccurate but fallacious, they burned a store belonging to Jacob Stollings, raided and burned houses at Millport and Grindstone Fork, then took cattle, food, and household goods.

What did happen was—the mob heard the Mormons were coming, so the mob grabbed a cannon owned by one of its members and took it 25 miles away to the Methodist campground.

David Patten pulled together 100 Mormon militia and a hastily assembled cavalry. They rode off to the campground looking for the cannon, knowing such a weapon could have disastrous effects against them. The Saints also knew it would be a mighty addition to their own armament and defense if they managed to capture it. When the mob got word they were coming, they hid the cannon in the ground and galloped away, planning to come back for it later.

To the Saints, looking for the cannon was like searching for a needle in a haystack. Until a hog came to the rescue.

As the men were searching for it in vain, a boy studied the hog and realized it was trying to uproot a large, round metallic-looking root that would not allow itself to be dug up. The men all gathered around, watching with smiles as the hog struggled to uproot the butt of the cannon. After laughing and chasing it away, they dug under the weapon, placed ropes beneath it, and lifted it out of the ground. It was a beautiful six-pounder (firing six-pound cannonballs). They hoisted it onto a cart and hauled it away with bags of balls and cannon powder to Adam-ondi-Ahman.

There, they mounted it at the most elevated part of town and, upon completing the task, cheered. Then they fired it where it could be heard for miles—announcing to the mob, with a bit of bravado, that they had found and absconded with the weapon. "It told the sad tale," reports Parley P. Pratt, "for some twenty miles around, that the robbers had lost their God of war."

Meanwhile, back in Far West, Joseph was determined to win the upcoming battle. He hoisted a flag at the town center flagpole to announce "free toleration of religion." Albert P. Rockwood declared that word was now out among themselves that the Saints should gather from all the villages to fight the war. He said Joseph had "unsheathed his sword," planning for it not to be sheathed again "until he can go into any county or state in safety and peace."

Dissenters twisted Joseph's words. They spread rumors that the Saints were now going to take the offensive.

Then two Apostles joined the throng. As if Joseph hadn't enough problems, Orson Hyde and Thomas B. Marsh apostatized from the church and spread rumors that the Saints proposed to start a "pestilence among the Gentiles" by poisoning their corn and fruit, and even planned to destroy the towns of all Missouri resistors and "make it one gore of blood from the Rocky Mountains to the Atlantic Ocean." They also claimed the Danites had passed a decree that "no Mormon dissenter should leave Caldwell county alive."

They went to the Missourians and signed an affidavit that sent them gnashing.

Joseph defended himself against the charge, labeling it pure slander, but it was too late—the Missourians were up in arms. They now redoubled their efforts to rid themselves of the Saints—they rode forth every evening through Mormon settlements, burning, plundering, killing cattle, and carrying off prisoners.

Local ministers, meanwhile, screamed anti-Mormon invective from the pulpit. One Methodist, a part-time minister and full-time Mormon-hater, was Samuel Bogart. He aspired to and was assigned as a militia captain and claimed he would shower

Far West "with thunder and lightning." Not waiting for orders
from state superiors, he ordered an attack on the Saints in the
southern part of Caldwell County, where his men proceeded
to burn the Saints out of their homes, taking two prisoners.
His next stop—Crooked River, he said, but the Saints learned
of his plan and decided to stop him dead in his tracks.

# CHAPTER 37

DETERMINED to stop the good Reverend Bogart on his warpath, David Patten, known as "Captain Fearnot," sounded the alarm at Far West on the night of October 25, 1838, as related by Brigham's brother, Lorenzo Dow Young:

"Perhaps I had slept two hours, when I was awakened by the bass drum sounding the alarm on the public square. I was soon out to see what was the matter. There were five men on the ground, of whom I inquired the cause of the alarm. They informed me that two of the brethren had been taken prisoners by the mob on Crooked River, tried by a court martial that day, and condemned to be shot the coming morning at 8 o'clock. A company of men was wanted to go and rescue them. Preparations were hurried."

Seventy Saints volunteered at the flagpole to go for the largest-scale, head-on clash yet between Mormon and Missourian. Among them were Porter Rockwell and Parley P. Pratt. Pratt records vividly:

"This company was soon under way, having to ride through extensive prairies a distance of some 12 miles. The night was dark, the distant plains far and wide were illuminated by blazing fires: Immense columns of smoke were seen rising in awful majesty, as if the world was on fire. This scene of grandeur can only be comprehended by those acquainted with scenes of prairie burning.

"The thousands of meteors, blazing in the distance like the campfires of some war host, threw a fitful gleam of light upon the distant sky, which many might have mistaken for the Aurora Borealis. This scene—added to the silence of midnight, the rumbling sound of the tramping steeds over the hard and dried surface of the plain, the clanking of swords in their scabbards, the occasional gleam of bright armor in the flickering firelight, the gloom of surrounding darkness, and the unknown destiny of the expedition, or even of the people who sent it forth—all combined to impress the mind with deep and solemn thoughts and to throw a romantic vision over the imagination, which is not often experienced, except in the poet's dreams or in the wild imagery of sleeping fancy.

"In this solemn procession we moved on for some two hours."

Advancing toward the river, their captain, David Patten, persuaded a non-Mormon lad of 18, Patrick O'Banion, to show them where Bogart's men were camping for the night. The lad pointed to the spot and told them exactly where the mob was. The Saints advanced in the predawn darkness toward the river. They entered the thick wilderness and trod slowly toward Crooked River.

Suddenly the Mormons heard noises. They halted.

Waiting for he signal to attack, the Saints remained silent in the cold, greying mists. And then . . .

A mob militia guard spotted them and called out, "Who comes there!"

The Saints never had a chance to reply—the militia opened fire before even waiting for a response.

Lorenzo Dow Young says that one Mormon, "who was one step in front of me, fell."

"Orders were issued to form in the brush and under cover of the trees," reports Pratt. "The fire now became general on both sides, and the whole wilderness seemed one continued echo of the report of the deadly rifle."

With one last assessment of enemy troop strength, commander Patten suddenly shouted the battle cry of Israel,

"The sword of the Lord and of Gideon!" Then he glanced across his men and shouted a final command . . . "Charge!"

As he arose, he saw his entire force drive into the vortex of the battle, with Porter Rockwell and Parley P. Pratt on the front line.

"As we rushed upon them the strife became deadly, and several fell on both sides," records Parley.

And thus the attack began. Porter and Parley fought side-by-side in hand-to-hand combat, overpowering a number of mobbers.

Lorenzo Dow Young continues, "A tall, powerful Missourian sprang from under the bank of the river and, with a heavy sword in hand . . . I succeeded in parrying the Missourians' blows until he backed me to the bank of the river. A perilous situation, for I could go no further without going off the perpendicular bank, eight or ten feet to the water. In a moment I realized my chances were desperate. At this juncture the Missourian raised his sword, apparently throwing all his strength and energy into the act, as if intending to crush me with one desperate blow.

"As his arm extended I saw a white hand pass down the back of his head and between his shoulders. For a moment his arm seemed paralyzed, giving me sufficient time to deal him a desperate blow with the breech of my gun, which parted at the handle, sending the butt some distance from me, and bending the barrel (as was afterward ascertained) 10 inches. As my enemy fell, his sword dropped from his grasp. I seized it and dealt him three desperate blows on the neck."

Another Missourian was then shot dead center and rolled down the riverbank. Parley adds: "At this instant a ball pierced the brave colonel, David Patten, who was then at my side, and I saw him fall. Being on the eve of victory, I dared not stop to look after his fate, or that of others, but rushed into the enemy's camp. This was located on the immediate banks of Crooked River, which was here several rods wide, and not formidable. The enemy, being hard pushed, flung themselves into the stream and struggled for the other shore. Those who reached it soon disappeared."

The militia had outnumbered the Mormons three-to-one, but the Missourians were now swimming away in a retreat. The Missouri militia, defeated and humiliated, never slowed down. And as they swam away, the Saints cheered.

The Mormons were victorious. They had in fact turned it into a rout.

They now invaded the deserted militia camp, confiscated the remaining enemy horses, guns, and blankets, and gathered their two wounded men, not realizing until later that a third, Gideon Carter, was dead on the ground, having been shot in the neck, the ball passing straight through his body. Then they returned to Far West.

But now the realities of the victory, rather than cheering the Saints, dispirited them. They saw their wounded Apostle, David Patten, in agony, the lead ball having passed through his body. The non-Mormon lad, O'Bannion, who was the 18-year-old who had helped them, was also barely hanging on, shot in the back.

On the way to Far West, they found a Mormon farm and took the wounded men inside, then sent for David Patten's wife. While he was in severe distress, she arrived and spoke with him briefly before he died. O'Bannion was taken to Sidney's home in the city, where he died in agony two days later. His parents came for his body.

Patten, Carter, and O'Banion all received military honors at the Saints' funeral ceremony. Joseph and Sidney, along with Hyrum, rode at the front of the procession, which included a small band, and made their way to a small cemetery outside town. Joseph said they had laid down their lives for their friends.

When Boggs heard Bogart's force had been routed, he was rabid. Especially as two Missouri settlers now added color to the tale: The two men, Joseph Dickson and Sashiel Woods of Carrollton, barged in breathlessly to see the governor; they claimed the Mormons were now moving on Richmond to lay it in ashes. "Our county is ruined—for God's sake give us assistance as quick as possible."

Since Boggs already had the Mormon apostates' affidavits—those of Hyde and Marsh—and he also had the same report from "good, honest, Missouri folk," he ordered 2,000 militiamen to the scene to oppose the maniacal, belligerent Latter-day Saints, who in fact were gloomily dealing with the deaths of the three men.

The last straw for the governor, however, was a filtered-down report originating from one of Reverend Bogart's men who claimed 10 of their force had been shot dead by the Mormons, with the remainder taken prisoners of war. By the time this report reached the governor, it was so blown out of proportion that he believed the Mormons had completely massacred the entire force at Crooked River, then had executed all the prisoners, and finally that the Saints were now marching on the whole of Missouri, with a large force of Indians joining them from across the Platte River.

Boggs felt he had to retaliate. Infuriated and without even investigating the claims, he issued his now famous "Exterminating Order." On October 27, 1838, he told General John B. Clark that the Mormons "must be treated as enemies and must be exterminated or driven from the State. . . . Their outrages are beyond all description."

When the Missouri citizens heard their governor's order, they volunteered for the militia and gathered in mobs by the thousands, grabbing weapons off the walls and excitedly riding out toward Caldwell and surrounding counties to kill them any way they could.

# CHAPTER 38

I<small>T</small> was a sunny Tuesday late afternoon when, on October 30, 1838, Mormon men peacefully gathered crops, the women performed chores in houses and tents, and the children played on the banks of Shoal Creek. Women were humming songs and children were laughing when suddenly they looked up and saw 240 mob militia coming forward on horseback, cocking their rifles.

Haun's Mill had about 30 families in 10 cabins plus additional tents, with a blacksmith shop, sawmill, and gristmill. They were happy where they lived and enjoyed their increasing prosperity. So when Joseph had told them to pack up everything they could and get out, they balked. Jacob Haun argued that if they left their homes, their property would be lost and the Gentiles would burn it. Joseph replied, "You had better lose your property than your lives, but there is no danger of losing either if you will do as you are commanded." But they disobeyed. Joseph did not force the issue, feeling they would consider him a tyrant if he did. At the settlement Haun's cohorts sided with him, and some of the women urged the men to stand firm and stay, offering to mold bullets if necessary. Why should they retreat to Far West when they had everything going for them there?

There were others just visiting the village. Warren and Amanda Smith and their six children had just moved from Ohio and were passing through on their way to Far West. Haun's Mill served as a convenient stopover place for visitors heading to the city of the Saints.

There was also a young fellow named Oliver Cox, whose sisters may have sensed something would happen because they had pleaded with him not to leave for Haun's Mill. But he was an adventurous lad. "If I die," he had told them, "I will die with my boots on." In fact he was quite proud of his new boots.

As for the locals who lived there, Nehemia Comstock had told the Saints just the day before that they would receive no harm, so the Saints felt they had nothing to worry about.

Except that Nehemia Comstock changed his mind. On that very day, he heard of the governor's extermination order and was now out for blood. So he led the 240-man militia toward Haun's Mill, taking a few highly esteemed citizens—among them a member of the state legislature and a Livingston County clerk.

The Saints, while on the surface having nothing to fear, looked up, saw the militiamen riding toward them, and immediately knew something was wrong. Not only was it in their facial expressions, but also in their demeanor as they slowly rode forward, guns pointed up.

One Saint, David Evans, swung his hat, calling for peace.

Comstock shouted, "Shoot everything wearing breeches, and shoot to kill!" Comstock fired his gun first, which was followed by a 10- or 12- second pause, then "all at once they discharged about 100 rifles," reports Joseph Young who was at the scene. They formed themselves into "a three-square position, forming a vanguard in front."

The women and children ran for the woods while the Mormon men in the fields appealed to the militia to spare them. Nine men and boys ran to the blacksmith shop for cover.

Then the militiamen began their charge. They opened fire again, killing men and boys in the open field.

"Our men took off their hats and swung them, and cried, 'quarter' until they were shot," says one witness. "The mob paid no attention to their cries nor their entreaties, but fired incessantly."

The militia galloped to the blacksmith shop, dismounted, and aimed their guns through the wide cracks in the logs. Then shot all nine men and boys inside.

Those families in tents behind the blacksmith shop ran for the woods in different directions "amidst a shower of bullets."

Amanda Smith ran with her little girls and darted about, looking for her boys. Not seeing any of the mob at the creek, she ran down its bank, across the millpond on a board, and up the hill with her girls. Shots rang out but missed them. "The bullets whistled all the way like hail, and cut down the bushes on all sides of us." One of her girls was wounded and tripped over a log. So Amanda pulled her up—then saw that her dress was riveted to a log. She ripped her daughter out of her dress and resumed running. They narrowly escaped. The militiamen jumped off their horses, ran into the woods, and saw in the near distance the log with the little girl's dress. Believing the young child to be trapped, they opened fire. Her dress was shredded with over two dozen shots.

Mary Steadwell was shot through the hand. As she ran, other shots pierced her clothes. "After running as far as she could, she threw herself behind a log, whilst a volley of balls poured after her, filling the log where she lay," says David Lewis, who further reports, "One small boy was killed, having his brains blown out . . . begging for his life."

Some of the Mormon men made their way to rifles and shotguns. They managed to wound only three militiamen. But, when fleeing, were shot down and mutilated with machetes.

One witness saw an old Revolutionary War veteran named Thomas McBride run for his gun. A militiaman named Rogers ordered him to surrender it. When he did, Rogers shot him, then pulled out a corn cutter and cut him to pieces, first slicing away his hands that he held up defensively, then his arms to his elbows, then his arms at his shoulders, then he beheaded him.

Andrew Jenson compiled later, "Brother Austin Hammer, who was mortally wounded—seven balls were shot into his body, breaking both thigh bones—had on a new pair of boots that fitted him tightly, and in the efforts to get them off, he was dragged and pulled out of the shop and about the yard in a barbarous manner. In his mangled condition this cruel treatment must have caused him the most excruciating pain. . . . He died 12 o'clock the following night." Jenson also says, "Two men also stripped Warren Smith of his coat, hat, and boots, and dragged him around before he was dead and kicked him."

One Livingston County man, William Reynolds, killed a 10-year-old boy and afterward boasted of it to another, Charles R. Ross, and described with "glee" how "the boy struggled in his dying agony."

Andrew Jenson records, "William Yokum was shot in the leg, which was subsequently amputated in consequence of the wounds received at the massacre."

The *St. Louis Globe-Democrat* reports, "Charles Merrick, another little boy only nine years old, had hid under the bellow. He ran out but did not get very far until he received a load of buckshot. . . . He did not die, however, for nearly five weeks."

Nathan Knight details, "Two men had Brother Warren Smith stripped of his coat, hat, and boots, and were dragging him around after he was dead and kicking him."

Amanda then found her husband Warren lying dead out in the open. Two other boys belonging to her had "hid themselves under the bellows," says Lewis, and "lay concealed from their view by being covered with blood and dead bodies of the slain." But the two boys were discovered below the bodies. "The elder of the boys, crying for mercy from his hiding place, was immediately put to death by putting the muzzle of a gun to the lad's ear and blowing off the top of his head. The other lad was supposed to have been killed, but they did not quite accomplish their object, the younger receiving a wound in his hip which carried off his hip bone." The church record later details from witnesses, "The little fellow himself states that seeing his father and brother killed, he thought they would shoot him again if he stirred, and so feigned himself dead, and lay perfectly still, till he heard his mother call him after dark." And he would live.

Her last son, age nine, was still alive when she found him, with three lead ball wounds, but he later died.

Oliver Cox, the young adventurer so proud of his boots, was lying dead, shot in the stomach, his new boots pulled off and stolen.

A few men escaped, including Joseph Young, Brigham's brother. Another crawled to safety. Margaret Foutz, who survived the massacre, says, "As we were returning I saw a brother, Myers, who had been shot through his body. In that dreadful state he crawled on his hands and knees, about two miles, to his home." There were miracles reported in the midst of the bloodbath. Andrew Jenson records: "Elder Walker stopped under some lumber leaning against the bank, which, however, afforded him but little protection; but in answer to his earnest prayer, the eyes of the mobbers were blinded, and although they looked directly at him, they apparently did not see him."

Nathan Knight says he was wounded in three places, including a ball lodging just below the pit of his stomach. "The last shot brought me to my hands and knees." Then he spotted Polly Wood nearby. "I motioned for her to come to me. I could not call her, neither could I stand up. She came and tried to lead me back, but I was too weak. She then kneeled down and placed her hands on my wounds and prayed the Lord to strengthen and heal me. I never heard a more powerful prayer. The Lord answered her prayer, and I received strength and walked back to Haun's house."

There were other miracles of escape. Isaac Laney was shot seven times, leaving 13 wounds in him, five of which were in the center of his chest. According to John D. Lee, he was found two hours after the massacre and taken nearly lifeless into camp and given a priesthood blessing. "He was promised, through prayer and faith in God, speedy restoration. The pain at once left him . . . . I heard Laney declare this to be a fact, and he bore his testimony in the presence of many of the Saints. I saw him four weeks after the massacre and examined his person. I saw the wounds, then healed. I felt of them with my own hands, and I saw the shirt and examined it, that he had on when he was shot, and it was cut to shreds." Wilford Woodruff, later to become president of the church, records a similar testimony of Laney, who "showed me 11 bullet holes in his body. There were 27 in his shirt, 7 in his pantaloons, and his coat was literally cut to pieces. . . . Also these shots were received while he was running for life, and, strange as it may appear, though he had also one of his ribs broken, he was able to outrun his enemies, and his life was saved."

As for the militia's mania, David Lewis, who was at the scene, recalls, "They burned all the books that they could find, they shot the hogs and cattle." Andrew Jenson reports, "One [Missourian] carried away an empty 10-gallon keg, which he carried before him on his saddle and beat as a drum. Another had a woman's bonnet, which he said was for his sweetheart."

The *St. Louis Globe-Democrat* reports the militia then looted the place, stealing at least 3 wagons and 10 horses. Two survivors stated "the place was pretty well cleaned out."

Amanda Smith adds that the mob howled wildly as they robbed them, then destroyed all the wagons and cabins.

After the massacre the survivors slowly made their way back to Haun's Mill. It was sunset. Dogs howled over their slain masters. Slowly, as children discovered their fathers and brothers, they too began crying. The *Missouri Historical Review* summarizes, "As they recognized one a husband and one a father, another a son, and another a brother among the slain, the wailings of grief and terror were most pitiful. All that night were they alone with their dead and wounded. There were no physicians, but if there had been, many of the wounded were past all surgery. [There were] dreadful sights in the moonlight, and dreadful sounds on the night winds."

Two men were still alive but in the throes of death. They would join 16 others who were dead, making 18 in all who would die. Another 13 wounded would survive. Almost 40 children were left fatherless. Later, the militia estimated that they had fired 1,500 to 1,600 shots.

The dead were dropped down an abandoned well by the surviving women.

Those Saints who escaped rode away to Far West on the few horses they could find, taking the wounded with them. A few had to stay, as their horses had been stolen. Among them were Amanda Smith and her surviving children, including her wounded sons, one of whom would die. All were in constant fear of the militiamen returning, but when they did, they were no longer out for blood. They were out for something else.

Nathan Knight reports, "A few days after the massacre the mob returned to the mill and ground up all the brethren's grain in that region of country. They numbered about 100 and remained about a month, killing hogs, robbing bee stands and hen houses. I and my family suffered much for food. At the end of six weeks I began to get around a little, and was again fired upon by a mob of 14. I escaped into the woods unhurt."

Those who had to stay behind practically starved. The Missourians would not feed the women. Amanda Smith reported to the *St. Louis Globe-Democrat*, "The next day the mob came back. They told us we must leave the state forthwith or be killed. It was bad weather, and they had taken our teams and clothes. . . . We had little prayer meetings; they said if we did not stop them they would kill every man, woman, and child."

Later she states, "We suffered greatly from hunger, cold and fatigue; and for what? For our religion."

When the parade of wounded and survivors stumbled into Far West, the people were sickened at the news. Joseph writes, "Thus are the cries of the widows and the fatherless ascending to heaven. How long, O Lord, wilt thou not avenge the blood of the Saints?" That response, the Saints believed, would come in 22 ½ years when the Civil War would commence and entire companies of Missouri volunteers—notably those from western Missouri—would be wiped out *en masse* and literally cut to shreds by shrapnel from close-range Confederate cannon and bayonet.

The same day as the Haun's Mill massacre, Boggs' army arrived at Far West, camping outside the Mormon stronghold in preparation for a major offensive.

J

OSEPH saw messengers galloping into town with the news—a huge mob was advancing. Soon the Saints spotted 2,000 militia appearing over the hill and across the prairie, where they stopped at a wooded area along Goose Creek.

Determined to defend the city, the Saints turned over wagons and log cabins, making breastworks. The populace gathered up their most valuable possessions, ready to flee.

Joseph led a group of 50 frightened men to the front, a half mile away and closer to the militia, to see if they were preparing to attack or camp down for the night. When Joseph's men saw them preparing camp, they hastened back to town.

A militiaman was seen coming into the city with a white flag, delivering a message to Joseph—the troops were planning to obey the governor's order and attack them. This note was from General Samuel D. Lucas, himself a mobber at Jackson County and who, unfortunately for the Saints, was now in charge of the state forces, being the first militia general to arrive on the scene.

All night the Saints fortified their fences to protect them from the impending onslaught. Women and children crowded the upper story of Sidney Rigdon's house, similar to those families who would do the same at the Alamo, which would take place eight years later at San Antonio.

There were some Saints who paraded bravely about, men like Luman Andros Shurtliff, who thought God would help them in battle and escape, and Porter Rockwell, who wanted to fight with the battle cry of "Remember Haun's Mill." Another parallel to the Alamo. However, numerous others were terrified. One captain in Far West told his men he would return shortly, but then simply buried his sword and silently left town, never to be seen by the Saints again. John Corrill reports that many state militiamen also seemed frightened.

In an act of cowardice that night, some state militiamen attacked farms outside the city and shot cattle, sheep, and chickens for sport, then trampled the cornfields, painted their faces, and drank themselves sick.

The militia continued to lay siege to the town. Some Saints tried to sneak out to gather corn to eat, as they were getting hungry, but the militia shot at them, turning them back. One of the Saints, Brother Carey, was knocked in the head by a rifle butt. He, with his wife and small children, had just arrived in town hours before the siege. He was left bleeding outside the city, and his wife was held back by the militia from helping him. Thus, without help, he died several hours later. The murderer would never be brought to trial.

On the next night, yet another Halloween, October 31, 1838, Joseph learned of Governor Boggs' extermination order. Sickened by the news, he was also told that Major General Clark was on his way with another 6,000 state militiamen.

The 2,500 militia already outside Far West were too nervous to attack the 600 male Saints. When they marched toward the city, Joseph told his men to stay calm. The militia marched nervously up to the barricade, glanced over it, and saw the Saints armed and at their posts. This caused the state militiamen to simply stand there like statues, not certain what to do.

Joseph did, however, and he ordered his men to take aim. Then he told each man to pick his target and hold sight of him—but not to fire until commanded.

Next, as a major surprise, he told the Saints to begin marching forward. The state militiamen, upon witnessing the advancing force, hightailed it out of there.

Joseph smiled, knowing he had a brief victory. The four-to-one outnumbered force of Saints still exuded a confidence that baffled their enemy. All it took was a few powerful men among them, like Lyman and Porter and Luman, pep-talking the Saints and simultaneously scaring the daylights out of their enemy—with their steely eyes, confident swagger, and determination. That the enemy was frightened is evidenced by the fact they gathered up enough courage three more times and marched toward the city, only to "chicken out" each time at the barricade upon seeing the Mormon soldiers briskly presenting arms and taking aim all three times. It is one thing to have your enemy vastly outnumbered, the state militiamen figured; it is another when you're the first several hundred who would take a lead ball to the heart for a doubtful cause. Others were of course devout, feeling they were on a crusade to protect their state from the "Mormon/Indian" coalition, but many had been among the mobs who had plundered the Saints when they had been deceived into surrendering their weapons at Jackson County before the onslaught there, or among those who had gathered with the 500 mobbers in Clay County and demanded the Saints leave from there, or among the 240 at the Haun's Mill Massacre. This time, though, they were facing Mormons with weapons who were defending their families. Thus, all three "attacks" by the militia never turned into attacks, as they advanced but retreated each time.

Then the state militia calculated there must be a better way. On the fourth try they tied a white flag to a gun and marched forward. This was General Lucas's idea, seeing his men were having problems obeying orders and attacking the barricades. But he was not the bravest man on the field himself. With his white flag he had 250 men accompany him. When he met the Mormon messenger outside town, he demanded their weapons and their leaders, saying he would treat them kindly. The messenger, Seymour Brownson, ran back to tell Joseph.

Joseph then sent Colonel George Hinkle, head of the Mormon militia, to meet the state militia delegation. There are some discrepancies as to whom Joseph sent to negotiate: Reed Peck's version says he (Peck) and Colonel Hinkle were sent by Joseph to sue for peace before General *Doniphan* (not Lucas), whereupon General Lucas (Doniphan's superior) galloped up and interrupted their negotiation and ordered that the church leaders must surrender. But John Corrill has a different version—he says *he* accompanied Peck and Hinkle to talk with the generals, plural, and that Joseph told him to beg for peace, adding that Joseph said he would go to prison for 20 years or be killed rather than have his people killed. Possibly, instead, a third version is correct—that James Henry Rollins rode out with Chauncey Higbee to negotiate with the state militia—although that version is not likely true because George Hinkle was not included in Rollins' account, and Joseph himself writes that Hinkle was Joseph's main negotiator with the militia.

It is not known what Joseph told his delegates, but Joseph later wrote that George Hinkle secretly agreed with the state militia leaders the following details of a betrayal: that church leaders would be tried and punished, that the Saints would give up all their weapons, and that the Saints' property would be confiscated to pay for "damages." In return, the militia would "protect" them while leaving the state.

John D. Lee details the events:

"Col. George M. Hinkle had command of the troops at Far West under Joseph Smith. He was from Kentucky and was considered a fair weather Saint. When danger came, he was certain to be on the strong side. He was a fine speaker, and had great influence with the Saints. Previous to the attack on Far West, Col. Hinkle had come to an understanding with the Gentile commanders that in case the danger grew great, they could depend on him as a friend and one through whom they could negotiate and learn the situation of affairs in the camp of the Saints.

"When our scouts were first driven in, Col. Hinkle was out with them, and when they were closely pursued, he turned his coat wrong side out and wore it so. This was a peculiar move, but at the time it did not cause much comment among his men, but they reported it to the Prophet, and he at once became suspicious of the Colonel. The Prophet, being a man of thought and cool reflection, kept this information within a small circle, as this was a bad time to ventilate an act of that kind. The Prophet concluded to make use of the knowledge he had gained of Hinkle's character, and use him to negotiate between the two parties. I do not believe that Joseph Smith had the least idea that he, with his little handful of men, could stand off that army that had come up against him. . . . Joseph wished to use Hinkle to learn the destiny of the Gentiles, so that he could prepare for the worst. Col. Hinkle was sent out by Joseph to have an interview with the Gentiles.

"The Colonel returned and reported to Joseph Smith the terms proposed by the Gentile officers. . . . The Prophet took advantage of this information, and had every man that was in imminent danger leave the camp for a place of safety. The most of those in danger [those who had fought at Crooked River] went to Illinois. They left at once, and were safe from all pursuit before the surrender took place, as they traveled north and avoided all settlements."

Joseph was disconcerted when more news came in of more Mormon villages being destroyed in all directions, and that 1,500 additional state militia had arrived outside the city.

At the end of the day, Hinkle came to Joseph and told him that militia officers wanted to visit with him and other church leaders. He says they wished to see if they could reach "certain terms" short of a massacre.

Joseph felt, naturally, he'd been betrayed. When his delegation came to inform him, he was probably too stunned to make an immediate decision of surrender, and ordered the Mormons to prepare for battle. Drums rolled and a trumpet sounded. The battle was ready. The Missourians marched forward. Porter and Parley were among those implanted against the breastworks and ready to fight for the Army of Israel. All along the line Mormons clutched their rifles and aimed at the oncoming, marching Missouri militiamen, who themselves were filled with terror.

B ᴜᴛ then Joseph surprised everyone. John D. Lee records, "Joseph Smith called all of his remaining troops together and told them they were a good lot of fellows, but they were not perfect enough to withstand so large an army as the one now before them, that they had stood by him and were willing to die for and with him for the sake of the Kingdom of Heaven, that he wished them to be comforted, for God had accepted their offering, that he intended to and was going to offer himself up as a sacrifice to save their lives and to save the church. He wished them all to be of good cheer and pray for him, and to pray that he and the brethren who went with him might be delivered from their enemies. He then blessed his people in the name of the Lord. After this he and the leading men, six in number, went with him directly to the camp of the enemy. They were led by a Judas, Col. G. M. Hinkle. I stood upon the breastworks and watched them go into the camp of the enemy. I heard the yells of triumph of the troops, as Joseph Smith and his companions entered. It was with great difficulty that the officers could restrain the mob from shooting them down as they entered." Other reports say General Lucas rode up, said not a word to the Saints, and ordered his men to take them. Lee concludes, "A strong guard was then placed over them to protect them from mob violence."

If John D. Lee's information is accurate—upon arriving at the militia camp, Joseph and the others were not surprised when they were ambushed and taken prisoner.

The church leaders were marched into camp by Cornelius Gilliam's men, who were painted like Native Americans, and shrieked and whooped. It was plain to Joseph that it would take somewhat of a miracle to save them from the ferocity.

Back in Far West the Saints heard the "Indian-like" shrieking. (General Lucas later reported to Governor Boggs that "the troops, with some slight exceptions, marched back in profound silence." Perhaps he lied, or perhaps he was referring to *later*, when there was a time the militia reportedly felt a soberness cast over them.) Immediately the militia leaders called for a court martial, which may have lasted the entire night. The Saints being tried were not allowed to attend.

That night it rained. Joseph and the others had to sleep in an uncovered pavilion, amidst taunts from the guards, telling Joseph to "show us an angel, give us one of your revelations," and save the man who is dying whom "we knocked his brains out with his own rifle [referring to Carey]," while, according to Parley P. Pratt, also bragging of raping women and girls in the newly captured city, Far West.

Then Joseph and his friends received word that the court martial declared they would be shot by a firing squad the next morning—in the public square before their people. And then they heard the firing squad begin practicing. Amidst that nightmarish sound, they turned to God by kneeling in prayer. When the sentence had been announced, the most fearless one among them seemed to be Mormon Colonel Lyman Wight, who defiantly told the mob, "Shoot and be damned."

That night General Lucas sent a message to General Alexander Doniphan to have the prisoners executed: "Sir, you will take Joseph Smith and the other prisoners into the public square of Far West and shoot them at 9 o'clock tomorrow morning."

Doniphan wrote right back: "It is cold-blooded murder. I will not obey your order. My brigade shall march for Liberty tomorrow morning, at 8 o'clock; and if you execute these men, I will hold you responsible before an earthly tribunal, so help me God."

Joseph was awakened at sunrise and learned of Doniphan's stance. It was clear that Doniphan had made a career-destroying decision, if he had any hopes of a future in politics, which many attorneys had. And he may have struggled through a sleepless night, knowing he may have been giving up a lifelong dream. But his conscience won out. Despite his courageous stand, he did walk away from Joseph, not staying to protect him. Perhaps he was confident that his stance would influence the other militia leaders to follow suit. But he may have been overconfident because, as Doniphan was leaving, rumors circulated among the officers that Joseph and his men might—or might not—be shot after all. Still, his stance apparently caused Governor Boggs to have second thoughts.

The next day, November 1, 1838, the male Saints were marched outside the "fort" walls, where they stood in line and had to lay down their weapons and their uniquely captured cannon. Hinkle rode up and handed over his sword and pistols to General Lucas. Then the Mormon citizenry was herded to the town square. The state militia watched as, under coercion, the Saints one by one sat at a desk under the Far West liberty pole and humiliatingly signed away their weapons and rights on a surrender document. Lee records, "We were to give a deed of all of our real estate, and to give a bill of sale of all our personal property, to pay the expenses of the war that had been inaugurated against us . . . and all of the Mormons were to leave Missouri by the first of April, A.D. 1839."

At that point, discovering a disarmed populace before them once again—just as in Jackson County—the troops stormed into homes and stole their property, then taunted and frightened the women. They also destroyed valuables. They told at least one woman, and probably many others, that they would never again see Joseph.

Joseph's house was trashed. Emma and her children were shoved into the street and saw most of their property carried away. Hyrum was ill, but forced at gunpoint to the prisoners' camp. Some women—the number is unknown—were pulled from their homes and tied to benches used for religious worship, then gang raped "in the most brutal manner," reports a formal complaint sent to Congress four years later. The militia officers, however, did send guards to try to stop additional trouble, according to John Corrill, who also doubted there were any rapes, but his account was vastly outnumbered by other reports, and his views were those of a Missouri apologist, being an apostate at this point.

Food and fodder were given by the Saints in return for promises by officers that the state of Missouri would pay for it later, but the Saints never got a penny. General Lucas marched his militia through town to give his troops the pleasure of "showing themselves off" to their victims, and simply to intimidate the Saints. Immediately, he sent a brigade to Adam-ondi-Ahman to confiscate the Saints' weapons. Lucas then wrote Governor Boggs that he was sending the prisoners to Independence to await orders.

No military action was ever taken against Doniphan for denying his superior commander's orders, and it was not ever even looked into. But his political career was demolished. Nor was any action ever taken against the troopers who pillaged and destroyed the Saints' property and raped their women.

On November 2 the Mormon leaders were marched in the rain to the town square. There, Joseph and the others plead for permission to see their families one last time, and to gather some clothing. They were finally granted their wishes.

Joseph found Emma at their home. She was surprised to see him still alive, believing he had been shot. He asked to visit her and his children alone for a few minutes, but his guards refused. He left his family feeling, as he wrote, that he was being torn away from them, who were left among "monsters" in the form of men, wondering if even their basic needs would be met. His young son clung to him as a militiaman pushed the child away with his sword, swearing at the boy and threatening his life.

Parley P. Pratt entered his home and found his wife down with a fever, his five-year-old girl standing there with no one to feed or care for her and his three-month-old baby. A woman lay on the same bed as his wife, having been forced from her home, and she was going through labor with no one to help her.

Hyrum Smith was forced to leave behind his pregnant and nearly bedridden wife.

All the prisoners were now pulled out of their homes, taken to the square again, and forced into two covered wagons. From there they began a 60-mile ride to Independence, where General Lucas fully expected the prisoners would be executed.

# 41

EFORE leaving town Joseph's mother and sister attempted to visit Joseph and Hyrum but were kept by the militiamen from getting within 400 yards of the wagons. Suddenly, however, someone helped them get through the crowd of soldiers. But as they arrived, the wagons began rolling forward, so they could only grasp Joseph's and Hyrum's hands and squeeze them for just one second.

Several days later General Clark arrived at Far West. The Saints asked him if they could see Joseph but were denied, so they wrote a memorandum explaining the facts of their case to the general.

In response, Clark grabbed 56 more men and took *them* prisoner. Then he gathered the whole town together and subjected them to a speech seething with hatred. It was on November 6, 1838, that he told them things they would not soon forget. He announced the terms of surrender, noting what they had complied with, then told them a new fact—that they would have to leave Missouri immediately. He added, "Whatever may be your feeling concerning this, or whatever your innocence, it is nothing to me." He confided that Boggs had told him to exterminate them and, if they had not cooperated as they had, they would have all been killed and their homes left in ashes. With a brazenness rarely seen in a speech to captives, he concluded, "As for your leaders, do not think—do not imagine for a moment—do not let it enter your minds that they will be delivered, or that you will see their faces again, for their fate is fixed—their die is cast—their doom is sealed."

Joseph Smith and the other prisoners were hauled over muddy roads for two days to Independence. On November 3, 1838, as they made their way, Joseph announced to his brethren that he had received a revelation the night before, stating that "whatever we may suffer during this captivity, not one of our lives shall be taken."

On the second day of the journey, they were assured by General Moses Wilson that while some of the officers planned to hang them, *he* would protect them. He said that when they reached Independence he would "let the people look at you, and see what a damned set of fine fellows you are." He also planned to protect them from General Clark and his troops, "who are so stuffed with lies and prejudice that they would shoot you down in a moment."

A woman came up to Joseph during one of their stops and asked who the Mormon Lord was among them. The guards pointed out Joseph, and she asked if he claimed to be the Lord. Joseph clarified he was only a man, but sent by Jesus Christ to teach. She was surprised, and listened, along with the guards, as he taught them. When she left she reportedly prayed he would be delivered.

On November 4, 1838, they approached Independence. Riders on lookout spotted them and returned to the townspeople, so that on the outskirts of the city in the pouring rain, a section of trumpets actually announced their arrival and a crowd quickly gathered. Joseph and his friends were paraded through town like animals, says Hyrum, but Joseph wrote his family that they arrived during a splendid parade, not wanting to worry his loved ones, although it was a parade of indignation. Joseph wrote Emma that they were put up in a good house, but the truth is it was vacant, and they would sleep on the hard floor. Joseph added to her an ironic note, considering her later course of action, "Oh, Emma, for God's sake do not forsake me nor the truth but remember me."

By November 5 or 6, they were given more comfortable treatment. They were taken to a tavern for room and board. But they had to pay their own way and were taken advantage of by being grossly overcharged. Nevertheless, they were allowed to catch up on much needed sleep, eat well, and walk about town freely. Joseph taught a number of people and persuaded them away from their prejudice, according to Peter Burnett, a lawyer who says Joseph changed the attitude of some of his enemies. "There was a kind, familiar look about him that pleased you." He adds that Joseph had the ability of "discussing a subject in different aspects and for proposing many views, even of ordinary matters." Burnett adds, "In the short space of five days he had managed so to mollify his enemies that he could go unprotected among them without the slightest danger."

Captain Bogart stole Joseph's horse, and it had a saddle and bridle worth $200, then he sold them to General Wilson. Wilson promised to return them to Joseph but, while admiring Joseph as he did, he never returned them.

A few days later Joseph and his friends were taken to Richmond in Ray County, where they arrived late on November 9, 1838. Seven of them were taken to an old log house and kept under guard. A Colonel Price entered with chains and padlocks, saying that General Clark had ordered them chained up. They were treated as prisoners again—and harshly. Their pocketknives were taken from them and their windows were boarded up. They were chained by their legs to each other and made to sleep on the floor, even though Sidney was out of his mind with a fever. During this confinement the guards abused and harangued them, and Colonel Price would do nothing about the mistreatment. Then they were told that General Clark had selected a firing squad to execute them. Once again they faced a near-sleepless night of worry.

To stop the execution from taking place, the next day they protested that they were civilians and thus were not subject military law. So General Clark had a messenger gallop off to Fort Leavenworth for a copy of the military code of laws. He studied them for days and finally announced (which was his way of conceding that they were right) that the prisoners would be handed over to civil authorities for a trial.

General Clark was so rabidly anti-Mormon that he then wrote Governor Boggs and told him that he visited Judge Austin A. King in order to initiate a civil trial, then stated that he was even at that moment "busily engaged in procuring witnesses." He added that since there were no civil officers in Caldwell County (as all were Latter-day Saints), he had to use the military to obtain witnesses from Caldwell (an illegal procedure), "which I do without reserve." He said he considered most of the prisoners guilty of treason. However, a major roadblock to his plan developed when he discovered that the law would require the trial to be held in Caldwell. He says that if the courts decided that the prisoners had to be tried in Caldwell, then he knew they would not be indicted there until the population changed. He brazenly suggested that if the courts did decide to try the prisoners in Caldwell, then he would have to take control of the matter and try them in the military court for mutiny. He said he would have taken that course already, but realized it was doubtful whether the military had that jurisdiction. Then he asked Boggs to forward to him the attorney general's opinion on that point. As an executor of the law, he was trying so hard to assist and even supplant the judicial branch of government that he was far overstepping his bounds.

Joseph now wrote Emma: "I received your letter which I read over and over again, it was a sweet morsel to me. O God, grant that I may have the privilege of seeing once more my lovely family." He then explained who was chained next to him—Robinson, then Wight, then Rigdon, then Hyrum, then Parley, then Amasa: "And thus we are bound together in chains as well as the cords of everlasting love, we are in good spirits and rejoice that we are counted worthy to be persecuted for Christ's sake." He added that Doniphan was his lawyer again, along with a Mr. Rees.

He did not tell her the horrors they faced there at Richmond Jail, but Parley outlined them in his riveting autobiography: Sidney's daughter, though of frail health herself, and caring for a baby, came to nurse her father in his dire sickness. In her presence the guards began telling obscene jokes about murder, rape, and robbery against the Saints at Far West. Parley sensed all the other prisoners were still awake, as was he, and declared that Joseph, although still in chains, arose, "roaring as a lion . . . in terrible majesty," and told them in the name of Christ they were "fiends of the infernal pit," and commanded them to stop, "or you or I die this instant!" Parley said the guards, though armed, shrunk, begged his pardon, and became silent the rest of the night.

On November 13, 1838, Joseph and the others finally had their chains removed. They were immediately taken by General Clark to the civil court where other church leaders joined them—nearly four dozen in all. And to their surprise they saw who their judge was—their old avowed enemy, Austin A. King, who was, technically, illegally presiding over the court, since he had already condemned the defendants in the *Jeffersonian Republican* ten days earlier, as well as in the *Missouri Argus* five days earlier. Also, rather curiously, King and the prosecutor, District Attorney Birch, had both been on the court martial team that had sentenced Joseph to be shot.

King was known among colleagues for being a religious zealot and having no sense of humor. A member of the state legislature asserts that King disgraced his position as judge and was "the most unfit man I know" to have sat in judgment on the Saints' case. *The Missouri Republican* adds that King was "almost universally condemned."

Despite the judge's own prejudice, the court began. And for the next two weeks the state called witness after witness against the Saints. Amazingly, none were placed under oath. The most distressing aspect of it all for Joseph—even more so than having a well-known activist bigot as his judge—was seeing a parade of turncoats brought before him to testify—including Sampson Avard, Oliver Olney (whom Avard had told that to save himself from the court he must "swear hard" against church leaders), George Hinkle, John Corrill, Reed Peck, John Cleminson, John Whitmer, and two others who would later repent of their misdeeds and return to the fold—W. W. Phelps and Orson Hyde—and whom Joseph would completely forgive. Hyde later admitted, after he had made his stand in court, that his conscience was tortured for months to such an extent, as Wilford Woodruff later writes, that his very flesh was wasted. And from that, he humbled himself to the dust.

Some of their testimonies were in regard to the Danites whom, as stated earlier, Joseph had not only denounced as a group, but had actually dissolved. These testimonies claimed the Danites intended to attack the countryside and were lead by Joseph. In all, the 45 Mormon defendants watched as one apostate after another was marched into the court and testified against Joseph, further feeding the myth of Danite attacks on innocents.

Their testimonies also supported what King seemed rather obsessed with—a distortion by the apostates of Daniel 2:44 in the Bible about God setting up a kingdom that "shall break in pieces and consume all these kingdoms." He was told by the apostates that the defendants also believed the prophecy in Daniel 7:27, which declares that the kingdom "shall be given to the people of the Saints of the most High."

When Judge King heard that, he turned to the clerk, "Write that down; it is a strong point for treason."

Immediately a defense attorney shot back, "Judge, you had better make the Bible treason."

King, realizing the absurdity of his own statement, immediately became silent.

But the perjured testimonies that he hungered for continued to spew forth from the dissenters and from those who were out to "save their own skin."

When Mormons at the trial attempted to counter these charges, they were, according to some sources, forced to silence at gunpoint.

King now commanded the Saints to come up with their own witnesses. So the defendants quickly drew up a list of 40 names and gave it to the judge. The judge acted on it immediately and sent Samuel Bogart with 50 soldiers to Far West. Quickly

Bogart rounded up the witnesses, brought them to Richmond and, instead of taking them to court to testify, threw them in jail. Only a handful were allowed to testify.

When King wanted the names of more witnesses, he was given 20. But the church leaders soon realized the game King was playing, and sent a messenger galloping off to Far West to warn the 20 to hide. All were alerted except one. Bogart found him, took him to Richmond, and threw him in jail also. Doniphan then gave obvious advice to Joseph—don't give the judge any more names. He also told Joseph that King already had his mind made up to get the Mormon leaders behind bars.

In the lopsided trial, 39 testified against Joseph and only seven were allowed to testify for him, three of whom had inconsequential testimonies, being women who could only vouch for their husbands being home rather than out on "Danite raids."

Despite Judge King's prejudice, he released most of the prisoners for lack of evidence. Others were released on bail. Six of them, however, the ones he was really after, were sent to Liberty Jail on November 28, 1838, to await trial on trumped-up charges of treason and murder, while five others were sent to Richmond Jail, including Parley P. Pratt.

The state legislature saw the court's clear violation of legal procedure. So embarrassing was it for them, in fact—knowing that such a sham of a trial had taken place in their state—that they debated whether or not to even release the trial's transcript for publication. They finally did so to the citizens of the state, with an apology. However, they decided to then cover up the state's actions against the Saints by refusing to even investigate the events that had taken place against them. This cover-up move was criticized in the *Missouri Republican* on December 18, 1838.

But on December 19, 1838, John Corrill, despite his turncoat actions against Joseph at court, made a brave and bold move—he appeared before the state legislature and read a statement signed by Brigham Young, Edward Partridge, and others, which gave the history of their persecutions in Missouri, from Jackson County to Far West, detailing the looting and destruction and murder they had suffered. Finishing his speech, he saw the place filled with stunned silence. Then a Jackson County representative stood and began shouting down what they had just heard, claiming it should never have been read on the floor. Others also stood and denounced the Mormons. However, one old codger stood and said he suspected—since they were trying so hard to suppress the Saint's petition—that it must be true, whereupon others called for an immediate investigation, claiming Missouri's honor was at stake.

Still, as the *Missouri Republican* pithily reports on December 24, 1838, the "right of petition was denied," adding that the Mormons' "only offense may have been that they inhabited fair lands that others coveted."

So with the executive branch having called for the Saints' illegal extermination or exile, and with the court backing it up, the third branch of government, the state legislature, was now merely turning its head. Thus, the Saints were left on their own, feeling they were being stripped of everything once again, to make their way to a new land.

Joseph and four others were now remanded to Liberty Jail and waited for their next trial. And waited.

At Liberty Jail the five men were held in a dungeon-like cell, the weeks dragging on, turning into months. And they soon began to lose hope of freedom.

The Saints in Far West meanwhile struggled without Joseph's help to evacuate the state before April 1, and continued to be plundered. With no law enforcement agencies willing or able to protect them, they were hampered by constant mob attacks— stealing their food and clothing—leaving many Saints subject to starvation and exposure. Some, including Porter Rockwell's father, were so severely exposed to the cold that they died months later. A non-Mormon named M. Arthur wrote the state representatives from Clay County on November 29, 1838, complaining: "These demons are now constantly strolling up and down Caldwell county in small companies armed, insulting the women in any way and every way, and plundering the poor devils of all the means of subsistence (scanty as it was) left them, and driving off their horses, cattle, hogs, etc. and rifling their houses and farms of everything therein, taking beds, bedding, wardrobes." He adds that the Saints are leaving the state daily and are "entirely willing to leave our state," and a number have already left.

Brigham Young then came to the rescue. Although having no resources to help them, he was able to provide much-needed leadership and encouragement. One major step he took was to form a committee to search out the needy. He had been made president of the Quorum of the Twelve two months earlier, in October 1838, when Thomas B. Marsh had apostatized, and now he began to magnify his position by encouraging the Saints to give all their means to help the poor. He even put his plan into *action* by enlisting 380 "subscribers" to his plan—a veritable army of Good Samaritans.

Still, the tidal wave of poverty, sickness, and exposure never let up till they reached the safety of Illinois. Their destination? The western border town of Quincy, right on the Mississippi River, where the 1,800 locals would soon receive the thousands of Saints with compassion. They let them sleep in their houses, barns, and sheds, and set up tents and lean-tos in their fields and along the riverbank.

Thousands left Far West from November 1838 through February 1839, traveling all the way across the state in wretched, cold conditions.

As with hundreds of other families, Porter Rockwell had taken the several-hundred-mile journey to Quincy, Illinois, with his parents, wife, and children. But he was one of the few courageous enough to return through dangerous roads and fields to visit Joseph, determined, in fact, to *set him free.*

# CHAPTER 42

At Liberty Jail, where Joseph and the other four were holed up like animals, Porter finally arrived. He found the prisoners anxious to hear the news of loved ones in their new home at Quincy. In the course of numerous dangerous visits over the months, traveling between Liberty and Quincy, Porter faithfully supplied them with refreshments "many times." "Someone," says Joseph, managed to smuggle shovels in to the five at the jail, but just before their escape, the handles broke. When Joseph requested replacement handles, the friend managed to find, buy, or "borrow" several handles, then snuck them in under his coat. But the jailor became suspicious of the "over-anxiety on the part of our friend," says Joseph, and the plan was botched. Porter was likely that friend, whom Joseph leaves unnamed in an act of loyalty.

It was perhaps the first and last time Porter ever disappointed his prophet.

Joseph then planned a second jailbreak. Alexander McRae, a fellow prisoner, reports Joseph suggested they attempt the break one evening during an opportune moment, but they disobeyed—procrastinating Joseph's suggestions until it was too late. They did manage to grab the cell door—only to see it shut in their faces.

Joseph writes that he felt inspired to attempt another escape, but his friends refused, so he concludes that their window of opportunity was missed.

Another time, just as they were about to escape, visitors came to see them, and their chance was ruined.

Emma and their oldest boy, Joseph III, age 6, came to visit Joseph in jail twice before they left the state. On their second visit Joseph gave him a priesthood blessing, which the youngster always remembered. Stephen Markham helped Joseph's wife and children move on February 6, 1839, while his parents left eight days later. They would make it to Quincy, where Emma and the children would stay at the home of a Judge Cleveland. Joseph's parents would find other shelter.

One group, typical of those who made the migration, consisted of about 130 families. Once at the Mississippi River, they waited for the ice to melt so they could cross. They lived off the wilderness, with no food or shelter except makeshift tents, using bedcovers as roofs, which, unfortunately, would not hold back the rain.

Meanwhile at Liberty Jail, Joseph and his friends suffered. By February 25, 1839, Sidney Rigdon was now so gravely ill that a county judge named Turnham released him on a writ of *habeas corpus*, but sent him right back into the jail for his own safety, since the locals were dead set against the prisoners' release. Because of the squalid, filthy condition of the jail, however, Sidney would have taken his chances with freedom.

And his wish was finally granted. Sheriff Hadley and the jailer, Samuel Tillery, either due to a momentary lapse into compassion or not wanting to be responsible should Sidney die under their watch, let him go. They warned him to get out of Missouri as fast as possible.

On his way to Illinois, he was spotted by locals and chased, but managed to get away, using the woods for cover, and finally made his way to Quincy.

Joseph's attorneys petitioned for *habeas corpus* three times. Twice they were refused but the third time it was granted. Just when the prisoners got their hopes up, they would be dashed—as each time they would be released for only a few hours, then would be grabbed again and thrown back into jail, a devastating psychological blow to any prisoner.

County Judge Turnham seemed sincere in his statement that the Mormons were innocent and that the legal action against them was nothing short of persecution, à la Jackson County, and he even stated why—that the locals feared the Mormons would become too numerous for the area.

The jailer, Samuel Tillery, even told the prisoners that Boggs was ashamed of the entire ordeal and actually felt inclined to let them free, but the sincerity of both the county judge and the sheriff is questionable because the prisoners were kept in such terrible conditions for six months. Despite the mistreatment, Joseph felt the jailer and the sheriff sympathized with their attempts to escape.

In addition to Porter and Emma, other close friends and family visited the prisoners. Each time they would bring food, clothing, and boots. The female members of the church brought pies and cakes, handing them through the windows. But the guards oftentimes pushed them away and abused the visitors when they tried to serve food or cheer the prisoners. Often food was snuck in under coats. At times it was discovered, and the visitors were sent away with a torrid of oaths, after having traveled 150 miles in extreme cold, being hungry themselves. The food the prisoners were served was disgusting, and it is possible the abuse from the guards was not sanctioned or even known of by the sheriff and the jailer. Joseph wrote his friends, telling them how appreciative he was of their visits. One visitor, Prescindia Huntington Buell, states that one guard was posted outside the jail and another inside, watching for tools or weapons being snuck in.

Joseph, through it all, grew personally and spiritually from his ordeal. "It seems to me my heart will always be more tender after this than ever it was before," he wrote. As for tribulation in general, he would record: "I think I never could have felt as I now do, if I had not suffered the wrongs that I have suffered. All things shall work together for the good of them that love God."

Also: "As for the perils which I am called to pass through, they seem but a small thing to me, as the envy and wrath of man have been my common lot all the days of my life; . . . deep water is what I am to swim in. It has become a second nature to me." And: "He that will war the true Christian warfare against the corruptions of these last days will have wicked men and angels of devils and all the infernal powers of darkness continually arrayed against him."

Amazing his friends, he continued running the church from prison, and did so effectively. He wrote numerous letters—some expressing gratitude for their faithfulness, others giving advice, consolation, and even a communication stating that their business would be overseen by a committee of authorities. He requested that minutes be forwarded to him, and also gave a directive to gather evidence of abuse by the Missourians while the details were still fresh in their minds. These affidavits would later be presented to the U.S. Congress. He also issued to the members a warning—stay away from secret combinations like the Danites.

And then he summarized his feelings on the reason for their suffering—"God hath said He would have a tried people, that He would purge them as gold." (As for him and his cell mates, he tells Emma they are "prisoners in chains, and under strong guards, for Christ's sake and for no other cause.") He also believed the intensity of the trial of their faith was "equal to that of Abraham" and, interestingly, so that the "ancients will not have whereof to boast over us in the day of judgment." Furthermore, he said that their faith "will be a sign to this generation, altogether sufficient to leave them without excuse" (meaning, perhaps, that those who persecuted them would be without excuse when they would face the judgment bar of God, or when they would face the judgment of cannon some years later).

Joseph declares to his people that "the Constitution of the United States is a glorious standard; it is founded in the wisdom of God." Nevertheless, even though the Saints were deprived of their rights, "we see what we see, and feel what we feel, and know what we know." And finally he testifies, "We say that God is true; that the Constitution of the United States is true; that the Bible is true, that The Book of Mormon is true, that the book of *Doctrine and Covenants* is true; that Christ is true; that the ministering angels sent forth from God are true; and that we know that we have an house . . . eternal in the heavens, whose builder and maker is God."

On March 21, 1839, Joseph writes, "My Dear Emma, I very well know your toils and sympathize with you. If God will spare my life once more to have the privilege of taking care of you, I will ease your care and endeavor to comfort your heart. . . . Try to take time and write to me a long letter and tell me all you can, and even if Old Major is alive yet and what those little prattlers say that cling around your neck. Do you tell them I am in prison that their lives might be saved?" Joseph next says that since God rules all things "after the counsel of his own will, my trust is in him." Poignantly he adds, "My nerve trembles from long confinement. . . . Doth my friends yet live? If they do, [do] they remember me? Have they regard for me? If so let me know it in time of trouble. My Dear Emma, do you think that my being cast into prison by the mob renders me less worthy of your friendship? No, I do not think so."

Joseph then asks Emma to request Judge Cleveland in Quincy to look after her and the children, and if they can stay there and not suffer for anything. He finishes, "I will reward him well if he will and see that you do not suffer for anything I shall have a little money left when I come."

While in Liberty Jail Joseph also received a revelation expressing that, despite their horrendous trials in jail, Christ had suffered far more and understood their plight. Finally one morning, after six months in jail, in April 1839, they were told they would be taken to trial the next day. Court would be held in Daviess County before a grand jury. Joseph writes Emma on April 4, 1839, that they have been "within the walls' grates, and screeking of iron doors of a lonesome dark dirty prison. . . . This night, we expect, is the last night we shall try our weary joints and bones on our dirty straw couches." Dirty indeed, probably with human waste and vomit mixed within them. He adds that they "lean on the arm of Jehovah, and none else, for our deliverance, and if he doesn't do it, it will not be done, you may be assured, for there is a great thirsting for our blood in this state." He adds that they will finally be moved from jail, "and we are glad of it. . . . We cannot get in a worse hole than this is. . . . My Dear Emma, I think of you and the children continually. . . . I want [this]: You should not let those little fellows forget me. Tell them father loves them with a perfect love. . . . Don't be fractious to them, but listen to their wants. Tell them father says they must be good children and mind their mother. My Dear Emma, there is great responsibility resting upon you . . . to form their young and tender minds, that they begin in right paths. . . . I suppose you see the need of my counsel and help. . . . Remember that he who is my enemy, is yours also, and never give up an old tried friend, who has waded through all manner of toil for your sake, and throw him away because fools may tell you he has some FAULTS."

Just as the last week of October had often been the Saints' darkest hour, the first week of April was often their brightest.

Joseph thought the night of April 4 would be their last there. But the jail would hold them still another night. That night of April 5 likely passed quickly, as they had hope for freedom and for at least some sort of change, even though they were heading off to yet another trial. But the biggest hope would come when Doniphan would tell him he planned to get their court venue changed to Boone County, where the people would be less prejudiced against them.

On April 6, ever an important date in church history, they were released forever from Liberty Jail.

The ride to Daviess County took two days, a trial for them because of their weakness. But they were filled with optimism, especially due to being out in the sun and fresh air for the first time in months.

They arrived at Daviess County on April 8, and the next day their trial began.

Before the grand jury, they were found guilty of "murder, treason, burglary, arson, larceny, theft, and stealing." (Some observers have facetiously noted that Missouri grand juries could not be accused of "piling it on".)

Waiting on pins and needles, the prisoners held onto the hope that a change of venue would come so they could be freed—not only from that court atmosphere (which was so decidedly against them), but from the mobs who harangued them each day as they walked to and from court. (At the court itself, most spectators and even court officiators were drunken and continually threatening them.)

Finally, on about April 15 they got their change of venue. They were ordered to go to Boone County for sentencing and were placed on a wagon. Four guards and Sheriff William Morgan took them away amidst threats from the now-raging mob.

Their journey through lone Missouri woodland roads proved most interesting.

Under the direction of Sheriff William Morgan, who either felt sorry for the prophet or was directed by a political superior, the law officers became drunk, and the five church leaders escaped into the woods. A day and a half into their journey, the sheriff apparently showed Joseph and the other prisoners a highly unusual paper—an order without a signature or date. The sheriff then told Joseph to never show it to anyone. Then came the clincher—he said he had been told not to reach Boone County.

According to Hyrum, the sheriff finally said, "I'll take a good drink of grog and go to bed. And you may do as you have a mind to." The prisoners, who had obtained honey and whiskey along the journey in case an opportunity arose to get the guards drunk, now gave it to the guards. Three of them drank away and fell asleep, while the fourth assisted Joseph and his friends in saddling the horses. Then the guard turned his back as the prisoners mounted up and galloped away for Illinois.

Joseph was finally free.

As Sheriff Morgan arrived at Gallatin, he was grabbed by angry locals and run out of town on a rail. The entire Missouri countryside then became a raging hornet's nest . . .

Their "Number One Enemy" had escaped . . . and they took it out on other Mormon settlers, a few of which, under defiance of Boggs' exterminating order, were still lingering in the state. Missourians swarmed over the countryside, completely destroying the last Mormon settlements, burning homes, shooting animals, and pillaging every Saint-looking thing in sight.

Joseph was concerned for his people still in Missouri, most of whom were older Saints and widows still languishing in Far West. Among them were members of Brigham's army of Good Samaritans, still trying to help the old and sick pack and move out.

There were also some non-Saints, and others who may have been members but chose not to tarry with the church any longer, who had stayed the winter. All those still in town were described by W. W. Phelps as showing "visible signs of discontent," adding, "I think myself they are quite lonesome." But even the non-Mormons now deserted the city.

On April 20, 1839, the old settlers herded the last of the Saints out, with the most feeble and oldest actually helping the sick as they stumbled out of the quiet settlement. These last people had to walk because all their horses had been stolen.

Six days later an eventful meeting took place in Far West. Members of the Twelve Apostles, including the leader, Brigham, along with Orson Pratt and Heber C. Kimball, rode in quietly and unobserved, and found their ruggedly built town in ruins. Their purpose in coming back was to fulfill Joseph's revelation of 9 ½ months earlier: On July 8, 1838, Joseph had predicted certain events would take place—and now they were coming to pass, despite the fact his enemies had claimed it would be impossible. They had even laughed at him over it—but here they were, rolling a large stone to the southeast corner of the main square, which for them was symbolic of laying the foundation of the temple. Then they conducted vital church business, excommunicated

31 apostates, and ordained new Apostles—Wilford Woodruff and George Albert Smith—to replace those who had left the church. Next, they sang hymns and prayed together, and finally had the chief temple worker roll the stone again, this time away from the cornerstone portion, to symbolically await the time when God would allow the temple to be finished—be it years, decades, or centuries later. Then the meeting disbanded and the men rode away. The group, according to W. W. Phelps, had met at 3 A.M. on April 26 and consisted of eight leaders and seven members—15 in all.

The once populous town bordering the western frontier was now in shambles and, before the end of the 19th century, completely disappeared, leaving no evidence whatsoever of the once powerful prairie city.

The last Mormons were finally out of Missouri.

Meanwhile, at the banks of the Mississippi, Joseph and his fellow escapees arrived. Across the river they could see their people establishing themselves in yet another land.

It was a joyful, indescribably beautiful day for Joseph as he drank in the view.

# Illinois

CHAPTER 43

ON the morning of April 22, 1839, Emma sent Dimick Huntington into town to learn if there was any news about Joseph. (Emma herself rarely made the trip, since the Cleveland home in which she was staying was five miles east of Quincy's town center.) Near the river, Dimick noticed a poorly dressed man. He took no further notice of him until the stranger was practically next to him—within several feet in fact. Then he looked at him once more and exclaimed, "My God, is it you, Brother Joseph!"

All Joseph said was, "Hush!"

Joseph was thinly disguised in torn, worn trousers and old, dilapidated boots. He had his coat collar turned up and a wide-brimmed black hat turned down in front. His condition was frightful—pale and sickly looking. Nevertheless, he was in high spirits and wanted only to see his family first.

Dimick Huntington took him straight home. Joseph desired to see his parents after he cleaned up and changed, not wanting to distress them. Walking down the street, Joseph was fearful the people there would treat him as the Missourians had. So he demanded that Dimick take him by the back streets, which made Dimick smile, knowing how friendly the Quincy locals were.

On the five- to six-mile walk to his new home, despite his precaution, many people recognized him. And he was surprised to find them so friendly. Finally realizing he was in no danger of being arrested again, he relaxed.

Within two or three hours they arrived at the Cleveland home. When Joseph arrived, Emma spotted him and went quickly to the gate, where she met and undoubtedly embraced him, just before the children came running out to him.

In all, 300–400 Saints had been murdered, leaving thousands who were driven out of Missouri. In 1839 currency, over $200,000 worth of land had been stolen, which was the amount the Saints paid for property at the U.S. Land Office in Missouri. This does not include, however, the hundreds of thousands of man-hours spent building structures and clearing land and irrigating. Additionally, Joseph spent $50,000 on attorney fees in the state. Doniphan was one of the few attorneys who actually helped him—the rest merely took his money and were for the most part incompetent, as they had, in Joseph's words, helped but a little, being afraid of the mobs.

In his journal Joseph records a stirring summary of the Missouri era, lauding the Saints in "their courage in defending their brethren from the ravages of the mobs; their attachment to the cause of truth, under circumstances the most trying and distressing which humanity can possibly endure; their love to each other; their readiness to afford assistance to me and my brethren who were confined in a dungeon; their sacrifices in leaving Missouri, and assisting the poor widows and orphans, and securing them houses in a more hospitable land; all conspire to raise them in the estimation of all good and virtuous men, and has secured them the favor and approbation of Jehovah, and a name as imperishable as eternity. And their virtuous deeds and heroic actions, which in defense of truth and their brethren, will be fresh and blooming." True, they had been slow to accept the Law of Consecration and adhere to other revelations, but Joseph saw beyond their weaknesses, loving his people; thus, heaping high praises upon them. Conversely, summarizes Joseph, "the names of their oppressors shall be either entirely forgotten or only remembered for their barbarity and cruelty."

At Quincy, in Adams County, Illinois, the 1,600 inhabitants continued to receive the Saints warmly. The citizens loathed the treatment their new guests had received from the Missourians and now looked down at the "pukes" (a nickname they gave Missourians) more than ever, as did their newspaper, the *Quincy Argus*, on March 16, 1839.

But life in Quincy was still difficult for thousands. James Hendricks had been wounded at the Battle of Crooked River and left paralyzed from the neck down. At Quincy, Joseph Smith Sr. and six others gave him a blessing, then assisted him to his feet, whereupon he walked 30 yards away and back. His wife Drusilla reports their hardships at Quincy:

"We had one small heifer that the mob [in Far West] did not take that gave us a little milk for twice a day, but in less than two weeks there came a drove of cattle from Missouri and they [the Missouri cattlemen] drove her off with them, so we were like Job of old and my husband as sore, for his blood cankered and he broke [out] in sores all over his body. . . .

"In two weeks we neither had bread or meat so we sent our oldest son, William, three miles out on the prairie to the man who had hired our cattle. [They were paying a man to watch and feed their few cattle that had pulled their wagon across Missouri; but now their son was retrieving one to butcher]. We had one spoonful of sugar and one saucer full of cornmeal so I made mush of the meal and put the sugar on it and gave it to my children. That was the last of the vegetables of any kind we had in the house or on the earth. We were in a strange land among strangers. The conflict began in my mind: 'Your folks told you your husband would be killed, and are you not sorry you did not listen to them?' I said, 'No I am not, I did what was right. If I die I am glad I was baptized for the remission of my sins, for I have an answer of a good conscience.' But after that a third person spoke. It was a still small voice this time saying, 'Hold on, for the Lord will provide.' I said I would, for I would trust in Him and not grumble."

Coincidentally, when the Saints of Kirtland, Ohio, had years earlier fled to Far West, Missouri, they had crossed the Mississippi River at Quincy, located in the middle of the state.

Living at Quincy was Illinois' governor, Thomas Carlin, and other state notables. It was the largest city in the area along the Mississippi River, and it overlooked the river from the eastern side with high bluffs.

Carlin became personally interested in the Saint's situation. He rolled up his sleeves and went to work helping the refugees. He encouraged the townspeople to collect money, clothing, and food. They even held public meetings. They gave them jobs and respect. There were about 5,000 refugees in town now, overflowing the town's borders into the countryside and along the riverbanks. Soon work became scarce. Other Saints were scattered throughout eastern Iowa.

Some of the good treatment afforded the Saints was based on economics. Thomas Carlin had inherited a huge debt from the previous governor, Joseph Duncan, with most of it coming from a big-spending state legislature. Duncan had taken over the reins of the state with a $250,000 debt, but when he left four years later, it had ballooned to over $6.5 *million*. Carlin wanted to increase the debt to keep up with progressive states on the east coast, and this "keeping up with the Joneses" mentality stretched the debt ever higher—with expensive projects, and nothing substantial to show for it, such as railroads or canals. So, straining under economic difficulty, the people of Illinois were welcoming an influx of workers and potential taxpayers.

The politicians welcomed them as well. All one needed to be eligible to vote was six months' residency, so the Saints were an easy target for the vote-hungry politicians who joined in helping them. But a less calloused view would be that for months the Saints were poor and dependent on others, and no doubt drained the resources of the people who took them in and fed them; thus, it was a charitable project that the people of Quincy stepped up to.

Carlin, whether sincerely wanting to help the Saints or acting under political opportunism, met with Sidney Rigdon while Joseph was in jail and told him the Saints were not only welcome in Illinois, but would find permanent protection. He even agreed to ask the governors of every state to write Congress and protest the Mormons' treatment as unconstitutional.

Quincy was in an area of newly divided counties and townships. The houses and citizens were similar to the western region of Missouri—crude log huts, lean-tos, cabins, sparse population, and a frontier lifestyle. They found the area abundant in wildlife—flocks of game birds that were quite edible, such as dove, quail, pigeons, geese, turkeys, ducks, and prairie chickens; as well as deer with its very edible venison. Additionally, dangerous animals could be shot for their useful fur—bears, wolves, and wildcats. There were also the lawless—bands of robbers and squatters—who would camp on other people's property and cut down the trees, marring the land for their own selfish use.

With both good and bad elements before them, the Saints were simply grateful for a place to stay. But they needed direction—and a place to go from there.

Visiting friends and associates in Quincy, Joseph learned that while he was in Liberty Jail his fellow church leaders had written the governors of other states, as well as the President, asking them to investigate the Missouri events. He hoped they would receive economic reimbursement from the national government for what had been taken from them—but knew it could take years, if it came at all. So they would at least for a while be in financial straits.

One helpful factor was that they were mostly together in one state, one community. But since they were crowding out the citizens of Quincy, it was evident to Joseph they needed a new place—an independent home.

After Joseph conferred with church leaders, he decided to purchase what land he could afford—which amounted to two parcels of swampland at Commerce, Illinois, 43 miles north of Quincy.

Despite its drawbacks, Joseph had high hopes. "The place was literally a wilderness," he writes. "The land was mostly covered with trees and brushes, and much of it so wet that it was with the utmost difficulty a footman could get through, and totally impossible for teams. Commerce was so unhealthful, very few could live there; but believing that it might become a healthful place by the blessing of heaven to the Saints, and no more eligible place presenting itself, I considered it wisdom to make an attempt to build up a city."

And build up a city he did. Joseph's people drained the swamp, cleared the land, constructed homes and stores, and within a year had hundreds of structures firmly planted in the new bastion. They renamed it "Nauvoo," meaning in Hebrew "beautiful" or "beautiful plantation." The designation for the city came either from Joseph or possibly George W. Robinson, Sidney's son-in-law.

The city mushroomed. European converts swarmed its ranks by the thousands . . . and Nauvoo became the second largest city in Illinois, rivaling Chicago in size.

And it all came about this way. . . .

Joseph became involved with a man who could help them, but who was out for his own gain and profit and, in the process, would not only assit them in settling in Commerce, but would also financially ruin several hundred Saints.

THE standard fare for Joseph over the years, past and future, seemed to be this—befriending and accepting into his circle those who would use him for their own career or financial advancement, then turn against him, causing him even further feelings of betrayal. One of his life's greatest trials was betrayal, since he was so thoroughly loyal to his friends that he looked past their weaknesses and felt a remarkable kinship with them. (On one occasion W. W. Phelps told Joseph he should do as Bonaparte did and just have a small table of food at mealtime, upon which Emma replied, "Mr. Smith is a bigger man than Bonaparte; he can never eat without his friends." At that Joseph responded, "That is the wisest thing I ever heard you say.") The Whitmers and Oliver had turned against him, and now there would be another . . .

This new financial guru and right-hand man was Isaac Galland, who, lecturing before the public some time before meeting the Saints, had even admitted he had no integrity. He had run for the state legislature five years previously, had been an Indian agent and, unbeknownst to Joseph, had actually belonged to the Massac outlaw gang(!) He was a recognized thief and counterfeiter. But he would help the Saints settle in their own land before harming so many.

When Joseph had been in jail at Liberty, Missouri, one of his followers, Israel Barlow, had come across Galland in Illinois and had informed him of the exodus to Quincy, saying they needed other land. Seeing dollar signs, Galland went to work to "help" the Saints. In February 1839 he wrote smooth letters of supposed friendship to Mormons Israel Barlow and David Rogers, telling them of deserted cabins available at Commerce, and of land available for building farms across the river in Iowa, including the Half Breed Lands. So the two men went to check out those lands. Galland convinced them he owned the cabins in Commerce and also had the rights to sell 20,000 acres in the Half Breed tract.

Meanwhile, three months before Joseph's April escape, in January 1839, Brigham Young had led 400 Saints to both Illinois and Iowa. The Iowa Saints had established themselves at Fort Des Moines. Brigham and fellow future church presidents John Taylor and Wilford Woodruff lived at the fort after fleeing Missouri, living in vacant army barracks. The fort had been built five years previously by the War Department, but in 1837 the army had abandoned it when more whites settled the area. Brigham had begun talks with Galland about buying the barracks, as well as two parcels of land across the river from each other—Commerce and Montrose / Fort Des Moines.

Still in jail, Joseph directed church leaders, in a letter dated March 25, 1839, to buy the land Galland was offering. Joseph also told them to become Galland's friend, since he was showing "friendly feelings" toward them.

The land of Commerce had been organized as a town in 1834 by two Eastern land promoters.

Before that, the area's earliest roots extended back to 1674. Two tribes, the Sac and Fox, had settled in nearby trading posts and small villages along the riverbanks of the Mississippi. They were two separate tribes living side by side, and they lived on a similar diet to what the whites would later survive on—corn, rice, melons, wild grapes, and game—buffalo, deer, turkey, and river fish.

Throughout the 1700s white settlers moved in—mostly French. In the autumn of 1779, white Americans had begun settling the area, mostly families from Tennessee and Kentucky.

Then in 1800 the whites had begun *pouring* in. By 1810 Illinois had 12,282 official inhabitants. Ten years later it had quadrupled to 55,221.

During this early period the village at Commerce City was called Quashquema. It was settled by the Sac and Fox, who merged in 1805. They also settled in a village across the river near the future Montrose, Iowa, on other acres the Saints would procure. By 1824, just 15 years before the Saints came, the Sac and Fox tribe had almost 500 members inhabiting the Quashquema settlement. That same year they were forced to leave Venus and all their villages.

That action precipitated the Black Hawk War of 1832, when they and other Native Americans returned to the state to try and resettle their original lands; however, the whites had by now completely taken dominion over the land and had power in numbers to stay off most attacks. It was an exciting time, to say the least, for white settlers pushing the borders of the frontier.

In the years just before the Saints arrived, settlers had poured into towns all along the Mississippi, in addition to Commerce City.

After Quashquema, the settlement was next called Venus, settled by one James White, a man who had purchased it from the Sac and Fox tribes for 200 bags of corn. The "Trading Oak" in Nauvoo marked the spot where that first transaction had occurred, and White's family was the first group of permanent white settlers there.

In 1829 when Hancock County was organized, Venus was actually the first county seat and had a post office. By the next year Venus had two dozen families served by the post office. Later, before Joseph's people settled there, the county seat moved to Carthage, closer to the center of the county.

Within four years Venus grew to 100 white settlers and spread for 1½ miles along the river. It was then surveyed and renamed Commerce in 1834 by two settlers—Alexander White and Joseph Teas.

C H A P T E R   4 4

Soon afterward it was mapped again as Commerce City. (Thus, Nauvoo had four names in just five years—Venus, Commerce, Commerce City, and Nauvoo.) But the town had only eight cabins and one store within the city limits when the Saints arrived in 1839. Nearby, however, perhaps just outside the new city limits of Commerce City, there were a number of other settlers and several more stores. The first two in the area were owned by men who would convert to the faith— Hiram Kimball and Amos Davis. They were rough sorts, true frontiersmen. (Kimball at one point would get into a fistfight with the rugged Porter Rockwell, yet they would remain friends and, in fact years later, work together on Brigham's successful and adventurous intercontinental mail system that would predate the Pony Express.)

The area around Commerce City was laid out like this: On the Mississippi River south was the farm of Hugh White. East of that and up the hill a way was the farm of Daniel H. Wells, who would later play an important role in helping the Saints. Across the Mississippi, in Iowa, was Montrose, a town of two or three buildings, plus the office of the New York Half Breed Land Company and Brigham's Fort Des Moines barracks, which was more inland from the river. Just south of Nauvoo about 12 miles and also on the Mississippi River was Warsaw, a much larger town of about 300 residents. Carthage was 12 miles east of Warsaw, and smaller, but was one of the two main towns in Hancock County. Commerce City was among several villages that had only a few families.

Meanwhile, in 1824 when the Sac and Fox villagers were forced out, they were given lands directly across the Mississippi River—119,000 acres of the Half Breed Indian Reservation, which ran for 20 miles along the water front and took up one third of Lee County, Iowa. The Saints would end up buying some of this land. This section in Lee County had been set aside as a reservation for the Sac and Fox, with the U.S. Government keeping a reserve interest.

In 1834, five years before the Saints came, the U.S. Government had given the merged tribe the right to sell or

*Richard Lloyd Dewey* | JOSEPH SMITH: A BIOGRAPHY

transfer that land. Unfortunately, speculators with false claims joined the legitimate claimers and soon there was a staggering number of claims—160. In 1836 one claiming company based out of New York began making numerous purchases. It had five agents, one being Isaac Galland. Galland had convinced the company he knew the land well, but the company soon lost confidence in him and may have fired him.

In 1838 the government passed a law that allowed the land to be partitioned off. Not much later, the act was reversed. Claimants then tried to adjust their titles based on when they had made claims. It was all such a mess that the government gave up on all attempts to regulate the lands. At least for a while.

When Joseph was still in jail, in fact about 16 days before his escape, on about April 1, 1839, Sidney Rigdon and his family moved away from Quincy, perhaps feeling a bit too proud to accept charity. Sidney and his family—including his son-in-law—then settled 50 miles from Commerce in Big Neck Prairie and rented a farm where they began work. But when he visited Isaac Galland in Commerce City, he decided he wanted Galland's two-story stone house. Being more stylish, complete with a stone porch, the home was one that people could look up to, perhaps more than any other in the area, and therefore seemed to suit Sidney's personality. Sidney bought it immediately and sent for his son-in-law, who transferred their rental of the farm to another church member. His son-in-law then moved to Commerce, not far from Sidney's new home.

Thus, there were now two church families in Commerce, even before Joseph was out of jail. When Joseph finally saw the area, he gazed upon it and saw both good and bad. The good points were that it was isolated; it was stationed along a main artery (the Mississippi River), which would be good for commerce (the fortuitous title for the town) and perhaps emigration and travel; it was teeming with wildlife; and it possessed beautiful views. The bad points were that the soil was untested; the land was low lying, which would be difficult to build on; the swamps would need to be drained just to get a wagon over or even merely to walk upon; the dense trees and underbrush were equally impossible to traverse; and, being swampland, there would be diseases associated with living there.

So when Joseph first stepped foot upon the soil of Commerce, it was likely a bittersweet experience, feeling it was the place where they should settle, but knowing it would require tremendous work. It would be the fifth community they would carve out of a wilderness—Kirtland, then Kaw township near Independence, then wilderness areas in Clay County, then Far West, and now this—and they knew it would be their hardest.

CHAPTER 45

J

OSEPH made his first big step toward moving to Commerce
City on May 1, 1839, just two weeks after his escape. On that
day he bought Hugh White's farm of 135 acres for $5,000, and
Isaac Galland's tract of land west of that for $9,000.

Two weeks later he and his family moved there. The White
farm had a log house where the Smiths lived and where church
meetings would be held. Two weeks later in early June, the
first Mormon-built house went up 200 yards away, built by
Theodore Turley.

So that Joseph could concentrate on building up the kingdom
and receiving revelations, as well as presiding over the church,
he was given the opportunity to erect this town, which, as
stated, he renamed "Nauvoo" upon moving there, while at the
same time receiving compensation by selling lots to incoming
church members. First, he and Hyrum planned out the city and
divided it into lots. The bluff overlooking the flatlands below
was set aside for the future temple. The streets had to be cut
out of the foliage by sawing down timber and clearing thick
brush and grapevines.

As the Saints poured in from Quincy and other parts to which
they had scattered, they pitched in to build their city. Many
lived in wagons and tents and hastily assembled wilderness
structures until they could construct framed houses and log
cabins. They also began planting crops outside town, as Joseph

had envisioned, so that the main living portion of the city would be occupied only by homes. By that fall they would learn from their first grand experiment if the sandy soil could grow their crops, which it did—so abundantly, in fact, that it did not even need cultivation.

Sections of woodland were cleared for habitation, but trees remained plentiful in the city, adding color and beauty to the settlement.

Outside town farms went up quickly because many wished to live away from the hubbub of city life and remain amidst their crops. Other Saints began fanning out to small villages in the area and throughout the county, even spreading to Iowa across the river, settling into a total of at least 31 townships and villages, 18 in Hancock County and at least 13 in Iowa, one of which—Brigham's barracks at Ft. Des Moines—was already settled when the Saints moved into the area. As for Hancock County, Joseph planned 18 communities, with Nauvoo being "the hub of the wheel."

Outside of Nauvoo the third and fourth towns of substantial Mormon population would be Lima in Adams County, Illinois, near Quincy; and Ramus in Hancock County, Illinois, closer to their chief headquartering city. (One peculiar fact is that there was already one branch of the church in Illinois when the Saints fled Missouri for Quincy. This branch had been lingering around since 1832 and was in Fulton County, east of Hancock County.)

As for Iowa, the 20,000 acres they had bought included parts of Keokuk, Montrose, and the town of Nashville. They were able to purchase them by issuing "Half Breed Land Company" stock. Of the 13 communities soon settled in Iowa by the Saints, the town of Zarahemla was the most populous and second largest Mormon town overall. Zarahemla alone would boast 326 members by 1841.

However, Joseph and other church leaders wished to keep most of their people closer to Nauvoo in order to help build the temple.

Thus, the Saints settled both sides of the Mississippi River, with farms expanding beyond the original plat map.

The city design was based on a plat laid out for the city of Kirtland, Ohio, and for Jackson County, Missouri (known as "City of Zion"), which was also to be the same for the New Jerusalem (later to be built at Jackson County). Wilford Woodruff said the Kirtland plat (which Jackson County, Missouri, the New Jerusalem, was to duplicate) "was given by vision" to Joseph. But the city blocks were smaller in Nauvoo. Each Nauvoo block consisted of four acres, and every family was given one acre on which to build their home. (The original plan for Kirtland and Jackson County called for 10-acre blocks for a city one square mile in size, with 15,000 to 20,000 inhabitants. Like Nauvoo, farms would be outside the city. While most of the city was for residential use, the center of town would have a large municipal building and temple complex. Unlike Nauvoo, the New Jerusalem would have 24 temples in the complex).

Nauvoo was actually planned out in 1839, before it was inhabited—a revolutionary concept for the day, of which the citizens were proud. The first city plan had been papered out on August 30, 1839, when the church owned 671 acres. And the town filled up in this manner: When a required number of people were ready to move in, new streets would be surveyed and "opened."

Interestingly, even after Nauvoo was inhabited, it would take almost two years to officially organize the place into a government. And it would finally be certified by the state on February 3, 1841. By 1841 nearly 80% of the original Nauvoo plat was in use. The town council, autonomous of but obviously influenced by Joseph, immediately went to work at their meeting place, Joseph's homestead office, beautifying the city, launching public works projects, and passing laws on building restrictions. (Joseph used his home from the spring of 1840 to January 1842—almost two years—as his office, but then it would move to the Red Brick Store, upper level.)

Due to low funding, many new building projects were slow to be completed, including new streets as well as road repairs.

But for Joseph it was a good problem—the place was crawling with converts aplenty.

The post office was in Sidney Rigdon's kitchen, against the wall in a corner.

Joseph's people began prospering faster than they had ever dreamed.

Since his home was near the ferry landing up the hill, Joseph would enjoy a view of the river to calm his soul on the distressing days that lay ahead, and there he would receive many a visit from his close childhood friend, Orrin Porter Rockwell, and others, like Brigham Young, Elias Higbee, and his own brother Hyrum—the few whom he could implicitly trust. His home was so busy with beloved friends visiting, and even his parents moving in, that he added on a substantially larger frame house to the James White cabin where he lived. So he now had a regular "Homestead," as he called his home.

Isaac Galland, meanwhile, was selling thousands of acres of the Native American land tract through "warranty deeds" to the Saints, which granted to the buyers no outright title. Some of this land was traded for highly valuable land in the eastern U.S., which the Saints owned. And the trade would come back to bite them.

Twenty and a half years before the Saints settled Illinois, the territory had achieved statehood as the 21st state, on December 3, 1818.

With regards to its white settlement history, Commerce City was indeed the "frontier" of the state: It lay 250 miles southwest of Chicago and 185 miles north of St. Louis.

The booming town with all its construction—this time of superior, large houses and buildings, compared to the small huts and cabins in all their previous communities—was a source of soaring morale among the Saints.

Under Joseph Smith's supervision, two hundred and fifty structures went up immediately, with several hundred more planned during the year. Because irrigation was such a fundamental part of their design, these hundreds of homes were laid out with the help of Joseph's associates who were skilled in large-scale irrigation.

Before and during this period, the Saints attempted to convert Native Americans. Some joined them and moved to Nauvoo, including some of the Sac-Fox and Potawatomi tribes.

Just as they were about to erect their new kingdom in Commerce, however, they were hit with their first problem—mosquitoes. More specifically, malaria. They were still weak from physical and emotional exhaustion created by the exodus from Far West, so malaria took an especially hard toll. This was before it was known that mosquitoes were disease carriers, so they had no idea how to control the problem; yet enough of the first settlers had faced the illness there that they had warned others to not move into the area. They were also plagued with measles and fevers. Many, especially children, were dying, while more and more became sick. Sidney and his family came down with the disease almost immediately upon moving in, and his 81-year-old mother didn't survive it.

Wandle Mace reports, "Joseph gave his house up to the sick, and moved his family into a large tent." He and Emma "took care of them" and rode on horseback as far as they could to care for them, going "from place to place visiting the sick" in order to "relieve their wants."

Emma worked night and day caring for them and treating them with herbs. Then Joseph was stricken. His friend Benjamin Johnson cared for him almost two weeks, flushing his colon with myrrh and warm water or with soda and a small portion of salt. Joseph's father was sick all summer. Some would shake for months and feel its effects for another year. Joseph finally healed from it and decided to get the Lord's work done by ridding the place of the pestilence. In short, he declared war on the disease.

ILLED with determination and the power of God, he rose up
and first went to those in his house who were sick and dying
and pronounced upon them priesthood blessings. Then he went
outside to others camped in his yard and gave more blessings.
Next, he went from tent to tent along the riverbank healing the
suffering Saints.

His next step—he asked for a boat, crossed the Mississippi
River, and went to the old military barracks at Montrose, Iowa.
There, he healed the sick who were filling the building—including
Brigham Young and others of the Twelve.

Returning home, he gathered some of those who were now
healed to help him, including Brigham and Wilford. Wilford
Woodruff, although living in Montrose, went back and forth
across the river with Joseph. He records that on July 22, 1839,
Joseph took each sick person by the hand and commanded
them in the name of Jesus Christ to rise and be made whole.
Wilford records one particular instance of a man, clearly on
his deathbed, unconscious, with his eyes set in his head "like
glass." After studying him a long time, then talking with him
and learning that the man felt it was too late to be healed,
Joseph asked, "Do you believe in Jesus Christ?" The man feebly
replied, "I do."

Wilford continues, "Joseph then stood erect, still holding
his hand in silence several moments. Then he spoke in a very

loud voice, saying, 'Brother Fordham, I command you, in the name of Jesus Christ, to arise from this bed and be made whole.' His voice was like the voice of God, and not of man. It seemed as though the house shook to its very foundations. Brother Fordham arose from his bed and was immediately made whole. . . . Then putting on his clothes he ate a bowl of bread and milk and followed the Prophet into the street."

William Huntington says that in this same year he lost use of all his limbs and his voice, and at one point he was apparently clinically dead. From the roof he could see people below mourning over him, and he could see his body below. He then saw Joseph and two others enter the room and lay their hands on his head and give him a blessing. He felt his spirit drawn back toward his body and enter it. By the end of the blessing, William could feel all his senses again. He sat up, hungry, demanding to eat. Huntington told those in the room what he had seen and witnessed, and Joseph explained that they had seen a man raised from the dead.

Joseph did lose friends and family members to malaria, but he also reached many as they were about to die and healed them, causing much rejoicing in the towns. He would write that some were not healed, lacking faith.

Both then and in the future the Saints saw similar events as miracles, and their allegiance to Joseph grew even greater.

In at least one case, Joseph would heal a man who was unconscious, having been down for two or three weeks. Suddenly the man was up and walking, fully conscious, and went to visit his daughter, whom he had not seen in a month. This man, Benjamin Brown, says critics accused Joseph of being an imposter, a false prophet, and never to have performed a miracle. He says that when any such miracles are too well attested of to be denied, these critics "attribute them to the power of the imagination over the body." Then he challenges those critics: "Was it the power of imagination over the body, that cured me, when I did not even hear Joseph's voice, or know that any operation on my behalf was going on, until I found myself well? The honest in heart will judge righteously."

A similar incident involved a woman who had lost her mind. David Whitmer went with Joseph to see her, and gave her a priesthood blessing, commanding her in the name of Jesus Christ to regain her senses and, says Whitmer, she was immediately returned to her right mind.

Jared Carter reported Joseph healing Carter's youngest child in a blessing, and on the same day, says Carter, a blind woman was healed and her sight returned by a blessing from Joseph.

The Nauvoo high council immediately obtained control of the ferryboat that ran between Montrose and Nauvoo. While Porter Rockwell had a love for river life, he did not participate in the operation of the ferry at Nauvoo because the pay, one must assume, was too low to support a family. He could better serve his family by working the farmland designated for the Saints east of Nauvoo, which was actually soil the Sac-Fox tribe had farmed. (Later, as stated herein, he would work as a taxi carriage driver from the steamboat to all parts of Nauvoo.)

While disease and hardship caused the Saints to dwindle, they would soon have a surprising influx of members from a place many had not even considered—overseas.

On July 2, 1839, Joseph and others crossed the Mississippi River, ate at the Woodruff home, and went to Brigham's house for an eventful meeting. The Presidency set apart the Twelve as missionaries, blessing them to convert many souls and to return home safely. Hyrum admonished them to teach only the first principles—especially repentance. Wilford states Joseph "presented some precious things of the kingdom unto us in the power of the Holy Ghost; yea precious principles that ought to be engraven upon our hearts & practiced in our lives." He told them to be forgiving, humble, and to not exalt themselves above another, to be honest, to give the Lord all the credit for what they would accomplish, and to not turn their backs on the revelations. Joseph advised them, "But whatever you do, do not betray your friend," ever sensitive to turncoats, who had and would always plague him. For the departing missionaries it would be a great trial, but they felt it was necessary to leave their families for Christ's sake, "trusting in him," as Wilford writes.

Isaac Galland then decided to be baptized—whether for career advancement or out of true conversion, one cannot ascertain, but on July 3, 1839, Joseph performed the ordinance himself, along with confirming him, then ordaining him to the office of elder, two hours later. Only 27 months passed before the *Hawk-eye and Iowa Patriot* editorialized that Galland had done so for his own advancement and to further his plotting.

Next item of Saint business—to start up another newspaper. Joseph had seen the power of the press in Palmyra, had been its victim there and everywhere since, and now was convinced of its importance in defending the church as well. Thus, shortly after his escape from Liberty Jail, he had sent several men back to Far West to find and dig up the press they had secretly buried. Dramatically, it had been buried in a member's yard the night the state militia had surrounded the town. They now found it full of mud, but they loaded it up in a wagon and towed it across the bumpy plains, then successfully transported it across the Mississippi River on a barge.

Now in Nauvoo they set it up in the basement of a warehouse along the river, where Joseph's youngest brother, Don Carlos, and his Canadian friend, Robert H. Thompson, cleaned out the mud and printed the prospectus for the new publication, which they called the *Times and Seasons*. However, working in the humid cellar workroom made them both ill. So the press was removed from the cellar, and work resumed on it in another building. The first regular issue came out in November 1839 and was printed by Ebenezer Robinson, who also became sick, possibly from malaria, yet he was able to run the operation from his bed. The first several issues dealt with persecutions in Missouri, which sparked an interest in non-Mormon locals.

But now the Saints struggled under a new burden.

Poverty. Most Mormons had been financially done in by the Missouri wars and were simply surviving form the surplus of more stable Saints. Their predicament reached such proportions that Joseph would embark on a new strategy: He would seek aid from Washington.

First he gathered a sampling of affidavits from many of the Saints who had been wronged, then prepared for the trip to Washington, D.C. Knowing he would be gone from his family even longer than the Zion's Camp expedition, he decided to take two reliable associates, Sidney Rigdon and Elias Higbee. He also felt it necessary to take two others who could be of significant service to them—Dr. R. D. Foster, who would join them two days later to attend Sidney in his illness, and Porter Rockwell, who would serve as their carriage driver and attendant as well as bodyguard. Porter had also proven both his loyalty and courage during the Liberty Jail episode. It was no secret that Joseph felt Porter had another mission in life—that of protector and church guardian—and the Saints were prepared to make full use of him.

So on October 29, 1839, two days before another Halloween, they set out with the package of affidavits and very impressive letters of introduction from the governors of three states and territories—Iowa, Illinois, and Ohio—in a two-horse carriage, with Porter driving. They were planning to see President Martin Van Buren, whom they had voted for in Ohio in 1836. (Part of the reason they had voted for him was because Van Buren's agent had promised them if they would vote for him he would get their Missouri lands back.)

The trip took a month—saddled with transportation delays and opportunities to explain the restored gospel to strangers. On this journey, as on most previous ones, trouble wasn't long in coming, but this time it was of their own making. In Ohio Dr. Foster embarrassed the others by flirting heavily with women, caressing and speaking "lewdly" in public, thus hampering missionary intentions wherever he did so. The rough roads made Sidney's illness worse and, after 11 days, they had to leave him behind, with Porter and Dr. Foster attending him and planning to catch up later when he would feel stronger. Meanwhile, Joseph and Elias Higbee transferred to a stagecoach and set out for Washington, D.C., without Porter's protection.

On the trip Joseph wrote Emma, on November 9, 1839, expressing his concern for their little boy Frederick, who was sick when Joseph departed. He states, "It will be a long and lonesome time during my absence from you," and adds that the purpose of the trip is to seek redress for his people out of a "sense of humanity."

Joseph had an exciting adventure on November 27, 1839. Not far from Washington on a hilly slope, the driver left the stagecoach parked precariously on a steep hill while he sauntered into a tavern to get a stiff drink. While the passengers were still in the coach, the horses were suddenly spooked and began galloping downhill. One lady wanted to toss her baby out the window to save it from the impending crash. Joseph talked her out of it. Amidst the panic and confusion, he persuaded the others to stay in their seats. Then he opened the door, climbed out, and crawled along the coach's exterior to the front. He swung himself onto the driver's seat, all the while barely hanging onto the coach as it pitched and jolted back and forth at high speeds over a bumpy road. After two or three miles, he gained control of the horses and brought the stagecoach to a halt.

No one was injured and the grateful passengers lauded him with praise. Congressmen on board talked about presenting his name on the House floor for a reward by public act. They asked his name. Their countenances changed. And they quickly dropped the idea cold.

On November 28, 1839, Joseph and Elias arrived in Washington and spent most of their time searching for a cheap hotel. The very next day they went to see the President of the United States.

ARRIVING at The White House, the mansion of the President of the United States, Joseph Smith and Elias Higbee merely showed up at the door and asked to see him. In that day the accessibility to the President was somewhat easier, one must think, because whoever answered the door simply let them in. Perhaps their timing was also good, because one account of an early president—Thomas Jefferson—reports that a visitor wished to meet him to launch the Lewis and Clark Expedition (which did materialize from 1803–1806), but the visitor was turned away at the door. So, finding a window at the opposite end of The White House, he broke in, wandered around the mansion looking for the President, and finally found him. He had his meeting with Jefferson. But life was easier this day for the two visitors from Nauvoo.

Inside The White House the two Mormon visitors were impressed by the veritable palace they found, decorated with the finest art from around the world. Even the wallpaper and furniture had been procured from Europe by Thomas Jefferson, the third President. They were taken without delay to an upper parlor where Martin Van Buren read their letters of introduction and agreed to meet with them.

Joseph then handed him several more letters—the first was from a Mormon outlining his destroyed property. Van Buren caught the gist of what the remaining communications contained because he then simply gave a small frown, looked up, and presented his response, which would be his final answer: "I can do nothing for you. If I do anything, I shall come in contact with the whole state of Missouri." It is possible he instead said, "Gentlemen, your cause is just, but I can do nothing for you. If I take up for you, I shall lose the vote of Missouri." Justice aside, he weighed everything on politics. Indeed, the national political uproar at the time was over states' rights, and it was an election year so, politically speaking, Van Buren might have been foolish to take on the Mormon problem; but as Commander in Chief, and the guardian of the Constitution, he completely neglected his responsibility.

Joseph, seeing that, forcefully told him so.

Van Buren would not back down, however, but did finally express some sympathy for their mistreatment and stated he would reconsider his position.

But Joseph knew that was it.

Van Buren did ask one or two questions about their religion—specifically how it differed from others'.

And Joseph's response was that there were two main differences: first, how they baptized—by immersion—and second, the gift of the Holy Ghost, which they possessed and passed on by the laying on of hands. He felt it unnecessary to talk further with the President on the subject, and left.

Joseph walked away from The White House stunned. His assertive nature would not let him give up so quickly, however, so he took his cause to Congress.

Joseph and Elias were for the next few days consumed with the task of taking their letters of introduction from the three governors to individual members of the House, in an effort to have their case brought before the entire House of Representatives. They found the Illinois delegation comprised of honorable men who promised to help any way they could, but were hampered by the prejudices of others.

Joseph Smith and Elias Higbee met with several representatives from both Houses. The most helpful were those from Illinois, whom Joseph considered worthy men who treated them well. These congressmen stated they would do all they could, but that they were constrained by people's prejudices. One was the most helpful of all—a senator from Illinois, Richard M. Young, who even offered to repay them for their travel expenses, which Joseph accepted.

Joseph then went to Congress as a quiet visitor and listened to their debates on other matters. On December 5, 1839, he penned a letter to his brother Hyrum: "There is a great deal of wind blown off on the occasion on each day. There is such an itching disposition to display their oratory on the most trivial occasions, and so much etiquette . . . to make a display of their witticism, that it seems to us rather a display of folly and show, more than substance and gravity, such as becomes a great nation like ours." He added, in parentheses, "However, there are some exceptions."

On December 7, 1839, Joseph and Elias finally had an official meeting in a committee room of the U.S. Capitol with the Illinois delegation. Congressman Robinson argued against presenting the Saints' case to the floor of the House because he felt it was not the concern of Congress; rather, that it was the business of the state of Missouri. Joseph argued for the Saints' constitutional rights, which obviously had been denied by Missouri. Countering Congressman Robinson was Senator Young, who agreed with Joseph. He frankly said he supported the Saints' position and added that he would obtain the opinion of others in the Senate. The delegation then decided that Senator Young would take their case to the Senate, but his hands were tied until the House could be organized—which was being delayed because of seats being contested. (The Senate meanwhile had been in session for a week.)

When word got out that Joseph was seeking over $1 million in damages for lost property, the Missouri delegation was sent scrambling for a defense. The honor of their state was on the line, and they looked not only foolish, but barbaric. They returned with the anti-Mormon fodder Joseph had heard so much before—of why they had expelled the Saints in the first place. Undoubtedly some of the Senate was swayed by it, while another part wasn't. The net result was that they would break for Christmas and reconvene with answers afterward. But in the meantime, they wanted one thing from Joseph—evidence. They told him to present it in January.

Joseph wrote the church's high council to gather and send the affidavits, then he took a train to Philadelphia on December 21, 1839. He stayed with several Saints there and tracted from house to house, teaching the restored gospel. Rockwell, Higbee, and Foster would soon meet him, but Sidney was so sick that he could not make the last leg of his journey, and never did arrive in Washington, D.C. On December 30, 1839, Joseph went to New Jersey for a few days, then returned to Philadelphia.

In early January 1840, the documents arrived. Joseph finally had his evidence: 491 Saints testified on paper of the injustices personally perpetrated on them, and to this stack, Porter and Joseph added their own. All told, claims totaled $1,381,044.

It apparently took the most part of a month to sort through and evaluate the documents, while likely doing missionary work, because they stayed in Philadelphia for a month—till the end of January 1840.

Joseph took the stack back to Washington to a Congressional committee and awaited their answer.

The committee sat on it and Joseph realized this would be their silent answer.

Crestfallen and quiet, Joseph and friends decided to give up on the government. But before going, Joseph did more missionary work. On February 5, 1840, he taught a large group of men, which included congressmen who stated they were curious to hear Joseph's views from his own mouth. One Mathew L. Davis (whom Joseph in his writings mistakenly labels a congressman but who in recent years has been discovered to be a newspaper reporter) writes to his wife in a letter: "He is not an educated man; but he is a plain, sensible, strong minded man . . . he is sincere. There is no levity, no fanaticism, no want of dignity. . . . He is . . . what you ladies would call a very good looking man. . . . His dress being that of a plain, unpretending citizen. He is by profession a farmer, but is evidently well read."

Significantly, Davis saw in Joseph's two-hour speech doctrine
that would "soften the asperities of man towards man. . . . There
was no violence, no fury, no denunciation. His religion appears
to be a religion of meekness. . . . I have changed my opinion of
the Mormons."

A winsome trait of Joseph was that he was, according to a
non-Mormon writer for the *Quincy Whig* newspaper, "divested
of all malicious thought and feeling towards his relentless
persecutors."

Joseph himself wrote of his public speaking style—not
possessing a "superabundant stock of sanctimoniousness,
complete with long-faced expression and drawn-out donkey-
like tone of voice."

William Clayton describes him, "Whilst you listen to his
conversation you receive intelligence which expands your mind
and causes your heart to rejoice." He also describes Joseph as
having an "abundance of intelligence." Lucy Mack, his mother,
offered in her own unpretentious manner, "You don't know
what a brain my boy has under that old hat."

Brigham Young analyzes him as "a comparative man,
regarding everything according to the circumstances of the
case, and every person according to their intrinsic worth." On
this note Edwin Rushton states that "in conversation with him
there was nothing . . . debasing."

As for public speaking, his brother Don Carlos says Joseph
stated "a speaker should always speak in his natural tone of
voice, and not . . . keep in one loud strain, but . . . act without
affectation." George Taggart says, "The information which comes
out of his mouth . . . is not in big words . . . but that which anyone
can understand." George A. Smith writes, "His manner and style
were very unassuming and affable" when speaking in public.
Christopher Crary adds that his style was "correct, forcible
. . . right to the point and convincing," although non-Mormon
Peter Burnett claims that in his private conversation Joseph
was "slow, and used too many words to express his ideas, and
would not generally go directly to the point." Numerous others,

by contrast, report Joseph's immense talent when speaking to groups. One is Parley P. Pratt:

"He interested and edified while, at the same time, he amused and entertained his audience." He adds that he could hold a congregation of "anxious listeners" for many hours, in the most adverse weather, "while they were laughing at one moment and weeping the next. Even his most bitter enemies were generally overcome, if he could once get their ears."

Yet, ironically, he was terrified of public speaking. Heber C. Kimball writes, "many times his legs trembled like Belshazzar's when he got up to speak before the world, and before the Saints."

Of significance to church members was his spiritual power. Lorenzo Snow says when he was filled with the Holy Ghost, "his whole person shone and his face was lightened until it appeared as the whiteness of the driven snow." Mary Ann Winters relates that once while standing near him during a discourse, "The Holy Ghost lighted up his countenance till it glowed like a halo around him."

Joseph by now realized that despite the opportunity to employ his powerful public speaking ability in the nation's capitol, he had accomplished all that he could. He left the city disappointed, especially in Van Buren: "I found him such a man as I could not conscientiously support at the head of our noble Republic."

As a last-ditch effort on the way out of town, Joseph stopped to meet with John C. Calhoun. He also got nowhere with him. So he, Porter, and Dr. Foster boarded the train to Ohio. With Sidney still in Philadelphia recuperating, Elias Higbee stayed alone in Washington to push the Saints' case forward, but to no avail. Elias would always prove to be an undeviating friend and ally, nevertheless. After his death three and a half years later, his two oldest sons would defect from the cause and seek Joseph's life, but the senior Higbee ever remained a stalwart friend to Joseph.

On the journey home Porter wished to part with Joseph's entourage at Hamden, Ohio, probably to visit his sister and her husband. Porter was not particularly excited about returning to Nauvoo where his wife, Luana Beebe, and he were having marital problems, but he did miss the children. Their differences stemmed from his being gone from her so much and spending much time with Joseph—and here he was just completing a four-month assignment once again helping Joseph. But, to make matters worse, he was not even returning directly to her. Joseph was unable to talk Porter into continuing with him, so Joseph was now forced to travel with only Dr. Foster, who had embarrassed him on their journey east four months earlier. Together the two traversed mud, snow, heavy rain, and other adverse road conditions, but Joseph did have positive moments along the way visiting with the Saints. On this journey he exposed President Van Buren whenever he could. "My heart faints within me when I see, by the visions of the Almighty, the end of this nation, if she continues to disregard the cries and petitions of her virtuous citizens, as she has done and is now doing." The *Alexandra Gazette* and the *Alton Telegraph* report Joseph saying the President was "not as fit as my dog for the chair of state."

Joseph and Dr. Foster arrived back in Nauvoo in March 1840. Porter Rockwell arrived later that month. Meanwhile in D.C., Elias Higbee attended a series of meetings and debates during February concerning the stack of affidavits, with opposition coming from the Missouri delegation, but on March 4, 1840, all came to a screeching halt when the Senate Judiciary Committee on the Case of the Saints versus Missouri handed down a unanimous opinion that the federal government should not become involved. On March 23 it technically all ended when the Senate passed a resolution that the committee be disbanded and that the Saints give up on their attempts. So that was it—no cash. Nor any offered assistance to return to their Jackson County (or Caldwell County) properties.

Joseph had done his best, but ironically all it had accomplished was raising the wrath of Governor Boggs in Missouri. He was now furious that his state had been embarrassed by the Saints in Washington—if not downright dishonored. He might have previously been happy just to be rid of the Mormons, but now with Joseph bringing to light their activities, it was time he declare a new war on them—this time by making every effort he could to get Joseph *captured in Illinois* and brought back across the river for yet *another trial.*

J OSEPH would now have to secure the services of Porter Rockwell even more heavily, along with other bodyguards, to keep his back covered—always looking out for bounty hunters and visiting sheriffs who were out to shackle him and steal him across the Mississippi. At the same time he had to move forward in a positive direction by building up the kingdom in Nauvoo.

A new obstacle arose before Joseph could upbuild the kingdom, however. His people were now being accused of pirating and counterfeiting.

A few Saints not properly practicing the faith felt justified in robbing outsiders because of their own losses. But the Saints as a whole and the church leadership decried it. Most of the thievery was taking place by non-Mormon professional robbers and river pirates, who would act out their deeds and then tell their victims they were Mormons, in essence framing them.

Thus, the Missourians blamed all thieving upon the Saints, and the reputation so damaged them that this misconception remained common in the Midwest for another 150 years.

A controversial incident occurred that further muddied the Mormons' waters. On July 7, 1840, a group of Missourians from Tully, Missouri, crossed the river in search of stolen property. When they found a gathering of goods on the riverbank, they kidnapped four Saints, taking them across the river and beating them into submission of admitting the stealing. Joseph got word of it and, assuming this was just another typical frame-up, complained to Governor Carlin, who then unleashed his wrath on Boggs across the river.

But it soon came to light that some church members may have been the thieves after all—at least logic was on the side of their enemies. The Saints were claiming the goods had been placed on the riverbank and that they just happened to have picked up the goods when they were caught. But when their enemies claimed the property was too sizeable to have simply been placed there to entrap the Saints, it left mud on the faces of the Saints. One was then found guilty in court—Alanson Brown. But the one left with the most dirt on his face was Governor Carlin, who had stood up for the Saints. Also embarrassed was Joseph. And in the end, because Carlin had defended the Saints, all he had managed to do was even further antagonize Governor Boggs against both himself and the Saints.

On September 12, 1840, Joseph's father, who had been sick all summer, took a turn for the worse, vomiting blood. The next day he called his family together to present a last father's blessing to each member. He told his wife Lucy, "You are the mother of as great a family as ever lived upon the earth." He told her the world hates them because they are not of the world, and that he dreaded to leave his children surrounded by enemies. He blessed Joseph to finish his work. Joseph reportedly called out, while weeping, "Oh, father, shall I?" Joseph of course did not know if his "personal mission" would be completed, especially with men like Boggs out to get him. Joseph Sr. then declared to everyone, surprised, "I can see and hear as well as ever I could." On the following day he told them he would live another seven or eight minutes. He then died calmly. He was 69 years of age. The next day at his funeral the eulogy was read by Robert B. Thompson, Don Carlos' earlier partner at the *Times and Seasons*. Joseph Jr. was deeply saddened at the loss of his father, stating, "He was the first person who received my testimony after I had seen the angel." Ever afterward his father had supported him, never doubting.

Malaria continued taking its toll, despite the swamp drainage that was still in process. Joseph's sister-in-law, his brother Samuel's wife Mary, succumbed. His brother Don Carlos then died in August 1841. (Joseph's own infant son was born a week later and named after Don Carlos.) Later that month the family friend Robert B. Thompson died, and the next month Hyrum's second son, also named Hyrum, passed away. Joseph's uncle Silas would also soon die.

Through it all the city multiplied and the economy boomed. Limestone was quarried locally for the temple being erected, and numerous shops and factories opened, with craftsmen of all sorts doing a remarkable business.

But most impressive was the quality of converts. And the converts began pouring in by the thousands—mostly from Great Britain, as a result of the Twelve in their missionary labors.

Before the Twelve had arrived in England, the missionaries had built a branch in Liverpool of 28 members, a remarkable feat in and of itself. But the numbers that the Twelve would convert were staggering. Fortunately for the Saints most of them were tailors, coopers, gunsmiths, tanners, blacksmiths, and brick builders, who responded to the idea of the gathering in America and to the opportunity of owning their own home on their own acre of land—which would be a miracle for them in light of Great Britain's poverty and slums. Also, most of these converts were of high morals, according to the British newspapers who reported of the Mormon conversion phenomenon. London, however, provided few if any converts, and Heber C. Kimball thought the reason was the city itself was filled with sin. The *Millennial Star* church newspaper was born in Liverpool in May 1840 and assisted in the conversion and retention of new converts in the British Isles.

Once they and the other converts from the U.S. and Canada immigrated to Nauvoo, most were delighted to be there and contributed magnificently, some fell away from the faith, and still others were not truly converted, but made it a point to enter and sow discord, according to Joseph, who warned them not to "expect perfection."

The church built a remarkable program to help the British immigrants get to Nauvoo—called the Immigration Fund. Brigham Young ran the office, which chartered ships and secured supplies so that British Saints could sail to New Orleans for less than five pounds—including food and provisions. The program so impressed the people of Great Britain that it was discussed in the House of Commons, and even non-Saints took up enquiry about emigrating with the Saints.

In Illinois Joseph's city attracted so much attention that visitors began pouring in to meet the prophet. Distinguished professionals from medicine, law, and religion were among them, and most were impressed with Joseph's warmth and candor. His clerk wrote, "He was always equal to the occasion, and perfectly master of the situation, and possessed the power to make every body realize his superiority"—not a pretended one, but one with natural powers, observed others.

Joseph's life now began to unfold in dramatic fashion. Just when he was settling down and his kingdom was leaping forward, along came a person who would bring the city great blessings (similar to Isaac Galland), then inspire much of the outside world against them. His name was John Cook Bennett. (As for Galland, his story and betrayal to the Saints would unfold concurrently now with John C. Bennett!)

CHAPTER 49

AN intelligent, short, dark-eyed, black-haired gentleman of much education and talent, John C. Bennett was a year and a half older than Joseph, had grown up mostly in Ohio, had been a student at Athens State University and a medical student under Dr. Samuel Hildreth in Marietta, Ohio. He had practiced medicine in several states, including as a surgeon for the military in the Black Hawk War. Even more impressively, he started the medical school at Willoughby, where he was the first dean and a professor of children's diseases and gynecology. Outside of medicine he helped to found colleges in Indiana, Ohio, and West Virginia. In 1838 he moved to Illinois, was appointed brigadier general of the Illinois Invincible Dragoons, and in 1840 was appointed by Governor Carlin as the quartermaster general (in charge of all supplies) of the State of Illinois militia. At one point he proved a genuine interest in religion by becoming a licensed minister in Ohio. When he was at Willoughby College, which was near Kirtland, he wrote to Joseph, seeking to assist him when the Missouri Saints were expelled from Jackson County. When the Saints were forced from Far West and moved to Quincy, he wrote Joseph again, offering to help, likely genuinely wanting to assist an indigent people. Joseph wrote back saying there would be essentially nothing in it for him if he was to help the Saints. But still, "my general invitation is, let all who will come, come and partake of the poverty of Nauvoo." He then invited

Bennett to come as quickly as possible, as he thought that Bennett could be "of great service to us." But he emphasized that he would have to pay his own way. Bennett packed up his wagon and came to Nauvoo in the spring of 1840.

Bennett offered to help Joseph locate the cause of the swamp diseases, adding that he had made a study of it in that area and was confident he could make Nauvoo healthful. Together the two men rode over the city and outskirts, where Bennett told him the remaining few marshes were the cause of the problem. Most of the others had been drained but, Bennett, along with the general medical community, worked under false assumptions on many issues, including swamp fever. Like the friend and associate he would become to Joseph, his advice was a mixed blessing of truth and falsehood that would so ironically characterize his relationship with Joseph. When Joseph asked what caused the disease, Bennett correctly answered that it was the marshes—but his incorrect follow-up answer was that the reason the marshes were responsible for the diseases was that there was a poison produced by rotting plants in hot, humid areas, and the poisons would cling to fog passing over the marshes, and then the fog would carry the poisons to humans. Thus, he recommended to Joseph that the Nauvoo citizens live on the second floors of their homes. But the mixed blessing he brought with that inaccurate diagnosis was his insistence that they fight the "fog poison" with quinine—which of course was the answer for fighting malaria, although he did not know it. And he just happened to have a quantity in his possession.

That summer Bennett accepted the tenets of the faith and was baptized. With the marshes drained and his quinine treating people, he was a tremendous blessing to the Saints. Joseph then saw talents in him that were needed to help establish Nauvoo politically. And with regard to assisting him on a theological basis, Joseph sought the Lord's inspiration on the matter and chose Bennett as his special counselor to take over much of Sidney Rigdon's work in the First Presidency, since Sidney was still sick. Joseph received a revelation for Bennett, saying that if he continued in the work, he would be crowned "with blessings and great glory."

Bennett's next assistance to Joseph came politically—getting the state legislature up to speed on what Nauvoo was all about and getting them to accept the Nauvoo city charter *and* grant them a charter for a city militia and a university. The power of having their own city charter would allow the Saints to protect themselves from spurious arrest warrants from outsiders who would try to drag church members out of the city and off to out-of-area jails. But with a writ of *habeas corpus*, which a city charter can grant local judges to issue, the individuals being arrested cannot be taken away by just anybody—or even by anyone, for that matter. As for the militia, with a charter for it in place, they could decide on their own militia officers and even receive a supply of weapons from the state.

Bennett was the man who got it all done. He had influence at the state government levels, since all were acquainted with him. He alone submitted the right forms and petition at the legislature in Springfield, and he alone hammered it through.

There were two main political parties at the time—the Whigs and Democrats. Joseph had sided against the Democrats, of whom Van Buren and Boggs were members. So the Saints now voted almost unanimously for the Whigs, except for one ironic exception—they had voted for James H. Ralston, a Democrat, because he had made friends with the Saints, instead of voting for the Whig candidate, an unknown lawyer—Abraham Lincoln.

John C. Bennett now gave Joseph his first advice. He said they should wait till after elections in 1840 had shown how much voting power they had. Only after that would he journey to Springfield to obtain the Nauvoo charter from the state. So, after the elections, he confidently took his trip to the state capitol and, having a track record, he began seeking representatives to assist him. They gladly did so, seeing the Mormons' recent power at the polls, and also because of his already established relationship with them. When Bennett proposed the city charter before the state legislature, he glossed over the actual powers that the charter would have, as well as the powers that the city militia would take. The city militia charter was especially interesting because it would make Joseph the highest ranking militia general in the United States should a war break out, giving him power as commanding general of the entire country's armed forces. Instead, Bennett cleverly presented the persecutions the Saints had endured in Missouri—the massacre at Haun's Mill, the expulsions from Jackson County and Far West, etc., and pulled attention to that aspect of his presentation, which allowed the charter to fly through with hardly a review.

Joseph was especially pleased with the city charter, feeling it gave them protection they had not hitherto had and, while Bennett got it through the right channels, Joseph was clear to point out that the charter itself was "my own plan and device. I concocted it for the salvation of the church, and on principles so broad, that every honest man might dwell secure under its protective influence without distinction of sect or party."

The charter called for a mayor, nine councilmen, and four alderman, and it allowed them to pass any ordinance that did not cross paths with the state and federal constitutions. The council (a legislative body) was also the municipal court (a judicial body), and this council had the power to organize the Nauvoo Legion (the executive body), although there was some separation of the branches. For example, only the mayor was in charge of using the legion, if necessary, to enforce city laws. (Additionally, of course, the legion could be used by the governor for state defense purposes if necessary.)

One of the distinguishing factors of the founding of the United States was the separation of the three branches of the federal government, which the Constitution became famous for worldwide. From that, state and city charters generally modeled their framework after the federal Constitution. So when state or city charters did allow for the three branches of government to not be completely separate, it had the possibility of raising "red flags" among critics, although there was no particular law covering it and, in fact, very few people cared. In further fact, there is no record of anyone anywhere caring if city charters intertwined the three branches of government—until Nauvoo. And not even Nauvoo, at first.

While Nauvoo's city charter mingled the three branches in a manner uncomfortable to its later critics, it was actually modeled after the Springfield state charter, which had been granted by the state legislature just a year earlier. One thing going for the Nauvoo city charter was that it was supported by Stephen A. Douglas, who was Secretary of State, as well as others. Perhaps he had studied it thoroughly and felt it was not much different from the Springfield charter—which it wasn't— or perhaps he merely glossed over it, which apparently both houses of legislature did at the state house in Springfield. In any case, it was signed by Governor Carlin on December 16, 1840, and Nauvoo found itself fully and legally protected in February 1841. Abraham Lincoln, despite being the one Whig not supported by the Saints, voted for it out of "magnanimity," states Bennett. Lincoln had even come to Bennett after it was passed and graciously offered his congratulations. Lincoln's political career would of course eventually soar, and in that career he would never make a negative comment about the Saints, despite their voting for Ralston. Lincoln holds a special place in the hearts of Latter-day Saints. They believe that Lincoln, as well as George Washington and certain other statesmen who were instrumental in the founding or furtherance of America, including all 56 signers of the Declaration of Independence, later accepted the restored gospel in the spirit world, after their deaths, as one of the later church presidents, Wilford Woodruff, received a revelation—even a visitation from these men—while in the St. George, Utah, temple.

CHAPTER 50

JOHN C. Bennett was voted mayor of Nauvoo, the only one on the ticket, for his industriousness in getting the charters for Joseph. A notable place for him to announce not only his election but that of other city officers, on January 2, 1841, was the store of Wilson and William Law, Canadian converts who, along with Bennett, would later help bring down Nauvoo, after making their way into Joseph's heart as the closest of friends—then betraying him.

Bennett was remarkably visionary about the city. In his inaugural address of February 3, 1841, he outlined his plans that would have made Nauvoo a major riverport city in the western hemisphere. At the south end of Main Street, he planned to build a wing dam, and from there a two-mile canal into the city so that goods could be loaded on ships and water power could be provided for steam to run mills and factories. He wanted to force taverns out of business, start a board of health, and drain out the lowlands along the river, while cutting down trees there. And he wanted to hire a fund-raiser to secure venture capital to start the canal project immediately.

The next day Joseph was elected lieutenant general of the Nauvoo Legion, and Bennett was appointed major general. Bennett was also chosen as chancellor of the university and president of the agricultural and manufacturing association. The university had 23 regents, including some non-church members. A committee made plans and chose a site for building the school, but no buildings were ever constructed. However, its organization went west with the Saints later, where it became the University of Deseret, then the University of Utah. Some professors did hold their courses in Nauvoo, however, from 1841–1842, charging $5 per quarter for tuition.

Joseph prophesied Nauvoo would become the largest city in the West, and it would have come to pass were it not for apostasy once again fighting the very infrastructure of the city and the church. Meanwhile, he directed land sales for the city and became the registrar of deeds, giving him power to sell or not sell land to individuals in Nauvoo. He set the prices for lots at $500, giving free lots to the handicapped from the Missouri persecutions.

After only 20 months, in January 1841, Nauvoo had shops, schools, paved streets, bridges, fields and gardens that were cultivated, orchards, a steam flour mill, several brick factories, a foundry, and two sawmills. Nearly all farming land was outside the city. For those who had no land of their own, there was a cooperative farm.

Joseph received a revelation in January 1841 stating that a hotel would be built for the increasing number of guests. And it would also be used as a place for Joseph's family when needed, although Joseph, Emma, and their children lived just across the street, west of the spot where the hotel would be (partially) built. The "Homestead" where they lived was the same home into which they had moved in May 1839, when they first came to Commerce. It was now added upon with a much larger structure built onto it.

The next month the Nauvoo Agricultural and Manufacturing Association was incorporated, as approved by Governor Carlin, and funded with $100,000 in stock shares.

Preparation then began on the new temple. It would be 83 feet by 128 feet by 60 feet high, with magnificently beautiful limestone from the local quarries.

One visitor to the city who wrote in the *Alton Telegraph* and the *Alexandra Gazette*, describing himself from Montrose, Iowa, said he heard Joseph comment that "our influence—as far as it goes—we intend to use." To the Saints this made sense for a people bullied about from state to state and who now had some power and influence in the state capitol *and* had their own charter and city militia with which to protect themselves. But the same newspaper article was critical of Joseph, who had power over people to follow him so devotedly as "to think and act in crowds." It also stated that Joseph had "awful claims to divine inspiration." Thus the local press was now becoming suspicious of both him and his power.

Some locals, especially the usual antagonists—ministers of religion—feared what they saw as their chief successful rivals. The reason—the Saints began claiming members of their congregations and converting some of the first settlers there. Others, like Reverend B. F. Morris, a Presbyterian missionary in the county, perceived that "nearly all of the old citizens are anxious to sell their property and many of them will no doubt move away." He believed most people did not want to live near them. What he feared most was that "this deluded, fanatical, and ignorant sect is about to be poured upon us by thousands . . . and thus like the locusts of Egypt consume every green thing in the land and wither away so far as they can every vestige of godliness." While the Saints' greatest critics included these ministers who saw them as "locusts," the fact is they brought undreamed of beauty to the area, draining the land of disease-infested swamps, laying out wide streets, and building magnificent homes on full-acre lots with gardens and flowers, bringing orderliness and even civility to a rugged frontier area. Nevertheless, the locals were becoming concerned, some even riled up against the Saints by the arguments of the ministers, but others were simply becoming envious. Still, envy can create a bloodthirsty enemy. The beauty and economic boon from hard work and careful planning by Joseph and others caused the envy to blossom into animosity. Still, other locals were simply appreciative of the Saints' progress.

One of the arguments used by their detractors was against the growing strength of the Nauvoo militia. By midyear 1841

they numbered 1,500. By early 1842, the end of the first year of
the legion's existence, they would number 2,000. (One report
says they had 5,000 men by the mid-1840s—three years later.)
They were well disciplined, divided into 26 companies of cavalry
and infantry, and had uniforms designed after the U.S. Army.
Furthermore, there was a boys' corps of 500, which drilled
with wooden swords. Their flag read, "Our fathers we respect;
our mothers we'll protect." Some of the locals who had been
heated up by their ministers saw the 500 boys as future adult
militiamen, becoming fearful even of them. While Joseph planned
the boys' drills and parades, many of the adult legion members
found their own legion just as fun. Many of the soldiers did not
have sharp-looking uniforms, but their leaders, whose uniforms
were patterned after the federal army, had plumes in their hats,
a common distinction between soldier and officer in the style
of uniforms among armies across the world.

Joseph's uniform was blue, with epaulettes, high boots,
and a hat topped with feathers, also like the federal army. He
carried a handsome sword. Bennett's uniform, however, was
even flashier, with tassels and gold braid. The legion drilled
mostly for show and recreation. Joseph would ride at the front,
flanked by a dozen bodyguard in white uniform. A band would
play music and their drills would become precise.

Many non-Saints would travel from miles away, taking a
riverboat to see the greatly heralded entertainment and parades.
But the purpose behind the legion was serious, as a protection
against future encroachment on their liberties.

They believed the Constitution granted them the right to
protect themselves. It was their only security amidst poverty
and sacrifice and sickness in maintaining the city. All males
had to join, unless exempt for a valid reason, and they could
even be fined if they missed meetings or parades.

John C. Bennett, still the quartermaster of the Illinois state
militia, obtained three cannons for the Legion and 250 rifles—
newer models than the old muskets that even some of the state
militiamen used, giving rise to even further envy.

Joseph believed that because the Legion had discipline, good uniforms, a stately appearance, intelligent training, and a knowledge of military tactics, it was "the pride of Illinois."

While some locals were entertained by the Legion's splendid parades, others were jealous and afraid, despite the fact that some of the troops and even officers were non-Mormons.

The U.S. Constitution calls for "a well regulated militia, being necessary to the security of a free state," and "the right of the people to keep and bear arms." To the Saints, this militia was another civilian militia under the power of the state, so the rising feelings against them were based more on emotion and propagandizing than on fact.

Bennett was meanwhile the trainer and organizer of the Legion. But Joseph was its figurehead and, as such, actually never did call out the Legion, except on one occasion. Dissidents claimed Joseph made threatening speeches, but they are not backed up by fact nor by Joseph's own journal, in which he confided the importance of the Legion. But more and more locals were beginning to side with the Saints' enemies, believing they would take the world by force if preaching did not work, as indicated in one letter to a friend by a settler named John Nevius, on May 2, 1841.

Preparations began weeks earlier on the new temple. But on April 6, 1841, that ever important date in Latter-day Saint history, the cornerstone was actually laid. It was a day they would celebrate with a parade, and it was among the last days of peace they would have as a city—before a new enemy would arise right under their noses.

A T the festivities on April 6, 1841, Joseph put on a show for his own people and the neighboring locals—complete with the marching Nauvoo Legion in their magnificent regalia, the firing of cannon, and band music. Up on Mulholland Drive where the bluff overlooks the city and the river below, Joseph sat with his officers, guests, and temple architects. They witnessed singing by the choir and a talk by the magnificent orator, Sidney Rigdon, who was regaining his health. Then they enjoyed a turkey feast. Joseph records the day as very gratifying, and was especially pleased that no profanity or drunkenness reared their ugly heads in such a large gathering, a common problem most anywhere else. He writes that liquor is "the bane of humanity in these last days," and is proud to announce it is "becoming a stranger in Nauvoo." (The Word of Wisdom, banning alcohol, was nevertheless still some time away.)

Sitting with Joseph on the stand and enjoying the dinner was the local editor of the *Warsaw Signal* newspaper, Thomas Coke Sharp. He had recently bought the paper and changed its name from *The Western World*. He was only 22, hailed from Pennsylvania, and had moved to Quincy, Illinois, in August 1840 to practice law. Then, because of a hearing handicap, he switched his occupation to that of a journalist and newspaper owner. So he bought the paper and moved 28 miles north to Warsaw, there to become heavily involved in county politics.

During the parade a strange thing happened that triggered him into becoming the worst enemy the Saints had ever had in the press and, to some extent, ever, period—even rivaling the viciousness of Governor Boggs. Sharp had, according to a man assigned by Joseph to watch his horse, been growing green with envy as the festivities unfolded. Norton Jacobs was studying Sharp on the stand, curious about his expressions, and Jacobs became convinced that all of Sharp's later animosity arose from that singular event. William, Joseph's brother, also observed him.

The very next day Sharp began his infamous anti-Mormon diatribes, apparently without cause. He not only condemned Joseph continually from that day forward, but leveled his wrath on all Saints, even those who accepted the Saints with any degree of friendliness or who simply displayed impartiality. He invented the popular phrase "Jack Mormon," meaning those who were not openly anti. (Later it would be turned by the Saints to mean those who were less active in the faith.)

The church began to make significant strides after that April event. Church conferences were held in New York City; Philadelphia; and Manchester, England, where the Twelve presided. In England alone, 6,000 members had been converted and lived in 28 cities, while 800 had already emigrated to Nauvoo. There would be 2,749 emigrating to Nauvoo in the two years of 1841 and 1842. While in England, the Twelve had published 5,000 copies of The Book of Mormon and 2,000 hymnbooks, and were still publishing the *Millennial Star* newspaper to help keep them tied together in the faith.

But the opposition to the kingdom was as intense as its progress. Not only was Thomas Sharp launching his newspaper attacks just 15 miles south to stir up anti-Mormon prejudice among the locals but, across the river, Governor Boggs was now taking greater strides to get back at Joseph for disparaging Missouri's honor before Congress. Boggs was now determined to get Joseph hauled across state lines to stand trial for the old accusations of treason at Far West. So, that very month of April 1841, as Sharp began his attacks, Boggs ordered Missouri law officers to go capture Joseph and extradite him back across the river.

Mysteriously, two months later, the formerly cordial and supportive governor of Illinois, Carlin, turned on Joseph. While accepting Joseph into his Quincy home on June 4, 1841, Carlin treated him with courtesy and respect. Then, when Joseph left, the governor sent a Missouri posse after him to arrest him and drag him across the river. He even sent the local Illinois sheriff to assist the Missouri constable in tracking him down on his way back to Nauvoo.

It was Joseph's first arrest in Illinois.

He was taken back by Carlin's betrayal and two-facedness. He was also literally taken back to Quincy, Illinois. There he was told to appear in court at Monmouth, Illinois. With the approaching court date, he became anxious, concerned about his fate, after having spent six months in Liberty Jail. Meanwhile, he had sent word to friends in Nauvoo, and now they came to join him, Porter Rockwell among them. Porter subtly threatened Joseph's captors and continually glared at them, making them uneasy. Also among the "protection party" was the African-American Saint, Elijah Abel, and six others who took a boat from the Nauvoo landing to Quincy, dealing with heavy river winds but determined to rescue Joseph if necessary.

On the appointed court day, Joseph, Porter, and other friends went with the constables to Monmouth but, before they could meet in court, they were swarmed upon by angry locals. So Joseph had to be kept upstairs in a house, where he was held prisoner, while the crowds literally pressed their faces against the glass to gawk inside.

On June 9, five days after his capture, Joseph was taken by the constables into a packed courtroom of curious and angry locals. There, his six attorneys conferred, and one of them, O. H. Browning, plead that Joseph could not be given over to Missouri because of the inhumane treatment the Saints had received there earlier, being driven out in the cold of winter and made homeless. Judge Stephen A. Douglas apparently agreed, but he based his decision on the legal aspect that the writ to take

Joseph had already been declined by the sheriff of Hancock County, who, in fact, was not of their faith, and that therefore the Missouri writ was now of no force. Additionally, said Douglas, he would not decide if the evidence was even admissible, since the same evidence in Missouri had previously not even been determined useable or not. Furthermore, Douglas indicated, the two states needed to first hash out certain problems, as there had been bad blood between them.

Joseph and his group rejoiced and, before noon, rode off triumphantly, leaving the constables in their wake, standing amidst mumbling, confused, disappointed crowds.

For a short time, while the forces of enemies regrouped, Joseph enjoyed another peaceful period. He rejoiced seeing members of the Twelve returning from Great Britain. He was thrilled at hearing their reports of miraculous success. Meanwhile, Parley P. Pratt had stayed behind to watch over the thousands of new converts, while Orson Hyde had sailed south to Jerusalem to dedicate the area of Israel to the return of the Jews, a blessings the Saints saw literally fulfilled 107 years later when the nation would be reestablished and the Jews would begin gathering there.

At their July 4, 1841, celebration, Joseph spoke to the Nauvoo Legion, declaring his concern for the national welfare "and his willingness to lay down his life in defense of his country," the church's record states.

Upon their return from Britain, another milestone occurred. It was decided the Twelve would now run the business operations of the church, while Joseph would merely preside over it. Brigham would also continue directing the immigration program, which included Britain, Canada, and the eastern U.S.

Having freed up more time to devote to spiritual matters and recording revelations, Joseph was now met with another problem—a financial disaster wrapped up with a heartrending disappointment by Isaac Galland. Although he did not attack the church for its beliefs, he left 250 families homeless. And it came to light that he had collected money from Joseph for his Eastern investors, then absconded with it.

The most distressing aspect to Joseph, however, was Galland's dishonesty. Joseph now learned his new friend had sold the 250 families land across the river in Iowa that didn't belong to him. He had in fact only owned a small undivided section of the reservation, and the net result was causing 250 families to lose their farms. They had poured their labor, souls, and life savings into building up farms they now had to abandon.

But there was another side to his swindle. It went down like this . . .

Galland had sold the Saints 500 acres in the middle of Nauvoo in August 1839, acting as agent for Horace R. Hotchkiss and his partners in New Haven, Connecticut. Galland far overcharged them for essentially useless swampland and, were it not for the Saints' industriousness, it would have remained worthless. But in this case the Saints happened to incur $6,000 interest, which was also far too high. Joseph was nevertheless willing to pay it, having made the deal and being a man to keep his word. But Galland was not. So when Joseph raised the $6,000 interest and gave it all to Galland to take east, Galland again absconded with it. On July 24, 1841, Hotchkiss wrote Joseph saying Galland had fled New York without paying the interest.

Joseph meanwhile received flak from some grumbling church members. In order to cover the cost of lots he had given free of charge to the widows and orphans of men killed in Missouri, and to cover the $6,000 interest on the land, Joseph had had to charge a small amount above the original cost of the lots to everyone else. Nevertheless, from that he was accused of pocketing the extra money.

Then Hotchkiss began writing Joseph, demanding his money. Joseph, not knowing yet that Galland had stolen it, told Hotchkiss off for harassing him. Hotchkiss also did not yet know of Galland's theft, so he accused Joseph of not paying up.

While still upset at Hotchkiss for his apparent harassment, Joseph decided now was a good time to tell Hotchkiss what he really thought of the whole overpriced deal in the first place—saying the property was a "deathly sickly hole" and that because of it he had lost his younger brother, Don Carlos, from malaria two weeks earlier. He also told Hotchkiss the Saints had not realized any profit from the land. But Hotchkiss still thought Joseph was just trying to evade payment.

Then on October 9, 1841, Joseph wrote the Hotchkiss officers again with the sad news that Galland had not returned to Nauvoo. They had both been ripped off. But Joseph would not yet accept the betrayal, seeing only the positive in people he trusted, and in this case it was no different—he wrote Hotchkiss saying, "He is on his way," believing he must have been delayed "by some misfortune or other." Joseph added about Galland, "He may return, however, as yet, and give a just and honorable account of himself." He asked Hotchkiss that they wait until spring to be paid, when Hotchkiss apparently was—but not with Galland's money. And in the whole process Joseph was left with egg on his face as he was shown trusting the wrong person, with the Hotchkiss company getting its money months late.

Galland was basically hiding out and, ironically, doing deals just 15 miles away in Keokuk, Iowa. When Joseph discovered he was there, he wrote to him on January 17, 1842. Galland wrote back with rude comments, including a refusal to pay, then ended up saying he was broke. The next day Joseph stripped him of his power of attorney to act for the church. The day after that Joseph wrote him again, asking him to settle up regarding notes Galland had given for lands in the East. Galland ignored him. Joseph then sent Brigham Young and James Ivins to meet with him and take papers for Galland to sign. That meeting was successful to some extent, and Galland sent the signed papers to Joseph on January 27. On February 27 Joseph met with him for the last time ever. They spent the day together, and one can only imagine the disappointment Joseph felt. But they reached some agreements, and it is possible Galland cashed in some notes he had previously acquired in order to reimburse the Saints, as they apparently got their $6,000 back. Joseph and Galland would only contact each other a few times by mail in the future, and Galland would isolate himself away from the Saints. As many a speculator who once had sizeable sums in his pocket, he could apparently not leave well enough alone, having to roll the dice yet again on other land or business deals, most of which went sour. The rest of his life was spent in Iowa, where he died penniless.

While bad press accumulated, Joseph went further downhill financially. By October 1841 all he owned was an old cow and a horse (both given to him as gifts), two pet deer, a dog, six turkeys, and a little furniture. Much of his problem was the fact he had not pulled out of his Kirtland difficulties—sacrificing everything for the kingdom, seeing his general store fail, and spending what little money he had left to assist others. Then in Far West he had slid deeper into debt from vexatious lawsuits by spending nearly every cent he could find on fairly worthless attorneys.

But then he began to prosper economically. And in the process he significantly enhanced the lifestyle of the Saints. He built The Red Brick Store west of his house, within a couple minutes walk. It opened January 5, 1842, to a large crowd of curious customers. All that day he worked behind the counters, selling goods from 13 wagonloads that had been brought from New Orleans and St. Louis. And on that day and many others, he managed the store while performing his other duties—civic, church, and family. The first day was "filled to overflowing," and he describes enjoyment in store work, loving to wait upon the Saints and being "a servant to all."

The Red Brick Store was a large general store for the day, painted by a British convert. It had marble, mahogany, and oak counters, with genuine marble touches. Shelves lined the walls. The bookkeeper kept up the accounting from a back room. Also in the back were stairs leading to the second floor and basement. Joseph invited the Masons to meet on the second floor. He believed the brotherhood of that organization could provide outside, non-Saint support and protection for him and his friends who belonged to it. On the top floor was Joseph's office, where he received revelations, did translating, and kept his sacred writings. On the south side was a window overlooking the river. Joseph labeled it "altogether a place the Lord is pleased to bless."

While in the midst of this peaceful, short moment, Joseph began to be the target of insulting articles spewed out by a large Eastern newspaper.

Editor James Gordon Bennett had started the *New York Herald* in 1835 in his basement and expanded it into a major publication of national influence, despite its sensationalistic flair and tendency to personally attack people in order to sell papers. So after James Bennett visited Nauvoo, he decided the Saints would make good fodder. At first, however, he was respectful. His initial article about the Saints, on November 18, 1841, treated Joseph well, calling him "the master spirit" whose ambition "is to found a religious empire that will reach the uttermost ends of the earth," even detailing the fact there were Apostles in Europe. Also in that issue he reprinted articles from the church about the status of building the new temple, the plans to buy 500 acres from Hotchkiss, and an article that described the most recent 1841 church conference. Joseph was pleased and the Saints reprinted articles in their *Times and Seasons* newspaper. Joseph, in December 1841, had the city council praise Bennett through a resolution for his positive portrayal of them and suggested church members subscribe to the *Herald*.

But James Bennett would turn on him. Within weeks, on January 10, 1842, he published a sarcastic article about the church's desire for growth, making church members look as though fanaticism, rather than the Spirit of God, was what drove them. Joseph continued to provide *Times and Seasons* articles to Bennett for reprinting, perhaps hoping some good would come of it, which it may have, but Bennett's editorializing poked fun at the Saints along the way. Nevertheless, Joseph would continue his "relationship" with the paper, providing them with news up through at least February 1843, so Joseph was evidently not as concerned as some in the community.

Although the *New York Herald* had national influence and caused people to lose respect for the Saints—even making missionary work more difficult in some respects—it was mild compared to the type of attacks coming from the local press. Not just Thomas Sharp's *Warsaw Signal*, but now a second paper joined the throng of what would be many local papers—the second now being at the state capital of Springfield, Illinois— the *Sangamo Journal*. On February 21, 1842, its attacks were based on Joseph having civil and military power. "He becomes a dangerous man, and must look to the consequences." It was an outright threat to Joseph. But it did not understand Joseph was this time determined to protect his people from the onslaught of potential mob violence like that which had plagued them in Missouri.

Joseph was more than busy with civic affairs. He was now also managing editor of the *Times and Seasons* newspaper, having taken over on February 15, 1842, doing so because church leaders were unhappy with the way it had been run since Don Carlos Smith had died the previous year. (John Taylor, as assistant editor and Wilford Woodruff, as business manager, actually ran the paper, but Joseph still had to spend a considerable amount of time in the business—overseeing the publishing of major documents heretofore unpublished, such as the *Articles of Faith*, *The Book of Abraham*, instructions on the building of the temple, articles about not being deceived by evil spirits, and a doctrinal article on baptism for the dead. Joseph served as editor for nine months, then John Taylor took over completely on November 15, 1842.)

Joseph also became consumed by other duties—making corrections to The Book of Mormon, making revisions to The Bible, preparing the hymnbook, revising and preparing the

*Book of Commandments* into the new *Doctrine and Covenants*, receiving revelations for (or translating) *The Book of Abraham*, selling city lots, meeting with the Twelve, visiting and healing the sick in their homes, writing and dictating numerous letters and journal entries, attending baptisms, counseling the women in launching The Female Relief Society of Nauvoo (to help the poor and ill), raising money for and overseeing work on the temple and on the Nauvoo House hotel (which was meant to provide comfortable housing for the Saints when they would immigrate to Nauvoo and which they would use as a place to stay until their homes were built, and which would also serve as a hotel for the many curious visitors flocking into the city), managing his general store (which gave him particular enjoyment), and starting up the Nauvoo Lodge of the Free Masons, which he did in March 1842.

This was in addition to keeping a home and family and taking time to play with his children, which he was well known for. (For example, he would often wrestle with them on the ground, and in the cold months he would slide down the hill on a sleigh with them onto the frozen river.)

He would also lead his people in dancing, parties, parades, singing, boat rides on the Mississippi River, and may even have led the first community to ever participate in what is now known as baseball. John Murdock said Joseph "scarcely ever met his equal as an athlete." He would play catcher, and when he batted "we used to holl[er] to the boy that was going for the ball [which Joseph hit far] to take his dinner. This used to make the Prophet laugh," says Aroet Hale. He also always conformed to the rules. Being beloved by his people, the crowds were likely sizeable, possibly pulling in not only hundreds, but thousands to watch the first baseball in America. And he competed in footraces, long jumping, and high jumping over horse corral fences. Joseph would also "leave a meal at any time to wrestle with anyone," says Jacob Jones. He could even wrestle, amazingly, for an hour at a time. The man who helped dictate Lucy Mack Smith's memoirs broke his leg when Joseph was "horse-playing" with him, tripping him in the street. "He immediately carried me into the house, pulled off my boot, and found at once that my leg was decidedly broken; then he got some splinters and bandaged it. A number of times that day did he come in to see me, endeavoring to console me as much as possible," says Howard Coray.

While believing home was the center of a pure and temperate lifestyle, the Saints naturally had no saloons, and what drinking did take place happened to be among the certain percentage of "backsliders" and non-Saints who inhabited the city. The one exception was a several-day business that Joseph set up in his home in behalf of his struggling friend Porter Rockwell, who had sacrificed greatly for Joseph. But when Emma returned from a furniture buying excursion in St. Louis, she had the bar dismantled immediately.

Far more serious was the one brothel that was secretly established, some say by John Bennett, in the guise of a grocery store, with a young man running it from behind a counter while selling groceries; however, suspicions quickly arose that more was going on in the back room when the "low-life" visitors to the store began filling the outside walls with graffiti, which more or less gave away the establishment's secret. The city council had it closed immediately upon finding out about it, and a handed-down story claims that it was dismantled by Porter Rockwell, who went riding up to it, tossed a lasso around the small structure, and pulled it to the earth, possibly with customers still inside.

The temple was a community effort overseen by Joseph. He constantly provided pep talks to the members asking them to sacrifice their time and substance for the holy house—10% of their time or 10% of their income.

The previous fall he had sent a large group of men to Wisconsin Territory, and they had returned with lumber on barges. That winter, just ending in March 1842, he had begun work in local quarries. There, 100 men were doing the actual quarrying and hundreds more were hauling stones. Women were knitting mittens and socks for the workers so they could continue through the winter cold. Many Saints pitched in by providing wagons, food, clothing, and hay for the work animals. Branches of the church from far and wide, hundreds of miles from Nauvoo, sent all they could in the way of money, cloth, yarn, quilts, shoes, and food to help build the temple. It was a monumental sacrifice for the entire community of Saints.

Some temple ordinances could not wait. So they built a temporary baptismal font in the basement that Brigham dedicated. This font rested on 12 carved oxen. Joseph was quite pleased with it because they had made the effort to build the oxen to resemble the most perfect-looking young steer they could find, which they had used as a model.

The doctrine of baptism for the dead involved baptizing living people as proxy for those who had died—most often the proxy work was performed for one's own ancestors—as Joseph taught that in the next life people would have a chance to not only mingle with loved ones again, but that they could hear the gospel if they had not in this life. He also taught that the ordinance being performed for those deceased individuals would allow them to have a higher degree of salvation if they chose (in the spirit world) to accept the gospel. Thus, by accepting the gospel after they died, they would have the opportunity to advance in glory and opportunity in the hereafter. Its precedent was laid out in the New Testament when Paul referred to baptism for the dead in 1 Corinthians 15:29.

Joseph foresaw the day when the sacrifice and hardships of the Nauvoo Saints would be appreciated: "Generations yet unborn will dwell with peculiar delight upon the scenes that we have passed through." He describes their sacrifices as " the all but insurmountable difficulties that we have overcome in laying the foundation of a work that brought about the glory and blessing which they will realize."

Joseph's newest enemy would rise to the surface during March and April 1842. The crusade against Joseph would reveal itself in the form of lies and personal attacks from none other than John Cook Bennett, who not only sought to ruin Joseph's reputation but, in retaliation, to heap persecution on the church.

It had started the previous summer when Bennett had taken Joseph's doctrine of polygamy and twisted it for his own purposes, seducing women under the guise of religious practice. Furthermore, he had represented himself as a bachelor, when in fact Hyrum had fortuitously come upon his wife and children in Ohio, who had fled from Bennett's abuse. Joseph had confronted him about his behavior in July 1841, and Bennett had, either sincerely or in a dramatic show, actually poisoned himself out of remorse, but had recovered. Joseph, feeling sorry for him, allowed him to stay in the church.

But Bennett went about town on adulterous escapades, ironically utilizing his close friendship with Joseph to further his selfishness, claiming Joseph sanctioned it and that it was his own form of polygamy.

When Joseph heard about Bennett's wild interpretation of the plural marriage doctrine, he believed Bennett was on dangerous personal ground. He also asserted that once a person had accepted the gospel, especially one who attained high church positions, and then turned away from it, they would be gripped by the adversary's influence. In this case he soon suspected Bennett was now seeking to literally supplant Joseph, even if by murder. His instinct in fact told him that Bennett might try to harm him during the Legion's parade on May 7, 1842.

On that day they held mock battles. Bennett, curiously, tried to get Joseph to take command of the first unit. Joseph, suspicious, refused. Bennett raised Joseph's suspicions even higher when he told Joseph to take position in the rear of the cavalry without his lifeguards. Joseph again refused. He chose his own place in the regiment, keeping his lifeguards with him, in fact very close to him. Joseph confided in his journal that day that Bennett was about to expose his real intentions. And time would soon tell all.

Hyrum then set out to uncover Bennett's lies. He found Bennett had been telling women that his activities were part of the mysteries of God, which would be revealed when the people were strong enough, and that it was all right if those women kept it a secret. He also told them he would give them medicine to induce abortion if necessary. One woman told Hyrum that when Bennett visited her during her illness, he stated he wanted to leave town with her and even begged her to let him kill her husband with a certain "medicine."

When the truth began catching up to him, Bennett went up to Hyrum on May 17, 1842, during a break in a Masonic lodge meeting held in Joseph's Red Brick Store, crying and pleading to not let the news out to the public. Then Bennett saw Joseph walking across the yard from his house to the store. He ran up to Joseph and grabbed his head, begging for forgiveness. Joseph asked him why he had been using his (Joseph's) name to carry on "your hellish wickedness?" Joseph then asked if he had ever taught Bennett such behavior. Bennett declared he had not. So Joseph asked him if he would sign a statement saying that. Bennett agreed and went into the Red Brick Store with Hyrum and wrote the affidavit, which stated that Joseph had never taught him to disobey the laws of man or God, then he swore to it before the alderman, Daniel H. Wells.

At that moment Joseph paved the way for Bennett's excommunication. He wrote a letter the same day to James Sloan stating that if Bennett desired to "withdraw his name from the church record," that he should be permitted to, "and this with best of feelings" between Joseph and Bennett. Joseph then signed it and gave it to Bennett. Bennett resigned immediately as Nauvoo's mayor, for personal reasons.

Two days later he stood in front of a crowd that had gathered for a city council meeting. He resigned his position, then Joseph asked him candidly if he had anything against him. Bennett responded, "I do not." Bennett confessed that in all his dealings with Joseph, "in public and in private, he has been strictly virtuous." Joseph was elected mayor and Hyrum vice-mayor.

A week later Bennett stood before Masonic officials and cried, admitting his promiscuity, and asking to be forgiven. Joseph believed him and actually spoke in his favor to be given another chance. But three weeks later the master of the lodge learned Bennett had been kicked out of the Masons in Ohio for "rascally conduct," and printed a notice to all members of the

CHAPTER 52 341

brotherhood to warn them. Five days before that, on May 11, 1842, Bennett's excommunication notice was written, but was not shown to the public for another month, on June 23.

However, Bennett's contriteness was short-lived. He began to fume over the facts, not accepting responsibility for his actions and stating he was basically too good for the church and did not wish to be around it. Then he said he had left the church before he had been excommunicated, and that the edict had been forged, since the three men whose names were on it were out of town when it was written. Another claim he made was that one man refused to sign the edict because he did not know of any unworthy actions Bennett had made. Steaming over being released as mayor and losing his church membership, Bennett then left town, promising to drink the blood of his enemies.

# CHAPTER 53

JOSEPH, meanwhile, did have his own witness. Lorenzo D. Wasson reported seeing and hearing Joseph tell Bennett off for his immorality and for lying, despite Bennett's claim that he was acting under Joseph's permission. Wasson later wrote Joseph more about Bennett: "If you recollect, I came down [the stairs] just before you were through talking [with Bennett]." Thus, Wasson had overheard important parts of their conversation. "There are many things I can inform you of, if necessary, in relation to Bennett and his prostitutes." Wasson then declares how he remembers Joseph taking him (Wasson) on numerous visits to the sick, not knowing why Joseph had asked him to accompany him, but now he realized why—so that no one could later impugn his character. Wasson adds that people might have been "watching you with a jealous eye." He further states, "I am satisfied of your virtue and integrity. . . and I now solemnly protest before God and men, I never saw a thing unvirtuous in your conduct."

Bennett went straight to the press, just like the dissidents in Far West. Whereas the *Warsaw Signal* had begun diatribes against Joseph from an outsider's perspective, the defection of a leading church authority—despite his short term with the Saints—was the first substantial spark to begin the next avalanche of abuse onto a Latter-day Saint community.

The *Sangamo Journal* jumped right into the fray with Bennett's "exposé" of Joseph. On July 8, 1842, the editor published an "extra," announcing the excommunication and adding a notice that Bennett would expose Nauvoo in a series of letters to the paper. The letters would be printed from July through September (and later would be reprinted in book form). They would paint him as an innocent victim. The gist of his story was that he had not wanted to sign the affidavit (which was a retraction that Joseph practiced polygamy) and that Joseph had forced him at gunpoint to sign it on May 17, and had also promised to make "catfish bait" of him or turn the Danites on him. So only then, he now claimed, had he signed the statement before Daniel Wells and presented the necessary statement in front of the city council.

Hyrum countered him, saying Bennett had no private discussion with Joseph on May 17, nor could he have, because Joseph was in the Masonic meeting all day; besides, Hyrum had the keys to the building and knew where Joseph was.

Bennett then claimed, through a published newspaper letter, that Joseph had established various levels of prostitutes, had used religion for its basis, and was a liar. He also claimed Joseph had made an advance on Sarah Pratt while her husband Orson was on a mission, and that she had told Orson when he came home, whereupon Joseph had denied it and tried to slander Sarah to her husband. An anti-Mormon book written by Wilhelm Wyl in 1886 attested to the same theory, wherein its author claimed to have spoken with Sarah years later, but Joseph's son, Joseph III, states emphatically that Sarah told him personally that Joseph had never spoken an improper word to her.

Bennett's claim had so upset Orson Pratt that he left the city in distress on August 29, 1842, and most of the city's population went searching for him. After a failed suicide attempt, he was discovered on the riverbank. For a few months Orson and Sarah left the church, but came back and were rebaptized in the Mississippi River on January 20, 1843, after the Twelve reconsidered his case in Brigham's home. There, Orson was immediately restored to the Twelve. Evidence that Orson was eventually convinced that Bennett was lying is found in a letter Orson wrote John Van Cott four months later: "J. C. Bennett has published lies concerning myself and family and the people with which I am connected. His book I have read with the greatest disgust. No candid, honest man can or will believe it."

Bennett did not stop there. He claimed Joseph attempted to seduce two other women—Sidney's 19-year-old daughter Nancy Rigdon and Martha Brotherton. An unreliable source from a disaffected family member of Sidney's claimed Joseph admitted to Sidney of proposing to her—not trying to seduce her—and that it was the first moment Sidney had heard of polygamy in the church. This report also states Sidney was further concerned by the gossip among neighbors regarding the matter.

Bennett then rounded up what ammunition he could from dissidents. Martha Brotherton had gone to the *St. Louis Bulletin* on July 15, 1842, and published a claim that Brigham had tried proposing to her without her parents' knowledge. She and her parents left Nauvoo, possibly over this, possibly over other matters that are not known, unrelated to polygamy, but they used polygamy as their reason to leave. She was in any case well within marrying age for the times, being 18. In his newspaper columns Bennett continued his accusations, claiming an outlandishly licentious lifestyle among the Saints, fabricating it with lurid details.

But what solidified the Illinois populace against the Mormons was his next theme—he claimed Joseph planned to take the area by force, and that his militia was far too strong for a religious leader to control. The *Warsaw Signal* had already paved the way for that argument. But Bennett took it a step further—he claimed Joseph planned to use the Legion to set up an independent empire, saying they had 30 cannons and an overabundance of rifles obtained from the state. He also lied by saying the Legion had members who were under allegiance to the Danites and would protect Joseph even if he was wrong.

The stage was set for the dry kindling wood to catch fire. Other area newspapers began reprinting Bennett's claims from the *Sangamo Journal.* The *Hawk-Eye and Iowa Patriot* issued, on July 28, 1842, a warning that most towns had Danites in them, warning its readers to be fearful. And there were numerous spurious claims. Even the *New York Herald* printed Bennett's letters for the national audience. While Saints throughout the country tried explaining the truth to their friends, some of the local settlers who had remained their friends through all the flak now began doubting them. Emma's nephew, Lorenzo D. Wasson, was on a mission in Philadelphia, and stated that people began opposing them there. Joseph learned from John Page in Pittsburgh on August 8, 1842, that missionary work in Pittsburgh had also been injured because of Bennett. While Page clearly saw young Martha Brotherton's efforts as slanderous, he requested Joseph to fight back. A week later he also requested the church authorities to furnish materials to argue the accusation because of the "high anxieties of the public mind."

Joseph did fight back. On July 9, 1842, he published Bennett's scandalous exploits in the *Quincy Whig.*

But Bennett's battle was effecting the gubernatorial elections of 1842. So was the national political schism that had been developing during the entire decade.

The emergence of two political parties had had its beginning just before Martin Van Buren's administration, during the tenure of Andrew Jackson. Jackson had refused to help local states if there was any cost to the federal government, had vetoed the charter of the second U.S. Bank (thinking it favored big business), and had made an unpopular stand on the tariff. Because of that, his opponents had begun a new political party. Jackson was a Democrat, and his opponents were Whigs, named from the Whigs in both American and British history who had fought despotism. The Whigs wanted laws passed to promote growth in the cities, and they wished to promote business, so they had less support on the frontier, where the Democrats were stronger. Party lines were divided and newspapers aligned themselves with their party of choice.

The Democratic presidential candidate, Martin Van Buren, had won in 1836, and followed fellow Democrat Andrew Jackson in not wanting to get involved with states' matters, hence his excuse for not helping Joseph Smith on the Missouri issue, despite the Constitution's call for protection of the peoples' rights.

So along came the Whigs. By 1840 the Whigs had mustered enough power to put William Henry Harrison in office. With a little spin-doctoring in marketing him, the Whigs had taken a Virginia aristocrat and made him look like a rugged frontiersman and Indian fighter, advancing him to the presidency under the slogan "Tippecanoe and Tyler too," the second part referring to his vice-presidential running mate, John Tyler.

The Saints favored the Democrats until Van Buren refused to help them. In state and county elections, the Democrats and Whigs were split 50–50 in a dead heat. But when the Saints went to the polls, it pushed the votes in one direction—and they elected the Whigs. Just before the August elections, candidates from both parties had visited Nauvoo and courted their vote, staying at the newly built Mansion House, which still acted as both Joseph's home and a hotel. (It was built just across the intersection and northeast of the Homestead.)

Once elected, President Harrison lived only one month, so his vice-presidential pick, John Tyler, took over. Unfortunately for the Whigs, President Tyler also proved to be a states' rights advocate, even though he was a Whig. So when fellow Whig Henry Clay submitted bills that made their way through Congress to the President's desk, it came as quite a shock when President Tyler would veto them. People saw the party splitting, resulting in the country going nowhere, so frustrated voters began returning in droves to the Democrats. Arrogantly, the Whigs thought they had the Mormon vote tied up, so their party-affiliated newspapers actually published anti-Mormon newspaper articles.

However, Joseph made it clear they would vote for their friends, and not by the party. On December 20, 1841, the *Times and Seasons* newspaper published his article, "The Prophet on the Attitude of the Saints in Politics." In it he stated: "We care not a fig for Whig or Democrat; they are both alike to us, but we shall go for our friends, our tried friends, and the cause of human liberty, which is the cause of God." He stated they had looked upon President William Harrison as their friend, but of course he was now deceased. He also said the Democrats had been their friends, so they would vote for them now.

This angered the Whigs. And helped heap more bad press against them. Thus, the next phase of anti-Mormon bigotry was actually spurred by politics, much overlooked by historians, including among Latter-day Saints throughout the past 175 years. The *Alton Telegraph and Democratic Review* (ironically a Whig newspaper, despite its title) on June 4, 1842, attacked Joseph for "commanding" the Saints how to vote, simply because he had signed that *Times and Seasons* article as "Lieutenant General of the Legion." The Alton newspaper also claimed Joseph's words "too bold a stride toward despotism." It did not help that in early 1842 Bennett, when he was in good standing, had written a series of articles for the Saints' newspaper. Nor did it help that he had undiplomatically stated in those articles that the Legion was so powerful they could bring justice to enemies and also restore "the inheritance of the Saints." Their neighbors had seen the drilling Legion but had only then begun seeing Bennett's words as acrimonious. On May 17, 1842, the *New York Herald*, in its series of anti-Mormon articles, published a warning by a U.S. Army officer stating that the Legion was led by talented officers, but with religious fanaticism, and would soon be up to 50,000 strong—an outrageous claim, of course. But his next claim was even more far-fetched—that it would be an empire that would "make this country shake to its centre."

This fear was used by the Whigs to denounce the Saints. Joseph Duncan, Illinois' Whig gubernatorial candidate, said he wanted to disarm the Legion and force them to train only with the state militia. He also promised to repeal the Nauvoo city charter. He had been the Democratic governor from 1834–1838, but had defected from the party out of principles and now felt his anti-Mormon stance alone would reelect him. The Whig newspapers would support him by attacking the Saints. On July 2, 1842, the *Alton Telegraph and Democratic Review* warned its readers—twisting Joseph's words—declaring that he alone would decide who would become elected in the state of Illinois. It also proclaimed that all readers should vote against any candidates who sought Mormons votes. On July 9 it published that a few entire southern Illinois towns were pledging votes to the Democrats to offset the bloc of Mormon votes. Another Whig newspaper, the *Sangamo Journal*, on July 8, reprinted the *New York Herald* article that claimed the Saints controlled Illinois politics and might later control U.S. politics. The *Warsaw Signal* now gathered a group of both Whigs and Democrats who would oppose the Saints, and started an anti-Mormon "club."

Sick of the onslaught by their neighbor to the south, Joseph's brother William launched *The Wasp* on April 16, 1842, which was published for about a year and, in defending his brother, he called the *Warsaw Signal's* editor Thomas Sharp a "complete jackass."

C H A P T E R 54

T

o Joseph's consternation, his brother William managed only to throw fuel on the fire. Meanwhile, on July 4, 1842 (the fourth of five Independence Day celebrations that Joseph would enjoy with the Saints in Nauvoo—although they were likely too sick to hold much of a party on the first one!) city visitors were brought in by three steamers from nearby towns and villages to witness the Legion march to the beat of drum and fife and see Joseph in full regalia, complete with feathered hat, as he sat atop his magnificent black horse that pranced to the beat of the band music. The townspeople sat on the ground enjoying the parade.

Adam Snyder, the Democratic candidate for governor of Illinois, suddenly died. They filled the vacancy by nominating Thomas Ford from northern Illinois, the Justice of the State Supreme Court. He was petite and shallow faced, 42 years old, and not particularly charismatic. He admitted that because he had no high ambition, he would be used as a pawn by more powerful figures who would govern through him. These unnamed individuals could have been the later strings—if they existed— that would politically and conspiratorially target Joseph, with Ford himself as the puppet, weak in psychological constitution and allowing it all to happen. Less importantly, Ford also felt he was nominated because no other Democratic candidate for governor would be nominated. Making matters worse for the

Democrats was the fact that the Mormons now backed them, so many voters would vote the opposite way. Ford therefore made the political stance of distancing himself, stating he had no knowledge of or involvement with the Mormons.

The Whig candidate, Joseph Duncan, may have printed thousands of John C. Bennett's statements that attacked Joseph. The purpose of the flyers was to turn people away from whatever candidate the Saints supported—namely, the Democratic candidate, Thomas Ford. A Whig newspaper, the *Alton Telegraph*, on July 23, 1842, boldly brags that Joseph Duncan did indeed push for Bennett's "disclosures" of Joseph Smith.

Ford was nevertheless elected, partially because the Saints turned out for him. However, he credited only the failing economy as the reason for his election, further distancing himself from the Saints.

After the elections the state legislature, which had considered repealing the Nauvoo city charter, changed its mind. It stated the charter was "strikingly similar to the powers and privileges embraced in the charters of the cities of Chicago, Quincy, and Springfield."

Ford was against the Nauvoo, Chicago, Quincy, and Springfield charters, and wanted them reformed rather than repealed, but the legislature had already made its stamp, and he did not have enough power over the legislature to make the changes he would have liked.

Now, with the elections over, John Bennett still attacked Joseph. His next strategy was to get Joseph extradited to Missouri. (Especially since Illinois was doing nothing about it.) And to pull that off he decided to take advantage of an event that occurred on May 6, 1842. Ex-governor Boggs was shot.

Boggs was assaulted while sitting quietly in his library, reading the newspaper. The would-be assassin shot him from behind, through the glass window, putting four lead balls into his head, one of which went into his neck and out the roof of his mouth. Another lodged in his neck muscles, and two others in his left brain lobe. He had been shot with a pepper box revolver.

Boggs, it turns out, had hundreds of political enemies, and for two months the Saints were not even mentioned as suspects. He was running for state senator and owned a newly opened store in Independence. He had made enemies by creating a tight money lending policy that especially hurt farmers. Thousands of angry farmers watched their families suffer and farms dry up and die because they could not get cash loans, and they blamed Boggs for their misfortune. He also reportedly had hundreds of business and personal enemies. A Mr. Tomlinson was first accused, but later released when suddenly they had one of their old enemies to blame . . .

Boggs' son William claimed that the gun used against his father was stolen from his father's store by an African-American. But when Porter Rockwell was reportedly seen about town on a family visit, William conveniently changed his story—saying he believed—without any facts on which to base his assumption—that Porter had done it. Others suddenly claimed there had been a man seen walking about Boggs' house for several days before the attack, and that the stranger—whose face no one saw—was a Mormon.

Porter barely escaped with his life, outracing his pursuers.

John C. Bennett read the newspaper accounts of Boggs' shooting. After some weeks, he came up with an ingenious frame-up. He claimed: 1) that Joseph had made a prophecy a year earlier saying that Boggs would die within a year; 2) that Joseph had hired Porter to fulfill that prophecy; 3) that Porter had told him (Bennett) he was the one who had shot Boggs, 4) that when Porter had gone to Missouri, Joseph told Bennett that Porter had left to "fulfill prophecy"; 5) that Porter was now living high on the hog about Nauvoo, with gold in his pockets and driving an attractive carriage around town (actually Porter had been hired as the cab driver from the steamboat landing to the temple, living very modestly); 6) that Porter had obtained these "sudden riches" by being paid by Joseph a reward of "$500 for any man who would do it"; and 7) that Porter had not told many people about his trip to Missouri (obviously not wanting the Missourians to be forewarned he was coming to visit family). Bennett's claims had several holes in them. Not the least of which is the fact that Joseph was near bankruptcy, as discussed below, and had no money to pay an "assassin."

Porter was so infuriated by Bennett's claims that he went to confront the dissident at a tavern near Carthage. There, Porter told Bennett he offered to whip any man who lied about him, and then Porter flat out denied the charges. Bennett backed down, trying to be diplomatic, saying he was Porter's friend, but Porter did not buy it. While Porter was every bit as rugged as his reputation suggested, he apparently was not an assassin—neither of Boggs nor Bennett, so Porter left, simply outraged by the man's insults and lies.

Joseph wrote the *Warsaw Signal* saying Bennett had lied about the prophecy, and claimed his innocence. When Joseph asked Porter if he had shot Boggs, Porter, who was known as an amazingly accurate shooter, replied in disgust, "What do you mean, did *I* shoot him—he's *still alive*, ain't he?"

C H A P **55** E R

J OHN C. Bennett was relentless in trying to bring down Joseph. He next went to Lilburn Boggs himself to get him to swear out an affidavit against Joseph. On July 20, 1842, Boggs signed it.

Then Bennett went to the new Missouri governor, Thomas Reynolds, with statements by Mormon detractors whom he labeled "the most respectable men" in and around Nauvoo. These men stated Joseph was the "sole cause" of the Boggs shooting.

Missouri's Governor Reynolds then may have filled out an extradition based on Joseph being a fugitive from years earlier. Or, as Joseph believed, it may have been Boggs who went before a judge at Bennett's inciting. In any case, the judge issued the extradition papers.

When Governor Carlin of Illinois received the extradition papers from Missouri on August 2, 1842, he likely mulled over whether or not to return Joseph to Missouri, and then for some unknown reason he signed it. Although he was simply serving out his term and would be replaced by Ford in December 1842, he acted under full authority of his position, having Joseph arrested in order to be taken across the river by Missouri agents.

Six days later, on August 8, 1842, sheriffs (from Missouri and Illinois) found Joseph and Porter Rockwell in Nauvoo and arrested them. By law, the sheriffs had to take them before

JOSEPH SMITH: A BIOGRAPHY | *Richard Lloyd Dewey*

the municipal court in Nauvoo. At their trial Joseph stated he had not been out of state during the previous two years. Using the Nauvoo city charter's power that granted a court the authority to issue a writ of *habeas corpus*, they were freed from the sheriffs. Then the Saints empowered themselves even further: That same day the Nauvoo City Council passed a law giving the municipal court the power to judge how valid every writ that might be served on its citizens was. This infuriated the sheriffs even further, and they galloped away angrily to Governor Carlin.

At that point Joseph escaped to an island in the Mississippi River. And Porter joined him. On this island Joseph advised him to flee for his life and go to Philadelphia to live with a church member. Porter, still having marital strife and fearful of losing his children, made the extremely difficult decision to heed his counsel and leave, which he did the next morning. When they awakened, Joseph hugged him goodbye and pushed him off in his skiff before dawn.

Governor Carlin then sent the sheriffs back to Nauvoo to arrest Joseph and Porter. By this time Porter was on his way east, and no one would tell the sheriffs where Joseph was. Only a few confidants knew his whereabouts.

The sheriffs returned once more to Governor Carlin and reported their failure, adding the postscript that everyone had been polite and seemed cooperative—but the sheriffs couldn't find Joseph.

The *Quincy Whig* reports with quiet indignation: "The Mormons treated the officers with every respect, and offered to assist them if necessary, in fulfilling their duty. The whole affair begins to look exceedingly like a farce."

This obvious ruse being played by the Saints angered both the Illinois and the Missouri governors. But what angered them more was that the Nauvoo city court had defied both states—the court had released the two men with writs of *habeas corpus*.

Carlin, perhaps taking out the frustration of his failed gubernatorial stewardship of the previous four years and the economic disaster into which he had plunged the state (including his inability to collect taxes to cover any of it), decided he could take a stand to rid the state of one last problem. He put up a "wanted poster" and reward for $200 for the arrest of either Porter or Joseph. The Missouri governor, Reynolds, would add another $300, and the total at one point, fueled by the anti-Mormon press and the anger it induced in some of its citizens, added up to $1,300—a genuine fortune for the day.

Rumors hit the locals that Joseph had given them the slip and escaped to Canada, England, or somewhere in Europe. Despite the rumors, the sheriffs kept raiding the town, convinced he was there and that if they simply could endure the smiles, the feigned cooperation, and the wild-goose chases elaborately staged by Nauvoo's citizens, they would prevail.

Joseph meanwhile was ingeniously spirited about town for the next four months from one secret spot to another. In the course of one several-day period, for example, he went to a farm outside the city, to a friend's home in Nauvoo, back to the island camping spot, and then to his beloved home, where a family member was always appointed guard. Joseph had the system down—when the sheriffs would come charging toward the door in a raid, he would race toward the trap door under the stairs and hide until they finished searching. Townspeople saw him traveling on a boat at night, possibly back and forth to his island hideaway, but the sheriffs never heard about it.

Trusted friends brought him food and correspondence, while the church kept sailing foreword with new converts pouring in. When away from home, Emma often visited Joseph, sometimes hounded and followed by the sheriffs, but always able to elude them and meet with her husband. The sheriffs then devised a new strategy—they made a major effort to keep her under constant surveillance. But she would still consistently manage to evade them. Joseph no doubt dealt with the drama well—the secret meetings and signal fires, the late-night travels and diversionary strategies. He reported he was in good spirits. Good indeed, as it may have actually been great sport for him. But at some point he tired of it, and even confided this in a letter to Newel Knight and his family, saying it was a time of affliction for him.

Joseph was touched by the faithfulness of certain friends, brothers, and parents, and by Emma's devotion. "They shall not want a friend while I live," Joseph records in his journal.

Then he learned the state militia might canvas the town to find him. So he made plans to flee the city northward. He wrote Emma on August 16, 1842, asking her to send supplies and clothes by boat with up to 30 of the best men. Their plan, said Joseph, was to "wend their way like larks up the Mississippi," until they found the north country, which would remind them of their home in New England. "Then we will bid defiance to the world, to Carlin, Boggs, Bennett," and the "motley clan that follow in their wake."

Emma wrote back to Joseph the same day, saying she was ready to leave with him. But the trip never materialized. One can imagine the nerve-wracking hours Emma and their friends went through, attempting to protect Joseph. Somehow, either through a spy or by an overheard conversation, Emma learned that Joseph's secret hideout had been discovered. So with no time to send a messenger to him, she and a friend shot across town to Joseph themselves, and found him hiding at the Edward Sayer farm. The two helped Joseph immediately move to his next hideaway—the Carlos Granger home, one mile northeast of town, beside Hyrum's farm. Here Joseph was given his own room.

From there he wrote to the Newel K. Whitney family. He tells them to be careful, even detailing that Newel should walk ahead of the others a little way, then knock at the southeast corner window near the cornfield. He then tells them to burn his letter as soon as they read it. "Keep all [this] locked up in your breasts; my life depends upon it." Joseph would later write that he appreciated Newell's faithfulness during that period. He would also state that Newel was among the friends he trusted. Joseph mentions in his journal how close he felt to Newel, particularly for his warm heart and his anxiousness about Joseph's welfare. Joseph describes himself now as "cast out and hated of almost all men." He adds, "Brother Whitney, thou knowest not how strong those ties are that bind my soul and heart to thee."

The next month Joseph had to escape to safety again.

On the night of September 2, 1842, Joseph learned of pursuers on his trail. So he, John Taylor, and two others planned an escape to John Taylor's father's home. They took a circuitous route to throw off the pursuers. Joseph then sent the others back to the city for news. While waiting, Joseph hunted in the woods for three days with William, John Taylor's brother. William asked Joseph if he was frightened with "all those hounding wolves" after him. Joseph responded that he knew the Lord would protect him, "and I have full confidence in his word."

Joseph would spend two weeks near the Henderson River at the Taylor's farm. William Clayton journeyed there to take Joseph's dictation, including Section 128 of the *Doctrine and Covenants*, which was then titled an "Epistle to the Church," regarding the doctrine of baptism for the dead, "as that subject seems to occupy my mind, and press itself upon my feelings the strongest since I have been pursued by my enemies." Within the revelation was a quote from John in Revelation 20:12 of the Bible. This would become a fundamental precept of Latter-day Saint doctrine that would, like a compass, guide the daily lives of the faithful through the years to come, giving them hope, inspiration, and direction:

"And I saw the dead, small and great, stand before God; and the books were opened; and another book was opened, which is the book of life; and the dead were judged out of those things which were written in the books, according to their works."

Emma loved Joseph and worked in his behalf, including writing Governor Carlin. On September 7, 1842, the governor wrote her back, slamming the Nauvoo court as an "intolerable usurpation of power." That response did not settle well with the determined Emma, so she wrote him again, setting him "straight." So the governor wrote back again—in fact several times, and finally admitted his admiration of her talent and judgment. He even expressed his surprise at her talents and judgment, but still he would not relent.

Governor Carlin was meanwhile taunted by the press for not being able to apprehend Joseph. The *Niles National Register* on October 1, 1842, and the *Warsaw Signal* on September 17, 1842, castigated the governor as well as Joseph, whom they claimed placed himself *above the law*, a catchphrase for the anti-Mormon press over the years to come.

By late September 1842, Joseph was still in hiding, but was now at his own residence, caring for Emma. She was ill with a fever. He thought she would die and was in tremendous distress over her. While not a practice in later years, she was baptized twice on October 5, 1842, to relieve her of physical discomfort. That night she worsened, but eventually began to improve. In 15 days she was walking again, but her road to health was slow, and she had numerous relapses.

Joseph's hiding adventures lasted a total of four months— from August 11, 1842, until mid-December.

Still not successful in taking Joseph down, John C. Bennett determined to find yet *another way to bury him.*

J OSEPH had given his all to the kingdom, but in the process was financially destroyed—much of his resources going to pay attorneys through the years, as heretofore stated. In consequence of these difficulties, he was forced to declare bankruptcy to free himself from the overwhelming debts that had accumulated. The National Bankruptcy Act, which went into law February 1, 1842, became his only way out. Joseph was bothered by the idea of declaring bankruptcy, but "I was forced into the measure by having been robbed, mobbed, plundered and wasted of all my property, time after time, in various places." So on April 14, 1842, he asked a Quincy lawyer to come to Nauvoo to talk with him about it. Four days later he, Hyrum, and Samuel went to Carthage to attest to their insolvency before the clerk at the county commissioner's court. By July 15, 1842, they were joined in bankruptcy by Sidney Rigdon and several other church leaders, as reported in Springfield's *Sangamo Journal*, with a statement that creditors must appear at the district court in Springfield on October 1, 1842, to prove why the men seeking bankruptcy should not be discharged from their debts.

One such debt was a promissory note for $4,866.38 for a steamboat Joseph and Hyrum had co-signed for on September 1, 1840. It had been bought from the U.S. Government by a Mormon businessman, Peter Haws, and several others, whom Joseph and Hyrum co-signed for. Several weeks after the boat had been bought, it was wrecked. The pilots, who likely had been guilty, disappeared. Peter Haws also fled, leaving Joseph and the others who had no money to pay the first note when it came due the following spring. A second note for the same amount was signed by three others who refused to pay it because the boat was damaged. The government wanted its money back and soon won a judgment in court against Joseph and other church leaders in June 1842.

A different sort of person then came into Joseph's life—who would later turn himself from current "enemy" to future "friend." He was Justin Butterfield, the U.S. Attorney for Illinois. For now he was Joseph's enemy, and fought against his bankruptcy, but later would defend Joseph's interests, detailed below. The reason Butterfield opposed Joseph was his fear that the judgment for the steamboat would be lost, and he was acting in behalf of the best interests of the U.S. Government. All others who had signed the loan were now insolvent, leaving Joseph and Hyrum his only hopes to get the steamboat loan repaid. But in trying to win a judgment against them, he had gone too far—being influenced by Joseph's old nemesis . . .

John C. Bennett.

Seeing Joseph applying for bankruptcy, Bennett decided to throw himself into the fray once again to harass and discredit Joseph. He wrote at least three letters to the *Sangamo Journal* on the matter. On July 15, 1842, he wrote the third letter, saying Joseph had hidden assets, and he accused Joseph of fraud, maintaining he used the bankruptcy act to not pay debts while he had the resources to, and claiming Joseph was personally benefiting from and misusing the bankruptcy act. Bennett then invented a list of details to substantiate his claim. Butterfield asked the Solicitor of the Treasury, C. B. Penrose, for authorization to check out the matter, using Bennett's newspaper letter as the reason.

Bennett also accused Joseph of transferring 230 city lots from Emma and himself to himself as trustee-in-trust for the church, which was legal, but Bennett says that fraud was involved because of the date on which Joseph had made

*Richard Lloyd Dewey* | JOSEPH SMITH: A BIOGRAPHY

the transfer—which he claims was the same day Joseph had declared his assets at the Carthage court—April 18, 1842. Joseph, however, claimed to have transferred them on October 5, 1841, six months earlier, which would have been the required legal amount of time, but Bennett claimed Joseph's October 5 date was fictitious. However, historical records show Joseph did indeed make the transfer on that October 1841 date.

One reason Joseph had made the transfer was because church leaders had become nervous that Joseph and other leaders had mingled church affairs with private ones, and it was a wiser accounting move to separate the two. One historian cites the example of Joseph, Hyrum, and Sidney using their personal credit to buy land from the Hotchkiss group for the settlement of the Saints. So, at the beginning of the year 1841, they began separating the two. Thus, on January 30, 1841, Joseph was appointed sole trustee-in-trust for the church. While a wise idea on the surface, for real estate it was a bad decision. Six years earlier an Illinois state law had been passed forbidding religious organizations from owning more than 10 acres. To compound the problem they were getting themselves into, when the Apostles returned from England in the summer of 1841, they transferred all the deeds they held in behalf of the church over to Joseph as trustee-in-trust.

Butterfield, the U.S. Attorney, saw the discrepancy. He knew Illinois state law. He could not let the church keep more than the allowed 10 acres, so he decided to sell off the Saints' 230 city lots (amounting to 300 acres) to pay for the government's judgment against the church regarding the steamboat loan. Butterfield therefore finally officially opposed Joseph and Hyrum's bankruptcy by filing an objection to the court on October 1, 1842, and the court set a hearing for December 15, 1842. He was confident he would stop them from obtaining their bankruptcy discharge.

At court Butterfield echoed Bennett's accusations point by point, possibly believing Bennett, possibly not, but using his argument nonetheless just to win the case. He wished merely to stop Joseph's bankruptcy so that his "client," his employer—the

U.S. Government—would be repaid in some fashion for the steamboat. That repayment, of course, would not happen if Joseph succeeded in getting his bankruptcy discharge. So Butterfield tried to prove to the court that Joseph had concealed assets and had made improper property transfers in order to come out ahead using the bankruptcy act. But the judge ruled against Butterfield. Joseph, in fact, had probably not even known of the bankruptcy law when he had made the transfers in October 1841, as the new law was never even mentioned in Nauvoo newspapers, journals, or minutes of meetings until two months after it went into effect, February 1, 1842. Once again, time demonstrated that Joseph's financial intentions were evidently honorable.

Joseph was still in hiding during this period, in order to keep from being arrested and extradited back to Missouri on the charge of conspiring to murder Lilburn Boggs. So he likely did not even attend the court hearing on December 15 in Springfield regarding his bankruptcy, although his delegates did. Hyrum received his bankruptcy discharge on December 16, 1842, and an arrangement was made with Butterfield to grant Joseph his discharge—but that was delayed until Butterfield could write to the office in Washington to have it granted.

However, Butterfield may have either changed his mind or been duplicitous with Joseph, because two days after the December 15 hearing, Butterfield wrote Penrose, obviously still planning to oppose Joseph, since Penrose wrote back to Butterfield suggesting that Butterfield stop opposing the bankruptcy. The reason Penrose wrote was because church leaders proposed paying a third of the debt in cash immediately and the remainder in four annual payments, with the deal backed by a real estate mortgage.

On May 25, 1843, Butterfield wrote Penrose again—this time to learn if the church leaders' offer would work. Nothing happened for a year. Then legal actions were drawn out for over a decade. But Bennett's fraud charges were never substantiated. Eventually the courts would rule that the church-owned property of over 10 acres was subject to a lien, and three foreclosure sales were held. Finally it was all settled on July 17, 1852, for $11,148.35, with only a small portion—$4,866.38—going for the steamboat, and the rest for typically outrageous attorney fees and interest on the 1842 judgment, with a small portion left over for Emma.

John C. Bennett nevertheless harassed Joseph all the way through bankruptcy, continuing to injure him with charges of fraud, not to mention the humiliation Joseph already felt in not being able to pay his debts. At the same time, Bennett was trying to get his own book published to "expose" Joseph. So he went to the lecture circuit in New York City to publicize his story in hopes of luring a publisher. James Gordon Bennett considered it for a while, but rejected the book when John C. Bennett insisted on including obscene engraved pictures.

Bennett did, however, find a publisher in Boston who agreed to publish it, excluding the pictures. Before the end of 1842, the book was published as *The History of the Saints; or an Exposé of Joe Smith and the Mormons*. The self-promoting was obvious, in which Bennett attached a label underneath a portrait of himself as "Gen. John C. Bennett, Doctor of Medicine." He "modestly" posed for the picture like Napoleon, in dress uniform with his right hand inside the buttons of his jacket. He also claims he joined the Saints merely to expose them and, in further "modesty," to save the government of the United States.

He immediately began touring with his book. And went straight to Illinois. He distributed flyers all over Alton, stating he would lecture to only gentlemen in the courthouse, charging 12 cents a head. He also went to St. Louis, where Joseph's land agent, Isaac Galland—even Isaac Galland—was mortified to hear Bennett's outrageous claims, and so wrote Joseph concerning them, stating that Bennett lied about everything Galland knew about. The kicker was when Bennett lambasted the Illinois state legislature for giving arms to the Nauvoo Legion and for passing the charter—*which Bennett himself had lobbied for* and, as the quartermaster general of the state militia, *had made the arming of the Legion his own special project*. The irony didn't escape Galland.

First came Bennett's book, then Bennett's lectures, and
finally Bennett's counterfeiting of phony commissions for
the Nauvoo Legion. For some odd reason, possibly to create
confusion, he falsified documents and distributed them to show
the appointment of new officers.

John C. Bennett knew he was lying left and right. James
Arlington Bennett confided to Joseph on September 1, 1842,
that John C. Bennett had told him there was no way an honest
jury would find anything against Joseph in the Boggs case. Then
James Bennett, Joseph's confidant, advised him to stay out of
Missouri anyway because of the intense hatred against him.

Thomas Ford took over office of governor in December 1842.
Joseph was still in hiding. Through the grapevine Joseph heard
that Justin Butterfield believed he could not be legally taken
by Missouri authorities. The reason? The crime took place in
Missouri while Joseph was in Illinois. So Joseph got his hopes
up. He sent Sidney and other church leaders to persuade Ford
to strip away Missouri's "requisition order." Ford thought it
over. Then announced his decision. He said he could not do it
because it would be interfering with the work of the previous
governor of Illinois, whose place he was taking.

Butterfield told Joseph the governor was right. But in a
twist of new hope for Joseph, he told him to go to Springfield
to stand trial, and that if he would, the State Supreme Court
judges would all free him under the laws of *habeas corpus*. Then,
in a friendly manner, Judge James Adams wrote Joseph, telling
him to gallop off to the court "without delay."

Four days before the end of 1842, Joseph set out for Springfield
with borrowed money and a coterie of friends. They arrived three
days later (after stopping to see friends and family, including
his brother Samuel at Plymouth, Illinois). At Springfield the
first stop he made was to see Justin Butterfield, his antagonist
through the entire bankruptcy ordeal. Now Butterfield was,
ironically, not only his proponent but his friend. So they went
over details of the trial that was to take place January 4, 1843.
Between the time Joseph visited Butterfield and the day of his
court, Joseph met with Thomas Ford and other state officials—

including senators, judges, and generals, who confessed their pleasant surprise at his demeanor and charming personality. He also met with church members in their homes.

On New Year's Day 1843, his people were given the Representatives' Hall to use as they saw fit. Orson Hyde taught the restored gospel at services that were attended by state dignitaries.

The day of the trial finally came. When Judge Pope entered the packed courthouse, he did so with ladies on both sides, probably as a ruse to poke fun at the polygamist prophet. Butterfield, possessing the ability of one-upmanship, won immediate points for Joseph with his opening: "It is a momentous occasion in my life to appear before the Pope, in defense of a Prophet of God, in the presence of all these angels." Meanwhile, he nodded toward the judge's ladies, then bowed in all directions right on cue. After the laughter subsided, Butterfield got down to business—he skillfully and logically pointed out that Lilburn Boggs had not shown in his affidavit that Joseph was charged with any crime and, furthermore, that the governor of Missouri had no jurisdiction in Illinois and could not order Joseph out of Illinois and back to Missouri.

On January 5, 1843, they returned to a courtroom filled with a respectable element of society, who were all for Joseph's acquittal. Judge Pope gave his opinion, which agreed completely with Butterfield's defense. The bottom line, he pointed out, was that, "This case presents the important question arising under the Constitution and laws of the United States, whether a citizen of the state of Illinois can be transported from his own state to the state of Missouri, to be tried for a crime, which, if he ever committed, was committed in the state of Illinois."

Pope read Boggs' affidavit. It claimed Joseph was an accessory to the crime before it was committed. Pope announced he had affidavits showing Joseph was in Illinois when Boggs was shot. He then pronounced, "As it is not charged that the crime was committed by Smith in Missouri, the governor of Illinois could not cause him to be removed to that state." He addressed the legality of anyone—while still in Illinois, who violates the law in another state—being subject to prosecution in Illinois, not in the other state. Pope then blasted Boggs as presenting no facts, only his "opinion" that Joseph was guilty. He concluded, "Mr. Boggs' opinion, then, is not authority. Let an order be entered that Smith be discharged from his arrest."

Freed and exuberant, Joseph and his party immediately obtained copies of the court transcript and, the very next day, marched over to Governor Ford's office to have them certified. Ford gave him a warning, an ominous one from the newly elected chief executive: "Refrain from all political electioneering." Ford, finding himself in the game of power and puppetry, knew the forces pulling his own strings and wanted Joseph out of the way.

The next morning, January 7, 1843, Joseph and his group shot off for Nauvoo through snow and slush, still elated. Willard Richards and Wilson Law then wrote the *Jubilee Song*, which they sang that night in high spirits on the road.

Back in Nauvoo, Joseph and Emma threw a party. This was actually a week later, and Joseph handed out printed cards with the "Jubilee Song" and another song written by Eliza R. Snow. The 70-plus guests sang with gusto and ate cheerily. Brigham was back in health, after a difficult sickness, and attended the party. Joseph and Emma served the food themselves; then they announced it was their 15th wedding anniversary.

Noticeably absent was Joseph's friend, Porter Rockwell, who was still in Philadelphia, lonely, missing his children, and unable to find work. He undoubtedly imagined Joseph holding parties in his absence, and such thoughts would have made him miss the society of the Saints even more. Joseph cared deeply about his friend and, though he himself was freed from being extradited to Missouri by Illinois sheriffs for now, Porter was still high on the wanted list and could not return. But Porter was anxious to return to family and friends, so he wrote Joseph. No record exists as to what Joseph told him upon writing back, but it was probably to remain in the East until the cold winds of extradition blew over sufficiently that he would be forgotten by Illinois sheriffs.

The sheriffs were still making trips to the city to see if Porter was back, but their trips were becoming less regular, so Porter was likely told that he just had to wait till he got the go-ahead to return, and that it would probably be just a few months away. He did stay with an Armstrong family in Philadelphia, who said he protected the Saints there, but he apparently became so discouraged with not finding work—and so lonely—that he finally decided to take off for Nauvoo in February 1843, hoping no one would nab him. . . .

In March 1843 Porter went down the Eerie Canal by barge, across several states on foot, and up the Mississippi River by steamboat. At St. Louis, Missouri, the boat stopped. Porter, rather than staying aboard, decided to disembark in St. Louis.

And that was his undoing.

CHAPTER 57

A bounty hunter spotted Porter and took him at gun-point. He then called for the sheriff and watched Porter get hauled off to jail. After a short stint there, he was taken aboard a stagecoach to Jefferson City, then to Independence where a mob awaited his arrival. The sheriff, Reynolds, held them at bay while Porter was escorted through the armed and angry crowd into the jailhouse.

And there, he languished.

Meanwhile, Joseph got word of Porter's capture and was distraught. He knew Porter would be treated like an animal, just as he had, with chains and horrid food. Joseph borrowed $100, a substantial sum for the time, to secure a top attorney for Porter. He wrote Justin Butterfield and James Arlington Bennet of New York. "Rockwell is innocent," said Joseph, "and must be defended." The two men did not take the case, but Alexander Doniphan in Missouri, purely as a stroke of luck—or a blessing, in Porter's case—drew Porter's name in the draw of free defense assignments, and Porter landed him. Later, Doniphan was paid for his efforts, although legally he did not have to be. Butterfield, in writing Joseph and declaring he could not take the case, stated his regrets, but still helped Porter and Joseph by giving detailed instructions—he said to find a respected lawyer and check out John C. Bennett's past to undermine his character as a witness against Porter.

Porter was hauled into a wild, rip-roaring courtroom that one could mistake for a saloon. The townspeople were soused and heated, and they practically threw themselves into a riot when the judge declared Porter was not guilty of shooting Lilburn Boggs.

But for political reasons Porter was taken back to jail to sit for several additional weeks, living miserably, being told he was there for his own good. However, the real reason for his incarceration came to light when Sheriff Reynolds offered him a high-on-the-hog lifestyle the remainder of his life, if he would act as bait. Reynolds told Porter to write Joseph to come get him, then they would nab Joseph. For that, Porter would be freed and set up for life. Porter considered his offer for all of one second, then swore at him.

The political forces would not free him, and held him illegally for additional weeks. Seeing no end in sight, he attempted an escape. This he did by befriending another prisoner but, because of his well-known, bigger-than-average heart, he could not pull it off—just as he was about to escape, with a free shot to the nearby woods, he noticed his jail buddy could not keep up with him, so Porter went back to help him. Together they were nabbed by the mob. Porter was now faced with the charge of escaping jail.

Alexander Doniphan wanted a change of venue so he could get a fairer trial. So Porter was taken, with mobs attempting to ambush him and his two guards in the night woods, all the way to Liberty. Once there, Porter was taken to Liberty Jail, the same dungeon in which he had visited Joseph.

With the Missouri political forces unwilling to even set a trial date, Porter sat additional weeks and finally attempted another escape. Crawling his way through a stovepipe hole one night, he scratched his body badly, but made it to the jail's lobby after several hours. Then exhausted and finding himself locked in from the outside, he fell asleep and was caught the next morning.

It was now June 1843 and Joseph was still worried sick over his tried and true friend. But life for the Saints was generally booming. Joseph saw Nauvoo prospering, immigrants still pouring in, commerce expanding, new shops and factories opening almost weekly, brick homes and large frame houses now outnumbering the log cabins, and farms and gardens flourishing like one would imagine in Eden. Missionaries were now heading out to even more exotic locales across the globe—Russia and the Society Islands in Polynesia—to bring in even more converts. The temple was rising higher and higher and now could be seen from miles around and across the Mississippi. On the first of June the city decided to buy a ferry boat to transport passengers across the Mississippi. The next day they actually made the purchase, with Joseph as half owner; she was called *Maid of Iowa*. On June 3, 1843, his friends and family boarded her and set out for Quincy, a band on board providing the music.

This short period of peace in his life—the first half of 1843—was the last. To some extent it ended in March 1843 when Porter was captured, which caused him significant worry. But his own problems mostly began the second week of June 1843.

At that time, Joseph's faithful friend Elias Higbee died of a fever. It was he who had gone to Washington with Joseph and had never deviated in his loyalty. Emma became terribly sick the same day, after already being ill many other days since moving to Nauvoo.

And then John C. Bennett attacked him again. This time through an old Jackson County enemy whom Bennett incited to write Governor Ford in Illinois. On June 10, 1843, this contact of Bennett's wrote Ford, saying that the Daviess County circuit court in Missouri had issued an indictment against Joseph for treason, and that papers were on their way from Missouri's Governor Reynolds to Governor Ford in Illinois requesting Ford to give Joseph up to the Missouri agent.

Ford talked with Judge James Adams of Springfield, Joseph's secret ally, and persuaded him to issue the writ of arrest. Moments later Adams turned around and secretly sent Hyrum a communique to warn him. Hyrum got it the very next day. Hyrum, knowing his brother was about to be arrested out of town, had to get word to Joseph to avoid the officers. Joseph was now actually with Emma, heading off to visit her sister, Mrs. Wasson, near Dixon, Iowa, a several-day journey from Nauvoo.

So Hyrum sent William Clayton and Stephen Markham to warn Joseph, and they left that night. They rode night and day, only stopping to sleep a couple hours and eat a quick meal, covering 212 miles in 66 hours. Finally they reached the Wassons' before dark on June 21. But they were too late.

They learned Joseph had just gone to Dixon proper to teach the gospel. At the point of exhaustive collapse, Clayton and Markham rode furiously forward, trying to catch up with Joseph before the Missouri authorities did.

They found Joseph on the road to Dixon. Joseph confidently stated "in the name of Israel's God" that the "Missourians cannot hurt me." But he agreed to turn back toward the Wassons'. He then sent William Clayton ahead for news. As Clayton rode forward a few miles, he passed two officers—Sheriff Reynolds from Missouri and the Carthage, Illinois, constable—but did not recognize them—they were disguised and rode right past Clayton undetected. The two authorities were shrewd. They had gone to Dixon, had hired a wagon in which to carry their prisoner once they snared him, and had told a church member there that they were Mormon elders looking for Joseph. The unsuspecting church member knew where Joseph was—so he sent the constables there—to the Wassons'.

It was 2 P.M. The Wassons and Smiths were at dinner when the two authorities knocked at the door. One of the Wassons answered. The sheriffs told her that they were elders, and asked for Joseph. Joseph just happened to be outside, not knowing the authorities were at the door. He was crossing the yard heading for the barn when Constable Wilson spotted him. Joseph looked up just as the two authorities were rushing to him. They pounced on him with pistol barrels and pressed their cocked weapons against his body.

According to his journal, Joseph said, "What is the meaning of all this?"

Sheriff Reynolds yelled, "I'll show you the meaning, by G--; and if you stir one inch, I'll shoot you, G--d--- you." Joseph's response was—go ahead and shoot.

CHAPTER 58

JOSEPH was tired of living. He was tired of the oppression. He demanded to see their legal papers. They did not serve him papers, as they did not have them yet, but they forced him into their wagon at gunpoint. Technically, this was a kidnaping.

Seeing the fray, Stephen Markham shot out of the house, ready to attack the authorities, who shouted at him to halt or they'd kill him.

The two sheriffs aimed their pistols back at Joseph again. Markham then dashed for the horses and grabbed their bits. The officers again threatened to shoot Markham, who, seeing rescuing Joseph was hopeless, knew Joseph could catch his death in the chilly night air, especially on a long journey, so, according to Joseph's journal, Markham yelled back, "No law on earth requires a sheriff to take a prisoner without clothes!" While Markham kept a hold on the horses, which blocked him from the authorities' aim, Emma ran out with Joseph's coat and hat. Joseph then yelled for Markham to ride to Dixon and tell the sheriff he was being kidnaped.

With Joseph sitting between the constables, he was taken at gunpoint the eight miles to Dixon, their pistols poking his ribs forcefully enough that his skin was bruised black.

At Dixon Joseph continued to be mistreated. His two captors refused to let him meet with an attorney or receive any guests. He was locked in a room of a tavern, where he threw open a window and shouted to a passerby that he was being held prisoner. Immediately, two attorneys from Quincy tried to visit him, but had the door slammed in their faces. This rose the ire of the Dixon citizens, who became indignant that a respectable Illinois citizen was being treated this way by a Missouri "puke," be he a lawman or not. So the hotel owner and his friends gathered outside the door, yelling to the two authorities that Joseph deserved justice. Caving under the pressure, the two authorities let the two Quincy attorneys in. Upon interviewing Joseph, the two lawyers immediately sent for Cyrus H. Walker, a noted attorney who was visiting the area and running for Congress. Joseph simultaneously ordered William Clayton to take the steamer to Nauvoo to summon Hyrum's help.

Stephen Markham then charged away in the night, heading straight for the justice of the peace and, upon finding him, swore out a complaint that the two authorities had threatened Joseph and himself. He also swore that the Carthage constable, Wilson, had turned Joseph over to the care of Sheriff Reynolds of Missouri, who was about to illegally take Joseph to Missouri. Because of Markham's complaints, the Lee County sheriff marched down to the tavern and arrested Joseph's two captors.

When the noted attorney Cyrus Walker arrived to visit Joseph, the master in chancery arrived as well, and issued a writ of *habeas corpus*, having it served on Reynolds and Wilson. He said they would have to appear before the judge at Ottawa. Meanwhile, Cyrus Walker spoke with Joseph and told him he would not help him unless he would vote for him. Walker then told Markham, "I am now sure of my election, as Joseph Smith has promised me his vote." But what followed, while a ringing victory for Joseph in the short run, ended up turning the state's populace against him even more than Bennett's rantings. And again it dealt with politics.

The two officers who had kidnaped Joseph now found themselves under custody of the Lee County sheriff. The local justice of the peace then lectured them, but allowed them to be released on bail. Strangely, he entrusted Joseph to their care again, but demanded they appear before the judge at Ottawa for the writ that the master in chancery had issued upon them. Reynolds was doubtlessly tempted to just go ahead and haul Joseph across the river, but that would have left the Carthage constable hanging to face the political consequences alone. One can only image the conflict, argumentation, debates, and subtle, if not overt, threats that took place between the two, but Wilson won out, and Reynolds stuck to the judge's mandate and headed toward Ottawa to see the judge, Joseph in tow.

Along the way they stopped at Pawpaw Grove, where the two authorities confined Joseph again, this time in a hotel room, allowing no visitors, apparently not learning their lesson. Meanwhile, Emma and the children returned to Nauvoo, learning of Joseph's ordeal.

At Pawpaw Grove word got out of the illegal detention, and a crowd assembled early the next morning, demanding to see Joseph and actually wanting to hear him preach. Sheriff Reynolds yelled at them to leave, but they refused. One old handicapped local, lacking use of one leg, pounded his cane on the wooden floor and yelled, "Stand off, you puke!" Then the old citizen told the two officers that their townspeople had a committee that would hear their case (instead of the judge at Ottawa) and would give them no appeal—apparently the threat of a lynching. The two officers stood back, once again mouths agape, as Joseph stepped outside. He taught the crowd for an hour and a half, asking them what they would like to hear about. When they answered, "marriage," he spoke about God's law of marriage. He felt his freedom began from that hour.

Fortunately for Joseph, he had friends racing about. The first problem they faced, however, was that the Ottawa judge was out of town, so they galloped off to Dixon where they got another writ and, while obtaining it, they overcame all future similar problems with this clever move: Stephen Markham had the document worded as returnable before the *nearest judge*.

On June 25, 1843, a messenger galloped into Nauvoo and told Hyrum of Joseph's plight. Hyrum did not know where Joseph and his captors were, and feared the worst. He quickly assembled a crowd on the city green and announced to them, panic-stricken, that Joseph was captured. He called for volunteers to find Joseph. So many stepped forward that it brought tears to his eyes. Over 300 brethren enthusiastically volunteered, and they immediately went to work. Fifty men were divided into small groups to begin the search. One large group of 75 set sail on the *Maid of Iowa* to check out boats on the Illinois River, in case Joseph had been taken captive on one headed for Missouri. While Dan Jones captained the crew of the search vessel, brothers Wilson and William Law set forth in a gallop with 175 others who rode out in different directions searching for Joseph. Wilson was a general in the Legion, and both were recent converts from Canada who would play heavily into Joseph's future. It took two days, but one squad finally found Joseph. Upon their discovery, Joseph broke out in tears, then said, "I am not going to Missouri this time! These are my boys!"

Two days later William and Wilson Law, with 60 of their group, also came upon Joseph. The Law brothers jumped off their horses, ran to Joseph, and joyously kissed him on the cheek. The consternation of the two officers who were escorting Joseph must have been substantial, especially when they suddenly overheard the Mormons plotting a move that would essentially end in the checkmate of the constables.

The checkmate went like this—Joseph's friends began galloping through the countryside as messengers, and others began showing up in droves to see how they could help. From their journals it is evident they had no intention of interfering, but wanted to make certain that Joseph was not suddenly spirited across the Mississippi by Reynolds. So as Joseph planned the long trip to Quincy, a 260-mile journey, he was accompanied by not only his friends and lawyers, but local curiosity seekers—all of whom planned to make the arduous journey with, of course, the two officers, who were becoming increasingly frustrated. Joseph's plan was to appear before Judge Stephen A. Douglas. He then hired a stagecoach, with the two officers riding among him and his friends, and the group rolled out on the morning of June 26, 1843. No more would he receive bruised ribs from being poked by pistol barrels.

Joseph suddenly realized something: the writ stated they could appear before "the nearest judge," so he informed his lawyers, and told them there happened to be a town—with a judge—closer than Quincy, which therefore was the closest place a writ of *habeas corpus* could be presented. Reynolds and Wilson saw the blade dropping as Joseph uttered the name of the town . . . Nauvoo.

He then announced that was where they were going next.

The two officers shouted objections—but found themselves having their horses turned around and headed back toward Nauvoo. Seeing the officers literally quaking from fear and anger, Joseph declared to them they should relax—they'd be treated better than they had treated him. Joseph took a break from the distressing events and entered a game of stick pulling—a game of strength and finesse—where "I pulled up with one hand the strongest man that could be found."

So onward they rode, Joseph as the prisoner of the two officers and the two officers as the prisoners of the Lee County Sheriff. All being escorted by the off-duty Nauvoo Legionnaires. Joseph, thrilled with the procession and entertained by the officer's angst, sent a messenger into the city to prepare for their arrival. His Legionnaires, meanwhile, were ordered to treat the two constables with the greatest kindness and hospitality.

The next day at noon, June 30, 1843, Joseph's strange entourage entered the outskirts of the city to a cheering throng. Hyrum, Emma, and a procession of carriages and wagons were heading out to meet him, with the accompaniment of music. The Nauvoo brass band was chosen for Joseph's triumphant return. The incoming volunteers who were accompanying Joseph placed prairie flowers in the bridles of their horses. Old Charley, Joseph's favorite horse, was then led out and he mounted the steed.

Throngs lined both sides of the street as he rode, with Emma beside him on another horse. The band played, "Hail, Columbia," and the thousands of people threw flowers at Joseph. It was a sight his two arresting officers, wishing they had never seen, would likely never forget. But that wasn't the end of it.

Cannons began firing and guns shot into the air. The cheering
became a roar, and the crowd followed him down the street to
his home. Arriving there, Joseph climbed on the side of a well
and began swinging his hat with one hand while holding a post
with the other as he called out, "I am thankful to the God of
Israel who has delivered me out of the hands of the Missourians
once more." People began crying for joy. Joseph's arresting
officers, overwhelmed with the spectacle but no longer shaking,
believed Joseph would keep his word and treat them well. But
their fear quickly turned to anger. Especially when, seeing the
crowd's adoration of Joseph, they realized the crowd was not
dispersing. The throngs of admirers and friends simply refused
to leave. Finally Joseph dispersed his friends and promised to
talk to them later near the temple at the grove.

An hour later at 1 P.M., 50 of Joseph's closest friends were
seated at dinner in the Mansion House, being served by Emma.
Joseph, keeping his word, wishing to either show he was above
his captors or, as a display of his subtle wit, placed the two
officers at the head of the table.

The people of Nauvoo then sent the citizens of Pawpaw
Grove, Dixon, and Lee County their sincere appreciation for
the "firm patriotism" they showed in adhering to constitutional
rights by protecting Joseph from Sheriff Reynolds.

Waiting for his hearing to be held at the Nauvoo Municipal
court the next morning, Joseph received permission from his
captors to talk to the crowds. At 5 P.M. the same day he arrived,
Joseph spoke to 10,000 people gathered in the grove. He held
them mesmerized with the account of his capture and rescue.
He excitedly told the audience, "I am well—I am hearty . . . I
feel strong as a giant." Of his captors he said: "They took me
unlawfully, treated me rigorously, strove to deprive me of my
rights, and would have run with me into Missouri to have been
murdered, if Providence had not interposed." He then told them
he would spill all his blood before being taken captive again.
"To bear it any longer would be a sin, and I will not bear it any
longer. Shall we bear it any longer?" There was, like thunder,
an uproarious, "No!"

He reminded the assembly: "The municipal court has all the power to issue and determine writs of *habeas corpus* within the limits of this city," and the city "has all the power that the state courts have, and was given [it] by the same authority—the legislature." Thus, Joseph believed in the power of city rights, especially if granted by a state legislature. Because it was so granted, he believed it was legal.

As he finished his discourse, Joseph had the noted attorney Cyrus Walker come to the podium. He told the crowd that his assessment of the Nauvoo city charter was that it held the power to try writs of *habeas corpus.*

The next day, July 1, 1843, Joseph went to court. Much testimony about Joseph's recent capture and the history of the Saints' problems with Missouri was heard. Joseph was discharged because the warrant was weak, the court stating it lacked substance.

Joseph's dismissal was legal and fair. But his enemies—both political and religious—would twist things, pronouncing that the municipal court should not undo an order issued by the state. But both Cyrus Walker and his congressional opponent, Joseph P. Hoge, agreed that Nauvoo did in fact possess such power. Ford disagreed, but shortsightedly did not look past the precedents of the charters already issued for Springfield and elsewhere that also granted a city such power, as stated earlier, and he in fact castigated the two lawyers running for office, saying they should have known better, even though Hoge was a member of his own party. Ford claimed they were both seeking the Mormon vote rather than acting out of integrity, but Ford himself was likely the puppet of greater political forces, so his position to criticize did not come from one of strength.

(Later, on December 8, 1843, the city council would make itself even more powerful by passing a city ordinance that stated any officer from outside the city who entered Nauvoo with a writ for Joseph's arrest would be subject to life imprisonment in the city jail, if it was based on the Missouri charges. And not even the governor could pardon him, unless approved by the mayor—Joseph himself. This was actually all within the

legal scope and powers of the city charter granted by the state
legislature.)

(On December 12, 1843, the council backed up the mayor's
power even further by passing an ordinance that required
each and every warrant issued in Nauvoo to be signed by the
mayor.)

Because of political and religious enemies who would
ballyhoo the situation, turning it into a critique of Nauvoo, the
statewide populace began to grow in resentment. Even the same
non-Saint citizens who had dismissed the anti-Saint newspaper
tirades going on for months in the *Warsaw Signal*, the *Alton
Telegraph*, the *Quincy Whig,* and others (as evidenced by their
warm reception of Joseph at Dixon and Pawpaw Grove, and
helping to protect Joseph from the two arresting officers there
just five months earlier) were now losing faith in the Saints. So
with the political and religious enemies in full throttle, people
who had been disinterested or leery of the one-sided press
attacks against the Saints were now reading the papers more
seriously, allowing their resentment of the Saints to fester, even
to the point of fear, and eventually hatred.

Despite the fact that these two new city ordinances were
meant to insure the Saints greater protection from Bennett and
Boggs, the public outcry against them by the citizens of Illinois
was so great that the city council would repeal the ordinances
on February 12, 1844.

Meanwhile, the state legislature refused to repeal the Nauvoo
charter, possibly because of the hypocrisy that would have
entailed while leaving other similar city charters in place, and
also in part because of political aspirations—the legislative
members still hoped to win the Mormon vote.

It was still July 1843, and Joseph had just been discharged
from his arrest by the Nauvoo Municipal Court. His arresting
officers—Sheriff Reynolds and Constable Wilson—immediately
galloped off to Springfield to complain to no less than the
governor himself.

Whatever their report included, others who had political
and religious axes to grind claimed Joseph had saved himself

by an armed militia and thus had placed himself *above the law*, the theme that would be hammered upon him repeatedly. Non-Mormon residents of Lee County meanwhile came to the Saints' defense—they claimed the two arresting officers were not disarmed, except temporarily, at Pawpaw Grove, and that the Saints who joined Joseph on his ride to Nauvoo were not armed and made no threat of force.

Sheriff Reynolds and Constable Wilson, basically outsmarted and outmaneuvered, went back to Governor Ford with their tails between their legs. They begged the governor to raise a militia to help them arrest Joseph. Word got back to Joseph on July 2 of their plan. Immediately the people of Nauvoo sent a statement in Joseph's behalf, defending him, and even Cyrus Walker personally went to see Ford to dissuade him from raising the militia to get Joseph. Walker then added his own request to Ford—stop helping the Missourians extradite Joseph. It was now up to Governor Ford to make the final decision . . .

NAUVOO was now the second-largest city in Illinois, and much busier than Chicago. In 1843 converts were still immigrating to the city by the hundreds—and there were 374 missionaries set apart that year alone. The Nauvoo bell would ring from atop the hill at the temple area at 7 A.M. every day to start the city's activities. The city had 35 stores and numerous factories—including match and powder, pottery, a wagon shop, two stone quarries, a water mill, two each of steam gristmills and sawmills, six brick factories, and an iron factory, plus cobblers, tanners, tailors, milliners, and blacksmiths. The two newspapers were the official church organ, the *Times and Seasons* (which published twice a month), and the regular newspaper, the *Nauvoo Neighbor* (which had initially been named *The Wasp* by William Smith, as stated earlier, before William became a state legislator and resigned from the paper on December 10, 1842). The paper's name changed three months later, on March 15, 1843, when it fell under the direction of John Taylor.

Each day an average of five riverboats would stop at Nauvoo, bringing in converts, business people, freight, tourists, and journalists. Visitors poured into the city on holidays because no one could throw a party like Joseph. There was often dancing; dinner parties; cornhusking parties; quilting parties; parades; and concerts from the city's three bands; riverboat trips from the city's own riverboat, which included dancing on board under the moonlight; and service project parties, which included afterward singing, dancing and games till late. Singers filled the streets on Christmas Eve and New Year's Eve. Theater was a large part of the city—with numerous plays, including Shakespeare and other serious drama, along with light comedies and melodrama such as *Pizarro*, in which Porter Rockwell performed with Brigham Young. Joseph attended many plays, including *Damon and Pythias* and *The Idiot Witness*.

Joseph and Emma's second home in Nauvoo, the Mansion House, was completed and moved into sometime in 1843. Before that they had lived, since 1839, in the Homestead, overlooking the river. Just across the street in the new home, Joseph had an escape route built in—consisting of a fake wall in a closet, behind which he could climb a ladder to the second story and from there ascend through a trap door to the roof. A tree hung over the roof, and from there he could climb up and then descend to the ground. Lucy Mack Smith, Joseph's mother, also moved into the Mansion House.

Joseph and Emma were gracious hosts—they had personally welcomed all visitors to the city who wished to see them, and even invited them to dinner. But the visitors became so numerous that they changed their strategy and were forced to start charging for meals and a night's stay, which, as it was broadcast far and wide, was the best of any hotel, not only in the state but on the entire Mississippi River. The actual hotel, the Nauvoo House, was slowly being built and would never be completed, so the Mansion House served as the guesthouse and hotel to most visitors.

In the summer of 1843, the Saints added a large two-story wing in back of the Mansion House, complete with a kitchen and dining hall on the main floor and 10 bedrooms upstairs. Across the street was a stable that held 75 horses. Emma filled the Mansion House with furniture, china, linen, a red carpet, a chandelier, and marble-topped tables from St. Louis. The grand opening of the Nauvoo Mansion, so noted by a sign outside the building, took place on October 3, 1843. They celebrated with a huge feast—breads, rutabagas, pumpkin pies, apple cider, turkey, and prairie chickens. Flags were placed around the house and on its outside walls for the event. Joseph and Emma dressed up in fine clothes, and they received 200 guests. Speaking after dinner was Robert D. Foster, who stated of Joseph, "If he has equals, he has no superiors." Dancing and music kept the party going till late.

Joseph still wrestled with his temper. On one occasion a "big man" named Josiah Butterfield insulted Joseph in his own house, whereupon Joseph literally kicked his rear end with the toe of his boot, as witnessed by his nephew, Joseph F. Smith. The man "lit on the sidewalk just by the gate." Also, on August 1, 1843, Joseph had an argument with Walter Bagby, a tax collector. When Bagby threw a rock at him, Joseph wrote that it "so enraged me that I followed him a few steps and struck him two or three times." Others stepped in to break up the fight, and Joseph gladly paid the fine for assault. (Afterward, Bagby became a fierce enemy of Joseph, inspiring Carthage meetings and stirring up former enemies against him.)

Joseph also fought with the issue of justice. On one occasion an African-American named Anthony was arrested for breaking the law by selling liquor, and was brought before Joseph, who was mayor. Anthony told him he had done so because, although he had bought his own freedom, as well as his wife's, he needed money to buy the freedom of his child. Joseph told him, "I am sorry, Anthony, but the law must be observed, and we will have to impose a fine." But the next day Joseph gave Anthony one of his best horses and told him to sell it to buy the child's freedom.

The same fall that the Mansion House was dedicated, in 1843, another African-American, Jane Manning James, a freeborn woman from Connecticut, came to Nauvoo with eight others of her extended family, walking all the way there. She details her arrival: "I only had two things on me, no shoes nor stockings . . . [which I had worn out] on the road. I had a trunk full of beautiful clothes, which I had sent around by water, and I was thinking of having them when I got to Nauvoo, and they stole them at St. Louis, and I did not have a rag of them. . . . One morning, before

[Joseph] came in, I had been up to the landing and found all my clothes were gone. Well, I sat there crying. He came in and looked around. . . . To sister Emma, he said, 'Go and clothe her up, go down to the store and clothe her up.' Sister Emma did. She got me clothes by the bolt. I had everything."

Joseph also took in numerous boarders, allowing them to stay free of charge, because they had no money. In one case a 14-year-old boy came on a cold night, penniless. He was there to find his brother, but learned he lived eight miles away. Joseph told him he would not have to pay and would be taken care of. He was fed and given a room, after being invited to sit by the fire.

Once Joseph took the coat off his back and gave it to a destitute member of the Twelve, John Page, who was headed on a mission to Canada without a coat.

Joseph's people were devoted for good reasons. William Henrie writes, "You could not be in [his] presence without feeling the influence and Spirit of God, which seemed to flow from him almost as heat does from a stove. You could not see it, but you felt it."

Joseph also won their respect. Jesse W. Crosby states that if Joseph borrowed a sack of flour from someone, he always repaid it with interest. He believed that "anything borrowed should be returned always with interest to the lender." And if he borrowed an ax, he would always return it sharpened.

He reportedly lived his religion, which made his people, for the most part, even more devout. Martin Harris says when Joseph worked on his farm in Palmyra he was "devoted and attentive to his prayers." Eliza R. Snow says he had family worship in Nauvoo "three times a day." Curtis Bolton reveals: "I have lived with him in his family; was with him morning, noon, and night, early and late. I saw him in most trying situations, with friends and enemies; and in all the time that I remained in his family, I never saw the slightest act, nor heard one word, unbecoming a man of God."

Joseph wrote the feelings of his heart: "O Lord glorify Thyself. Thy will be done and not mine." Also, "I desire to be with Christ. I count not my life dear to me—only to do His will."

Yet he was frustrated. Heber C. Kimball reveals: "He said sometimes that he felt pressed upon . . . as though he were pent up in an acorn shell, and all because the people did not and would not prepare themselves to receive the rich treasures of wisdom and knowledge that he had to impart. He could have revealed a great many things to us if we had been ready," but "we lacked that diligence and faithfulness that were necessary to entitle us to those choice things of the kingdom." One of the major weaknesses among the Saints, if not their major one—as revealed over the coming months—was the inordinate importance they placed upon property. His summarizing statement about property is "a good man will endure all things to honor Christ, and even dispose of the whole world, and all in it, to save his soul."

On July 4, 1843, with Nauvoo packed with visitors to see the ever-entertaining gala of events, parades, and band music in celebration of the nation's birthday, Joseph decided to address the crowd about Latter-day Saint politics. Three steamers brought 1,000 guests from St. Louis, Burlington, and Quincy, and other guests rode across the prairies to attend. When each boat landed, the Nauvoo citizens saluted them with firing cannon and band music, and each guest was then escorted, as though he were a dignitary, to his seat of honor. Despite the mistreatment the Saints had received, they never turned inward or introverted, and Joseph did know how to celebrate far above and beyond the frontier mentality of the day, always wanting to treat guests as celebrities.

Joseph spoke to the crowd of 15,000 that afternoon and explained that he did not dictate to the Saints how to vote, but that Ford had been voted into office because of them, simply because Ford had maintained neutrality and supported peoples' rights, while his opponent, Joseph Duncan, had said he would take away their charters and exterminate them; "hence the members of the church universally voted for Mr. Ford." He then explained that the very first time the Missourians had made a demand for Joseph's arrest, however, Ford capitulated and issued a writ, then turned around and did it again, "which has caused me much trouble and expense." Joseph then gave the account of his capture by the two officers. Wilford Woodruff records the effect of Joseph's speech: "Much prejudice seemed to be removed."

When speaking to crowds—whether vast or intimate— despite his fear, Joseph had a remarkable charisma. One young man named Job Smith, who had moved to Nauvoo, records this historical gem: "The stand from which he spoke, was, I think, between twenty and thirty feet long, and it was his custom in addition to his arm gesture to walk the stand from one end to the other and sometimes call upon the audience for an expression of approval which was usually answered by a loud "Aye" from the congregation. I have never but once since heard a preacher or lecturer exercise the mental power and earnestness manifested by that great man. He was large in stature and powerful in invective, and occasionally sarcastic."

On July 7, 1843, Ford's representative—his actual agent—a Mr. Brayman, arrived. Joseph assigned several of his own agents to spend all night making copies of Joseph's hearing from a few days previous.

Then a new political problem began to unfold that spun out of control for Joseph. It began with the congressional election. Democrats, of which Ford was a member, tried to convince the Saints that the state militia would invade them if they voted for the Whigs. To learn the Democrats' *true* position, the Saints sent Jacob Backenstos, a non-Mormon from Carthage who was active in civic affairs and a Democrat himself, to Springfield to learn what Ford really thought about them. While Backenstos was in Springfield, one week before election day in August, Hyrum received a revelation saying that the Saints should support the Democratic candidate, Joseph Hoge. Aside from that, it is possible Hoge had made a deal to support Hyrum in running for a seat in the state legislature.

Because of this momentous decision by Hyrum, all Hades would begin unraveling against the Saints. The rise of new turncoats in their midst and new political storms broiling up would come striking down on the Saints in complete devastation.

First, the turncoats. Because of Hyrum's support of Hoge (and Hyrum's possible eyeing of the state senate seat), William Law, of the church Presidency no less, took to criticizing Hyrum— vehemently. The *Nauvoo Neighbor* newspaper announced its support of Hoge and editorialized that they should vote as one, because if they split their vote they would lose political power. Joseph meanwhile said nothing. There would be more turncoats in the coming weeks.

Second, the political storms. When Backenstos returned from Springfield a day or so before the elections, he reported that the Democrats had assured him the Saints would receive favorable treatment if they would vote for their party. Later, Ford said he was in St. Louis at the time and that another Democrat had given Backenstos such assurances—a prominent party member, but without Ford's consent.

Ford's agent, Brayman, then sent a letter to Joseph via Backenstos, dated July 29, 1843. In it Brayman declared he was surprised that most Mormons thought Ford was hostile toward them. In a pure political cover-up, he stated that Ford had *reluctantly* sent the sheriffs to arrest Joseph, feeling it a constitutional obligation to arrest Joseph, and that it was the most painful thing he had done in his administration, but that he had to enforce the laws. Brayman further said in his letter that he knew Ford's feelings, implying they were positive toward Joseph. Brayman then told Joseph what he had reported to Ford—that neither Joseph nor his people were guilty of violence or unlawful conduct whatsoever, and further, as he states in his letter, "Throughout the whole of the unpleasant scene connected with your arrest, and the ill treatment which you received, your and their conduct was that of peaceful, law-abiding and good citizens." Brayman then confided in Joseph that the Missouri requisition order was now dead and that nothing more would come of it unless a new requisition was to be produced by the Missouri governor. Brayman opined that, after Ford would read the results of Brayman's investigation, which he was carrying to him, Ford would doubtlessly write the Missouri governor and put a stop to all future demands. He also added that Ford had never intended to call out the state militia, and that only a half-crazy politician would seek "to inflame your people against the Executive." He then addressed the rumor that Ford had held off invading the Saints with the state militia "for the purpose of 'holding a rod over you,' to influence the votes of your people in the coming Election." Next, he claimed Ford "has nobly disregarded political considerations" and that his decision in their case will be "precisely the same whether he makes it before the election" or after, no matter who they vote for. Finally, Brayman insulated Ford by saying these were his own views and not Ford's, but that he was certain the results would be as he stated.

On July 26 Ford did write to Sheriff Reynolds, saying he would not send the militia to arrest Joseph. His reasoning was sound—it would set a dangerous precedent for a governor to reverse a court's decision when a governor thought the court exceeded its powers. Ford would actually be greatly abused for this decision by other politicians and the press within his own state and, perhaps because of that and out of fear of further reprisals, he would take a later course that would dramatically harm the Saints. If there were conspiratorial powers above him, perhaps this fear was compounded by "orders" from those power brokers who had placed him in office in the first place.

With Backenstos' report of what the Democrats in Springfield had told him, the Saints felt an alliance with the Democrats, and consequently decided to change their minds and vote for them.

But the Saints were now in a quandary because the Whigs had courted them and expected their vote. And because Joseph had promised Democrat Cyrus Walker his own vote for helping him, Walker likely assumed Joseph would bring the entire Mormon vote to the polls as well; however, the sudden and surprising deciding factor was Hyrum's revelation, which he made public two days before the election—that the Saints should support Hoge, the Whig candidate.

The first sign of apostasy from first counselor William Law seemed to be his aforementioned criticism of Hyrum on July 31, 1843, when Hyrum announced they should support Hoge and that he (Hyrum) hoped to gain a seat in the legislature. Law out-and-out opposed Hyrum's announcement. Law's second sign of apostasy came when Hyrum announced five days later that he *had received a revelation for the Saints* saying they should vote for Hoge because God wished them to. That stunned William Law, who declared that since Joseph was voting for Walker, Hyrum's revelation must be false.

The day before the election, on August 6, 1843, Joseph clarified the situation: "In relation to Mr. Walker [the Whig candidate for Congress who had helped free Joseph], he is a high-minded man. Mr. Walker has not hung on to my coattail to gain his election as some have said. . . . When Mr. Walker came to my house, I voluntarily told him I was going to vote for him. . . . When I was arrested, Walker made Reynolds come to me and beg my pardon for abuse he gave me." Significantly, Joseph says that afterward Walker withdrew all his claims to the Saints' vote, if it would be "detrimental to your interest as a people."

Joseph adds, "Brother Hyrum tells me this morning that he has had a testimony that it will be better for this people to vote for Hoge, and I never knew Hiram [to] say he had a revelation and it failed."

Hoge collected 3,000 votes the next day from the Saints, and won the election by less than 800 votes.

The Whigs were so disappointed, having expected the Mormon vote, that with the loss of the election they began to view the Mormons as traitors. Bitter feelings arose. Cyrus Walker's true feelings are not known but, if Joseph's assessment of the man was correct, he would have understood that the Saints had the right to vote as they wished, without retaliation from him. Ford's assessment is that it was from this time forward

that the Whigs as a whole—and some Democrats—became
determined to drive the Saints from the state.

All that the Whigs needed to get rid of the Saints was
another spark to light the wildfire that would sweep down
upon them. And that spark would once again come from the
apostates . . .

CHAPTER 60

FIRST would come the dawn of a pivotal day—August 12, 1843. The locals of Hancock County would try to stop the Mormon doctor Robert D. Foster from going to Carthage to be sworn in as the new school commissioner. Fifteen of these locals stopped him, letting him know of their anger over the election and over Joseph's placing himself *above the law*, as they saw it, by not submitting to being carted off to Missouri.

At Carthage the same locals tried to intimidate the court into withholding the oath of office from Robert D. Foster. When they failed, their anger went through the roof. In retaliation, they promised to take on and destroy Joseph's political power and keep all the Saints out of public office.

So they organized a mass meeting. They held it one week later, practically foaming at their mouths, and from that spun off a series of other meetings that incited some of the populace to arms.

Meanwhile, on August 12, 1843, a momentous event occurred—an event that would separate the "wheat from the tares"—Joseph announced to his high council the revelation on polygamy, declaring that it was for the general church membership.

In his announcement he revealed the Saints no longer had to live on milk, but were ready for "strong meat," according to William Law. Open rebellion among the Saints' leadership created a schism that would lead to catastrophic events.

A month earlier on July 12, Joseph had received the revelation while with Hyrum and his clerk, William Clayton. Hyrum then told Joseph that Emma might accept the revelation if she saw it in writing. Joseph replied with a smile, "You don't know Emma as I do." She knew Joseph had been practicing it and she had agreed to it with reluctance, accepting that it was a commandment from God as in Biblical times, but at times she had difficulty with it, as Joseph likely did as well, since it was a difficult, if not extremely trying, practice.

This July 12 revelation is Section 132 of the *Doctrine and Covenants*. It had come about when Joseph had asked the Lord why the ancient prophets of the Old Testament had multiple wives. It also stated that marriages were of no force in the hereafter if they were not performed by the proper authority, which Joseph, as president of the church, possessed. As with the Old Testament prophets who practiced polygamy, the Lord was now restoring "all things," including not just polygamy but the ordinance and doctrine of sealing, defined as "what was to be bound on earth would be bound in heaven." Joseph nevertheless dreaded telling her or the church of this new revelation.

So Hyrum took the revelation to Emma.

When Hyrum returned from her, says William Clayton, he was visibly worn out, having been thrashed by Emma with the worst tongue-lashing of his life. Joseph's only comment was, "I told you, you did not know Emma as well as I did." So Joseph placed the revelation in his pocket, uncertain what to do with it, still reticent to reveal it to the church.

The next day, July 13, Joseph merely writes, "I was in conversation with Emma most of the day." Likely over this issue.

During this period Emma pleaded with Joseph to destroy the revelation. One account states that he handed it over to her, and she took it to the fireplace. She placed a candle under it and burned it. Because of that, reports Brigham, "she thought that was the end of it." This burning would have been a major act of defiance toward a revelation and the beginning of what seemed to be Emma's series of choices that eventually lead her away from the mainstream church.

William McLellin gives another version of the story (three years later, after defecting) — he says that when Emma and Joseph went to bed that night, Joseph told her that polygamy would ruin the church. So he asked her to rise and burn the revelation, but she refused to touch it, not even with tongs. So he arose, placed the revelation into the fire, and burned it.

But a copy of the revelation had been made on July 12 by Newel K. Whitney. And a second copy was made the next day by Joseph C. Kingsbury.

A key to Emma's changing attitude, which may have begun that year of 1843, was later presented by William Law. He might have invented this report, or it may have been accurate—he claimed that when he and Emma would come upon one another on the street, she would complain to him privately about the revelation. But since it stated that if she did not comply she would be destroyed, she confided, "Well, I guess I will have to submit."

While anti-Mormons had been meeting for three weeks and gathering arms, Joseph's worst enemies—the apostates—were now creating an uproar right in Joseph's face.

At the August 12 high council meeting, trouble began when someone asked Hyrum if there was truth to the rumors about polygamy among them, and then this person asked for the truth. Hyrum went outside, crossed the road, entered his house, and grabbed the revelation, then took it back to the meeting and read it to them. Several of the council members exploded. Three opposed the revelation immediately—they were William Marks, the high council president who would become a major apostate; Austin A. Cowles, whose daughter had married Joseph a year earlier; and Leonard Soby. The conflict became intense, and they found themselves in a virtual war.

New complaints began unfolding against him, and his enemies began growing in number. Joseph's life would always be in danger from the moment of this meeting on August 12, 1843, according to one of his lifeguard and council members, Thomas Grover.

But, as in the past, the fire that smoldered among the militant non-Mormons in the county did not become explosive until the apostates poured fuel on it. What the apostates did—as they always had before—was bring an excuse to the non-Mormons to declare open war. The apostates accomplished this by going to their enemies and laying out all their complaints against Joseph—apparently with half-truths and distortions. But it was enough fuel to incite the anger of the neutral non-Mormons and to push the already militant faction into taking up arms. The end result was—the non-Saints were now polarized and ready to crush Joseph any way they could.

As the months plowed forward, from 1843 to early 1844, Joseph was faced with mounting tensions caused by enemy from both fronts. The locals were already heated up from the anti-Mormon newspaper campaign about his "avoiding arrest," but it was not until dissident Saints went to the locals with distortions over polygamy and his quest to "conquer" that they went on a virtual warpath. What the locals feared now was being subject to Joseph's domination, based on what they were hearing.

The men who had tried stopping Robert D. Foster from taking oath as the new county school commissioner on August 12, 1843, were the same who had staged the mass meeting at the Carthage courthouse on August 19. At the mass meeting six men had been chosen to write resolutions, then had presented them at the next meeting on September 6, 1843. In the preface to the resolutions, they wrote: "We are necessarily and irresistibly forced to the conclusion that a certain class of people have obtruded themselves upon us, calling themselves Mormon, or Latter-day Saints, and under the sacred garb of Christianity, assumed, as we honestly believe, that they may the more easily, under such a cloak, perpetrate the most lawless and diabolical deeds that have ever, in any age of the world, disgraced the human species." They attacked Joseph as having a "heaven-daring assumption claiming to set aside, by his vile and blasphemous lies, all those moral and religious institutions which have been established by the Bible." They were at that point attacking his practice of polygamy. Then they twisted the events that had recently taken place, claiming Joseph had been violent against a legal officer (Wilson, the county constable), claiming further that Joseph had passed ordinances in the city council that were in violation to laws of the state, that the Nauvoo court had issued a writ of *habeas corpus* that was out of its jurisdiction in order to protect him from the arresting officers, and that the same municipal court had tried and acquitted him of those same charges made in Missouri; they further claimed Joseph had placed men in office whom he controlled, and that the Legion had been sent out against officers authorized to arrest him. All of their allegations twisted the facts. Their next complaint was that he merged "all religion, all law . . . in the knavish pretension that he receives fresh from heaven divine instructions in all matters pertaining to these things; thereby making his own depraved will the rule by which he would have all men governed." Thus, they concluded, "We pledge ourselves in the most solemn manner to resist all the wrongs which may be hereafter attempted to be imposed on this [non-Mormon] community by the Mormons, to the utmost of our ability—peaceably, if we can, but forcibly, if we must." They next decided not to support any candidate who sought Mormon votes, and chose committees to act as watchdogs over every election precinct in the county. The Warsaw committee chairman was none other than anti-Mormon editor Thomas C. Sharp. The central committee that would work with the various precinct committees had its headquarters in Carthage and included Frank A. Worrell, Levi Williams, and Harmon T. Wilson.

But what caused the earth to rumble was the decision to ally themselves with Lilburn Boggs and the Missouri authorities. They resolved to petition the Missouri governor to try again to get Illinois authorities to arrest Joseph for trial in Missouri. They even offered a posse to help the Illinois authorities capture Joseph. The meeting's resolutions were then sent by horseback to as many newspapers as they could find, in order to polarize the populace against the Saints. To effect this, they shot out messengers in every direction across two states and a territory—Illinois, Missouri, and Iowa Territory—hitting every newspaper they could find.

The Saints would not be pushed around, however. The *Nauvoo Neighbor* on September 13, 1843, fired back that if the Carthaginians came to make war on Rome (Nauvoo) they would be turned back like "Hannibal of old."

What added to the locals' fear and anger was the misunderstanding of the Saints' activities. Sidney Rigdon in April 1844 admitted they had "secret meetings," but that "there was no evil concocted" in them as they planned for a combined spiritual and temporal church government. This church government was misconstrued as a dominating "kingdom of God" that would subdue all other kingdoms, not taking into account Joseph's admonition and clarification on May 12, 1844: "I calculate to be one of the instruments of setting up the kingdom of Daniel by the word of the Lord and intend to lay a foundation that will revolutionize the whole world. . . . It will not be by sword or by gun that this kingdom will roll on; the power of truth is such that all nations will be under the necessity of obeying the Gospel." It is clear that his intentions for the kingdom of God had nothing to do with force, but the conversion of people's hearts.

Yet the locals were in abject fear that Joseph planned to set up a worldwide government by forcible dominion, not understanding his plans and twisting what small truths of the situation they did have. They knew from these pieces of information that the Saints had denounced the federal government as corrupt—which only added to their fear that the Saints would try to take over the government. Because of the "secret meetings" regarding Joseph's Council of Fifty, the locals thought Nauvoo was planning subversive measures, including plans to overthrow the entire country and abolish the Constitution. Joseph, by contrast, merely wanted to build the kingdom of God by converting people spiritually. But the apostates had lit the fire of misunderstanding under them.

Six years earlier at Far West, after the Saints had been driven out, several dissidents had similarly gone to Judge Austin A. King and stated that Joseph planned to build an earthly kingdom of God that would subdue all other kingdoms—then added their lies—that he planned to do it by force. Among the dissidents was Oliver Cowdery, who obviously should have known better. His pride, however, was evidently bent out of shape and, at the same time, he was withdrawing his support on the doctrinal matter of polygamy. The biggest conflict he had with Joseph, however, seemed to be over the subject of property. He wanted to sell property he owned in Jackson County, which Joseph had advised the Saints not to sell. In essence, Oliver's problem, until he would later return to the church, was material based. So when he went to Judge King to denounce Joseph, he declared that Joseph was planning to make church government overpower all secular government, and that he, Oliver, could not go along with it. Similar to the arguments made by the dissenters at Far West, six years previous, the new apostates brought up the same old issues.

In the beginning days of the church, the leaders had plans for the gospel to roll forth across the entire earth, but it was clarified more in later years in Nauvoo. There, they actually had classes on government. Those attending were members of a newly organized Council of Fifty that would oversee temporal matters. But now, being riled up by the apostates, their enemies would read much more into the council than really existed. The council itself was comprised of even non-Mormons, along with the Twelve and some of the other church authorities; it also included Joseph's most trusted associates who were not leaders, including Porter Rockwell. Two of the non-Mormons in the group were Thomas L. Kane (who attended council meetings on the trek west) and Daniel H. Wells (a justice of the peace and officer in the Legion, who would later join the church in the West.)

On April 17, 1842, Joseph had announced a revelation that detailed the political kingdom of God. The council may or may not have been the officiating body of that kingdom, but in any case it was officially organized in 1844. From April 1842 to spring 1844, Joseph had conducted occasional meetings of a group that was the forerunner to the Council of Fifty that did not relate to religion. On September 28, 1843, that group unanimously chose Joseph as president. Everyone who attended this meeting would join the council when it was organized six months later, except his second counselor in the First Presidency, William Law, who was turning against him. (William did attend an evening session of the meetings on September 28, 1843.)

As for Joseph's beloved general store—the Red Brick Store—he had worked there when he could for almost two years, till December 20, 1843, whereupon he now had to turn it over to two men, Butler and Lewis, because he was too busy. He was also no longer finding it so beloved because it was having problems collecting debts—some customers thought he should readily forgive all debts, being a prophet. Other customers gave him another problem—if he would not give them store credit, they would apostatize. Brigham reports Joseph finally saying, in wanting to get rid of the store, "These goods will make the people apostatize; so over they go, they are of less value than the people." Rather than closing the store, however, he solved the problem by simply walking away from it.

The very next day, on December 21, 1843, despite their history of rejections, the Saints tried once again to get help from Congress—this time by getting federal protection for Nauvoo. They again explained their grievances regarding what had happened in Missouri and now asked Congress to protect them from future *similar* problems by granting Nauvoo city the same rights, power, "privileges, and immunities" as a *territory*, so long as these privileges were not contrary to the Constitution, and they also asked Congress that Joseph be granted the power to summon U.S. forces to help protect them from mobs. Further, they requested that the Nauvoo Legion be paid the same as the U.S. Army during such actions.

This calling on the U.S. Government for assistance caused newspaper editor Gregg to blast out a threat against Joseph on February 7, 1844: "Your career of infamy cannot continue but a little longer! Your days are numbered!"

On March 11, 1844, Joseph *formally* organized the Council of Fifty. There were, according to Presiding Bishop of the church George Miller, 53 members, with Joseph chosen as "king" on the earth, likely a symbolic and preparatory title to when the true kingdom of God would be established and the Savior would be king over the earth. And that, the Saints believed, would be during the millennial reign of the Savior, after his Second Coming.

Dissidents purposely leaked word to their enemies, which caused them additional upset over Joseph's title. Governor Ford feared Joseph sought to be a monarch, as informed by "the best men who had seceded from the Mormon Church"—the apostates. These "best men" also told him the Saints looked upon the U.S. Government as "utterly corrupt," needing "to be replaced by the government of God." The apostates conveniently overlooked the millennial reign concept.

Because the meetings were secret, imaginations went wild. Rumors spread among the locals that they were reviving the Danites, an absurd accusation but—with the local populace already in fear of the Mormons—an accusation that sparked additional fears. (Only six members of the council had belonged to the Danites in its brief history, including Porter Rockwell, before Joseph had set them straight.)

At the first meeting of the Council of Fifty, Joseph conducted business, with 23 members attending in the room above Henry Miller's house. There, they discussed the possibility of migrating to a new home. Eight months earlier, in July 1843, Joseph had sent Jonathon Dunham to explore the western U.S. Meanwhile, in February 1844, Joseph had told the Twelve to send 25 volunteers to Oregon and California to search for a safe haven. Joseph likely had acted in the capacity of an ecclesiastical leader regarding those two assignments, since the Council of Fifty had not been organized (until March 1844), but apparently the council would now continue investigating new locales for the Saints to settle. They assigned Lucien Woodworth to talk with Sam Houston and the Texas congress about land they could colonize, preferably as an independent nation. Texas needed money, so the council hoped the leaders in Texas would allow the Saints to take a large tract of land in the lawless area—from the Nucces River to the Rio Grande—if the Saints would help defend Texas against the Mexicans. In their March 11 meeting they discussed two letters they had received from Lyman Wight regarding the lumber camp in the woods at Black River Falls, Wisconsin. The men there were disenchanted with the lumber camp and asked if they could sell the mill and move to Texas to lumber and prepare a place for the Saints to gather. The council also considered securing "a resting place in the mountains, or some uninhabited region, where we can enjoy the liberty of conscience guaranteed to us by the Constitution of our country, rendered doubly sacred by the precious blood of our fathers, and denied to us by the present authorities."

On March 13 and 19 they met again, with Porter Rockwell and Sidney Rigdon attending the latter date, along with two men whom Joseph did not know were in the process of apostatizing— William Marks and Orson Spencer. At these and future meetings, the council studied the doctrines and principles of national government and discussed how government should function. (The council would continue operation under Brigham Young and John Taylor in the West and would also have separate functions from that of the church.)

As part of the council's continuing plan for a westward migration, on March 26, 1844, Joseph petitioned Congress to appoint himself as a U.S. Army officer with the authority to raise 100,000 volunteers to open up the West and defend U.S. borders.

On March 30, 1844, Joseph wrote President John Tyler asking the same, in case Congress rejected his request. Tyler did have a particular interest in building forts along the Oregon Trail to protect settlers from the Native Americans. But Tyler evidently turned it down.

Joseph then sent Orson Hyde to carry the petitions to Congress and to learn if it would seriously consider the annexation of Texas. But Hyde would learn that the Texas annexation was unlikely as he listened to debates in Congress and wrote summaries of their discussions to Joseph. On May 25, 1844, the House of Representatives rejected Joseph's petition to appoint him as an Army officer to open up the West with volunteers and to protect the nation's borders, without even reading it on the House floor.

But the Texas possibility remained open. Woodworth returned from Texas on May 2, 1844, with solid results, holding a treaty, and reported to the Council of Fifty on May 3 that "it was altogether as we could wish it." Woodworth and George Miller were appointed by the council to "ratify the said treaty," which had been entered into by Woodworth and the Texas cabinet. But nothing came of the treaty and obviously the Saints never moved there.

The very first exploration for a westward migration likely came in 1843 when Joseph sent Jonathon Dunham to explore the western region of Iowa, 800 miles west of Nauvoo. Dunham returned August 26, 1843, long before these other exodus considerations came into play.

Because of the locals heating up over their misunderstanding of the secret Council of Fifty, spurred on by dissidents, they were becoming increasingly alarmed over their own safety by May 1844, and were arming themselves for all-out war.

C H A P T E R

62

I N early October 1843, shortly after Joseph's "open house party" for the Mansion House, Joseph became so distrustful of Sidney Rigdon's loyalty that he convened a special conference of the church. Showing no evidence of being the "dictator" or "despot" his enemies accused him of, he actually went to the church membership to sustain him in releasing Sidney as first counselor. Joseph feared Sidney had begun writing John C. Bennett and ex-governor Carlin and therefore was betraying him. He also feared Sidney had supplied information earlier that had told them where Joseph was traveling, which had allowed Sheriff Reynolds and the Carthage constable to arrest him at Dixon, Illinois. He also claimed Sidney had failed in his responsibilities as first counselor in the presidency and had badly bungled his management of the post office, which had been run out of Sidney's house. At this special conference called by Joseph, Sidney's eloquence got to the people—he spoke all that day and the next, defending himself, reminding them of his suffering through so much with Joseph and of their former close friendship, and then he sadly offered to resign. The people were moved and voted against Joseph—they wanted Sidney to remain as first counselor. Joseph retorted, "I have thrown him off my shoulders, and you have again put him on me."

Joseph was of a highly forgiving nature and possibly felt Sidney had repented and changed his ways, because a few

*Richard Lloyd Dewey* | JOSEPH SMITH: A BIOGRAPHY

months later he picked Sidney as his running mate for President of the U.S.

Joseph initially decided to determine the best candidate to support for President of the country. In the *Times and Seasons* on October 1, 1843, the church leaders promised to find the best man running for President. Joseph, John Taylor, and Willard Richards wrote letters to the five existing U.S. candidates—John C. Calhoun, Henry Clay, Martin Van Buren (the incumbent), Lewis Cass, and Richard M. Johnson. They received responses from them all, but none agreed to help the Saints with past grievances or future protection more than what the states themselves would provide. One response they received was as ludicrous as they could imagine. Henry Clay, who was later chosen to face Van Buren in the presidential race in the electoral college, wrote the Saints saying that if they desired justice for the abuses they had suffered in Missouri, perhaps they should "go to Oregon" and "get justice from the Indians!" The other candidates' replies weren't much better.

Joseph fired back replies, lambasting them in detail. In good conscience, he could not recommend anyone, so on January 29, 1844, he met with the Twelve and others, and they unanimously voted Joseph as their man to run for the presidency of the United States on an independent ticket. They felt, according to George Miller, that if Joseph was elected, the locale of the Saints would be in the U.S.—and if he was not elected, then "we would fall back on Texas and be a kingdom notwithstanding."

Joseph announced to the men that they would need to send every man who had the ability to speak in public to campaign for him, simultaneously preaching the restored gospel. Confident that he could get elected, he added, "Tell the people we have had Whig and Democratic Presidents long enough; we want a President of the United States." In a highly unusual move, he decided not to campaign for himself, feeling that his missionaries and other recruits could carry the day.

Joseph dictated his presidential platform to W. W. Phelps. They called it *General Smith's Views of the Powers and Policy of the Government of the United States*—a 12-page pamphlet published on February 7, 1844. Joseph's campaign directors immediately mailed it to a couple hundred leaders throughout the country. The platform was solid and would appeal to voters in both parties. And it was revolutionary in nature—calling for prison reform (turning prisons into educational centers for the convicted), physical labor for felons (putting them to work on roads and public projects), cutting state and national government budgets and offices (by decreasing their number, power, and pay, which would cut taxes), and doing away with archaic laws.

He had as much chance of some platform items passing as he did carrying the vote of Illinois and Missouri. Some of his plans were: 1) petitioning slave states to abolish slavery and reimbursing slave owners by selling public lands (abolitionist attempts to free slaves had only resulted in anger, and Joseph's attempts would likely result in the same antagonism); 2) establishing a national bank with branches in every state (but that too had been shot down by President Tyler twice in 1842); 3) expanding the country—from the Atlantic to the Pacific, but only with the approval of the Native Americans—and adding all of North America to U.S. borders if Mexico, Canada, and Texas (which then was a separate republic) so desired; 4) grant the President the power to stop mobs with the U.S. Army—without having to go through any state's governor (which would happen in time but was unheard of in Joseph's day).

As for abolishing slavery, Joseph had received a revelation 11 years earlier stating, "It is not right that any man should be in bondage one to another." The record is unclear whether Joseph believed African-Americans should not hold the priesthood. Abraham O. Smoot believed that was the case, although he stated they could be baptized with the consent of their masters. The limitation could have been made because they were slaves rather than based on the fact they were Black. Joseph did befriend an African-American named Elijah Abel, who was converted in Ohio and ordained to the priesthood on March 3, 1836, under Joseph's direction. Elijah lived in Joseph and Emma's home for a long time and was ordained a seventy and sent on a mission to Canada and Ohio at age 73, giving his life for the cause; there he experienced exposure and contracted a serious illness, dying shortly afterward.

Joseph's only clear statements about African-Americans were in regard to his anti-slavery views.

The church's policy of African-Americans not holding the priesthood—although they could be baptized into the church—did not become official until Brigham made it so in 1852, once in the West. (That doctrine was reversed by the president of the church in June 1978 after Spencer W. Kimball stated he spent much time and effort supplicating the Lord on the subject.)

Anson Call held to the belief that Joseph told him certain spirits in the pre-existence had remained neutral and as a result came to the earth as Blacks, through the lineage of Cain, whose black skin was perpetuated through the descendants of Ham after the flood. Some other Saints believed the same.

But that opinion was strongly repudiated by Brigham Young in 1869, who proclaimed that Joseph had stated the descendants of Cain were black because of the mark God had set upon them as a protection after Cain had committed murder. Brigham then declared he would not believe anyone who claimed to have heard Joseph say the spirits of Blacks were neutral in heaven, because he had heard Joseph say the opposite. Brigham declared Joseph's belief—"All spirits are pure that come from the presence of God."

As for Joseph's anti-slavery views, he was at first "hands off" on the topic while living in Ohio, stating in the *Messenger and Advocate* in April 1836 that he feared the abolitionists might stir up war and that the people of the North did not have the right to dictate to the South that it should not hold slaves any more than the South should say to the North that it should—"What can divide our union sooner, God only knows."

While against slavery personally, he stated the time of slavery was not yet ended, and while so doing he echoed the ideas presented in the literature of the slave owners of the South, whom he did not want to antagonize. There seemed to be two reasons why: 1) He had missionaries there and did not want to see them harmed, and 2) he probably truly was swayed by what he read, as what he likely read and what he said are remarkably similar—that it was indicated in the Bible that the sons of Canaan were cursed with servitude by God's decree, and that the curse was not yet lifted, but that "God can do his work without the aid of those who are not dictated by his counsel" (the abolitionists). Joseph stated he was speaking his own opinions as a person, rather than as a prophet dictating doctrine.

But his personal views regarding abolishing slavery would change drastically over the next several years—perhaps from his own pondering or perhaps from inspiration. In 1842, for example, Joseph learned from John C. Bennett—at that time a member of the faith and mayor of Nauvoo—that a well-known doctor in Chicago had written Bennett asking for support for three abolitionists who were being held in a Missouri prison. Joseph responded to Bennett that slavery and the manner in which abolitionists were treated made his "blood boil." Joseph published the Chicago doctor's letter in the *Times and Seasons* and added a note in favor of liberty for all.

From that point on, Joseph was always expressly anti-slavery. On December 30, 1842, Joseph told Orson Hyde, in the company of Judge Adams, at whose home they were staying in Springfield, in answer to Hyde's question concerning what he would advise a man joining the church who owned 100 slaves—"I have always advised such to bring their slaves into a free country and set them free—educate them and give them equal rights." While he did not think Blacks were ready for their own government yet, he also did not consider them as inferior—which was a common belief of the day. Joseph saw them merely being held back by lack of opportunity to improve.

On January 2, 1843, he stated to Orson Hyde and others: "They came into the world slaves, mentally and physically. Change their situation with the whites, and they would be like them." He supported fully educating them. He did not support mixed marriages, however, and that was likely another personal view stemming from societal pressures. (As another example of admitting he had personal views that differed from inspiration, on February 21, 1843, he said, "In relation to politics, I will speak as a man; but in relation to religion I will speak in authority.") He also supported segregation, but having full and equal rights, perhaps still persuaded by the slave holders' propaganda literature he had read. He stated on one occasion that the slaves should be freed and eventually turned over to Mexico. But overall, his views were extremely liberal for the day, even revolutionary, and very courageously expressed in states filled with activist slave holders.

Joseph's official candidacy for presidency was announced 3½ weeks after his platform was published, on March 1, 1844, by the *Times and Seasons*. Six days later he said, "We will whip the mob by getting up a President."

Three days later Joseph chose as his running mate James Arlington Bennett, a recent convert of sophistication and savvy in New York City. Willard Richards wrote him, "General Smith is the greatest statesman of the 19th century." Willard also challenged him to be a missionary during his campaigning, and to set out for Nauvoo, teaching and advocating the presidency/ vice-presidency along the way, and to "expose the wickedness of Martinism" (Van Buren). J. A. Bennett wrote back declining, but in any case was ineligible, being born out of the U.S., in Ireland. He told Joseph he had no chance of winning even one state but knew if elected Joseph would govern in good faith. But if it would further the cause of the church's teachings, then, in that sense he might succeed. Some witnesses felt Joseph believed he could actually win, but Joseph may have been hiding his true feelings, wanting the hundreds of missionaries and their new converts to spread the word not only of his candidacy but also of the restored gospel, which could only bring good results. The presidential campaign was, if for no other reason, a fresh approach to missionary work. One visitor to the city stated that Joseph told him the Lord would "turn the hearts of the people" to elect him—but how much Joseph truly believed it is questionable.

A state convention was held in Nauvoo on May 17, 1844, where he was formally nominated. It was then that Sidney was announced as his running mate. A presidential campaign convention was planned for either New York City or Baltimore on July 13, 1844. Brigham then began organizing committees, visiting area newspapers, and writing letters to drum up support for Joseph.

They went after the Catholic vote. Willard Richards wrote a letter on May 24, 1844, to the alderman of Philadelphia: "The Mormons and the Catholics . . . are the only two who have not persecuted each other and others in these United States, and the only two who have suffered from the cruel hand of *mobocracy* for their *religion*."

Over 45 conferences were planned that spring and summer in 14 states and in the District of Columbia. Missionaries were assigned to all of them to once again fulfill Joseph's mandate— to both preach the Restored Gospel and proclaim Joseph's platform. The Twelve were assigned to visit as many of the conferences as possible. Missionaries canvassed states with the messages—speaking to large and small groups alike. Some, if not most, believed they really had a shot at electing Joseph. Aboard the steamship *Osprey* a poll was taken among passengers showing that Joseph led the two main candidates—Van Buren and Clay. Lyman Wight wrote Joseph from Philadelphia where he was campaigning and teaching, stating, "You are bound to be the President of the United States." He was proud to say that he had also been proclaiming "you are the Prophet of God."

The missionaries' new converts also took up the electioneering. Wight wrote Joseph on June 26, 1844: "We ordained ten as promising young elders as we ever laid hands upon. They pledged themselves to start this week and go through the state of Delaware from house to house." From the feedback he received in Philadelphia, Wight felt it was actually an even race among not only the two main candidates but all six candidates — who were now Joseph, Van Buren, Clay, Tyler, Polk, and Bering. Perhaps Philadelphia was more receptive to new political ideas and, being away from the hotbed of anti-

Mormon press (although still influenced by the national, but far fewer anti-Saint articles), found people more willing to accept Joseph's extremely pragmatic political ideas, not having an emotional reaction one way or the other toward the Saints, like the locals who had been stirred up by religious and political opponents.

Perhaps other states along the eastern seaboard gave similar feedback to the hundreds of missionaries and members stomping the political hunting ground. Or perhaps Wight was just one of the many who were so positively charged when they proclaimed both the gospel and the platform that they were not entirely objective as to the numbers they thought were accepting them, as most people, then and today, are polite even when they disagree or, in the case of many voters, perhaps simply did not know where they stood and needed time to think about it, leaving Wight's assessment of Joseph and the other four candidates "evenly divided" on votes.

In any case, Wight's message to small and large groups was refreshing to the populace who were used to seeing political campaigning take place almost solely in the party-affiliated newspapers—while Joseph's was a one-on-one message born with tremendous conviction, similar to Wight's when he reported to Joseph of his newly converted young men hitting the campaign trail, saying they would "bear you up as the *only* suitable candidate for the next presidency." If the election had come down to two main candidates seeking the necessary electoral votes, James Bennett's savvy likely would have borne out—especially when the opposing candidate's electioneering machine could and would have resorted to the vast newspaper network to slander Joseph, as it had in each local area in which the Saints had lived. Joseph's once-close associates who turned bitterly antagonistic would have certainly spent whatever means and time they had to oppose Joseph through local newspapers throughout the nation, as well. And that number of riled up, determined apostates was about to grow in number—and show their determination to not rest

until their once-close friend was not only defeated politically
. . . but was literally buried in the earth.

CHAPTER 63

J

OSEPH'S story is completely intertwined with his friend Porter Rockwell's. While Porter was in the Missouri jails, he came upon disturbing news—he learned from Sheriff Reynolds that there was a plot to capture Joseph, which had resulted in Joseph's arrest in Dixon. But more significantly he learned there was a traitor in Joseph's circle. This "turncoat," as they were often designated (referring to British loyalists who wore colonial blue for a time, then turned their coats in for red), was cooperating with Missouri officials to that end. This was startling news for Porter, and he was determined to either get released or escape in order to warn his closest friend.

As for the Dixon, Illinois, event months earlier, Joseph either never learned who the real culprit was or, if he discovered it was Sidney, found it in his heart to forgive him. The turncoat was the one Porter learned about from Sheriff Reynolds, who had reported to the Missourians Joseph's whereabouts on his trip to Dixon *and* whom the sheriff referred to as one of Joseph's circle. But Porter never learned his name. As events would unfold in the coming months, it would seem the culprit was someone other than Sidney.

But Joseph at this point did not even know there was a turncoat. Only Porter knew. And he was determined to somehow get the news to Joseph. After languishing a few more months in jail, he was finally brought before a magistrate. Alexander

Doniphan defended him again, and this time the court declared that although Porter was guilty of attempting to escape jail, he could not be found guilty of escaping someplace where he was not legally supposed to be held—as pointed out by his adroit attorney, Doniphan. Porter had already been declared not guilty of Governor Boggs' assassination attempt.

So Porter was released. Or he would be, declared the jury, after a five-minute sentence. Porter therefore was escorted in handcuffs back to jail for the brief sentence, which actually lasted several hours, while his enemies ran about town seeking to drum up additional charges to keep him in jail.

Doniphan, not knowing Porter was still incarcerated, later that night just happened to check at the jail and found Porter still there. In a tirade against the jailor, he demanded Porter be released at once.

Porter was taken outside by Doniphan and directed into the woods alongside the road. In hushed tones Doniphan warned him to keep out of sight all the way back to Illinois—as there was a plot to snare him.

Before leaving, Porter told Doniphan this—he had been visited by his mother weeks earlier, and she had given him all the money she had, most of it from Joseph's own pocket (which was money he borrowed and repaid in a timely manner, much to his own credit and willingness to sacrifice for his friend). Porter was now able to pay Doniphan for his services, even though his services had been technically free. Then Porter would use his remaining money to pay various farmers and horse owners for short rides along his journey back to Nauvoo.

Doniphan bid Porter farewell and watched as Porter, unarmed, made his way to freedom. Soon Porter heard a hunting party searching for him. But he made his way stealthily through thick forests, traveling the first 25 miles only at night.

His feet became bloody, and he had to stop for three days to let them heal enough to walk. He was in a race against time, however, knowing his best friend on earth had to be warned of the turncoat. Finally Porter made his way clear of the hunters on horseback and was able to hire various farmers for short rides. He slept in the woods, ate wild game and fish, and did everything he could to keep a low profile.

He was able to secure room and board, finding farmers who would let him sleep in the house or barn and eat their wives' cooking. His beard was long, his hair uncut and unkempt for over nine months, and he smelled awful. On the final leg of his journey, he rented a horse and rode 25 miles, then walked another 25 miles the same day. Despite his aching feet he walked another 40 miles the following day. After waiting a day, he hired someone to take him the last three days to Montrose, across the river from Nauvoo.

He crossed the river at night in a small boat. It was Christmas Eve 1843 when he arrived on Nauvoo's shore, ready to kiss the ground.

Rather than going home, he went directly to the Mansion House. He saw a huge gathering inside through the windows, with dozens of buggies and horses tied outside. He knocked on the door.

When someone answered it, his one-of-a-kind sense of humor took over and he suddenly saw potential for both drama and a practical joke—he feigned the role of a drunk Missourian. From the doorway he yelled out so all inside could hear, "Where's Joe Smith? I'm gonna string 'im up!" The party hushed. Joseph strode through the crowd to the door, ready to manhandle the soused Missourian, when, grabbing the stranger's shoulders, he looked Porter "full in the face." Searching Porter's eyes, Joseph realized, to his astonishment, it was none other "than my sorely persecuted friend, Orrin Porter Rockwell!"

The two men embraced and the party continued, more vibrant than ever. Joseph brought Porter in, where he received a hero's welcome. After the attention, toasts, and celebrations subsided, Porter took Joseph into a private room and told him of the plot on his life—that it was one of Joseph's right-hand men. Joseph, not wanting to believe this was happening to him yet again, finally allowed himself to accept the news. Porter was then given a bath and fresh clothes. Afterward, in a side room with several friends, including James Jepson who recorded the event, Joseph laid his hands upon Porter's head and gave him a priesthood blessing—an astonishing one that would lift the name of Orrin Porter Rockwell to that of a legend—Joseph promised him that if he would keep the Lord's commandments, and never again cut his hair, no bullet or blade would harm him the remainder of his life. From that moment, Porter became not only a larger-than-life figure, but a veritable folk hero, a protector of the innocent, and a loyal confidant to Joseph. This blessing seemed to set him apart in a stranger fashion than anyone on earth since Sampson. And from that moment Porter would miraculously amass from numerous witnesses dozens of eyewitness accounts of facing mobbers—and later, outlaws—in rather amazing shoot-outs, with enemy bullets literally missing him from point blank range, while he would mow down those who faced him and, in the end, tally up numbers against attackers and assassins in the dozens and, if all apocryphal accounts were added, even the hundreds. (See the author's work, *Porter Rockwell: A Biography,* Paramount Books, New York)

Porter, reeling from the events of the past year—the heartbreaking loss of his wife, the heart-wrenching departure to Philadelphia where he had gone jobless for weeks, the nine months in Missouri dungeons followed by a race-against-time return to Nauvoo while dodging enemy hunting parties in order to warn his closest friend, all capped off by the miraculous blessing he had just received from Joseph—was now freshened and cleaned up to go visit his children and parents.

He would be returning the next day and practically every day thereafter to the side of Joseph as his special bodyguard.

But in the meantime, Joseph got the word out immediately—probably after a near-sleepless night—that he needed help. He recruited 40 special Nauvoo police on December 29 to protect the city and himself 24 hours a day. Then he told them at a swearing-in ceremony that his life was in danger from enemies within the church. He told them, "My life is more in danger from some little dough-head of a fool in this city than from all my numerous and inveterate enemies abroad." He said enemies without the church could do nothing were it not for someone who sat in council with him and called him brother. He said the secret was out, as Porter Rockwell had brought it back with him from Missouri, that "we have a Judas in our midst."

This one speech set off waves of strange behavior from the guilty party—who was not just one person, it seems, as his enemies now began showing themselves very early and very clearly. He was actually stunned when they began complaining so vociferously, saying they were being singled out, when Joseph had done nothing to point fingers at anyone in particular.

The first to step forward was William Law, Joseph's second counselor in the presidency for the past two years. Law had become prideful since coming from Canada with wealth. He was investing in farming, building, land, and industry, and Joseph's policy of controlling real estate had gotten in the way of his speculating and turning a big profit. He had become critical of Joseph's slow handling of the Nauvoo House hotel construction. He claimed Joseph was misappropriating funds meant for the hotel and using them to buy lands to sell to incoming converts. He wanted work on the hotel stopped—as well as on the temple—so that they could focus on housing.

He and Dr. Robert Foster had purchased lumber from Wisconsin that had been earmarked for church buildings, then had turned around and used it for houses and commercial buildings. The two men paid wages, rather than the city scrip that laborers who worked on the Nauvoo House and temple were paid. Joseph had told them it was wrong to compete with church and city projects, but he could not persuade them to stop—nor could he get the Nauvoo male workforce to stop working for Law and Foster's projects.

The pull of the dollar held sway over the prophet's words in too many cases. Emma, also, was becoming extremely attached to her gracious Mansion House and its fine furnishings, and that love for her property would come to a head in Joseph's life within five months.

William Law complained to Hyrum that he feared the police were going to put him "out of the way." On January 2, 1844, he went to the city council, saying some policemen had told him they had promised under oath to "take care of" the traitor close to Joseph, as that traitor was also planning to be Joseph's assassin. Joseph's response was that he had only given instructions to the policemen to protect him from the Missourians. The council was thorough in their investigation of Law's claim and interviewed the police nearly all day. Law was finally satisfied his life was not in danger.

But the next night, on January 4, 1844, someone built a fire on the riverbank near William Mark's house, just a few blocks west of Joseph's home. Marks was president of the high council, and now he was terrified, thinking it was a signal by the police that he had been singled out. He was so concerned the next day that he, also, demanded a session with the city council to question the police.

At that city council meeting on January 5, 1844, he joined Leonard Soby, who protested that he, too, had been threatened— by actually two policemen—the second of whom had allegedly said that both he (Soby) and William Law were the traitors and would be killed.

Joseph felt the accusation was bogus. That same day he wrote in his journal, "What can be the matter with these men? Is it that the wicked flee when no man pursueth? . . . Can it be possible that the traitor whom Porter Rockwell reports to me as being in correspondence with my Missouri enemies, is one of my quorum?"

The next downward turn in the spiraling whirlpool of apostasy was William Law's claim that Joseph had just propositioned his wife Jane.

Law tried forcing Joseph into a corner—he demanded that either Joseph confess and repent before the high council or Law would see to it that Joseph's "sins" would be exposed to everyone in the world, meaning, of course, by Law going to the area newspapers to incite the locals into a mob.

According to Joseph, the real reason for that threat is this—William had earlier approached Joseph, requesting him to seal William and Jane together for eternity. When Joseph prayed about it to the Lord, he returned with the answer that it could not be done because William was adulterous. When Jane asked Joseph why he would not seal them, Joseph wished to protect her feelings and did not tell her. Several days later Joseph had passed her doorway on the street. She asked him to come inside, then threw her arms around him, hugging him, and said, "If you won't seal me to my husband, seal myself unto you." Joseph declined, and put her aside gently, then left. When her husband William returned, Jane told him that Joseph had come to see her, wanting to marry her.

Apparently it was at this point that William Law formed a group to oppose Joseph. William claimed in public he was afraid to act against Joseph because of retaliation from the "Destroying Angels"—undoubtedly the nonexistent Danites—whom he said Joseph had ordered to get rid of him.

In reality the attacks were likely a cover-up of his own plans—to rid himself of Joseph in order to pursue two specific paths to power—he wanted to lead Joseph's followers religiously himself and, perhaps more importantly, to take advantage of the financial windfall that would be his if Joseph were out of the way. Law happened to be sitting atop the aforementioned major profit-making projects of housing and real estate speculating that were being hampered by Joseph (because Joseph was using the town's labor force to work on the Nauvoo Hotel and the temple).

Additionally, Law wished to have the approbation of his wife and was not getting it, not even being allowed by Joseph to marry his wife in the temple. The final straw was likely the emotional one of his wife Jane's report about Joseph's advances. A final possible reason for William Law's violent opposition may have its underpinnings in church doctrine. It was and is a Latter-day Saint tenet that adultery is considered a grievous sin, next to murder in seriousness, and that once a church member has purified his life by repenting of it and then makes covenants in the temple, then that member is committed to God to never engage in that practice again, but if they do so after entering the covenant, they are open to extremely powerful influences of the adversary—Satan.

William Law became a new and powerful opponent to Joseph. It had possibly been he who had been the Judas that Porter Rockwell had learned of in Missouri, but in any case he was now Joseph's full-fledged enemy. He claimed publicly that he had believed for some time that Joseph was a fallen prophet but did not want to come out against Joseph until he figured his own life was in danger—a convenient victim position to gain more followers, which, with his charisma, he was able to do, along with organizing a campaign of whisperings by his closest friends throughout the city in order to achieve his goal.

That campaign of "divide and conquer" began by meeting with his closest associates in order to conjure up a way to bring Joseph down.

# CHAPTER 64

S PECIFICALLY, the co-conspirators began their operation in this manner. William Law met with his brother Wilson, who was head of the Nauvoo Legion, and his own wife Jane, then others of notability in the community who were disaffected—William Marks, Leonard Soby, Austin Cowles (the latter two of whom were also members of the high council, while all three were opposed to polygamy), and two sons of Joseph's now deceased friend Elias Higbee. Elias had never wavered from Joseph, but his two sons, Chauncey and Francis, were now dedicated to overthrowing the prophet. Both had not been in full standing with the church since they had been discovered associating with John C. Bennett after Bennett's apostasy. It is possible Bennett was still involved in Joseph's overthrow and, if so, it was likely through these two young men, both in their early twenties. Another conspirator was Dr. Robert D. Foster, who, like William Law, had those financial gains at stake and could profit greatly from Joseph's downfall. All of these had been close to Joseph, which made it especially painful for the prophet.

Another key in the group was Joseph H. Jackson, who had befriended Joseph but had not become a member of his closest circle, as had the others.

It was now March 1844. William and Wilson Law were both leaders of this band of dissidents, and they began a series of secret meetings. One or more such meetings were held in the Keystone Store in a back room.

But the band was soon discovered. M. G. Eaton was invited to and attended the meeting and was so alarmed at what he heard that he reported it to Joseph, then signed a sworn affidavit regarding it. He says that at the meeting Robert D. Foster and the Higbee and Law brothers talked about polygamy, and that Foster claimed he had returned home one day to find "a person"—later identified as Joseph—talking with his wife over dinner. When "the person" left, Foster says he confronted his wife, who refused to talk. He stuck a pistol to her head and placed another in her hand, telling her she must talk or shoot him or he would shoot her. She fainted dead away. He says he revived her and she then told him that the man had been preaching the spiritual wife doctrine to her. Foster told the group that he was so afraid that he would not go out at night. The group all then decided to stop these activities. One of the group said they could get the people at Carthage to help them if things were to lead to an all-out insurrection. As to whether they really believed each other's tales or were using the meeting to recruit the innocent, one can only guess.

In any case Joseph, upon learning of the meeting, decided to put a quick end to the newest rumor. He took his associate William Clayton and a friend of Mrs. Foster, a Mrs. Gillman, for a visit to Mrs. Foster's home. Joseph told her that he had been told—apparently by Joseph's new "spy," M. G. Eaton—that her husband, Dr. Foster, had claimed Joseph had made indecent proposals to her. In the presence of his witnesses, Joseph asked her if she had ever known him to be guilty of immorality, and she answered, "No." He asked her if he had ever preached any plurality of wives doctrine to her or if he had propositioned her to engage in intercourse with her—especially when they had had dinner during her husband's absence. She replied, "No." Then they left. It was apparent that Foster had made up the entire story after learning Joseph had dined at his home in his absence, leaving Joseph susceptible to such charges.

From that one pivotally important informant, M. G. Eaton, Joseph went to address a crowd of followers. On March 24, 1844, he told them he had learned of a conspiracy against him, his family, and all the church leaders, then boldly named the conspirators—which must have sent an amazed hush through the crowd—Chauncey L. Higbee (but not his brother Francis, yet), Robert D. Foster, Joseph H. Jackson, and William and Wilson Law. Joseph records in his journal, "I ask, did I ever exercise any compulsion over any man? Did I not give him the liberty of disbelieving any doctrine I have preached, if he saw fit?"

Three weeks later on April 13 Joseph confronted Robert D. Foster before the municipal court—"Have I ever misused you any way?" Foster refused to answer. Joseph asked again. He got the same response. Joseph asked him a third time, and Foster only said that Joseph had been friendly to him. Joseph then asked him to name the wrong he had done to him and he would ask his forgiveness, then added that he wanted Foster to testify that Joseph had treated him honorably. But Foster refused to testify.

Before a church high council meeting Joseph then brought charges against Foster for lying, for slandering his character, and for conspiring against both his life and the peace of his family.

On April 15, 1844, Foster received notice to appear before the high council on April 20. Assuming his membership was in question, Foster rounded up witnesses. But they weren't needed because the trial for his and the Laws' memberships was held without their being present, perhaps in fear of their raising an uproar. At that unannounced April 18 church meeting, Foster and the Laws were excommunicated, and news of it was printed in the *Times and Seasons*.

The conspirators, as they came to be known among the Saints, were not like some apostates who merely moved away. (Oliver Cowdery and others, however, had followed Joseph from Kirtland to Far West, seeking to sell their Jackson County property, so in that sense they had similar motives as these conspirators who remained with the Saints.) These dissidents had vested interests in Nauvoo and were still fighting for them, wanting Joseph out of their way. So, of course, they stayed, at least for a while.

Joseph meanwhile resorted to strategy in self-defense. He put a spy in the house of William Law—a 14-year-old lad named Charles Stoddard who applied for and was hired in the position of houseboy. The boy's mother records the incident fully in her diary. . . .

In April 1844 William Law and his associates spent all night planning a way to trap and kill Joseph. Law awakened young Stoddard and assigned him to oil his gun, telling him he was going to shoot Joseph. "Poor Charles was frightened beyond description," reports his mother Sarah. "But Mr. Law stood over him and prodded him with his foot when Charles hesitated. . . . Finally, when Mr. Law was satisfied with the way the gun was working, he put one bullet in (he boasted he could kill the Prophet with one shot). He sent Charles to bring the Prophet.

"He [Charles] ran as fast as he could and delivered the message, but he begged the Prophet not to go to Mr. Law's. . . .

"As they walked the few blocks from the Mansion House to the Law residence, the Prophet assured Charles that no harm would come to him that day. Charles was frightened, and he said that it kept racing through his mind, 'I am the one that cleaned the gun that is going to be used to kill the Prophet,' until he was sick with fear. The Prophet, in a final attempt to calm my dear son, uttered the fateful words, 'Mr. Law may someday kill me, Charles, but it won't be today.'

"As they approached their destination, Mr. Law came staggering out of the house, shouting out what he intended to do.

"The Prophet said kindly and unafraid, 'You sent for me, Mr. Law?' To which Mr. Law replied with oaths that now he was doing the whole a favor by disposing of the Prophet with one shot.

"Calmly, the Prophet unbuttoned his shirt and bared his chest, then said, 'I'm ready now, Mr. Law.'

C H A P T E R

**65**

SARAH Stoddard finishes her account of William Law's attempt to kill Joseph:

"Mr. Law paced a few steps, turned, aimed, and pressed the trigger. There was complete silence. Then the air rang with profanity, and Mr. Law turned on Charles, accusing him of fixing the gun so it would not go off and threatening to kill even Charles. . . .

"The Prophet, to divert Mr. Law's blame of Charles, suggested that a can be placed on a fence post for Mr. Law to take a practice shot. Relieved, Charles ran for a can and laid it on its side on the post. Mr. Law paced back, took aim, and fired. His 'one shot' streaked through the exact center of the can.

"Even Mr. Law was quiet, as if stunned.

"The Prophet buttoned up his shirt, gave Charles a meaningful look, and then said, 'If you are finished with me now, Mr. Law, I have other things needing to be done. Good morning.'"

Robert D. Foster was the next to confront Joseph, though less violently, but still with vitriolic antagonism. He went straight to Joseph, who records, "He charged me with many crimes, and said that Daniteism was in Nauvoo; and he used a great variety of vile and false epithets and charges." Foster also wanted to face him at a public meeting and publish the results in the Warsaw newspapers.

Joseph instead wished him "to be quiet, and not attempt to raise a mob." So Joseph's counterproposal was that he would face him in a public meeting and that the results be published in the *Nauvoo Neighbor.* But Foster refused to agree to be "quiet" and not go to the anti-Mormon press. Joseph writes, "I then told him I had done my duty; the skirts of my garments were free from his blood; I had made the last overtures of peace to him; and then delivered him into the hands of God, and shook my garments against him as a testimony thereof."

The next day, April 28, 1844, Foster, along with the others who had been excommunicated, as well as a few sympathizers, decided to start their own church. They called Joseph a fallen prophet and appointed William Law as their leader to "take Joseph's place." They chose a committee among themselves to visit and persuade as many Saints as possible to join the new church. Then, most significantly, they ordered a printing press and drew up plans to start a new, "alternative" newspaper—the *Nauvoo Expositor.*

From canvassing the entire city, they were able to gather 300 sympathizers at regular meetings, in which their first item of business was to, coincidentally—since the non-Saints had the same agenda—demand that the city charter be revoked.

Nine days later their new press arrived from St. Louis. It was quite a public spectacle as it was unloaded from a steamboat and hauled atop a wagon. Word spread quickly through the county with much excitement as it was slowly and carefully pulled by horses through the main city streets, winding its way up Mulholland Drive to the bluff above, without any interference from city or church authorities. Then it was set up at an office on the main boulevard, just a block east of the temple. The staff of dissidents quickly set up the equipment and began setting type for their prospectus. In this bold one-sheet publication they proclaimed disobedience to the "political" revelations and proposed to censure the "monarch"—Joseph Smith.

Three days later that prospectus came off the press. And on that morning, May 10, 1844, Robert D. Foster was dismissed as surgeon general of the Nauvoo Legion, and Wilson Law was

CHAPTER 65

427

fired as major general. William Law was officially released as second counselor, and both Law brothers received a complaint filed against them in the Masonic Lodge.

Infuriated by that newest move, William Law went to Carthage and filed a charge against Joseph for adultery and polygamy. Foster also charged Joseph for false swearing.

Joseph would not stand still. On May 26 he made a public defense against the charges of adultery and false swearing, but covered up his practicing polygamy, believing it was not safe for him if the world knew about it. He stated, "I should be like a fish out of water, if I were out of persecutors. . . . I glory in persecutions." He then faced the adultery charge straight on, saying that for the last three straight years he had clerks follow him everywhere and record his every action and word. He shot a sarcastic barb at William Law, the new church's leader: "It appears a holy prophet has arisen up, and he has testified against me: the reason is, he is so holy." He finally faced the accusation of being a fallen prophet and no longer virtuous: "I am the same man, and as innocent as I was fourteen years ago; and I can prove them all perjurers. . . . As I grow older, my heart grows tenderer for you. I am at all times willing to give up everything that is wrong, for I wish this people to have a virtuous leader."

The next morning Joseph and his entourage rode to Carthage for his trial. But once there he learned almost immediately that his case had been delayed until the next term of the circuit court. While leaving, he was threatened by a mob, and sensed the entire town was ready to explode. He realized he and his associates could never again go to Carthage—for any reason—legal or otherwise.

Arriving back in Nauvoo, Joseph began exposing Francis and Chauncey Higbee. Reporting through the *Nauvoo Neighbor,* he accused Chauncey of misusing the spiritual wife doctrine as John C. Bennett had—of seducing three women whom he had promised to make his "spiritual wives." Joseph also exposed Chauncey's brother Francis Higbee of adultery, seduction, and perjury, and obtaining a venereal disease from prostitutes.

JOSEPH SMITH: A BIOGRAPHY | *Richard Lloyd Dewey*

Within a week, the Higbees, Laws, *et al* retaliated. On June
7, 1844, they published their first and only issue of the *Nauvoo
Expositor.* The editor was a non-Mormon member of the city
council and an attorney, Sylvester Emmons, who filled his paper
with invectives directed only against Joseph. The full group
of dissidents likely contributed in some form or another as
they attacked Joseph's control of the land near and in the city,
which was obviously part of William Law and Robert Foster's
agenda. The paper attacked Joseph for abusing the rights of
the city charters, accused him of political intrigue, and cut him
down as the "lawgiver to the church" and "king" of the church.
Interestingly, they did not attack him with the later accusation
of wanting to be a "temporal" king over an "earthly" kingdom.
But their newspaper did attack him for "moral imperfections"—
specifically, polygamy. Austin Cowles, William Law, and Jane
Law wrote statements in the paper claiming they had seen or
heard read a revelation from Joseph that allowed men to marry
up to 10 virgins—a blatant distortion of the truth.

Nathan Cheney reports the general feeling of the Saints
about the attacks—"They printed all the lies the devil could
think of and some that he could not think of."

The newspaper accomplished what the conspirators wanted
it to—it fanned the flames among the non-Saints in the area and
angered the local faithful who saw through the lies. Joseph and
his closest associates felt they had to take some kind of action,
but did not know what. On the verge of pulling their hair out,
they wondered how to deal with this latest, most public attack
yet by the apostates.

When they met, they discussed the possible repercussions
of both allowing and stopping the apostates's publishing. If they
allowed them to continue, they feared it would only goad the
mobs to possible violence and even ruin Joseph's chance for
the presidency. But they knew if they stopped the paper from
publishing, they would be violating freedom of the press, so
they debated its ramifications. Finally, they decided the *Nauvoo
Expositor* was more of a "slanderous rag" and "libel sheet,"
which the New York City government had established case

law concerning—that such presses could be destroyed, since they were not considered subject to the protective umbrella of freedom of the press. If the city sued the paper, there would be sensationalism over the issues. Furthermore, the court would be held outside of Nauvoo, where they knew enemies could rig the jury and win the case, leaving Joseph and friends in an even worse situation—appearing guilty—since they would lose the case on the "issues." At that point, the leaders who would be declared "guilty" by a court of law could be recognized as the administrators of the city charter. And with that established, the state could easily revoke the city charter, causing the city government to be dissolved and allowing the dissenters to take power. From that, Missouri marshals and bounty hunters from three states could swarm upon the town, hunting down whatever fugitives redneck courts could issue warrants against—including and most especially Joseph. Mobs could even throng into the city, playing out the entire Missouri outrage all over again.

One of the major issues to the apostates was polygamy. But William Marks claimed that during this time Joseph said he would stand before the church and preach against polygamy and have it stopped. He also said Joseph would even bring charges against himself (Joseph) and all who practiced it, and that those who would not "repent" of it would be excommunicated. Marks reported Joseph as saying "there must be every exertion made to put it down," and that unless it could be abolished it would destroy the church. Even if Joseph had told him that, Joseph would have meant it in a public relations sense, as he never denounced polygamy as ungodly but, on the contrary, saw it as a sanctifying practice.

However, even if Joseph did say what Marks reported, Joseph changed his mind. Because on June 8, 1844, he called for the city council to investigate the *Expositor.* The meeting lasted parts of three days. In it Joseph read to the council the *Expositor*'s charges and denied them point by point. Then the council members each spoke their peace about what they should do. Many stood and accused the publishers of seduction, theft, and even counterfeiting. Hyrum called the paper a nuisance.

They used a noted legal reference work, *Blackstone*, to determine what a public wrong was. They discussed other case law and viewed it as allowing them to destroy nuisances, since a nuisance destroys the peace. Another council member said their whole community was disgraced by its lies, and proposed suppression of such publications. Hyrum was evidently the first to suggest they destroy the press. Warrington, a non-Mormon, proposed they instead levy a fine of $3,000 for every libel. On the surface that looked good, but Joseph countered the proposal with its reality—that no Saint could go anywhere near Carthage to prosecute the *Expositor* for libel since he himself had just been threatened there.

Both Mormon and non-Mormon historians have for a century and a half conceded that Joseph and his city council acted rashly and made a mistake by having the press destroyed, even calling the action illegal. But the facts as outlined above point out two factors: 1) They carefully considered and debated the matter, and 2) They actually used case law (the historical precedent set by other cities in similar circumstances) in dealing with the situation and, in fact, used sound judgment in their decision, which, unfortunately, writers have been quick to condemn for so many years.

So the council determined the *Nauvoo Expositor* publishers guilty. Specifically, of libel—proclaiming the paper a nuisance—and they ordered Joseph, as mayor, to have the nuisance removed. Joseph, as head of the executive branch over the city, then ordered Marshal John P. Greene, with the assistance of Jonathan Dunham leading the Legion, to go destroy the press. A squad was immediately sent for and gathered to destroy the press, and among their number was Porter Rockwell.

I T was 8 P.M. on June 10, the same day as the council meeting, that Porter marched with a squad of Legion and the city marshal up Mulholland, past the temple, and another block eastward. They stopped at the *Expositor* office door, which was locked. The order to destroy the press was read, but no one inside would open the door. One of the men was ordered to break the lock with his rifle butt, which he did, then the men slowly and without conversation entered—amidst threats and swearing from the dissidents. They grabbed the press and pulled it out into the street, smashing it. They took the type outside and poured it out of its wooden container into the street. Then they grabbed the inside portions of issue number two of the *Expositor* and burned them inside the office.

A crowd of several hundred was gathering outside by now, watching the proceedings, then followed the squad as it was marched back to the front of the Mansion House. There, Joseph made a speech, saying the press was rightfully destroyed and that the men had done the proper thing. He said he would not allow a libelous newspaper to be published in the city again. The people cheered.

When William Law returned from Carthage and discovered his press destroyed, he was livid. On horseback he rode over the type and, he claims, over his broken furniture. The dissidents fled town. The Law brothers and their families boarded a steamboat and went upriver to Burlington, Iowa. No longer was William Law out to fight for rights over real estate and turn Nauvoo's male population into a workforce to make a fortune, realizing, even with Joseph out of the way, he would never polarize the Saints in his direction, a point no doubt driven home when he saw the thousands celebrating the demise of his press. He also doubtlessly realized his paltry group of 300 followers wasn't worth staying in Nauvoo for either, so he decided to rid himself entirely of his ties to Nauvoo. He sold his farms, lots, sawmill, store, steam flour mill, and homes at a $30,000 loss, he later claimed.

Others of the dissidents remained. Their first course of action—head straight for the anti-Mormon press. Robert D. Foster immediately rode off to see Thomas Sharp at the *Warsaw Signal* and make a statement that appeared two days later, June 12, reporting the destruction of the *Expositor,* while calling Joseph "that unprincipled wretch." Then he called for "the Public to avenge this climax of insult and injury."

Thomas Sharp jumped into the fray, finally having the ammunition he had been craving. He finished his diatribe with a capital-lettered call to arms, "CITIZENS ARISE, ONE AND ALL!!!"

Joseph H. Jackson then wrote an anti-Mormon pamphlet in Warsaw, likely using Sharp's printing press.

Thomas Sharp spent the next six days preparing the largest anti-Mormon issue to date. On June 18 he published an "extra" that called for "friends at a distance" to come to their assistance in order to "rid earth of a most heaven-daring wretch."

The next day, June 19, 1844, Sharp published his regularly scheduled issue, stating they must all be determined "to strike the tyrant to the dust. . . . You, fellow citizens, are justified before the world, and in the sight of heaven. Strike then! For the time has fully come."

Mass meetings were staged at Warsaw and Carthage. Rumors were announced as fact that Hyrum Smith had posted a reward for the destruction of the *Warsaw Signal* and had threatened Sharp's life.

Hyrum denied it as "false as hell."

At the Carthage mass meeting they resolved, "We must resolutely carry the war into the enemy's camp.... We will sustain our press and the editor at all hazards." Then they announced they would "cooperate with our fellow citizens in this state [Illinois], Missouri, and Iowa, to exterminate, utterly exterminate the wicked and abominable Mormon leaders."

Joseph suspected that his enemies were now making inroads to the state government, so on June 14 he fired off a letter to Governor Ford explaining their action against the *Expositor.* He said the city council had issued the order, that it had come after "a long and patient investigation," and that it had been carried out without riot or disorderliness—unlike enemies had claimed. Two days later on June 16 he wrote Ford again, clarifying that the Legion was at Ford's disposal to put down any disturbance. Significantly, he invited Ford to Nauvoo to investigate the entire affair.

But by destroying the *Expositor,* Joseph and 17 others were now charged at Carthage for inciting a riot. A sheriff came to arrest him. Joseph knew the trial would not be fair, and he refused to surrender—so he persuaded the Nauvoo court to issue a writ to keep him in Nauvoo while they held their own trial.

In that trial Joseph, Hyrum, W. W. Phelps, and John Taylor, among others, were tried on the same charges as issued in the Carthage arrest warrant and, on June 17, they were acquitted by Daniel H. Wells, a non-Mormon judge in Nauvoo.

But when the sheriff returned to Carthage without the prisoners, a mob of 700 angry locals rushed into a meeting, claiming Joseph was acting "above the law." The meeting was attended with "such excitement I never witnessed in my life," records a member of the Carthage Greys militia.

At Rushville, Illinois, 3,000 men volunteered to fight the Mormons. Hundreds more joined up at Keokuk, Iowa, as well as Green Plains and McDonough Counties in Illinois. Anti-Mormon messengers charged off to Governor Ford to ask him to add the state militia to their invasion. If Ford would not give them the militia, they said, they would just go without them.

On June 18 Joseph responded by calling the Nauvoo Legion together and, standing atop a new building near his home, faced over 4,000 men, with the event recorded by Willard Richards: "'I call God, angels and all men to witness that we are innocent of the charges which are heralded forth through the public prints against us by our enemies. . . . Will you all stand by me to the death, and sustain at the peril of your lives, the laws of our country, and the liberties and privileges which our fathers have transmitted unto us, sealed with their sacred blood?' ('Aye!' shouted thousands.) He then said, 'It is well. If you had not done it, I would have gone out there (pointing to the west) and would have raised up a mightier people. . . . I call God and angels to witness that I have unsheathed my sword with a firm and unalterable determination that this people shall have their legal rights, and be protected from mob violence, or my blood shall be spilt upon the ground . . . and may the thunders of the Almighty and the forked lightnings of heaven and pestilence, and war and bloodshed come down on those ungodly men who seek to destroy my life and the lives of this innocent people.'" That last sentence would literally be fulfilled, many Latter-day Saints believed—along with the earlier Missouri persecution problems prophecy—just 16 years from then with the start of the Civil War, in which entire divisions of men from western Illinois and western Missouri would be wiped out in the most horrid scenes of battle that America had ever seen. It would also be the last war of no morphine or sterilized amputation instruments, and where over 90% of those wounded would die—usually in agony, compared to the opposite statistic of 90% who would live after they were wounded in the following wars.

Joseph believed all the forces of evil were coming to a head and were focused directly on him. He sent immediate word for the Apostles in the East on missions, and all the other missionaries, to head home right away. Among those out of state were Brigham Young in Boston, Orson Pratt, Heber C. Kimball, Orson Hyde, and William Smith.

The enemy, meanwhile, was passing "cannon, ammunition, and men over the Mississippi" by the hundreds from Missouri to Illinois, wrote Willard Richards.

Joseph directed the Nauvoo Legion to dig trenches and pitch tents at the eastern side of town. He also ordered them to begin manufacturing artillery, but then he gave a prophecy. He said no gun would be fired by the Saints during this pivotal period. He begged Hyrum to leave town with his family on the next steamboat to Cincinnati. Hyrum said, "Joseph, I can't leave you."

Governor Ford decided things were getting out of hand and went to Carthage personally on June 21. He found the city militia, known as the Carthage Greys, drilling four hours a day and standing guard at night under the direction of the county constables. Another militia had been called out at Warsaw under Levi Williams. As for reinforcements, Ford directed his general, Minor Deming, to call up local militia in huge numbers from the anti-Mormon populace of Schuyler and McDonough Counties.

Mob meetings, speeches, and horsemen with messages were galloping back and forth among the towns 24 hours a day, filling the cities with excitement. Those non-Mormons who wanted peace were threatened by the anti's, Ford would later write. The anti's spread rumors that the Saints were stealing horses, murdering, and torching property, but whenever those stories were investigated, they were found false. Ford capsulized 10 reasons for the eruption—besides the destruction of the press, of course—their religious views, military strength, polygamy, the new rumors of Hyrum's calling for the *Warsaw Signal* to be destroyed, the Saints' ties with the Native Americans, the land being consecrated for only the Saints' use, Joseph being crowned king, the Danites being revived to shed the blood of non-Mormons, and most importantly their bloc voting. On the same day he arrived, Ford wrote Joseph and the city council, saying that charges had been made against them and to ask that they send representatives to Carthage and give him their account of the situation.

Joseph pulled together affidavits and sent them via two representatives—John M. Bernhisel and John Taylor.

The next day, June 22, 1844, the two men met with Governor Ford. They showed him the affidavits and a letter from Joseph saying it was not safe for him or the council to go to Carthage, and they asked instead for Ford to come to Nauvoo to review the case. In the process, the two men were treated rudely by Ford's staff and kept waiting for hours. When they finally did get in to meet with Ford, he was surrounded by the apostates—the Laws, Higbees, Robert Foster, and 15 others. As the two men tried giving Ford the facts, they were interrupted with shouts and profanity. Ford made up his mind right at that meeting, and even admitted so in his writings later—that Joseph and the city council were all guilty. Ford told Joseph's two representatives at that momentous meeting that Joseph and the others had to come to Carthage for trial, which would demonstrate their compliance to the law and also dissolve public excitement. Even when the two Mormon representatives explained how Joseph's life had been threatened during their last visit to Carthage, Ford would not budge—either from complete naivety, or from the hope that Joseph would be eliminated and the whole problem might go away, or possibly because his decision had been earlier determined by his own political bosses before leaving Springfield, causing Ford to not even listen fairly to the two representatives—one can only speculate. But Ford at this point disregarded the constitutional guarantees of protection and demanded that Joseph and the council members comply with his directive and come to Carthage immediately. He told the representatives to wait while he prepared a message for Joseph and the council. Adding blatant insult to the situation, he made them wait five to six hours, then presented it to them.

The two representatives galloped back to Nauvoo, arriving at 10 P.M. Joseph and the others anxiously opened Ford's letter and read it: "I now express to you my opinion that your conduct in the destruction of the press was a very gross outrage upon the laws and the liberties of the people. It may have been full of libels, but this did not authorize you to destroy it. There are many newspapers in this state which have been wrongfully abusing me for more than a year." Ford failed to consider—or conveniently overlooked—the fact that Joseph's situation contrasted, rather than paralleled, his own—Ford's life was not in danger from mobs being riled up by a libelous press. In any case, he was now passing judgment and acting as a judicial body, rather than as an executive, being the governor. Joseph quickly saw the hypocrisy of Ford's next criticism—that the Nauvoo city council's legislative and judicial powers had been combined. Ford was illegally doing what he was accusing Joseph of doing, although Joseph was technically not illegally blending functions, since the state had granted a certain combination of powers in the city charter. Further, Ford was not even hearing Joseph's side of the story and was passing another judgment on Joseph after hearing only the one-sided case presented to him by the apostates. Therefore, Ford was not only making an ill-formed decision but was acting on it unlawfully. Worse, Ford was not even providing constitutionally guaranteed protection to Joseph and the council members from avowed threats in Carthage, even though he knew full well the volatileness of the mobs and even admitted them in his letter to Joseph and the council, "Excitement is a matter which grows very fast upon men when assembled." In essence, Ford's letter to Joseph was more of an illegal summation before passing sentence—it was not at all worded like a plea for the defendants to appear in court, where everyone is innocent before proven guilty.

Joseph wrote back to Ford just two hours later—now in the early morning hours of June 23, 1844: "We would not hesitate to stand another trial according to your Excellency's wish, were it not that we are confidant our lives would be in danger. We dare not come. Writs, we are assured, are issued against us in various parts of the country. For what? To drag us from place to place, from court to court, across the creeks and prairies, till some bloodthirsty villain could find his opportunity to shoot us. . . . Yet, at the same time, you have expressed fears that you could not control the mob, in which case we are left to the mercy of the merciless. Sir, we dare not come."

Joseph then talked over an idea with his two representatives who had returned from Ford, and with Hyrum, of going to Washington to consult with President Tyler. Among the group of men with Joseph that night were Porter Rockwell and Abraham Hodge. Hodge reports that Joseph was conflicted as he tried to determine what to do.

"All at once Joseph's countenance brightened up and he said, 'The way is open. It is clear to my mind what to do. All they want is Hyrum and myself; . . . they will not harm you in person or property, and not even a hair of your head. We will cross the river tonight, and go away to the west.'"

CHAPTER 67

JOSEPH sent word to Emma detailing what she should do, then he told Hyrum to carry out the plan—Joseph's and Hyrum's families should pack up and board the *Maid of Iowa* steamship, then head down the Mississippi and up the Ohio River to safety, while Hyrum and he would head west.

Just over an hour later, at 2 A.M. on June 23, 1844, Porter Rockwell rowed Joseph, Hyrum, and Willard Richards across the Mississippi in an old leaky rowboat, the men bailing water out with their boots. It was a moonless night and the men could barely see one another. At dawn they made it to the opposite shore. Dead tired, they trudged to the home of a faithful follower in Montrose, Iowa.

Inside, Joseph wrote Emma a letter: "I do not know when I shall go, or what I shall do, but shall if possible endeavor to get to the city of Washington. . . . If you conclude to go to Kirtland, Cincinnati or any other place, I wish you would."

Joseph gave the letter to Porter and sent him back across the river to both deliver the letter to Emma and obtain Joseph's best horses. When Porter presented the letter to Emma, however, she insisted Porter return to Joseph with Reynolds Cahoon and deliver her own letter to Joseph. It was evident she did not want to budge. Cincinnati was out of the question. Porter, obviously disconcerted at her reaction, obtained the horses and agreed to take Cahoon across the river with him. They boarded a barge and crossed the river, where Porter lead Cahoon and the horses to Joseph. Meanwhile in Nauvoo hundreds of people were leaving the city, although considering the city's population of 12,000, probably over 95% were staying, despite the fact most of the merchants on the hill had left.

When Cahoon handed Emma's letter to Joseph, he opened it, only to receive the most devastating communication he had or ever would receive in his life. She asked him to come back and surrender himself. Her property, she said, was too valuable to just walk away from. She hoped and was optimistic that all would work out—after all, he had been arrested and released so many times before that this was just one more time. However, she must have also known how the county, indeed the entire section of the state, was up in arms more than at any point in their lives, and Joseph had made it clear that if taken, this time he would be killed. He also had communicated to her the Lord's will—that she and their people should just walk away from their property and flee west and, in her case, should first go to Cincinnati for protection. She refused. Upon putting the letter down, Joseph then witnessed Reynolds Cahoon fulfill his purpose for being there—forcefully and vocally he reiterated Emma's demands. He told Joseph that people were looking upon him now as a coward for leaving them. That their property was just too valuable to leave. That he should come back and give himself over to the authorities. Cahoon told him, "You always said if the church would stick to you, you would stick to the church; now trouble comes and you are the first to run." Cahoon then said the governor had promised his personal protection. Joseph knew better but was so utterly disappointed in Cahoon and Emma's refusal to accept his counsel, that he stated in complete despair, "If my life is of no value to my friends, it is of none to myself." He then turned to Porter Rockwell, "What shall I do?"

Porter humbly stated, "You are the oldest and ought to know best. As you make your bed, I will lie with you."

Joseph then turned to Hyrum, "Brother Hyrum, you are the oldest, what shall we do?"

Not having Joseph's prophetic insight or perhaps simply equally distraught, his answer was simple, but it was the wrong answer, as it went directly against the prophecy Joseph had made just hours before when his face had lit up at the Mansion House, "Let us go back and give ourselves up."

Joseph informed him, "We shall be butchered."

Hyrum, obviously overly optimistic, stated, "The Lord is in it. If we live or die, we shall be reconciled to our fate."

The men retired to the river shore and there Joseph wrote Ford a letter while they waited for a boat. He told Ford that he would go to Carthage the next day. He also began his court defense, immediately sending for witnesses and attorneys.

Joseph and his friends returned across the river. While he had spent this short time in Montrose, he had what some may describe as a metaphoric vision of what lay ahead: He and Hyrum boarded a steamer that caught fire. They jumped into the ocean and with faith were able to walk upon the water. They saw the boat they had been on float into the nearby town and catch the city afire as the inhabitants looked upon it in horror. What he saw next could have also been merely representative or it could have been a vision of what Joseph had earlier labeled the "paradise" portion of the Spirit World, which awaits those who lived an honorable and moral life on earth (yet which is prior to the Final Judgment and resurrection into one of three degrees of heaven).

He says they began to forget all their earthly troubles as the sun shone brightly upon them. Their brother Samuel soon joined them, and they journeyed together toward the western shore of the ocean, where they could see a city of heavenly beauty. "Its order and glory seemed far beyond the wisdom of man," describes Joseph. A boat came up to them. They boarded it and were warmly greeted. They heard music "such as is not of earth." When they arrived on the shore, they were welcomed by friends, and they could see that the light of the Lord shone throughout the city. Joseph told W. W. Phelps afterward that he felt comforted with joy and peace and that he had truly been in heaven. At the Nauvoo shore, Joseph told them he wished to speak to the Saints one last time, upon which Porter said he must do it by starlight. But they decided there was not enough time. So Joseph went to the Mansion House, greeted his family with hugs, and entered his home, knowing it would be the last night he would spend with them.

Joseph's closest friends came to him early the next morning. At 6:30 on June 24, 1844, Joseph, Hyrum, Porter Rockwell, John Taylor, W. W. Phelps, and 13 other members of the city council started for Carthage, accompanied by Willard Richards and a group of friends. It was warm and sunny, and Joseph talked with a number of people who passed him, telling them he was going like a lamb to the slaughter. He added to Eliza R. Snow, "But I am as calm as a summer's morning; I have a conscience void of offence towards God, and towards all men; I shall die innocent, and it shall yet be said of me—he was murdered in cold blood." The last time he had publicly spoken in Nauvoo he had also said the words, "I go like a lamb to the slaughter," says Eunice B. Snow. But on this day, journeying to Carthage, as he passed the Snow family, he made an interesting nonverbal gesture: "My mother and I," says Eunice, "were standing in the dooryard and, as he passed, he bowed with uplifted hat to my mother." Eunice also says of Hyrum that his behavior was different, as he "seemed like one in a dream, sad and despondent, taking no notice of anyone."

When Joseph's group reached the hilltop, he gazed over the city filled with flowers and neatly kept green yards and proclaimed, "This is the loveliest place and the best people under the heavens. Little do they know the trials that await them." They rode past his farm and he turned back several times to gaze at it. He said, "If some of you had got such a farm and knew you would not see it any more, you would want to take a good look at it for the last time."

They proceeded southeast, down roads that cut through fields and farms, and at 10 A.M. they arrived at a spot four miles west of Carthage, at the farm of Albert G. Fellows. There they came across Captain Dunn with 60 state militia cavalrymen. Dunn gave him Ford's order, which said to confiscate the state-

owned weapons that had earlier been given to the Nauvoo
Legion. Joseph agreed and wrote a note for his senior Legion
officers to "comply strictly and without delay." Dunn, obviously
afraid of marching into what he assumed was a hornet's nest
with his mere 60 troops, requested Joseph to accompany him
back to Nauvoo to make certain there would be no resistance.
Joseph then sent a note to Ford explaining his delay in reaching
Carthage.

Once in Nauvoo, Joseph helped obtain the 200 arms and
three cannons that the state had granted them. Then at 6 P.M.
he and his entourage started back with Dunn for Carthage.
Seeing potential problems with Porter Rockwell accompanying
them—knowing he was a firebrand with confidence and swagger,
and seeing nothing good coming out of gunplay in the streets
of Carthage—he ordered him to stay behind. In an agonizing
decision, Porter complied with his order and rode his horse off
the road to watch Joseph pass. The two men saluted for what
appeared to Porter—believing Joseph's prophecies to always
come true—would be their last.

As Joseph's entourage continued toward Carthage, with their
shadows growing long, they passed Abraham Hodge returning
from Carthage, where he had been sent by Hyrum for news.
Hodge had one comment: "If it was my duty to counsel you, I
would say do not go another foot, for they say they will kill you
if you go to Carthage." But the decision had been made and
they continued on.

They arrived back at the Fellows farm again, four miles west
of Carthage, where they stopped to eat and rest. Catching up
with them was Captain Dunn and his militia with the cannons
and 200 arms. Dunn thanked Joseph for complying so peacefully
with Ford's demand. He promised he would protect Joseph
and his friends even if it cost him his life. Joseph then asked
his friends to return to the safety of Nauvoo, but they refused
to go.

Joseph's group of 17 accompanied Captain Dunn and his
60 cavalrymen into Carthage, where they entered at 11:55 P.M.
into the midst of a broiling mob. Among them were 1,400 local

militia, the most out-of-control being the Carthage Greys, which consisted of 30 men. The pot had been boiling all day, the men getting more intoxicated with each passing hour. As the Saints were brought in, the Carthage Greys militia tried breaking through the cavalry, shouting threats. Dunn took the prisoners through the maze of men toward Hamilton's Hotel and Tavern just east of the public square.

Not far behind the Carthage Greys in anti-Mormon hatred was the militia from McDonough and Schuyler Counties, so it was ironic that the Carthage Greys were shouting and, according to witnesses, trying to push the McDonough militiamen, who were protecting the prisoners, out of their way so they could harm the prisoners. The Greys then began throwing their rifles into the air and watching them fall with the bayonets sticking in the dirt, all the while whooping and threatening.

Captain Dunn led the prisoners into the safety of the hotel. The Greys crowded outside its windows and doors, shouting for the prophet. To quell the noise, Governor Ford, who was lodging at the same hotel, finally stuck his head out a window and called for quiet: "I know your great anxiety to see Mr. Smith . . . but it is quite too late tonight. . . . I assure you, gentlemen, you shall have that privilege tomorrow morning as I will cause him to pass before the troops upon the square, and now I wish you to return to your quarters." The mob turned away, one yelling, "Hurrah for Tom Ford."

Early the next morning, now June 25, 1844, the city was filled with excitement. The prisoners were marched from the hotel to the constable's office and were officially surrendered to Constable Davis Bettisworth, their guards telling him that the governor had promised his protection and would see they were granted a fair trial. The constable then allowed state officers to take the prisoners for part of the morning.

At 8:30 A.M. Governor Ford sent the various militia to the public square. He climbed atop an old table and addressed them till 9 A.M. Illegally acting as judge and jury, he declared the Smiths guilty of all charges against them, then said the law must take its course. Perhaps he was trying to soothe their feelings with this speech, but possibly not, as the end result was to rouse them up into a veritable lynch mob. With the people in a near-riotous state, Ford went to the Hamilton Hotel and collected Joseph and Hyrum so they could be paraded among the troops, in order to keep his promise to the troops.

As they walked out of the hotel and into the street, Ford marched several paces in front, leaving General Minor Deming to protect the two prisoners. Deming took Joseph on his right and Hyrum on his left. Following them were three Saints in the second flank—W. W. Phelps, John Taylor, and Willard Richards.

The prisoners were possibly then taken to Deming's headquarters, where the Greys were on guard. The Greys, still the most unruly of all the militia, ironically now found themselves protecting the prisoners, walking in a triangle with rifles raised, keeping the raging nonmilitia mob back. The Greys, no doubt, were toeing the line due to the fact Deming and Ford were in their midst. With the mob pushing the Greys and shouting at the prisoners, the Greys nevertheless managed to escort the party 300 yards to the 57th Regiment's position.

There, the prisoners were paraded by Ford before the troops of that regiment. Then an unexpected twist occurred. Ford introduced Joseph and Hyrum as generals about 20 times as they passed through the troops. According to one source, it was General Deming who introduced the two prisoners incessantly as "Generals of the Nauvoo legion." The troops were offended by Ford or Deming using the term "generals," as titles for Joseph and Hyrum. The Greys threw up their hats and drew swords in defiance. The same source, Samuel Williams, an officer of the Carthage Greys, claims that as the prisoners were marched back with Deming, the Greys began "hissing, groaning, and making all sorts of hellish sounds" because they thought they had been commanded to march with the Smiths as an "honor guard." Williams writes he "had no more command over them than I would have had over a pack of wild Indians." He then claims Joseph fainted, and rumors spread that he fainted three times, but those with him disagree, and it is highly doubtful that Joseph showed such vulnerability, being used to violent opposition and mobs, having been threatened many times before in Palmyra, Kirtland, Far West, Liberty, Dixon, and Carthage, while actually being violently abused in Kirtland and Dixon.

General Deming possibly ordered the Greys to be put under arrest, upon which one Grey reportedly jumped atop a wagon and told his fellow militiamen to place powder in their muskets and not surrender their arms. This man atop the wagon, according to the *Warsaw Signal*, was the Grey's captain, Robert F. Smith, who shouted at his men, asking if they would submit to arrest. When they yelled "No!" back to him, he ordered them to load their weapons with ball cartridges. Deming demanded their weapons but they refused to surrender them. The *Warsaw Signal* concludes that the Greys were "wrought up" and ready to shoot the prisoners—and would have, had Deming pushed his order any further—but he backed down. Deming, however, claimed he never called for the Greys' arrest—only for their officers to see him at his quarters.

Governor Ford, hearing that the prisoners were being escorted about with "honor"—with the militia acting as their "honor guard," since Joseph and Hyrum had been introduced to them as "generals"—and learning the militia was angry about it, hurryied to the local militia and told them the prisoners were not being "honored." He explained he just wanted to show them the prisoners, and claimed it was not his idea to introduce them as "generals." It is very possible that he was backstepping, because, as stated, it had been either he or Deming who had come up with the idea of introducing the Smiths in that manner. At this explanation the crowd cheered for about two minutes, "and we made some noise," reports Williams.

The parade was over now and the prisoners were escorted to the hotel. Up in his room, Joseph wrote Emma a letter of reassurance—reporting that the governor was treating them kindly. His words reflected those of a man who did not faint: "When the truth comes out we have nothing to fear. We all feel calm and composed." Despite the premonitions of never seeing his city again, he seemed optimistic, because of Ford's and

Deming's determination to protect him and Ford's reassurance of a fair trial. Hyrum similarly wrote his wife that the governor wished to "put down mobocracy." He expressed optimism that they would have a fair hearing since they knew they were "innocent of any crime, and, 'truth will prevail.'" He added there were many people passing to and from Nauvoo, which would continue daily, "so that you will hear the news regularly."

Joseph also wrote Porter Rockwell. He advised him to remain in Nauvoo and not be taken prisoner by anyone. Porter, unable to read, had others about town who could and did read Joseph's letter to him.

At 4 P.M. the prisoners faced Justice of the Peace Robert F. Smith again. Ironically, he was also captain of the Carthage Greys and held active membership in the anti-Mormon party started by Thomas Sharp. He charged Joseph and company with riot, because they destroyed the *Expositor*, but released them on bail of $500 each, demanding they appear at the next term of the circuit court. Now free to go, most of Joseph's party returned to Nauvoo. But Joseph and Hyrum decided not to go with them—instead, always acting as the peacemakers, they chose to talk briefly with Ford and then go on to the Hamilton Hotel—a decision that would forever change the face of church history. While there, at 8 P.M., a constable appeared with a *mittimus* that Robert F. Smith had conjured up, saying they had to be held in jail until they could be tried for treason. Joseph's attorneys, James W. Woods and H. T. Reid, were present, and they argued that the *mittimus* was illegal because the charge of treason had not been made at their *hearing*. Woods said a justice could not send a man to jail on any criminal charge without first having a preliminary investigation of their possible guilt. Woods then went to see Ford, still in his nearby hotel room, to complain. Ford refused to get involved, saying he could not get in the way of a civil officer, such as the constable who was merely doing his duty.

Justice of the Peace Robert F. Smith then illegally acted as the executive branch, the captain of the Greys, by sending his soldiers to carry out the *mittimus* he had issued as the judicial branch. The difference between his blending of powers and that afforded to the Nauvoo city council was twofold: 1) Nauvoo had legally been granted a melding of powers by the state legislature (plus the three branches of government, though closely tied together in Nauvoo, were still spread out among various individuals), while the Carthage city charter did not grant such provisions; and 2) Robert F. Smith was overstepping all legal bounds by acting as judge and executive administrator at once.

Joseph and Hyrum were taken by the Greys through an angry crowd. They were escorted from the hotel to the jail a half block from the town square. It is possible Captain Dunn and his state militia guarded Joseph and Hyrum on their walk to the jail, probably to better protect them from the mob, since the Greys were not so inclined. Joseph and Hyrum were also joined by eight friends, including Dan Jones and Stephen Markham, the latter whacking away at the drunken mob with the large hickory cane he dubbed "the rascal beater."

AT the jail the prisoners entered a small foyer with a room on the right for the jailor and his wife, which led to a stairway that went upstairs. On the second level to the right was the debtors' jail, where Joseph and his group would sleep. Directly ahead of the stairs was the actual jail, complete with bars inside. The debtors' cell was a well-lit, open, and larger room than the actual jail cell room. Two windows faced the east and south. A fireplace lined the north wall, and the room had a double bed and several chairs. There was no lock on the door. Jailor George W. Stigall treated them well, giving them the debtors' room. Joseph and Hyrum's eight friends were allowed to stay with them that night, and most would sleep on the floor.

Before going to bed, the prisoners were visited by several officers and guards. Joseph asked them if he appeared to them guilty of the charges being leveled against him—an enemy to mankind, murderer, etc. One answered that it was not apparent to them outwardly, but they could not tell what was in his heart. Joseph responded, saying that was true enough, but he could see clearly what was in their hearts—they wanted his blood spilled—and he told them he was not being persecuted for any crimes that he had actually committed. He then prophesied that because of their bloodthirstiness they would behold scenes of bloodshed to more than their satisfaction—apparently another reference to their future date with destiny in the Civil War.

Joseph and Hyrum both told Dan Jones this night that they were "about to finish their race and go to their joy."

On June 26, 1844, the next morning, Joseph requested Ford to see him, which he did. They spoke a long time, having a friendly chat, and disagreed mainly over the destruction of the *Expositor*—Ford felt it violated freedom of the press, while Joseph viewed it like a putrefied carcass that needed removing. Joseph told Ford that he had heard that Ford was going to Nauvoo. He also told Ford that he, Joseph, would not be safe with the governor gone. Ford then promised to take Joseph and Hyrum with him if he did go to Nauvoo.

Once Ford left their meeting, Joseph spent the day dictating to Willard Richards the events of the past several days. Jones and Markham meanwhile carved at the door with a small knife to make the latch work, in case they were attacked.

That afternoon Constable Davis Bettisworth wanted to take Hyrum and Joseph to the courthouse for Robert F. Smith to examine them on the charge of treason. Stigall, the jailor, knew this attempt was illegal and initially refused to let the prisoners out of his jail, but the Carthage Greys threatened him, so he let the prisoners go. When Joseph and Hyrum met with Robert F. Smith, their attorneys decided to subpoena witnesses from Nauvoo. The judge told them to have the witnesses there at noon the next day, June 27, whereupon Joseph and Hyrum were sent back to jail.

Staying with them that night were three fewer friends— now five total, who read together The Book of Mormon; then Joseph bore his testimony to the guards telling them of his divinely appointed mission, of the restoration of the gospel, the visitation of angels, and that the kingdom of God was again upon the earth—and reiterated that was the real reason he was imprisoned, not because of breaking any laws. Different shifts of the Carthage Greys had been assigned to watch the prisoners from outside the jail, but occasionally they would visit him inside. Late at night they finally lay down to sleep, but Willard stayed up writing until the last candle burned out. Although Hyrum and Joseph slept on the only bed, when a gunshot was heard outside, Joseph left the bed to sleep on the floor with his friends. There, Joseph asked Dan Jones if he was afraid to die. "Has it come to that?" asked Jones, who added that he was not afraid. Joseph next gave a prophecy—which would be his last. He told Jones he would live to see Wales and fulfill a mission there, which came to pass.

Meanwhile there was an anti-Mormon meeting held at the Hamilton Hotel each day that week, which was so well organized that delegates attended from every state in the union except three. They were conspiring over the best way to "stop Joseph and Hyrum Smith's career." They were told that if the Illinois and Missouri representatives would combine together to kill Joseph, they would not be brought to justice for it. How one could make that promise without having substantial ties to judicial and/or executive branches of Illinois state government, one can only surmise. Stephen Markam, a friend of Joseph, climbed up the hotel stairs and suddenly entered the meeting. The proceedings, obviously, came to a quick halt.

The next day, June 27, 1844, the prisoners and their friends arose. Joseph asked Dan Jones to go downstairs and find out what had caused the gunshot he had heard during the night. Jones was surprised when he ran into Frank Worrell, the officer on duty of the Carthage Greys. He was especially surprised when Worrell told him: "We had too much trouble to bring old Joe here to let him ever escape alive, and unless you want to die with him you had better leave before sundown. . . . You'll see that I can prophesy better than Old Joe." Panicked, Jones ran to the Hamilton Hotel to tell Governor Ford. On his way Jones heard more on the town square—a Warsaw militiaman telling a crowd, "Our troops will be discharged this morning . . . but when the Governor and the McDonough troops have left for Nauvoo . . . we will return and kill those men, if we have to tear the jail down." The mob cheered.

Jones hurried to the hotel, ran up the stairs, found Ford, and reported to him the threats he had overheard. Ford's reply was:

"You are unnecessarily alarmed. The people are not that cruel." Dan Jones then demanded of the governor that the Greys be replaced as Joseph and Hyrum's guards. "If you don't," added Jones, "I have only one prayer—that I will live to testify that you have been warned."

Back at his cell, Joseph told one of his attorneys he would not live another day, "so fully was he impressed with the belief that he would be murdered."

Soon John P. Greene, marshal of Nauvoo, entered Ford's quarters and told him that if he went to Nauvoo and left the prisoners in Carthage, they would be murdered. Ford's response was—Greene was overenthusiastic. One of Ford's own aides then told the governor that a conspiracy was out to kill the Smiths, but Ford remained recalcitrant.

Next, Cyrus Wheelock went to Ford and told him that while *technically* the law might protect them, *realistically* nothing could shield them from assassins. Ford finally might have wavered from his arrogant position, but not enough to change course, when he replied: "I was never in such a dilemma in my life, but your friends shall be protected. . . . I have the pledge of the whole army to sustain me." But what he did with that army was amazingly ineffective.

At the jail, Joseph dictated a letter to Emma. He informed her there would be no exterminating order. He also reiterated his innocence, and he told her to have Jonathan Dunham tell the Saints to remain home unless the governor came to visit and talk to them. He said it was the duty of all men to protect themselves and their families. He finally told her to give his love to the children and all his friends. After finishing his letter he dictated a postscript.

At 9:40 A.M. he dictated a second postscript to Emma, saying he saw that Ford was about to disband the troops—all but a small guard to protect the prisoners, as Ford planned to go to Nauvoo to address the people. He concluded, "This is right, as I suppose," but he did not express his grave disappointment that Ford was breaking his promise to take the prisoners with him if he was to leave the city.

One can imagine Joseph's feelings when he saw Governor Ford leaving town with the only band of neutral troops—the state militia—led by Captain Dunn. Ford later wrote his reason for going without Joseph—that Joseph's life would be in danger had he taken him to Nauvoo, which, although true, was a weak excuse in light of the fact Joseph was in far greater danger staying in Carthage with only his enemies, the Carthage Greys, to guard him, and also because of the fact he had made a promise to Joseph to take him if he went to Nauvoo.

One reason Ford was leaving was to intimidate the Saints in Nauvoo with talk of extermination if they should retaliate in the event Joseph was harmed. A second reason was that he had evidently heard the Hancock County militia planned to march on Nauvoo, searching for counterfeit money and, in the process, show off their numbers so the Saints would be dissuaded from fighting, and also to prevent future Mormon "problems." Ford later wrote that he at first liked the idea, but then he heard the Hancock County militia were threatening destruction and killing in Nauvoo. He also saw that the Hancock County troops were growing more excited as they prepared to march out, so he changed his mind, wanting to prevent them from finding an excuse to start a battle. The county militia would have lost such a battle, Ford points out, but many innocents would have been killed. Still, Ford's decision for deserting Joseph to accomplish these things in Nauvoo was questionable at best.

Ford then made his biggest mistake. In Carthage, when he saw the Hancock County militia all excited about starting a battle in Nauvoo, he changed part of his plans. He disbanded half the Carthage Greys right on the spot—a huge blunder if he was trying to protect the prisoners, because the Greys now had no military orders or commander to follow and keep them in line.

Then, part way to Nauvoo, Ford made another tremendous error—he sent a messenger to the Warsaw militia to disband. That militia was marching to a halfway point between Warsaw and Carthage called Golden's Point, planning to meet the Carthage Greys there for the march into Nauvoo. When they had gone about eight miles from Warsaw, on their way to their rendezvous spot at Golden's Point, they received word from Governor Ford to disband. But Ford did not simply send an order for the Warsaw militia to disband—he simply cut them loose.

With no military leaders directing them at that point, Thomas Sharp took over, inciting many of them to march into Carthage, joined by some in their ranks who shouted they must go and kill the Smiths. While certain members of the Warsaw militia refused to go along with the plot and started back for home—which was Ford's apparent intention—other disbanded Warsaw militiamen decided they wanted more excitement. They plastered their faces in mud mixed with gunpowder and struck out for Carthage. They were about 85 in number.

As they made their way to Carthage, one of the Carthage Greys came upon them and told them the governor was gone now and that the Smiths had to be killed quickly, before he returned.

CHAPTER 69

O N his march to Nauvoo, Governor Ford, with Deming's state troops, had been gone only about two hours when Ford decided to send a message to the Carthage Grey's captain, Robert F. Smith, saying he feared violence against the prisoners, so he expected Robert F. Smith to do his military duty. Captain Smith agreed he would and sent the message to the governor.

Joseph then wrote a quick note to Jonathon Dunham, requesting the Nauvoo Legion to come to his rescue. Joseph got the note downstairs to several horsemen, who took off for Nauvoo, but for an unknown reason Dunham never received it or, if he did, never sent the troops as Joseph requested.

Joseph next sent a letter to an attorney he had once hired— the very capable Orville H. Browning. Browning had defended Joseph before Judge Stephen A. Douglas in June 1841, seeking a writ of *habeas corpus*. Had Browning failed on that occasion three years earlier, Joseph would have been extradited to Missouri. Now he wrote Browning, asking for his services in defending him once again—this time against charges of treason for a hearing scheduled for June 29.

After writing this letter, Joseph's friends were forced to leave, except for John Taylor and Willard Richards. When Jones came outside with the letter, a guard shouted to the mob that the letter was destined to the Nauvoo Legion ordering a rescue. The mob charged him, but Jones outran them.

All his escape managed, however, was to galvanize the mob. They wanted to kill Joseph before the Mormon army would arrive, not knowing that the letter was merely meant for a lawyer.

In jail Willard Richards took ill. Joseph sent Stephen Markham out for medicine but, when Markham returned, the mob forced him out of town at bayonet point.

Cyrus Wheelock entered the jail, sneaking a pepperbox pistol under his overcoat, the guards not finding the coat suspicious since it was raining outside. It was a loaded, primitive six-shooter, known for misfiring as much as it fired. John Taylor had owned it and given it to Cyrus before going to Carthage. Joseph asked Cyrus if he shouldn't keep it for his own safety, but Cyrus said it was meant for Joseph, because it was an act of heaven that he was not searched when he entered the building. Joseph took it from him and then handed another weapon over to Hyrum—a single-shot pistol that had been snuck in to him earlier by John S. Fullmer. Joseph then said, "We may want to help the guard defend the prison." Hyrum took it, but said, "I hate to use such things or see them used."

Joseph responded, "So do I. But we may have to defend ourselves." They asked Cyrus to get several more pistols or revolvers in case they needed them. They also sent him back to Nauvoo with messages for friends and family. Cyrus's orders were to tell the Legion not to take any military action and to keep the city calm. This was not a reversal of Joseph's earlier order to Jonathon Dunham to come rescue him—it was an order to not get into aggressive actions with their enemy in or outside the city, separate from the rescue operation he had ordered.

Joseph and Hyrum felt "unusually dull and languid, with a remarkable depression of spirits," reports Cyrus, adding they felt "gloomy and surcharged with indefinite ominous forebodings."

At about 3:15 P.M. Hyrum asked John Taylor to sing the new hymn, "A Poor Wayfaring Man of Grief." The sad, serious tune of the song fit their feelings, says Taylor. In Nauvoo Ford arrived with the state militia and wished to address the Saints.

Obeying Joseph's requests, the Saints had stayed at home, but now assembled only for the purpose of hearing out the governor. Before the assembled crowd, Ford gave one of the most insulting speeches the Saints had ever heard, as he first passed judgment against Joseph on the "crime" in which he was already at Carthage to be tried for, and in the process Ford amazingly blamed the entire city, telling it that all its citizens must atone for its council's decision:

"A great crime has been done by destroying the *Expositor* press and placing the city under martial law, and a severe atonement must be made. . . . Depend upon it—a little more misbehavior from the citizens, and the torch, which is already lighted, will be applied, and the city may be reduced to ashes, and extermination would inevitably follow. . . . If anything of a serious character should befall the lives or property of the persons who are prosecuting your leaders, you will be held responsible."

In Carthage the only troops left to guard the prisoners were half the Carthage Greys, camped out at the public square, nearly a half mile from Carthage Jail. (The other half had earlier been disbanded by Ford.) Only six or eight soldiers were left to guard the jail at one time, in rotating shifts. The conspirators met with the guards and persuaded them to load their weapons with blanks, according to Major Deming (while Frank Worrell would plead the 5th Amendment when questioned about it).

It was in the debtors' room upstairs that Joseph and the other three dealt with the heat and likely high humidity. John Taylor and Willard Richards still refused to protect themselves by leaving. The other three men then asked Taylor to sing "A Poor Wayfaring Man of Grief," which is about a man who, the listener realizes at the end of the song, is Jesus Christ. When Taylor finished singing, Joseph asked him to sing it again.

All four men heard a rustling outside at 4 P.M. It was the changing of the guard, with their captain, Frank Worrell, taking charge—the same who had made a threat to Dan Jones that morning. (Captain Robert Smith was in charge of the rest of the Greys still on duty in the public square.) The prisoners then sent for some wine to revive their spirits (this was still before the Word of Wisdom became a commandment). The men shared it with their guards, who probably entered their room. This may have made an interesting moment, because Worrell and some of the others were part of the plan to attack the prisoners at any time. One can picture Worrell graciously drinking with his guests, even laughing and charming them. At 5 P.M. jailor Stigall came to the prisoners and suggested they go into the cell. Because of the increased heat in that room, Joseph was likely hesitant, but willing, and told the jailor they would go in after supper. His two friends spoke up and said they would go in with them. But they never went into the cell. They finished supper in the debtor's room while the following events were occurring elsewhere:

The Hamilton Hotel owner's son William and his friend were sent by William's father, Artois Hamilton, to spy on the Greys. They climbed the courthouse cupola and watched everything going on below from a telescope. At about 4 P.M. they saw men gathering on the prairie two miles outside of town—probably in the northwest. One of the boys scampered down from the courthouse and ran off to tell Captain Robert F. Smith, who told both boys to stay on watch and tell only him if the men out on the prairie came toward the jail.

Young William saw the men 45 minutes later closing in on the jail in single file at a quick step. They were sneaking along at the north end of the rail fence, where no one on the ground could see them. They were moving toward the jail and keeping their guns low and out of sight. William again scampered down from the courthouse and went running to tell Captain Robert F. Smith, but could not find the captain. He kept looking, however, and finally found him, after the invaders actually reached the jail.

The rank-and-file men of the sizable Greys unit still on duty at the public square apparently knew nothing of the attack and were not in on it. One officer of the Greys ran into his home and told his family that men (likely the off-duty Greys, combined with the just-disbanded painted-face Warsaw militia) were heading toward the jail to grab Joseph and take him to the public square to hang him. After buckling his sword on his belt, he ran back to his company of Greys on duty at the public square. His sister-in-law, Eudocia Baldwin Marsh, then rushed to the door and saw the Greys at the public square running about to form up as troops, and they looked frightened. She then heard that the Mormons were coming to rescue the prisoners.

The Greys at the public square were sleeping on their bunks when Captain Robert F. Smith awoke them and tried snapping them into formation. Being half asleep, they obeyed listlessly. One of them, the younger brother to Eudocia, was upset that they were not being organized more quickly to protect the Smith brothers. Because of the commotion he was raising, one officer grabbed him several times and shoved him back into formation. He finally pulled free and yelled to his fellow troops: "Come on, you cowards, d - - - you, come on! Those boys will all be killed!" He then ran with his gun as fast as he could toward the jail.

After many delays, according to young William Hamilton who still watched from the courthouse cupola, the Greys finally formed up and marched with no particular haste to the jail, their flag flying and their weapons on their shoulders. Anti-Mormon Samuel O. Williams may be accurate, or may be covering up for their incompetency, as he claims the Greys practically ran in double quick time, the reason being they thought they were being attacked by 400 Mormons, because their lookout thought it was the Saints who were sneaking through the meadow and along the fence toward the jail, not the disbanded Carthage and Warsaw militia. The more reliable version, however, is from Eudocia Baldwin Marsh.

One of the disbanded Greys, named Darnell, writes he was east of the jail getting his horse, when he saw a file of men stooping and sneaking forward, wearing hunting shirts and having brown-painted faces. He says they were approaching from the northwest corner of the pasture. He ascertained by their body language that the guards at the jail were *expecting* these men.

Meanwhile in the jail, Hyrum asked John Taylor to sing the same song as two hours earlier. Taylor said, "Brother Hyrum, I do not feel like singing." Hyrum said, "Oh, never mind; commence singing, and you will get the spirit of it." So Taylor began singing. Soon after, he was sitting by one of the windows when he saw men with painted faces coming around the corner, heading for the front door.

Meanwhile, young William Hamilton, the spy from the courthouse cupola, arrived at the jail and saw the guards clearly acting like they knew what was about to happen. They fired at the attackers from only 20 feet away, but no one was hit. Others claimed they saw the guards shoot into the air. The attackers then jumped over the low fence and ran toward the jail, surrounding it. Only one guard of the eight or ten tried holding them off, obviously not part of the conspiracy, but the attackers told him not to fight back. Others claim the guns had blanks in them.

From upstairs in the debtor's cell room, the four men heard the commotion downstairs. Then came a shout for surrender, accompanied by three or four gunshots, possibly as warning shots to the jailor Stigall in order to intimidate him. Willard Richards then ran to the window and saw attackers outside. Immediately came the thundering noise of the mob charging up the stairs. The mobbers began firing their guns, but were actually firing into the wrong room—not the eastern debtor's prison where the prisoners were. Rather, they were shooting toward the northern room, where the celled room was located. When the four men in the debtor's room heard the shots, they slammed the door shut.

Hʏʀᴜᴍ went for the single-barreled pistol. Joseph lunged toward the six-shooter. Richards grabbed a cane and Taylor picked up Markham's big "rascal beater." Because the latch was still not usable, both Richards and Taylor propped themselves against the door. Gunshots now came from the doorway. When the mob shot at the door latch, the four men inside jumped back—Joseph, John, and Willard to one side, while Hyrum stayed right in front of the door.

One shot came through the wood door panel and hit Hyrum in the left side of his nose, the ball going into his brain. He was also hit at the same time by a ball coming from the open window behind him. Then was shot two more times. He fell, groaning, "I am a dead man."

Joseph dropped his defense and leaned over Hyrum, saying, "Oh, my poor dear brother Hyrum!" He watched Hyrum die, then rushed to the doorway, opened it a few inches, stuck his gun through the opening and fired all six shots. Only three of the shots fired, hitting and wounding three different men.

He then pushed his fist through the door and punched one man in the neck, a disbanded young militiaman from Warsaw. The *Atlantic Monthly* reports Joseph's bravery and defiance— shooting a Mr. Wills, an Irishman, in the arm; a Mr. Gallagher from the Mississippi river bottom, in the face; a young man named Voorhees from Bear Creek, in the shoulder; and a man named Allen, who was 6'2". Willard Richards and John Taylor then pushed against the door to shut it.

The mob on the stair landing pushed several times against the door, using their combined weight to force it open. But the men inside were strong, and the door only opened slightly. Gun barrels poked through. With Joseph bracing against the door, Richards and Taylor were able to take some of their weight off the door and now had both arms free to swing their canes. For at least several seconds they smacked the gun barrels away. Shots went into the room, hitting the ceiling and walls. But the sheer force of the mob overwhelmed the prisoners, and eventually the door opened several more inches.

John Taylor continued knocking down gun barrels with his cane. Still, more rifles were poking through the door and firing into the room. Joseph said, "That's right, Brother Taylor, parry them off as well as you can." Willard Richards continued beating away barrels as best he could.

The mob members who had fired their single-shot weapons were not about to charge into the room, acting cowardly enough to retreat out of the way and let other mob members, those with loaded weapons, replace them at the doorway. The new men also created a force as they were pushed from behind, by virtue of the increasing size of the mob down the stairs, and the door finally swung open.

Being overrun at the doorway, Richards and Taylor were forced away from the door.

Taylor ran to the window. A lead ball from the doorway went into his left thigh. Paralyzed, he stumbled on the window sill and began slipping outside. A lead ball fired from outside hit him in the chest and knocked him back into the room. The same lead ball hit the backside of his watch in his vest pocket, stopping it at 5:16.

When he fell to the wood floor, he was shot in the left wrist and then again below the left knee. He began crawling and was shot a third time in the left hip, cutting open his flesh and spurting blood onto the wall and floor. He managed to crawl underneath the bed but was hit twice more.

Richards was never hit straight on, but was grazed on the left ear. When the door had been flung open, he was thrown against the wall behind it and found himself out of the path of lead balls. Over the next few seconds, he saw Joseph scramble to the window sill, where both Richards and Taylor claim Joseph was trying to draw gunfire onto himself to save his friends—which he did. As he prepared to leap out of the window, he was shot four times—from the door and from outside—hit in the right side of the chest, his right collar bone, his lower abdomen, and his back. At the window he swayed with an arm and a leg outside. Willard Richards adds that as he fell out the window he said, "O Lord, my God."

Thomas Dixon, standing about 10 steps away from the well, said Joseph "raised himself against the well curb, drew up one leg and stretched out the other, and died immediately." Another said that after Joseph braced himself against the well curb he said "in a low but distinct voice, 'God's will be done.'" Two witnesses say he was untouched once on the ground, but some accounts say he was stabbed or shot again. However, the body showed no additional wounds.

Another account says that while the mobbers surveyed their handiwork, they saw a light shoot through the clouds onto Joseph, and the scene became solemnly still. A pamphlet published the next year said that one witness, William Daniels, claimed there had been a light that stopped a man from beheading Joseph with a sword. But in court the next year Daniels repudiated the contents of the pamphlet, which had been published by Lymon Littlefield in Nauvoo, saying the pamphlet misquoted him. He could have made the retraction under pressure and ridicule, however, (as described later herein at Joseph's murder trial) because another witness in Pontoonsuc, Illinois, backs up William Daniel's report. A homeowner there says that about 10 of the mob went to Carthage upon learning Joseph was jailed, then came to her home the day after the murders, all 10 telling her that "the Smiths were killed and a great light appeared at their death."

Meanwhile, upstairs, Willard Richards was scrambling for safety. When Joseph had fallen out the window, someone called out, "He's leaped the window!" At that, the mob ran back down the stairs. This left Willard Richards free to grab John Taylor from under the bed and take him to the jail cell by going out the debtor's room doorway and to the end of the wall in front of the stairs and around the corner to the right. Richards laid him down on the floor and covered him with a mattress. He told Taylor: "I'm sorry I can't do better for you, but maybe this will hide you. I want you to live to tell the story." Richards actually expected to be killed himself any moment, as there was nothing to cover his large, 300-pound frame and tall height. For the moment, the mob was still outside, so Richards found another spot to hide momentarily.

The mob did charge back up the stairs, but went only into the debtor's room, where they found Hyrum's body. They ran back down the stairs to search for the other two—John and Willard—when suddenly they heard, "The Mormons are coming!" The mob panicked and ran for the woods, leaving Richards' escape as a fulfillment of Joseph's prophecy a year earlier, when he had said that one day Willard would be caught in a hail of gunfire and would see his friends fall to the left and right but would not receive one hole to his clothing.

The mob itself consisted of perhaps half disbanded Warsaw militia and half Carthage militia—the "first unit."

The second Carthage Greys unit—the one still in uniform and still on duty—finally arrived at the jail just as the mob went fleeing into the woods. The Greys made no attempt to pursue the mob. The leaders of the Greys' unit on duty set up a guard at the jail, but probably all but seven took their weapons home and fled town with the other citizens of Carthage. One report, from Samuel O. Williams, stated that only six men stayed in town, and he probably meant the Greys militiamen, not the townspeople because, for one, he was their officer and, for another, it would be seven (not six) Greys who would assist one townsperson and three Saints the next day in taking the bodies away. (The next day, a number of people likely returned to Carthage, including their seventh militiaman.) Another report, from the young man William Hamilton, stated that four families stayed—his father Artois' family and a widow with a sick child, being two of the four families. The two young spies now dutifully helped the city by carrying out an assignment, apparently from their father, to shut all the doors and windows left open when the people dashed out of the city in terror.

At the jail, with a small guard of Greys outside watching— or at least on the premises—Willard Richards kept an eye on things, probably through the ground floor window, and finally went outside when he saw it was safe. He apparently went back upstairs, carried Hyrum's body downstairs, and finally went outside. There he retrieved Joseph's body and carried it inside, laying it beside Hyrum's. Eventually, Artois Hamilton arrived with a wagon.

After both men loaded up the two bodies, they drove to the hotel, where they remained until coffins could be hastily built. Richards scurried about for a doctor, food, and water for his suffering friend, John Taylor, and finally found a doctor just before midnight. Doctor Thomas L. Barnes cared for Taylor, finding that the straw from the mattress used to cover him had stuck to the coagulated blood of his wounds. Barnes cut the lead ball out of his hand with a small, dull knife and a carpenter's compass, making the operation excruciatingly painful. Barnes later said Taylor had "nerves like the devil."

Meanwhile in Nauvoo, other drama was unfolding. Porter Rockwell went into the Mansion House, seeing a number of militia horses tied outside and a state militia guard posted at the entrance. Porter likely intimidated the poor fellow with his wild animal image, having not cut his hair in over a year and a half, and his confident swagger; so he managed to get inside.

Up the stairs of the Mansion House he climbed to retrieve the hat he had left there the previous day, when he walked in on an embarrassing moment for Thomas Ford. One of the Illinoisians was looking at his watch and muttering, "The deed is done before this time." It was just after 5 P.M. Porter did not think much of it, but his appearance produced a huge gasp from the officers and staff. He swaggered outside, climbed atop his horse, and realized something was amiss. He recalled the words he had just heard and the looks on the state officials' faces—and knew Joseph was in trouble. He took off galloping for Carthage.

On the way there he recruited a friend, Gilbert Belnap.

Together the two men rode as quickly as possible down the Old Carthage Road. About halfway there they passed a horseman, George D. Grant, who stormed past Porter and blurted out the news that Joseph and Hyrum were dead—killed by a mob. Porter and Belnap were shocked and grief-stricken. They dismounted and took cover. The mob, still riding full gallop, and spotting only the two men, were feeling their "oats" and confidently decided to take them on. They pulled out weapons and began a charge. They assumed nothing could keep them from ambushing the two Saints. Only Porter was one Saint not to be ambushed.

As the oncoming horsemen charged him, Porter Rockwell dismounted and took aim, while Gilbert Belnap stood petrified at the side of the road. Snatching weapon after weapon from his belts, then catching several tossed to him by his "recovering" companion, he fired at the oncoming horsemen, shooting until his weapons were empty—knocking one horseman from his roan, then another, and another, piling up one corpse after another on the moist dirt road.

Porter began reloading his weapons, so the remaining horsemen stopped for better aim and fired—but their lead balls only splattered mud around Porter. Nothing could hit him. As he continued reloading his weapons, the last remaining mobbers blazed away at him. Still, nothing hit him. Finally, Porter opened fire again, knocking one man off his horse to the mud, then another. And another. The remaining few horsemen realized they were up against something unlike anything they had ever seen and, in awe and terror, turned their horses, beating a hasty retreat, their horses kicking up mud toward Nauvoo as they galloped back toward Carthage.

Porter and Belnap decided to return to Nauvoo, Porter knowing he still must heed Joseph's last admonition, to not let himself ever be taken prisoner.

In Nauvoo Joseph and Hyrum's youngest brother Samuel, age 36, was working on his farm when a messenger rode up and announced the news of his brothers' incarceration—but neither the messenger nor Samuel knew yet of their deaths. So he saddled up his horse and galloped off for Carthage, hoping to protect his brothers from the mob.

Some of the killers, still with painted faces, saw Samuel just outside of town. When they saw him, they chased him. But he made it safely to Carthage. And there the mobbers stopped, afraid to return to the murder scene. Samuel rode forward into the deserted town, likely wondering why the mob stopped chasing him. Making his way on horseback to Carthage Jail, he arrived to find both his brothers' bodies. Moments earlier he had been terrified from the chase, but then, upon discovering his beloved brothers, his mood turned another direction—he sunk into complete despair. From the combined stress, he would take on a high fever and die 32 days later.

Governor Ford probably left the Mansion House just after hearing the news of Joseph's and Hyrum's deaths. He arrived in Carthage with his state troops late at night and spoke to the few remaining citizens on the public square. He told them to desert the city because the Mormons would likely burn it. Then he took off for Quincy, by a circuitous route through Crooked Creek, Augusta, and Chili, as fast as his troops could manage without harming their horses. At his first stop, nine miles south at an inn, he watered his horses and rested. One woman at the scene reports he was scolding others, storming around, and impatient to leave.

He finally arrived at the next major city—Quincy. He immediately ordered someone to ring the bells as an alarm, fearing the Saints might attack even that far south. He then dismounted and wrote letters to Emma Smith and General Dunham of the Nauvoo Legion, saying that the Saints would have justice. He obviously sent these messages to keep the countryside from being annihilated; but this was a promise he wouldn't keep. Also in the letters his first item of business was to cover himself—he claimed he had no part in the conspiracy, and later, either truthfully or as a cover-up, he claimed that the mobbers had hoped all along the Smiths would be murdered while Ford was in Nauvoo, so that the Mormons would retaliate and kill Ford, which would give the mobs an excuse to then attack Nauvoo.

Ford was either misinformed or lied when he stated that after Joseph's death the church leaders preached sermons with profanity, revenge, and hate as their themes, which is not true, judging from numerous early Mormon letters and journals.

The people of Warsaw fled in droves across the Mississippi. Carthage was still a ghost town—food left on plates, livestock grazing, and farms left unattended. John Taylor was still at the tavern being cared for by Artois Hamilton and the doctor, but they and the seven-man guard detail of the Greys were almost the only ones in town, as the woods and villages throughout three counties were filled with frightened, nervous people, certain the Saints would lay torches to all three counties and possibly shoot everything in sight.

The Saints, meanwhile, obediently complied with their leader's request—stay at home. They were told to not seek revenge and they obeyed. Even Porter Rockwell sat in despair, waiting to let justice take its course, wondering with thousands of others who would lead them next.

A few feared Nauvoo would be attacked, and they left across the river for Iowa, but most stayed low and at home, not fearing for their safety, but overcome with grief.

In Carthage the two caskets were probably constructed late at night. Samuel Smith, having discovered his brothers' bodies after the mob chased him into town, helped Willard Richards and Artois Hamilton prepare the bodies for the caskets and load them onto the wagons.

The next morning, Friday, June 28, 1844, the citizens of Carthage and Warsaw began returning to their homes, realizing there would apparently be no onslaught of Nauvoo Legion retaliation.

Heading out of Carthage at 8 A.M. were the two wagons carrying the bodies of the slain. Driving one of the wagons was Samuel Smith. A Carthage Greys militiaman drove the other. Another militiaman sat beside Samuel Smith on the buckboard, and six others rode alongside them, possibly being the detail left behind at the jail the night before, when the Greys were disbanded and fled into the woods with the rest of the citizenry. Among the group driving to Nauvoo down the old Carthage Road was Willard Richards, riding a giant horse to carry his huge frame.

The road was still muddy from rain, and the procession made its 18-mile ride in silence to Nauvoo in the cloudy balminess. The coffins, having no lids, were filled with prairie brush to keep heat and bugs away as much as possible. Joseph's body was also covered with a torn Native American blanket. At 2 o'clock in the afternoon they arrived at the outskirts of Nauvoo.

The Saints did not open stores or go to work that day. When the wagons came rolling into town, hundreds began gathering along Mulholland Street, up on the bluff where the temple stood. Many converts from Ireland and Wales commenced a moaning that was part of their tradition. As the Saints poured into the city from the numerous outlying villages and farms, they packed the street even tighter. They began walking as a massive crowd toward the oncoming wagons as the wagon procession reached the town, then they surrounded the wagons and turned around, following them as they rolled down the streets, going northward until reaching Mulholland, then westward, and finally southwestward down the bluff. Now thousands were walking with the wagons as they made their way to the flatlands below and south to the Mansion House near the river.

Emma and her four children watched along the street, standing among the thousands who lined both sides all the way from the bluff to their home. There were now up to 10,000 grief-stricken people watching, not the least of whom was the pregnant Emma.

Arriving at the Mansion House, Willard Richards announced he would speak, despite his exhaustive ordeal. The massive crowds grew instantly quiet. They knew he had been with Joseph and Hyrum and had experienced the onslaught firsthand. He first asked the crowd to remain peaceful. He stated that he had pledged his life on their good behavior, and drove the point home by saying that John Taylor still lay wounded in Carthage at their enemies' mercy. He told them to leave vengeance to God.

Joseph's and Hyrum's bodies were taken into the Mansion House. The people were asked to return to their homes until morning. The Mansion House doors were closed, and the bodies were immediately washed and the wounds plugged with cotton soaked in camphor, the task being performed by three men, possibly including Elijah Abel, who was not only the African-American close friend of Joseph but who was an undertaker by trade. The two bodies were dressed up, complete with white neckerchiefs, and the two widows were finally granted their wish to see them.

The next day the bodies were ready for viewing—in coffins with a white cambric lining, covered with black velvet, supported with brass. Over the men's faces were glass lids held by brass hinges. The caskets were laid out in the dining hall. At 8 A.M. the doors were opened, and 10,000 people slowly and respectfully filed past, looking at Joseph and Hyrum one last time. At 5 P.M. the last remaining people were asked to leave so the families could grieve in private, and the doors were closed.

George Cannon preserved the most accurate depiction of the two brothers by making "death masks" from their faces. The molds were then filled with plaster. Cannon was the father of George Q. Cannon, the talented biographer mentioned earlier and first counselor to four of Joseph's friends and future church presidents.

Joseph and Hyrum were then secretly buried, so enemies could not molest the bodies, especially since there was still a reward offered for Joseph's head in Missouri. Before going to Carthage, Joseph had left instructions to the Twelve regarding the details of his funeral. The coffins were removed from the pine box caskets and taken into a small bedroom at the northeast corner of the house until the next day. In the pine boxes that people assumed were the real caskets, the undertakers substituted rocks and sand, and then they were nailed shut.

When the funeral took place, the boxes of sand were carried in a horse-drawn hearse to the graveyard and buried amidst a public ceremony at which church leaders spoke.

At the funeral, W. W. Phelps left the Saints an inspiring legacy of the men he loved. Of Joseph, Phelps said: "He came to . . . teach men to walk in the light of the Lord. . . . His words lit up a sacred flame in the heart of the Saint that showed an ocean of existence unexplored by the vain philosophy of the world. . . . He was a man of God . . . who knew what was right and did it, independent of consequences."

The bodies were taken out at midnight on June 29 by armed men and buried across the intersection at the Nauvoo House, which was under construction in the newly dug basement. The earth was smoothed over and covered with wood chips to hide them. Later the bodies were reburied near the southwest corner of the Homestead, and their graves were not marked.

In the weeks following the murders, the perpetrators scurried about, plotting every way they could to get out of trouble.

During these chaotic weeks gossipmongers and speculators threw out opinions on the murders—some claiming Joseph and Hyrum were killed by lead balls fired by mobbers *and* Mormons when the Nauvoo Legion invaded Carthage to free them(!) Others said Missourians were the perpetrators. For over a hundred years most Saints believed it was the Carthage Greys who committed the crimes. But the truth is, it was mostly the disbanded Warsaw militia, led or at least inspired by Thomas Sharp, with only some of the disbanded Carthage Greys.

Sharp and other anti-Mormons had actually hoped that with Joseph gone, the church would dissolve. But the exact opposite occurred, and they witnessed the Saints solidify firsthand. Joseph was now a martyr. Missionaries could build around that, testifying that prophets through the ages had often been martyred. Rather than dissipating, their numbers mushroomed. Soon Nauvoo had 15,000 Saints, with thousands more in other villages throughout the area. Because of the murders there was a settling in by most of the locals, but this was a mere calm before the next storm.

# CHAPTER 72

URING this calm, the church was able to regroup. The Twelve, who were on missions (for both the church and Joseph's presidential election), began hearing the news from local newspapers where they were laboring and from family letters, and they began returning to Nauvoo as quickly as possible. William Smith, however, was advised to stay in the East, because his two brothers had been killed and he might be targeted next. The only two Apostles still in Nauvoo were Willard Richards and the still-recovering John Taylor. Thus, it was Willard and likely leaders of lower quorums who negotiated in behalf of the church, promising Ford that the Saints would be peaceful and not avenge Joseph's and Hyrum's deaths, but rather leave it to the state. Possibly it was Ford's idea that such a covenant should include the following promise from the Saints as well—that they bring no charge against the governor. Willard agreed. Sidney Rigdon may or may not have been involved in such negotiations, but likely was not. He was the one other church leader remaining—as Joseph's first counselor in the presidency. William Law, Joseph's second counselor, had of course apostatized.

This left the church leadership up in the air, confusing many of the Saints. Those vying for church president knew they had precious little time to make their pitch, as the church was one of order, and they were obviously used to having a solid leader.

The "candidates" therefore knew the matter would be settled quickly. Several claimed that Joseph had secretly appointed them to replace him, including Alpheas Cutler, who had married Porter Rockwell's ex-wife and who would later apostatize and start his own small gathering in Iowa.

Another was James Strang, a convert of a few months who would take a group to Beaver Island, Michigan, publish the *Voree Herald* newspaper, hand down revelations, send missionaries to England, and for a time would even attract the likes of Martin Harris, John E. Page, and even John C. Bennett. (His neighbors thought him a thief, however, and in 1850 he proclaimed himself a king. He also went so far as to wave about a letter he said came from Joseph, giving him the authority as next church leader. Brigham, however, pronounced it a forgery. In 1856 he was murdered by two of his followers and his church dwindled.)

Next among the presidential "hopefuls" was Lyman Wight, who led a small group to the Colorado River, near Austin, Texas, and then on to several other locations before dissolving.

Another contender was David Whitmer, whom Martin Harris claimed Joseph and his counselors had laid hands upon on July 8, 1834, and appointed him to lead the church if Joseph died.

Emma meanwhile threw her support to her son, Joseph III (who would end up leading the largest faction outside the main body of Saints that would go to Utah); this was based on her belief that Joseph had ordained their son while in Liberty Jail in 1839 and later confirmed it in 1843. The boy was 12 when Joseph died.

William Smith became another contender. He returned from the East after his brothers' deaths, was made patriarch, but was not content. He asked Brigham to be above all other authorities so that no one would stand at his head. On June 30, 1845, Brigham wrote him back. He said the Twelve would not sanction it "because the president of the church stands at the head of all the officers in the church." He also told William, rather diplomatically in fact, that it was his right to officiate as patriarch to all the world, with no one to control him except the Twelve." William apparently did not take to the idea of being reigned in by the Twelve—or anyone. He had publicly opposed his brother Joseph on one occasion, which in fact brought tears to Joseph, to think his own brother would turn against him, so now he joined with Emma in promoting Joseph III. On October 5, 1845, he wrote a friend, "Brigham Young is a tyrant and usurper and he shall not prosper. . . ." Then William added that he would not "trouble Nauvoo" with his presence much longer. William, who ironically had started the *Nauvoo Wasp* years earlier as a rival newspaper to Thomas Sharp's *Warsaw Signal*, now crossed over enemy lines and *went to Sharp* to publish against Brigham. On October 29, 1845, the *Warsaw Signal* quoted William Smith, saying that Brigham Young was a tyrant encircled about by men who would perform almost any crime at his request. On November 1, 1845, the *Times and Seasons*, the paper that had evolved from *The Wasp,* wrote that William had been excommunicated. Not to be outdone, William excommunicated Brigham Young in St. Louis with his own new council of high priests.

Others believed the church leader "next in line" should take over—which some thought to be William Marks, the president of the high council. Still others, including George Miller, felt the Council of Fifty should select the next president, even though the council was a political, not an ecclesiastical body, which included non-Mormons.

However, in the eyes of the 15,000-plus Saints, it came down to two main choices—Sidney Rigdon and Brigham Young. Brigham being president of the Twelve Apostles.

Brigham's claim apparently stemmed from a letter Joseph had written in Liberty Jail in 1839, stating that the longest-standing member, the "oldest" of the Twelve, should be the president of the quorum. The Twelve determined from that that each new church president would come from the president of the Twelve as well. A stronger position was taken by Wilford Woodruff, then of the Twelve and later church president: "He [Joseph] told us that he had received every key, every power and every gift for the salvation of the living and the dead, and he said, 'Upon the Twelve I seal these gifts and powers and keys from henceforth and forever. No matter what may come to me. And I lay this work upon their shoulders.'"

Sidney's argument was that he was Joseph's first counselor and the only member of the First Presidency remaining. As Joseph's running mate for the President of the U.S., apparently he and Joseph had reconciled their differences after Joseph had accused him just months earlier of conspiring with the Missourians for his arrest. Rigdon's health had failed him for five years, but he still had the energy to pursue the position of church president. He was in Pittsburgh when Joseph was killed, and shot back to Nauvoo, arriving August 3, before the Twelve returned.

The next day he gathered the church membership together in a huge crowd and spoke to them, maintaining that when Joseph was killed he had received a vision from God revealing that he would be the church's guardian until the right man would take Joseph's place. Sidney then requested a special conference for the following Tuesday, but it was delayed until Thursday. On Tuesday evening Brigham returned. The next day at a closed meeting for church authorities, Sidney and Brigham both spoke. There, Sidney again recounted his vision. Brigham stood and said he did not care who led the church, but that he must know "what God says about it." He reminded them, "I have the keys and the means of obtaining the mind of God on the subject."

The next morning, August 8, 1844, the conference requested by Sidney was held. Speaking from atop a wagon in the grove, Sidney spoke for an hour and a half and did not seem his old powerful self, evident, some thought, from the lack of holding God's authority in seeking to lead the church. Brigham called for a second session that afternoon. At 2 o'clock, Brigham spoke to the crowd of thousands: "You are like children without a father and sheep without a shepherd. . . . You cannot take any man and put him at the head; you would scatter the Saints to the four winds, you would sever the priesthood. . . . I tell you in the name of the Lord that no man can put another between the Twelve and the Prophet Joseph. Why? Because Joseph was their file leader, and he has committed into their hands the keys of the kingdom in this last dispensation, for all the world." He addressed them in the stifling heat for two hours.

Later that day Brigham would pen in his journal: "Now Joseph is gone. It seemed as though many wanted to draw off a party and be leaders, but this cannot be. The church must be one or it is not the Lord's." He adds, "The Saints looked as though they had lost a friend [Joseph] that was able and willing to counsel them in all things. In this time of sorrow my heart was filled with compassion." He writes that he had the Holy Ghost with him and was able to comfort the mourning Saints.

Certain members attending wrote afterward of a miracle that took place—they saw the image of Joseph and the voice of Joseph when Brigham spoke—even his personality appeared to be Joseph's. Among those who witnessed the manifestation was Wilford Woodruff. Anson Call states, "Before he had spoken many sentences I discovered that it was the voice of Joseph, and had I have been where my eyes could not have beheld him I should have believed that Joseph had been speaking. It was Joseph's voice and Joseph's gestures through the entire discourse." Witnesses even claimed Brigham took on the facial appearance of Joseph. "The whole assembly heard, as they thought, the voice, saw the form and felt the spirit and influence of the Prophet Joseph. And even nonmembers of the church were startled, and expected to see the presence as well as hear the voice of the departed Seer," reports Andrew Jenson. George Q. Cannon further details: "Who that was present on that occasion can ever forget the impression it made upon them? If Joseph had risen from the dead, and again spoken in their hearing, the effect could not have been more startling than it was to many present at that meeting; it was the voice of Joseph himself; and not only was it the voice of Joseph which was heard, but it seemed in the eyes of the people as though it was the very person of Joseph which stood before them. . . . The Lord gave his people a testimony that left no room for doubt as to who the man he had chosen to lead them was. They both saw and heard with their natural eyes and ears; and then the words which were uttered came, accompanied by the convincing power of God to their hearts. . . . There had been gloom and, in some hearts probably, doubt and uncertainty; but now it was plain to all that here was the man upon whom the Lord had bestowed the necessary authority to act in their midst in Joseph's stead." The apparent miracle was enough for the leaderless Saints: The Lord was endowing the "mantle of Joseph" on Brigham Young.

Sidney then asked that the vote be taken for those supporting the Twelve. The crowd sustained the Twelve with a raise of hands, after which Brigham stated, "This supersedes the other question" (of having Sidney lead the church).

Sidney was crushed. He would not follow the Twelve, feeling he was superior, being Joseph's "right-hand man" for so long. And now he flat out refused to follow their counsel. They met with him and attempted to alter his opinion, but he was defiant. They told him they needed his ministerial license. He would not surrender it.

Not much later Sidney said he would head back to Pittsburgh and expose the entire history of Nauvoo and its evil persons, whether living or dead. On September 8, 1844, Brigham laid out before the high council that Sidney threatened to either lead or destroy the church. Sidney refused to attend, saying he was ill. The council excommunicated him.

In Pittsburgh Sidney returned as promised and started a newspaper, his own version of the former Kirtland paper, with a slightly altered title, *Latter-day Saints' Messenger and Advocate*. In it he denounced the Twelve as polygamists and apostates. He would never return to the faith. Joseph had warned, indeed the Lord had warned through revelations, said Joseph, that men would aspire to honors and succumb to pride and, according to the faithful rank and file, that was especially true of many of the most capable and brightest minds of the day. The egos of some of the most talented, many felt, could not be tamed, but those faithful to Brigham would plow forward, with Brigham at their head.

Meanwhile, because of the church leadership challenge and the Saints trying to readjust from the martyrdoms, the political fury that had begun before the martyrdom was now taking a distant backseat to them; nevertheless, church leaders advised the Saints to vote in the August national elections.

A mass meeting was called to determine who to vote for. They decided to vote for General Minor Deming as the county sheriff and, as coroner, Daniel H. Wells, still a non-Mormon who would, as stated, later convert on the trek west. For state representative, they voted for Jacob B. Backenstos.

With the landslide of pro-Mormon candidates winning the local county elections, the anti's went into a furor. Leading them was Franklin Worrell, the officer of the Greys who had been in charge of the guard at Carthage Jail when the brothers were shot. Worrell seemed particularly incensed that Sheriff Deming had promised to bring the murderers to justice. He wrote to Thomas Gregg, an anti-Mormon writer in Warsaw: "I hope Deming will attempt to arrest some of the mob. If he does, we will then have some more sport—and [make] no mistake."

Deming rented out his farm to a Mormon family in order to serve as sheriff. As a result, he and his young family were continually abused by the roughnecks.

Soon after Deming's swearing into office, the official "wolf hunts" were organized. They began with a public notice that a military camp would be held in Warsaw from September 27 to October 2, 1844, to keep the local militias "excited" in the form of a "proper military spirit." Some of the captains received printed notices that the camp was to be a six-day, blatantly labeled "wolf hunt" in the county. They defined the "wolves" as the Saints and those friendly to them, the so-called "Jack Mormons."

The purpose may have been deeper than many supposed: It was not to harass the Saints so much as it was to coerce the non-Saints who were determined to see justice in the murder trial of the Smith brother's suspects—specifically, Sheriff Deming and others. Four of the 10 militia leaders conducting the wolf hunts were soon indicted for the murders and a fifth was suspected—Robert Smith of the Greys.

The wolf hunters harassed and threatened the people connected with choosing the jury. As Deming says: "There were about 200 directly or indirectly engaged in the murder and they are bound . . . to commit almost any act to save them from infamy and punishment. This number with their relatives and friends forms a bold, desperate and ferocious band, that expect by their perjury and violence to overawe the courts and evade justice. They have so long and often threatened me that I have become familiar with the talk of lynchings and death."

Ironically, the local press blamed the Mormons for destruction and robbery—but they were not guilty—it was the bandits and organized wolf hunters. The Whig newspapers all over the nation sent the false information, however, that it was the Mormons who were guilty. Even late into the 20th century such reports were believed, especially in the Midwest. And ironically the Democrat-connected newspapers would not come to their aid with the truth, even though it was Democrats whom the Saints had elected. So the national press, along with the surrounding counties' newspapers, were all completely one-sided against them. Only the Nauvoo newspapers published the truth about the wolf hunters.

Ford may have been true to his claims that he was the lone man in the wilderness trying to obtain justice for the Saints. He denounced his own party for not coming to the Saints' rescue after seeking their votes and getting elected by the Saints' voting bloc. He also castigated all politicians for turning their back on the Saints in order to avoid unpopularity. Ford claims he sought to keep the peace and obtain justice for the Saints. He called for 2,500 volunteers to ride with him to Warsaw on September 25, 1844, to bring peace to Hancock County. Thomas Sharp attacked him in the *Warsaw Signal* for this and lied, saying the flyers calling for wolf hunts had not been distributed. Part of the reason for the 2,500-man force was "to arrest the murderers," Ford would later write. But because of the press's influence, he could only muster up 450 men—still, it was a large enough force to intimidate the wolf hunters into stopping their plans of attacking Sheriff Deming and the county commissioners.

Because of Ford's bold measure, the leaders of the wolf hunters skipped the state, crossing over to Missouri, as did nearly all the Carthage Greys and three other men who were later indicted, according to Ford.

The murder trial for Joseph and Hyrum Smith began in October 1844. Sixty suspects were presented to the grand jury, yet there was only enough evidence to bring indictments against nine. Among them were Thomas Sharp and three of the four whom Joseph wounded with his pistol during the attack. Four of the nine were never found and thus could not be arrested—including the three who were wounded. Even while under arrest and awaiting trial, Sharp remained unrelenting in his anti-Mormon newspaper campaign. An anonymous writer in the *Illinois State Register* of November 8, 1844, reports of Sharp: "He it is who invents and publishes all the lies about Mormon stealing, Mormon murders . . . for the purpose of exciting the people to riot and murder." The writer also adds a reason that was heretofore unknown: that Sharp's paper is the voice of "a gang of town lot speculators" in Warsaw who are afraid that Nauvoo is about to economically choke Warsaw and ruin their real estate speculations—a motive never mentioned until that article was published.

Brigham, Porter, and others had the safety of the city charter to provide them writs of *habeas corpus*—which kept out-of-town sheriffs and bounty hunters from arresting and spiriting them off to jails throughout Illinois and Missouri—but the city charter was yanked in January 1845, leaving Brigham to become creative in keeping his people from being arrested left and right.

O N one occasion Brigham sent a look-alike from a meeting, wearing Brigham's coat and hat. This was William Miller, who was arrested and taken to Carthage—only to be recognized there as not being the real Brigham Young. In jail that night, the imposter Miller laughed till his sides ached, and the non-Mormons in the tavern joined him in laughter, as the constable had now been tricked twice in the same manner, giving the locals plenty of fodder to laugh at him. Adding to the situation's humor, Miller describes the constable's absolute certainty that he had the right man as he hauled Miller away from Nauvoo: "On the way to Carthage the marshal was very social, and remarked [to me] that the people had got quite a joke upon him for letting Turley [another Mormon who had similarly tricked him] give him the dodge." Miller adds that upon his arrival, "the troops began to whoop and holler and went into town in high glee." They all thought they had snared Brigham Young—until two men later that night came and saw Miller, then trudged into the constable's office and told him once again he had been outsmarted.

Brigham continued to confuse the constables. Whenever they would come into town, Brigham's messengers would send them away on wild goose chases. Ford actually attempted to have the charter merely amended, while newly elected and neutral state representative Jacob Backenstos aggressively fought to keep the Nauvoo charter intact, but to no avail.

Ford then came up with an ingenious idea that helped Brigham—he suggested they make part of Nauvoo a town, so it could have the protection of *habeas corpus*. But the catch was that a town could be only a maximum of one square mile wide. The other main difference between a town and a city was that a town could only have a justice of the peace, who could act as a judge to some extent, but a city could have a full-fledged judge. To cover all of Nauvoo and thus protect all its inhabitants, 12 towns would need to be incorporated—but only one could, and it was. While this did not protect the Saints from marauding sheriffs with arrest warrants, it did give the Saints a semblance of law and order among themselves, and Brigham filled in the very large blank by extending the order of the township to the entire area of Nauvoo by utilizing bishops who worked within the church government to keep peace and civil order in each ward. And each bishop had special deacons to assist him. Even civil disputes and legal problems were for the most part handled respectfully and orderly in this manner. Because of their faith and loyalty to their restored gospel, they kept civility foremost among themselves. So Ford's recommendation had paid off and then been expanded upon.

The temple also continued to be built. One hundred and fifty gigantic stones were placed atop the temple using ropes. Men would work through rain and cold, only briefly pausing when it snowed, so the temple could be finished remarkably quickly. On May 24, 1845, the final capstone was placed on the southeast corner. Brigham stood on the stone and knocked it into place. A band played music, then Brigham spoke, saying he prayed that they would be defended by God and sustained until they could all receive their "temple endowment," a special ordinance necessary for exaltation.

At the temple dedication stood officers of the law, who afterward escorted witnesses to the murder trial in Carthage. Yet the Saints had no hope of protection from the mobs there. Ford also knew the witnesses were in danger of never even arriving, so he wrote Sheriff Deming to warn him and even authorized Deming to call on the militia for help, even from Nauvoo citizens, if need be. Perhaps Ford's conscience was kicking in, because he had no support from either political party at this point and was apparently feeling a semblance of humility, especially since he had so bungled the Smith situation.

At the Carthage courtroom the mobs raged within and without. The witnesses arrived to a broiling mob. Still, the witnesses received no protection because no militia would come to their aid.

Hundreds of locals in Hancock County descended on the courthouse with weapons, ready for war if the Saints decided to show force. At least a few believed the Mormons were going to attack the courthouse if the verdict did not please them, and the rumor seemed to spread strategically to rile up the citizens. Instigators of the rumor seemed to hope the populace would attack the Mormons to drive them out of the state before the court would even be held.

But the rumor did not inspire that action—it only incited the locals to bring their guns, which were not used, at least not yet. So the court was held, despite the disruptions and intimidations, and no one was convicted. And the Saints did not retaliate.

Two trials were actually planned—one for the murder of each brother. The five who were brought to trial for Joseph's murder were four officers of the Warsaw militia and Thomas Sharp. One of the officers, Mark Aldrich, had been forced into bankruptcy when his land scheme failed to attract Mormons in Warren, Illinois—another economic reason for the persecution. The other officers tried for murder were Levi Williams, colonel of the 59th Regiment (Aldrich commanded a battalion under him); Jacob Cunningham Davis (a state senator and captain of the first company under Aldrich); and William N. Grover (a Warsaw justice of the peace and captain of the second company under Aldrich). The judge was Richard M. Young, a capable judge and justice of the state supreme court who could normally keep order, but not in this excited courtroom.

Josiah Lamborn was the prosecutor. He was a heavy drinker and would die due to alcohol two years later. The defense had four attorneys, including, ironically, Orville H. Browning, who had helped Joseph before Judge Stephen A. Douglas when he faced extradition to Missouri in 1841, and whom Joseph had called upon the day he was killed.

When the court convened, the defendants should have been convicted—they had no alibis and had in fact all been seen in Carthage—but the trial broke down because of weak witnesses who would not testify of a conspiracy. And that was the only evidence on which to nail the men, since no one could prove who fired the shots. The witnesses did establish that the defendants were in the militia, which was discharged at Golden's Point, and that these defendants had indeed taken volunteers with them to Carthage—but the witnesses refused to say what the purpose was for going to Carthage and also refused to say whether or not any of them had talked of killing the Smiths.

The prosecutor Lamborn then dropped the ball when one witness claimed that defendant Davis said he would not kill men in jail and left, going the opposite way—which means there were indeed plans to actually kill the Smiths. But Lamborn did not pursue that very obvious line of questioning. And that line of questioning would have easily proven a conspiracy and therefore convicted all the defendants present, except Davis.

The spectators cheered when witnesses refused one after the other to admit damaging testimony against the conspirators.

Frank Worrell was then called as a witness. When Lamborn asked if he and his men on guard at the jail had blanks in their guns instead of live ammo, Worrell plead the 5th Amendment—refusing to answer on grounds that he might incriminate himself.

Lamborn then made the biggest blunder of the trial when he called his chief witness, William Daniels, who, unlike all the other witnesses, defied the crowd in the courtroom and named names. The crowd's incessant cheering suddenly came crashing to a halt with Daniels on the stand. He laid out the facts clearly—that Sharp had riled up the accused men at Golden's

Point to kill the Smiths, that Grover was the first to volunteer, and that all the others had joined the mob to kill them, except Davis.

But the defense countered by undermining Daniels' credibility as a witness. Lyman Littlefield had published the aforementioned booklet stating that a mobber with a Bowie knife had attempted to cut off Joseph's head, but that a light from heaven had come down like a chain, keeping the mob from getting near Joseph. It then said that the man with the Bowie knife froze in fear, unable to move until he was carried off by others. The booklet further claimed that Joseph had appeared to Daniels in a vision and given him his blessing to relate the account. Daniels repudiated the book, saying it misquoted him, but there were too many doubters who wanted to see him as unreliable. Browning continued hammering away at him, discrediting him on several issues—that the light was incredulous, that the book had made money and therefore made Daniels suspect, and that Daniels had since moved to Nauvoo, recently joining the Mormon Church, and was now not even a solid citizen there, having no job. Nine witnesses were then brought up to undermine Daniels, some saying he had been offered money to testify, although that accusation was never proved.

Then Lamborn made the most ridiculous mistake of the entire trial—perhaps of his career as a trial lawyer and state supreme court justice—he trashed his own witness. He claimed Daniels' book was ludicrous and his testimony not reliable. He then threw in the proverbial towel, acting as judge over the court by declaring that the state witnesses had been successfully repudiated by the defense. He even said he had no case against two of the five defendants and that the evidence against the other three was circumstantial. The defense smiled all the way through its conclusion, simply quoting the prosecution that the evidence was not conclusive and that the witnesses were not credible. Then the defense intimated that a verdict of guilty could actually incite a civil war, which was an attempt to frighten the jury, as though they even needed further reason to indict the men, given Lamborn's capitulation. The jury met for less than three hours, including a lunch break, and brought back a verdict of "not guilty." The trial was over. It had lasted less than a week.

Next was Hyrum's trial, so the defendants were not yet free, but they were released on bail. The new trial was set for June 24, 1845.

Upon reconvening for Hyrum's murder, the court waited for Lamborn or some other state prosecutor to arrive. But he never showed. So the judge reset the trial for the next day. Again, no prosecution. With the spectators cheering, the judge dismissed the case.

Lamborn actually wrote Ford on June 11 asking if he should prosecute at Hyrum's trial, but Ford's reply is unknown. It is quite possible that Ford figured Joseph's murder trial was enough, and that public opinion was satisfied, despite Ford's claims that he was always a proponent of the law.

The next wave of tragedy struck the Saints on June 24, 1845. The county clerk, a dedicated anti-Mormon, got in an argument with Sheriff Minor Deming at the courthouse, and it turned into a fight. The clerk attacked the sheriff, choking him with his strong hands. Deming warned him repeatedly, and finally shot him in the abdomen, whereupon the clerk died 15 minutes later.

Obviously innocent to his friends who labeled it self-defense, Deming was nevertheless indicted by the anti-Mormons for first-degree murder, calling it premeditated. So distraught was Deming that he resigned from his sheriff's position and, while waiting for his trial, secured a high fever, likely brought on by the stress, from which he died on September 10, 1845. His final request to his wife was that she teach their sons to stand up for the right, no matter if it made enemies or friends.

The mobbers running Carthage learned of his death and literally threw their hats up in the street and cheered, says his widow.

The night before, a strange incident occurred. As the people of Lima and Green Plains, Illinois, gathered at a courthouse to discuss how to get rid of the Mormons at Lima, someone rode past and fired shots into the schoolhouse. This one incident so embroiled the mob that they used it as an excuse to once again start attacking the Saints. However, Brigham saw it as a frame-up. He says the mobbers themselves shot at the schoolhouse to provoke their own mob. Even Governor Ford and the anti-Mormon newspaper writer Thomas Gregg agreed with him.

But the next day, especially with the sheriff out of the way, the mobs galloped into the night, burning Mormon barns and crops, even throwing the sick out of their homes and laying the torch to their houses.

A new sheriff was immediately chosen—Jacob B. Backenstos. He went out recruiting a volunteer posse to stop the destruction. But not one man would join him. The 300 mobbers attacked other nights, burning 175 houses and driving out all the Saints at Morley Settlement, which was part of Lima.

Sheriff Backenstos was then attacked in Carthage—he was forced out of his house and chased by horsemen. Jumping into his wagon, he took off for Nauvoo. On his way he happened to ride past Porter Rockwell, who had ventured into the county to help Saints who had recently been burned out of their farms. As he stopped to water his horse, the sheriff charged past him, slowing only long enough to deputize him right on the spot.

Porter took out his weapons, stood on the same road as when the mob had charged him the day Joseph was killed, and now again faced an oncoming cluster of horsemen. When seeing the long-haired figure before them, who they knew had shot some of the mob earlier on that road, the horsemen stopped dead in their tracks. But their leader, none other than Captain Frank Worrell of the Carthage Greys, told his men to wait behind. He would take care of Orrin Rockwell himself. Frank Worrell pulled out his weapons and charged the Mormon from horseback.

# CHAPTER 74

R IDING closer and closer, Worrell fired, and the lead balls bounced up in the dust around Porter's feet. Finally, Porter lowered his pistol, took aim at Worrell's belt buckle, and fired—hitting him dead center. Worrell flew six feet into the air, crashed to the dust, and died, with blood geysering from his wound and his men gaping at him in horror. As far as Porter was concerned, it was just one more of Joseph's murderers taken care of. As far as the mob was concerned, Porter was now an opponent they were determined to put away in jail for a long, long time, hoping they would never have to face him again. They gathered up Worrell's body, took it back to Carthage, and began proceedings to have Porter arrested.

The city was now livid. Their popular captain of the Greys was dead, and Brigham's man Rockwell was responsible once again.

Backenstos meanwhile went to Nauvoo with Porter and his friend. Backenstos immediately recruited several hundred Saints for his posse and headed south to stop the marauders. First stopping at Carthage, they drove the mobbers away from town and set up a guard at the courthouse. Then they went to other settlements where the mobbers were attacking outlying Mormon farms and driving people into Nauvoo. While slowing down the destruction and harassment, Backenstos and his huge posse were not able to stop the persecution, but the Saints in

Nauvoo were stepping up for a major conflict in the event they were invaded.

Ford decided there was only one solution—to get the Mormons out of Illinois. It was time, he said, they simply had to leave. So Ford sent a four-man delegation to Brigham to issue the ultimatum—one of whom was Stephen A. Douglas.

And Brigham, somewhat surprisingly, agreed. It was obvious to him they were at the end of their rope.

He also agreed that the Mormon leaders and a thousand families (perhaps 7,000 people) of the now-numbered 16,000 Saints in Nauvoo and surrounding villages would leave in the spring. The remaining Saints were to leave soon thereafter if they could, being more indigent.

Brigham of course could have made a stand. But he chose the role of peacemaker. Even with his conciliatory position, the delegates still threatened the Saints, saying, "violent means will be resorted to, to compel your removal" if they did not go as promised. At that, many a leader would have told their enemies they were going on their own terms and to leave them alone or they wouldn't go at all. But Brigham, despite his strong personality, thought of the Saints' best interests and wished to avoid conflict at all costs.

So they began the largest migration in the history of the United States—with the biggest wagon-building project in the nation's history as well. The citizens were assigned companies, and within each they would start a wagon shop or two. Each company would also take two ferryboats on their trip and a specific list of supplies—food, fishing and farming supplies, cattle, cooking utensils, weapons, tents, ropes, and oxen.

Craftsmen, wagon builders, and blacksmiths worked in shifts around the clock. And the project went on for months. Each family would need $250 worth of supplies, a hearty sum for the day, especially in light of the fact no one could sell their property for more than pennies on the dollar, if even that. They basically had to walk away from their homes and farms. Brigham negotiated the sale of the entire city, including all their property in Hancock County, to a private buyer in Iowa, and also to a group of Catholic bishops, for half the market price—$1 million, with the extremely valuable temple building thrown in for free. (After leaving, of course, the Saints would have no need for it, but they requested of their potential buyers that it be kept up and treated respectfully.) However, sales never materialized and only a few individual properties were ever actually purchased.

Meanwhile the Saints were finishing their temple with the greatest handiwork possible, despite their poor economic state and considerable sickness and stress while preparing for their departure. Workers even carried weapons with their tools while laboring on the temple, as the mobbers would attack farms closer and closer to the city as the weeks progressed.

Finally on December 10, 1845, the temple was open for the temple "worthy"—those who were full tithe payers and who kept the other basic commandments—who received special instructions and participated in holy ordinances within. These included eternal marriage—the ordinance of sealing husbands and wives together for the eternities—and these ordinances were performed for over 5,000 adults, even while the greatest of care was being placed into finishing the interior—laying the floor, plastering, and installing seats.

Brigham and the other leaders organized the entire migration into far more detail than just companies, down to small units as well, so that their exodus would run like clockwork. The leaders studied maps and assigned guides and hunters. Brigham was especially bent on assigning Porter Rockwell as guide, chief hunter, and protector. But Porter was now in jail.

Sheriff Backenstos and Porter Rockwell were indicted for the murder of Frank Worrell. Ironically, Backenstos, whose life had been saved by Porter, had to arrest him, obviously against his own wishes, and put him in jail. To accomplish this, Backenstos had to plan the arrest carefully. He arrived at the hotel in Carthage where Porter was visiting and surrounded the hotel with a posse of sharpshooters. There, he found Porter asleep in his room. (And armed to the hilt.) He awakened Porter and took him captive. Of further irony, Backenstos was able

to continue serving as sheriff, while Porter would languish
in the Galena, Illinois, jail for four months in similar horrid
conditions as in the Missouri jails. This time, once again, he
was acquitted by a grand jury—one consisting of neutral Illinois
citizens who found the killing of Frank Worrell not an act of
aggression. Backenstos not only testified in his behalf but was
himself acquitted.

Brigham and the Saints, meanwhile, had taken off for the
West on February 5, 1846, crossing the Mississippi River.
The main camp made it to Sugar Creek, Iowa, and waited for
Brigham, who left Nauvoo on February 15, 1846. Ten days later
a crippling snowstorm blew in above Montrose, Iowa, enabling
some to cross the frozen river for several days, although many
suffered from the 12-below-zero temperatures.

That same month more than a thousand wagons—
representing nearly a thousand families—crossed the river to
Iowa, exceeding Brigham's promise for that number of people
to be out by spring. Many suffered and lingered on the Iowa
banks of the Mississippi until they could muster the strength
and means to push on to Sugar Creek to join the others. Many
died en route, some of starvation, some of illness.

At Sugar Creek the main body of Saints resumed their trek
west, making Council Bluffs, Iowa, their next stop-off point, 400
miles away. From there they would camp and gather strength to
make the 1,000-mile-plus journey over mountains and plains to
the Great Salt Lake Valley, the place they finally designated as
their destination. Just 10 weeks later, in mid-May 1846, 16,000
Mormons were traveling by wagon train toward Council Bluffs,
Iowa.

About a thousand Saints, however, were still in Nauvoo,
including dissidents, certain others that could be described
as simply lazy, and those doing final business, plus the ill and
the elderly, such as Lucy Mack Smith. Additionally there were
several hundred "new citizens" consisting of non-Mormon
workers, store owners, doctors and attorneys. This group
included Lewis Bidamon, who would wed Emma.

When Porter Rockwell was released from jail at Galena, Illinois, he went straight to Nauvoo to find his people—and found the city nearly deserted. He did happen to come across Joseph's oldest son, Joseph III, and tearfully hugged him. He confided in him regarding his father. "Joseph," he said, "they have killed the only friend I have ever had." They parted, and the boy watched Porter walk down to the shore and hire a barge to ferry him across. It was the last time the boy would ever see Porter, as Joseph III records in his memoirs.

When Porter arrived at the tent of Brigham and other church leaders at Council Bluffs, Iowa, they hugged and tearfully embraced him. Brigham sent Porter back to Nauvoo several times, as a messenger and to help the infirm and destitute.

And what Porter witnessed on his last trip was the unfolding of a major drama . . .

Feeling drunk with power, and seeing the Nauvoo Legion gone and having full sway over the remaining Saints, the mobs took full advantage. They viciously attacked more homes and farms. Their leader was Thomas Brockman, a man Ford described as an "uncouth, ignorant semibarbarian" who sought notoriety.

Brockman gathered almost 800 men and took command of them, even bringing in artillery, and on September 11, 1846, he attacked Nauvoo. In what has become known as "The Battle of Nauvoo," he attacked the 150 men of the Saints, several of whom, and one boy, were killed, while others were wounded. But they held firm until the mob finally obtained more ammunition from Quincy. Realizing the war was futile, the Saints surrendered.

Brockman took the city on September 17, 1846. The previous night the Saints fled to join Brigham's group west, but they had to leave without money or tents, while carrying household items in their hands. Six people, old or ill, were actually hauled away on their beds, and the Saints crowded the ferryboats.

Brockman marched in and forced the remaining residents to line up and talk with him. He decided who would stay and who would go, including the "new citizens." Most were told they had to leave within two hours. Bands of his men broke into houses and tossed the residents and their property into the street.

On September 23, 1846, rain fell on the 640 refugees across the river, where they were camped on the bank. On October 5, at the direction of Brigham, certain men were assigned to go back for the refugees, bringing food and wagons, which preserved their lives. But it was a race against time, as Brockman's forces hurriedly set up several cannons along the riverbanks on the Illinois side of the river and began firing, sending cannonballs over the river into the camp of the Saints on the Iowa side. Seeing the cannonballs crashing into their camp and panicking the defenseless Saints, Porter Rockwell arrived and stared at the scene. And what he saw made his blood boil.

P ORTER witnessed the attack by Brockman's forces—the cannon continuing its fire—and he had to make a choice: either to sneak upstream, cross the river, and circle back to Brockman and his men, so that he could surprise them from behind and level them to the earth with the small battery of weapons he carried, or stay and help the Saints get out of range and save their lives. He decided to stay and assist the terrified Saints, watching the cannonballs crash left and right about him as he helped family after family flee into the woods, driving their few wagons out of range of the cannon, one after another, until they were all safe.

After all the Saints had completed the 400-mile journey to Council Bluffs, losing family members from exposure along the way and burying them beside the trail, they finally gathered in Iowa—all except the few remaining Saints in Nauvoo, some of whom would join them later. However, because of Brockman, the remaining Saints had by now basically divided themselves between those who would leave and those who would stay. A small number of faithful did remain, and for some reason Brockman let them stay, perhaps feeling they were needed for the continuation of the community, due to their skills.

Those who had apostatized from the main church splintered off—some staying in Nauvoo, some moving to Iowa, and some moving away from the area, taking their followers. Some stayed with the main body of Saints, crossing into Iowa, and *then* splintered off, leaving the church after they had fled Nauvoo.

Other dissident groups tried staying in Nauvoo but were forced out by Brockman's band. The vast majority of Saints, however, stayed with Brigham and, in April 1847, began the great migration west. It all began with 148 people—three of whom were women and two being children—as the advance company that was led by Brigham Young. As stated, Porter was chief scout and protector of the party, as well as, apparently, chief hunter. Crossing the plains and mountain passes, they arrived on July 24, 1847, with Porter being the third man among them to see the Great Salt Lake Valley. Soon the 17,000 Saints followed as the main migration.

Because of the nation's press, few Americans cared about their hardships and injustice. But one ally who came to their aid was Thomas Kane, a law clerk from Philadelphia who met a Saint traveling to Washington to try to get help. Kane was touched by his story and changed from being a critic to an admirer of the Saints. He actually went out to visit the refugees on the bank of the Mississippi River and traveled another 400 miles west to Council Bluffs.

Of the deserted Nauvoo, Kane reports: "I never saw more abundant proofs of intelligent industry and quiet domestic thrift. . . . Ropewalks, boat yards, smith shops, tanneries, all the marks of mechanical skill and enterprise were in the town. The farms were large and well enclosed, well cultivated, beyond any that I had met in that portion of the West." But at the temple he saw drunks "who had much defiled it with their vomit and filth." Brockman's band meanwhile roamed the streets and stopped all visitors, forcing them to obtain a passport from their warlord.

He summarized, "The Mormons have been as grievous sufferers by slander as by any other wrong, and that so far from being the creatures they have been represented by their enemies and as I myself once believed them, they are a people of singular virtue in every sense of the word. Pious though not austere—honest, frugal—self sacrificing, humane, decorous; such are the Mormons as I have known them."

Over a year after the Saints arrived in the Great Salt Lake Valley, on November 19, 1848, the Nauvoo temple was burned by an arsonist, and in 1850 a tornado destroyed the remaining portion of it, freeing it, in Brigham's view, from defilement.

Porter would be a mainstay in scouting, exploring, and protecting the Saints, once in the new territory, and would in fact establish a reputation second to none in the history of the American West in dealing with outlaws—acquiring a file of stories that seemed so miraculous that many have found them difficult to believe, while others have ascribed it to the divine protection promised by Joseph. Porter would face and fight the lawless, leaving witnesses who would relate firsthand accounts that would astound many.

An equally amazing chapter of Latter-day Saint history details the account of a comparative handful of Mormons holding back the elite of the U.S. Army—the top 2,500 American soldiers sent by President James Buchanan in 1857 to invade Great Salt Lake City—only to be stopped cold in their tracks by the likes of Porter Rockwell and Daniel H. Wells, through ingeniously designed rockslides, dams, flooded roads, and stampeding cattle. (And, of this account, the *London Punch* newspaper would publish a cartoon—of the flower of the American Army, 2,500 strong, being herded by 10 Mormons.) The history of the Saints under Brigham would be replete with miracles and new antagonists—some of them federal judges and the ongoing anti-Mormon press that would only let up later in the 20th century.

As for Joseph's family, Brigham assigned Newel Whitney and Benjamin Johnson to return to Nauvoo to visit Emma. They attempted to persuade her to join the migration. She refused. She stayed in Nauvoo and ran the Mansion House as an inn, and soon met her next husband, the aforementioned Lewis Bidamon, to whom she was happily married. Brigham also tried talking Joseph's mother Lucy into going west but, because of her feeble health, she decided to stay in Nauvoo. She lived a while with her daughter and son-in-law before the exodus, and finally spent the last two years of her life with Emma and her new husband.

Before the exodus, the Twelve asked her to write a history of Joseph's life, which she did, despite the anguish of seeing four of her sons and her husband give their lives to the cause. It is the only source of many events in Joseph's early years—including his childhood, his visits from Moroni and other angels, the gold plates, and dealing with the early years of the restoration. With the help of scribes, Howard and Martha Jane Coray, she finished her book before the main migration west. Due to the chaos and overwhelming work of organizing and preparing for the hurried exodus, however, the Twelve did not publish it then, and would not until a half century later. But Orson Pratt did, in 1853, while in England researching genealogy. The book was later revised somewhat by church historians, with important sections taken out on the whim of various editors over the next century and a half. (The latest and most comprehensive version—indeed, the complete and unabridged original version—was compiled by R. Vernon Ingleton and published by Stratford Books in 2005 as *History of Joseph Smith by His Mother: the Unabridged Original Version*. This version is the only one to use the complete, original 1853 text as its backbone and, in footnotes, to include all the corrections later placed by church historians; additionally and very significantly, it is the only version to include all the facts contained in her *rough draft* that did not appear in her *final manuscript* that went to press. [To make it easy to read, the editors use a different type font for the rough draft material so that the text of the original published version flows easily into the rough draft material and back again to the published version.] Using this ingenious system makes it a gem of a book, as told in her feisty and engaging manner.) Three years after her book came out, she died, in 1856.

From the West, Brigham tried but failed to retrieve Joseph's and Hyrum's bodies, as Emma would not allow it, keeping them in Nauvoo where they lie today.

None of Joseph's children who lived past childhood stayed in the church led west by Brigham. Joseph III became president of

the Reorganized Church of Jesus Christ of Latter Day Saints when
it was officially organized in April 1860, pulling in independent
congregations that for 13 years had remained separated from
the main church, which had migrated west in 1847. Its name was
later changed to Community of Christ, the largest church with
ties to Joseph outside of the one Brigham led. (By 2005 it would
have approximately a quarter million members, compared to the
12 million members of the Utah-based church. Both churches
are worldwide, but only the Utah church uses the designation
"Mormon" as a nickname.)

William, Joseph's last living brother, never returned to the
church now led by Brigham.

Over the decades in the Great Salt Lake Valley, the church
and settlement flourished under Brigham Young. Missionaries
brought in tens of thousands, and eventually hundreds of
thousands, of converts, and the church finally asked the
gathering to Zion to stop. Instead, the Saints were asked to
live in their own communities throughout the world and build
up Zion there, Zion being defined as a place where the pure in
heart dwell—specifically, the individual homes of members
(with another definition being the actual dwelling place of the
Savior someday, which the Saints still believe will be Jackson
County, Missouri, expecting a migration of sorts to take place
there in the future).

Polygamy was the most-known tenet of the Mormons
but was repudiated by the church in 1890. Members found
practicing it today are promptly excommunicated. Some
"fundamentalist" church communities—defined by some
as "break-off groups"—ranging from several dozen to a few
thousand members (throughout the West in particular) still
practice it, but they are not in any way affiliated with the
Utah church, and their members are not on the membership
records of the Church of Jesus Christ of Latter-day Saints (or
the Community of Christ).

The issue of separation of church and state continued to be
a sore one for national leaders during the first few decades the
Saints were in Deseret Territory, but by the time they acquired

statehood in 1890, the powers of church and state were well divided, with the Saints no longer feeling the need to combine the two in order to maintain strength and effective government. Brigham had governed through both entities as the president of the church and territory's first governor. (For a brief study of life in the West, including attempts by the government, the machinations of federal judges, the continued work of dissidents and anti-Mormon newspapers, and the various enemies who would attack the Saints from numerous directions, and how Brigham handled it all, the aforementioned work *Porter Rockwell: A Biography* details that history. It was written as not only a biography of Joseph's friend Porter Rockwell, but also as a history text, which has been used in schools.)

Brigham would say on his deathbed in 1877 that he could see Joseph Smith before him, coming to take him home. And since then, the Utah church has continued to maintain a president, who has always come from the ranks of the Twelve Apostles, even the senior member.

The second half of the 20th century was a turning point for public relations in the church, finding prominence and positive public images in political, entertainment, and athletic arenas, coupled with a phenomenal growth that more than quadrupled during that 50-year period alone; thus the church finally found news media exposure turning around after a hundred-year public attack on the institution.

The temple in Nauvoo was reestablished by the Church of Jesus Christ of Latter-day Saints in 2002 and, since the 1960s, the church has devoted tremendous resources and attention to rebuilding dozens of original buildings in Nauvoo as part of a major restoration project, adding to the area dozens of retired couples serving as missionaries alongside the usual younger missionaries, who greet hundreds of thousands of visitors to Nauvoo each year, many of whom come out of curiosity or, in the case of Latter-day Saints, come for inspiration and as a sort of homage, wishing to visit Joseph's final earthly home and resting place. A pageant is also held there each July.

Similarly, an annual large-scale pageant, which plays for seven days and attracts over 20,000 visitors nightly during July, is held at Hill Cumorah near Palmyra, New York, where Joseph reportedly found the gold plates that he translated into The Book of Mormon. The pageant presents the story of his finding the plates and of the First Vision, in which the Father and the Son appeared to him.

The Saints view Joseph's First Vision, in the spring of 1820 when just a lad of 14, as one of the cornerstones of the church. In the final analysis, critics and dissidents were either unable to accept the heavenly visitation or never truly embraced it. However, those active in the faith maintain that if Joseph was indeed visited by the Father and the Son in the Sacred Grove, later being given priesthood authority to act in Christ's name, and subsequently following Christ's directive to reestablish his church, The Church of Jesus Christ of Latter-day Saints must be Christ's true church. So the mission of Latter-day Saints is unique and rather simple—first, they invite the entire world to read Joseph's own words, as contained in a pamphlet entitled The Joseph Smith Story, which gives his account of the First Vision in the Sacred Grove near Palmyra, New York. Secondly, they invite the world to read and study The Book of Mormon itself in its entirety, which Joseph declares he translated by the gift and power of God. And thirdly, they invite the world, after reading these two accounts, to ask God if these two accounts are true.

The man who was riding with Porter Rockwell on the day of Joseph's death and who saw Porter take on a small mob, Gilbert Belnap, knew Joseph well and bears this testimony of Joseph:

"I loved [his] company. The sound of his voice was music to my ears. . . . In his domestic circle [he was] mild and forbearing. . . . Although opposed by the combined powers of earth and hell, by the inspiration of God he restored the gospel to the earth, organized the Holy Priesthood, consecrated the land of Zion, planted a great city, gathered his thousands around him, and laid the foundation of a mighty work. At the same time he endured the most unparalleled persecution of any man in the history of our country."

The final testimony of Joseph's life is born by John Taylor, who knew Joseph intimately and was with him when he was martyred. He says Joseph was "our prophet; he approached our God; had obtained for us his will." He also states, "Joseph Smith, the Prophet and Seer of the Lord, has done more, save Jesus only, for the salvation of men in this world, than any other man that ever lived in it . . . and like most of the Lord's anointed in ancient times, has sealed his mission and his works with his own blood."

# E P I L O G U E

MANY people, both friend and foe, who were acquainted with Joseph left their observations of him for us to consider. Among them were Joseph's first cousin Jesse, son of his uncle Silas, who said, "I am unable to fully describe my sensations when in the presence of this wonderful man. . . . I have never heard any human voice, not even my mother's, that was so attractive to me. Even his bitterest enemies, if they had the privilege of hearing him speak, became mollified, and forgot their anger. . . . His domestic animals seemed to love him. . . . The dog and the horses rejoiced when they saw this man. . . . His children rejoiced when he was present." General Wilson rode with Joseph to his trial in Missouri and said, "He was a very remarkable man. I carried him into my house a prisoner in chains, and in less than two hours my wife loved him better than she did me."

Emma stated that whenever Joseph went to work in the garden there would soon be a small crowd around him that "would tramp the ground down faster than he could hoe it up."

Governor Ford says, "It must not be supposed that the pretended Prophet practiced the tricks of a common imposter; that he was a dark and gloomy person, with a long beard, a grave and severe aspect, and a reserved and saintly carriage of his person; on the contrary, he was full of levity, even to boyish romping."

As early as 1831 Ezra Booth, who would leave the church shortly after converting, wrote to Edward Partridge with an insightful comment about Joseph, although critical: "Have you not frequently observed in Joseph, a want of that sobriety, prudence, and stability which are some of the most prominent traits of the Christian character? Have you not discovered in him, a spirit of lightness and levity, a temper of mind easily irritated, and an habitual proneness to jesting and joking?"

Brigham stated, before even meeting Joseph and while defending his doctrine to a critic: "I have never seen him, and do not know his private character. The doctrine he teaches is all I know about the matter—bring anything against that if you can. As to anything else I do not care. If he acts like a devil, he has brought forth a doctrine that will save us, if we will abide it. . . . I never embrace any man in my faith. But the doctrine he has produced will save you and me and the whole world."

As to Joseph's athletic skill, Newel Knight, who knew Joseph since their boyhood, said, "In all his boyish sports and amusements, I never knew any one to gain advantage over him."

Benjamin Johnson, who also knew him well, said Joseph "would allow no arrogance. . . . Criticisms even by his associates were rarely acceptable, and contradictions [against him] would rouse in him the lion at once." This was probably one of the self-criticisms Joseph referred to when he spoke of his follies.

A non-Mormon wrote of his attributes and weaknesses: "He possessed the most indomitable perseverance . . . and deemed himself born to command, and he did command." The same writer reports that John McDaniel, a non-Mormon, doubted he could prophesy, which sparked Joseph's temper to the point of almost instigating a fistfight, as Joseph reportedly responded: "Nobody can slander me! If my brethren cannot protect me I will do so myself!"

Despite being quick to anger over personal attacks, Joseph was known for his self-confidence and pleasant and easy personality. J. B. Newhall writes, "He is a jolly fellow and, according to his view, is one of the last persons on earth whom God would have raised up a prophet or priest. He is so diametrically opposite to that which he ought to be in order to merit the titles or to act in such offices."

Joseph was aware of his weaknesses, and some revelations pointed them out even more clearly. The first to do so was in 1829, in which he was rebuked for allowing himself to be persuaded against the Lord's will, in allowing Martin Harris to take The Book of Mormon manuscript. His weaknesses were referred to in the plural as the revelation states, "And behold how oft you have transgressed the commandments and laws of God." Later in 1829 another revelation said, "I command you my servant Joseph to repent and walk more uprightly before me." Four years later another revelation stated, "Verily, I say unto Joseph Smith Jr.—you have not kept the commandments and must needs stand rebuked before the Lord." Seven years afterward, a revelation indicated that God works among men through those who are far from perfect: "Unto this end have I raised you up, that I might show forth my wisdom through the weak things of the earth."

In Ohio on June 6, 1832, Joseph handwrote the following letter to Emma, which not only shows his concern for improvement, but the manner in which he should do so—through pondering and prayer in a secret place: "Dear Wife . . . I have visited a grove which is just back of the town almost every day where I can be secluded from the eyes of any mortal, and there give vent to all the feelings of my heart in meditation and prayer. I have called to mind all the past moments of my life and am left to mourn and shed tears of sorrow for my folly in suffering the adversary of my soul to have so much power over me as he has had in times past. But God is merciful and has forgiven my sins, and I rejoice that he sendeth forth the comforter unto as many as believe and humbleth themselves before him. . . . I will try to be contented with my lot [of imperfection], knowing that God is my friend. In him I shall find comfort. I have given my life into his hands." This pondering took place as well while he wandered the streets of New York City, although he did not report facing self scrutiny then—he was discerning and pondering the hearts of the people. From that, his followers might learn that a secret wilderness can sometimes be in the midst of a bustling city, as long as one is detached and able to ponder.

Others who knew and adored him were specific in their descriptions of him. William Clayton wrote in a letter: "He [is] a man of sound judgment, and possessed of abundance of intelligence and, while you listen to his conversation, you receive intelligence which expands your mind and causes your heart to rejoice. He is very familiar. . . . I can converse with him just as easy as I can with you."

Howard Coray said: "I sat and listened to his preaching at the stand in Nauvoo a great many times when I have been completely carried away with his indescribable eloquence—power of expression—speaking as I have never heard any other man speak."

George Q. Cannon said: "He could at other times unbend and be as happy and unconventional as a boy. This was one of the most striking characteristics; and it was sometimes held up to scorn by his traducers."

Jane Snyder Richards, wife of an Apostle, wrote: "[He] was able to foretell the mysteries of the future with a marked degree of accuracy, and nearly as much readiness as the ordinary individual could relate the happenings of the past. . . . As the Leader of his people he was ever active and progressive but always modest and considerate of them and their trying circumstances. Socially he was an ideal of affability and always approachable to the humblest of his acquaintances."

Parley P. Pratt adds, "In short, in him . . . the gifts, wisdom, and devotion of a Daniel were united with the boldness, courage, temperance, perseverance, and generosity of a Cyrus."

Emmeline B. Wells writes: "His expression was mild and almost childlike in repose, and when addressing the people, who loved him it seemed to adoration, the glory of his countenance was beyond description. At other times the great power of his manner, more than of his voice (which was sublimely eloquent to me) seemed to shake the place on which we stood and penetrate the inmost soul of his hearers, and I am sure that they would have laid down their lives to defend him. I always listened spellbound to his every utterance—the chosen of God in this last dispensation."

Jacob Butterfield writes that Joseph was "a man that sets good examples in his family and in the streets and labors diligently to have the church deal justly, walk humbly and to have mercy."

Joseph Smith's life, in its entirety, is one of keen discipleship, generosity, and charismatic influence viewed by his followers. His mission was one of a kind, and his claims are of such importance that a certain respect should be paid by students of his life, perhaps even to take him up on his admonition to study those claims, beginning with, it seems apparent, The Book of Mormon, as well as the abbreviated works of his life, in his own words, mentioned earlier in the booklet *The Joseph Smith Story.*

# Appendices

# Money-diggers and Rodsmen

Porter Rockwell's sister stated that Sallie Chase, a Methodist, had a stone which she would consult in behalf of people who came to her for help in finding lost and stolen items. She further explained, "There was considerable digging for money in our neighborhood by men, women, and children," most of whom were not of Joseph's religious persuasion. On February 16, 1825, the *Wayne Sentinel* reprinted an article from the Windsor, Vermont, *Journal*, which said that respectable citizens had been digging for treasure in the Green Mountains for years and believed stories that said the treasure was "enchanted by the Devil or Robert Kidd." The *Sentinel* also stated that "a respectable gentleman" in Tunbridge, Vermont, had stated he had found a gold chest with the help of a vision and a mineral rod. On March 2 the same newspaper reported a wood chopper saying he had found gold in the trunk of a tree near Utica, New York. A woman in New London, Connecticut, used a small transparent rock, according to an article in the *Lyons Advertiser,* August 29, 1827, saying it had "the power of opening to her view the recesses of the earth," which she used to help two men dig for a box of coins stolen from a Spanish galleon, the box having been buried in mud under six feet of water near the wharf.

On February 1, 1831, the Palmyra *Reflector* stated that many people throughout the countryside were seeing visions of treasures in the earth—men and women of all ages.

In Wells, Vermont, in about 1800, there was a religious cult that used rods to hunt for buried treasure and find lost objects.

A P P E B N D I X

# Theories Attacking The Book of Mormon

While the nation's press—religious writings in particular—denounced Joseph and The Book of Mormon, the *New Yorker* wrote a surprisingly sympathetic view, yet obviously believing Joseph wrote the book himself rather than translating it from the plates, by stating that Joseph "shows a degree of talent and research that in an uneducated youth of twenty is almost a miracle of itself." While complimentary, in its own way it was a form of detraction from Joseph's declaration that the book came about by divine means.

Another detractor was Philastus Hurlbut, a former Mormon who had been excommunicated for adultery. (While one's sins are considered wiped clean by baptism into the restored church, if afterward a member commits certain "grievous" sins such as adultery, murder, or a felony, they are generally excommunicated.) Hurlbut claimed the book came from the "Solomon Spaulding manuscript," a novel written in 1812, whose author died four years later. Spaulding's brother John and his wife still had the Solomon Spaulding manuscript, and Hurlbut met with them. From his interview with them, he learned there were some similarities to The Book of Mormon but, when he found the manuscript, he was chagrined to find very few similarities—the Spaulding manuscript was merely a weak adventure novel about pre-Columbus immigrants to America. The main similarity was that it claimed to be a translation of ancient scrolls discovered in a cave. It had no religious aspects to it and was written in an entirely different style. Hurlbut, in vain, then went searching for another manuscript of Spaulding's, despite the widow's claim that there was only one manuscript. Since Sidney Rigdon had known the publisher who had rejected the Spaulding manuscript, Hurlbut tried to tie The Book of Mormon to Rigdon's authorship, but there was one major obstacle—Rigdon had joined the church *after* the book was published. (Rigdon never even saw The Book of Mormon until well after it was published, and he maintained that claim all his life, even after he later left the church.) Nevertheless, this highly fictitious tie-in theory was accepted by numerous if not most people in the 19th century and even by some in the 20th century. Even fairly intelligent people such as Rigdon's old partner Alexander Campbell jumped on the bandwagon—switching his belief from Joseph fabricating the book to using Spaulding's manuscript.

However, by 1904, the theory pretty much died. That year Charles Matthews wrote that neighbors of the Smith family discounted the Spaulding theory, believing the Smiths had written it with Oliver Cowdery's help. This was a seemingly logical explanation since Oliver was around much of the translation period and was highly literate, but Latter-day Saints believe that most anyone who reads the book will realize that an illiterate family and one educated scribe could not possibly write such a work, possessing numerous literary "footprints"—different styles of writing—with intricate and complex plot weaving (especially among the accounts of the Nephites during their numerous conflicts with the Lamanites throughout the book). But the problem with this theory is that Oliver came along only after much of the book had already been written, and proponents of the book say that proof of this lies in the additional fact that only part of the manuscript was written in his handwriting. Oliver died active in the faith, but during a large portion of his life he had been disassociated from the church and, during that period, point out the Saints, he had numerous opportunities to claim authorship or fraudulence regarding the book, but never once did so. In fact, he said that he did try to translate part of the book at one time but could not even manage to translate one line.

Later in the 20th century a historian claimed Joseph formed his main idea from a Vermont Congregationalist minister named Ethan Smith, the author of *View of the Hebrews*, published in 1823. One idea advanced by Ethan was that the Native Americans descended from the lost tribes of Israel. Joseph would later mention that book in a positive way as supporting the theme of The Book of Mormon, but that's as close as it ever got to The Book of Mormon, one book being entirely different from the other.

Rather than being a novel of romance and adventure, Joseph purports The Book of Mormon as pure scripture, maintaining, "The Book of Mormon was the most correct of any book on earth and the keystone of our religion, and a man would get nearer to God by abiding by its precepts than by any other book."

# What Happened to the Three Witnesses and the Eight Witnesses?

While all of the three witnesses left the church at one point—
although two later returned—they never recanted on their
testimony about the plates. Nor did the three witnesses ever
claim they were pressured by Joseph into doing or saying
anything. Of the eight witnesses, however, Governor Ford later
said some of them told him (obviously after they had apostatized)
that they never saw any plates in the box, but that Joseph had
them pray for two hours, reprimanding them as having little
faith, until they were able to finally see something—at least the
box. Ford, however, was known for twisting numerous reports
and accounts to his benefit and viewpoint.

Three Palmyra citizens—Reuben Harmon, John Gilbert, and
Reverend Jesse Townsend, along with Stephen Burnett—claimed
Martin Harris had told them he never saw the plates with his
natural eyes, but with his spiritual eyes—"only in vision" as
Burnett states in a letter, which is not exactly surprising, since
Joseph himself first saw the plates in vision, but these enemies
tried making an issue of this point. Burnett adds that Martin
later said, in the Kirtland Temple, that he knew The Book of
Mormon was true and that he had more than once lifted the plates

while they were in a box with only a tablecloth or handkerchief over them. Burnett, nevertheless, desired to focus on what he could criticize in Martin's testimony, and left the faith. Others, of course, had no problem with Martin's description and were not in the least bit shaken by what he said.

Martin Harris, despite his written testimony of the truthfulness of The Book of Mormon, did not remain active in the church. First, he and Dolly, ever disagreeing over The Book of Mormon, divorced. He then married another woman, an active Latter-day Saint, and had a second family with her. But from Kirtland, he did not go westward with the Saints to Missouri nor later to Nauvoo, and from 1838, when Joseph left Kirtland, to 1844 he was withdrawn from the church and even joined a different religious group. But his second wife remained active, so she and her children went west with the Saints to Salt Lake City.

Finally in 1870, poor, broke, and failing in health, Martin went west to see his family. There, he reunited with the Saints in full faith. In the Salt Lake Tabernacle he testified of the truthfulness of The Book of Mormon. He gave numerous talks declaring he had seen the plates as clearly as his own hand. His popularity among the Saints returned, and he testified of his experiences everywhere he could until 1875, when he died at age 92.

The second witness of the three, David Whitmer, also became disillusioned with Joseph, although he never became bitter toward him and always proclaimed his love for the man. His main problem seemed to be one of faith: When he saw Joseph give up the seer stone, he figured Joseph must have lost the powers of prophecy, and thus, Latter-day Saints believe, David's faith weakened. He even decided that Joseph led the church astray. He left the fold in June 1838, when he feared that the Danites—whom Joseph quickly excommunicated for militancy — were including him in their threats. Despite being disaffected from the church, and *because* of that actually, he became the target of many newspaper writers who sought to interview him—but none could draw from him anything but a firm testimony of the gold plates, which he always declared he saw and felt with his own hands. In 1882 he wrote a pamphlet to the Christian world declaring his faith in The Book of Mormon. He did denounce his belief in Joseph's establishing polygamy and other matters, but added that that should not dissuade people from the book itself, stating, "How plain and simple is the doctrine of Christ set forth therein." He proclaimed that belief until his death.

The third witness, Oliver Cowdery, also left the church in 1838. He did so because he opposed both the doctrine of plural marriage and being "controlled" by church leaders in earthly matters. He stayed in Ohio and practiced law in the town of Tiffin. He also became a Methodist. He decided to return to the fold, however, and went to Council Bluffs, Iowa, to join the Saints on their way west. There, he was rebaptized. He planned to join the main fold of the church in the Great Basin, but died before leaving Iowa. Just before dying, he stated again that he had viewed and touched the plates and had actually received the priesthood from heavenly authority.

All three witnesses had personal problems with the direction the church went or were prideful regarding following a youthful church leader, in Joseph Smith, but none retracted his testimony of claiming to see the plates delivered by an angel to them and of handling the plates themselves.

APPENDIX D

# Polygamy

Joseph F. Smith, Hyrum's son, and later president of the church in Utah, wrote in the *Deseret News* of May 20, 1886, that Joseph had first received a revelation about polygamy in 1831, but was told not to make it publicly known, so he told only his closest and most trustworthy associates—Oliver Cowdery and Lyman E. Johnson. Orson Pratt would learn about it the following year from Johnson.

Joseph apparently learned about the doctrine in Kirtland, as Joseph B. Noble says Joseph told him he received the information while translating the scriptures, which would have indeed been in 1831. It was in Kirtland that the first rumors spread that the practice of polygamy had begun. In response to the rumor, while Joseph was visiting Michigan, W. W. Phelps prepared and read a statement stating that, while they were being accused of practicing polygamy, they believed in monogamous marriages.

Also, as early as July 17, 1831, Joseph prophesied that white church members would marry Native American women. At that time, Joseph, W. W. Phelps, and five others had journeyed west of Jackson County, beyond the U.S. boundaries into Indian territory. There they prayed, and Joseph told them that they would mix with the Indians through marriage; then three years later Joseph told Phelps how that would be done—through polygamy.

While polygamy was revealed for the general church in 1843, it is possible Joseph tried to introduce it two years before that to the general church membership. In 1841 he may have taught the principle to a congregation, after which Emma, Vilate Kimball (wife of Heber C.), and others became upset, according to Heber C.'s daughter Helen. And according to another source, though not as reliable, even Don Carlos Smith, Joseph's brother who was otherwise faithful, became angry. Helen Kimball adds that Joseph concluded the time was farther off than he had realized and that the Lord would help them accept it if they continued their faithfulness in other areas.

But to his closest associates and the Twelve, Joseph did apparently introduce it in 1841. That year, Joseph was anxious for the Apostles to return from England so he could teach them. On July 1, 1841, when seven of them returned, he taught them the doctrine until late at night. As for how Joseph learned the time was right for others to practice it, he told Joseph B. Noble that an angel had announced to him that the time for plural marriage had arrived.

Joseph attempted to persuade his closest associates to follow his example immediately. He confided to John Taylor that the church could not continue until polygamy was established. Saints in retrospect believe it simply needed to be established for a time and not necessarily permanently. In Joseph's day, it would be a test for his followers, as many, if not most, would have difficulty accepting it. But the test would end for the church—at least for the mainstream church that would be headquartered in Utah, 47 years later—when, as stated, polygamy was renounced in 1890 by the First Presidency.

Orson Pratt found it equally unsettling, but after pondering and apparently praying upon the matter, he determined it must be a heavenly revelation "because it is utterly impossible . . . to believe a part of them to be divine, from God, and a part of them to be from the devil."

Once Joseph announced polygamy to the church, most had great difficulty with it, being raised with strict traditional values on marriage. Brigham Young said he literally wanted to die: "It was the first time in my life that I desired the grave."

Brigham finally came to grips with polygamy, but when he reported such, he inadvertently chose his words poorly, apparently not thinking them through: "I foresaw, when Joseph first made known this doctrine, that it would be a trial, and a source of great care and anxiety to the brethren, and what of that. We are to gird up our loins and fulfill this, just as we would any other duty."

There were misconceptions among some of the Saints—that the first wife would be the superior wife with a higher status, etc., but such misunderstandings were clarified. Eliza R. Snow was one who clarified it, detailing the fact that the ceremony was identical for all.

To the public, Joseph either avoided the topic entirely or possibly denied supporting or practicing it, at least until the Nauvoo period. He was in a quandary because the Lord had told him not to reveal the doctrine to the public—and that directive, under inspiration, would have taken precedence over laying everything out to his enemies, and even to the general church population at large, as they were not ready for it—this despite his total commitment to honesty in business and all other matters.

One typical scholarly study (by Thomas O'Dea in *The Mormons*, published by the University of Chicago Press in 1957) thought it "odd" that Joseph may have written letters from Liberty Jail denying practicing polygamy when no one at that time was even accusing him of it. But the study neglects to consider that Joseph had received incessant criticism from enemies and perhaps could foresee another round coming. He also knew his enemies had a long memory and would pull up anything from his past they could criticize—for example, his "treasure digging" days were not forgotten for over a hundred years by enemies who thought in some way that should take away from the truth of The Book of Mormon. Furthermore, while in jail, he might have heard criticisms, possibly even from his jail guards, about the rumors they very well could have heard regarding polygamy, or someone may have written him about it, or one of his visitors may have received "flak" from friends or relatives concerning the topic. Such scholarly studies typically overlook such possibilities and simply try ridiculing or criticizing Joseph as overly defensive by his bringing up the subject, when they do not comprehend all the information and pressures he was receiving, while still trying to remain true to directives to not let the general church population—much less the general public—know of the doctrine and his practice of it yet.

Joseph apparently was well aware of his own shortcomings. Regarding those shortcomings as related to polygamy, Joseph felt the Lord pointed out a weakness to him on the subject, since he received a revelation that was a request for Emma to forgive him for his trespasses. He recognized his weaknesses and on May 21, 1843, stated in a lecture, "I do not want you to think I am very righteous, for I am not very righteous." The statement, however, was within the context of his earlier admissions—which did not include any "malignant" or major category of sin. Whatever Joseph's transgressions were, even in respect to polygamy, and possibly related mistakes that the Lord asked Emma to forgive him for, they did not include adultery, according to his acquaintance Joseph Lee Robinson who writes, "He felt [so] anxious with regard to himself that he inquired of the Lord [and] the Lord told him that he, Joseph, had never committed adultery."

Some, such as Vilate Kimball, wife of Heber C., had difficulty at first, to the point of finding it an Abrahamic test—a tremendous trial of faith—then afterward became fully convinced of its origin from God. Helen, in fact, not only saw her husband take a second wife, Sarah Noon, but she witnessed her own daughter Helen marry Joseph as a plural wife, causing her heart to "bleed," says her daughter. Joseph knew the parents' difficulty in giving the hand of their only daughter to him, so he told Helen: "If you will take this step, it will insure your eternal salvation and exaltation and that of your father's household and all of your kindred." It was, interestingly, Helen who would become such a strong advocate of the practice that she would later write detailed treatises on it.

The Saints felt that the Lord helped them accept the practice and eased the difficulty of living it. Eliza Partridge, who, along with her sister Emily (daughters of the ever-faithful Edward Partridge, who had died of malaria upon moving to Nauvoo), married Joseph, and records: "I thought my trials were very severe in the line [of duty] and I am often led to wonder how it was that a person of my temperament could get along with it and not rebel, but I know it was the Lord who kept me from opposing his plans, although in my heart I felt that I could not submit to them. But I did, and I am thankful to my Heavenly Father for the care he had over me in those troublous times."

Meanwhile, reports and rumors spread throughout town about polygamy.

Emma seemed to float in and out of acceptance of the doctrine. She was an emotion-filled, passionate person, which no doubt had its draw to Joseph. But with it came the challenge to be more patient and understanding. Regarding their children, for example, as stated earlier, Joseph wrote her on April 4, 1839, admonishing her to be kinder to the children: "Don't be fractious to them, but listen to their wants."

Allen J. Stout, one of Joseph's lifeguards, reports that while on duty in the Mansion House he overheard Emma through the door discussing polygamy: "This impulsive woman from moments of passionate denunciation would subside into tearful repentance and acknowledge that her violent opposition to that principle was instigated by the power of darkness; that Satan was doing his utmost to destroy her, etc. And solemnly came the prophet's inspired warning: 'Yes, and he will accomplish your overthrow, if you do not heed my counsel.'"

Orson Pratt similarly reported: "She was embittered against Joseph, her husband, and at times fought against him with all her heart; and then again she would break down in her feelings, and humble herself before God and call upon His Holy name."

Joseph obviously loved Emma and sought to serve her. Benjamin Johnson wrote that once while he was visiting their house: "Two of Emma's children came to him [Joseph], as just from their mother, all so nice, bright, and sweet, and calling to them my attention, he said, 'Benjamin, look at these children; how could I help loving their mother; if necessary I would go to hell for such a woman.' And, although at the time he had in the Mansion other wives, younger and apparently more brilliant, yet Emma—the wife of his youth—to me, appeared [to be] the queen of his heart and of his home."

Brigham also spoke of Joseph's love for her, stating that he had a habit of declaring he would have Emma in the hereafter even if he had to go to hell for her.

While Joseph's first plural wife was Fannie Alger, noted earlier, many mistakenly believe his first plural wife was Louisa Beaman, who was sealed to Joseph by her brother-in-law, Joseph B. Noble, on April 5, 1841. Joseph told Noble he had placed his life in his hands. "Therefore do not in an evil hour betray me to my enemies." Louisa also firmly believed the doctrine was from God, says Noble.

Eliza R. Snow was the most well known of Joseph's plural wives, a sophisticated, elegant educator, known for her dignity. They married June 29, 1842. She states that when she first learned of the practice: "The subject was very repugnant to my feelings—so directly was it in opposition to my educated prepossessions. . . . But when I reflected that I was living in the Dispensation of the Fulness of Times, embracing all other dispensations, surely plural marriage must necessarily be included. . . . I increased in knowledge concerning the principle and . . . today esteem it a precious, sacred principle." She was secretary of the Relief Society while Emma was president, and she lived with Emma and Joseph. Her occupation was running a school of 65 children.

One purpose of marriage, states Joseph, was the "holy purpose that the myriads of spirits waiting for tabernacles might have pure healthy bodies."

Joseph was disgusted by the gossip from idle thinkers throughout the city who, in his mind, did not understand or appreciate the doctrine of polygamy. On October 15, 1843, he spoke in church, saying, "Set our women to work and stop their street yarn and talking about spiritual wives."

It was an important principle to Joseph, although not to be presented to the church in general for a dozen years, nor especially to the world at large, subjecting the church to ridicule. It was also a reason some would turn on him to the point of taking his life, and he suspected this would happen beforehand. Helen Kimball, the first wife of Heber C. Kimball, writes, "He charged them not to divulge it, as he was harassed by day and by night by his enemies [apostates within the church], and on their secrecy depended his life."

Men who practiced it had high obligations placed upon them, Joseph taught. His attitude toward women was one of the greatest respect and kindness, say those who knew him well. Lucy Walker, to whom he was married, reports that Joseph taught the brethren that a man's wives "should be his bosom companions, the nearest and dearest objects on earth in every sense of the word. He said men must beware how they treat their wives." Because of mistreatment of women, said Joseph, "many would awake in the morning of the resurrection sadly disappointed; for they, by transgression, would have neither wives nor children, for they surely would be taken from them and given to those who should prove themselves worthy."

As for the "opportunity" of men misusing polygamy to fulfill their lustful desires, Helen Kimball reports, "The prophet said this order would damn more than it would save, because it was a holy principle that could not be trifled with."

Church leaders were caught in a quandary between revealing the truth of their actions and trying to cover them up for the sake of protecting themselves and the church. As with several similar incidents throughout scriptural history, this did in fact occur. Joseph wrote in the *Times and Seasons* that John C. Bennett's "secret wife system" was a matter Bennett manufactured himself—which, in fact, was true. To protect himself Joseph's rebuttal to Bennett's accusations was to characterize them as "a foul and infamous slander." A more clear-cut denial was printed in the same newspaper, signed by several church leaders: "We give this certificate to show, that Dr. J. C. Bennett's secret wife system is a creature of his own make, as we know of no such society in this place, nor never did." But among those signing it were Newel K. Whitney, who had consented to the marriage of his daughter to Joseph two months earlier. Furthermore, 19 women signed a similar statement, including Emma, Eliza R. Snow, and Elizabeth Ann Whitney—all of whom were married to Joseph.

Of this apparent prevarication, the church would explain in the *Deseret News* in 1886: "The Almighty has revealed things on many occasions, which were for his servants and not for the world. . . . When assailed by enemies and accused of practicing things which were really not countenanced . . . they were justified in denying . . . and at the same time avoiding the avowal of such doctrines as were not intended for the world. This course, which they have taken when necessary, by commandment . . . is all the ground which their accusers have for charging them with falsehood."

The years following Joseph's death resulted in a greater practice of the doctrine. The Nauvoo temple was used for ordinances of plural marriage in the winter of 1845–1846. In 1852 Brigham publicly announced it as a church tenet. But an official statement later declared only three percent of Latter-day Saint families in Deseret Territory practiced it.

Emma seemed to have lost the fear of being spiritually destroyed if she did not accept it. After Joseph died, she went public that she was against it.

As stated, and not related to polygamy, Emma married Lewis Bidamon. Noteworthy, she wrote her son Joseph III, saying that she now had a new happiness that she had not expected.

After Joseph's death Emma tried to convince others that Joseph's other wives were "spiritual wives" only and that he had not been married to them in the traditional sense. Emma also said the Twelve had "made bogus" the principle by actually living with their plural wives and having children. George Albert Smith's wife Lucy went to her husband and reported Emma's statement. He replied, "Emma knows better." It is possible that some of Joseph's plural wives were married to him only in a spiritual fashion, for eternity, and did not live with him in the traditional sense, but some did, according to certain friends and acquaintances of Joseph.

In October 1879 Emma claimed polygamy was Brigham's invention, saying: "No such thing as polygamy, or spiritual wifery, was taught publicly or privately, before my husband's death, that I have now or ever had any knowledge of. He had no other wife but me, nor did he to my knowledge ever have." The following portion is the only part on which, according to other Latter-day Saints, she stated the truth: "He did not have improper relations with any woman that ever came to my knowledge."

Eliza R. Snow countered her comments: "I once dearly loved 'Sister Emma,' and now, for me to believe that she, once honored woman, should have sunk so low . . . as to deny what she KNEW to be true, seems a palpable absurdity. If what purports to be her 'last testimony' was really her testimony, she died with a libel on her lips. . . . Sister Emma, of her own free will and choice, gave her husband four wives, two of whom are now living, and ready to testify."

Eliza's account of Emma echoed others. Years later Eliza writes: "After these many years, I can truly say; poor Emma, she could not stand polygamy, but she was a good woman, and I never wish to stand in her way of happiness and exaltation. I hope the Lord will be merciful to her, and I believe he will. . . . Perhaps she had done no worse than any of us would have done in her place."

Emma's son Joseph III, as also stated earlier, would become president of the later-named Community of Christ. He told his first cousin, Samuel H. Smith, in 1860 that his father never practiced nor taught polygamy, and that was the stance of his church, and it always had been.

The Community of Christ church believed Brigham Young established polygamy, so they never practiced it. They cite a verse in The Book of Mormon that condemns it (Jacob 2: 23–25). The Saints, however, believe that revelation continues and updates previous revelation, and that commandments given to one generation can be updated for another. They refer to the differing directives given in the time of Moses versus those of the time of Christ as examples.

Lucy also implies that Joseph had very few children from these marriages and explains why: "Could they but realize the hazardous life he lived, after that revelation was given, they would comprehend the reason. He was harassed and hounded and lived in constant fear of being betrayed by those who ought to have been true to him." There were in fact only two recorded children born to Joseph through polygamy. One was to Emily Partridge, daughter of Edward Partridge. Their baby boy David was born five months after Joseph's death. The other is unknown, but George Albert Smith was visiting Joseph when Joseph and Emma both assisted in the birth. Eliza R. Snow may possibly have had a miscarriage in the spring of 1844, although the sources for that are highly suspect.

Pertaining to the attitude that was necessary to make polygamy successful, Benjamin Johnson recorded his perspective at age 85: "While I can believe that to some plural marriage was a great cross, yet I cannot say so from my own experience, for although in times that tried men's hearts, I married seven wives. I was blessed with the gift to love them all and, although providing for so many was attended with great labor, care and anxiety, yet there was sympathy and love as my reward."

The kind of service-oriented woman it would take to make it work was exemplified by Vilate Kimball, Heber C. Kimball's first wife, as recorded by his second wife, Lucy Walker: "She was dearly beloved by his wives and children, as well as by all who intimately knew her. Too little has been said of her exemplary life. She was as a ministering angel to those in distress, ever ready to aid those who had not been so fortunate as herself in regards to the comforts of life. She never seemed so happy as while seeking to make others happy."

Lucy Walker was married to Joseph and lived in the Mansion House with Joseph and Emma. Reporting of others who were married to Joseph and residing in the house, she says of the spirit in their home: "Instead of a feeling of jealousy, it was a source of comfort to us. We were as sisters to each other."

As for his personal purity, Angus Cannon, brother of George Q. Cannon, said that Joseph and Hyrum "were pure and chaste and worthy of the people's love" and that Joseph "is beyond doubt in my mind . . . a humble disciple of Jesus."

# Important and Little-known Teachings of Joseph

Joseph also taught from his revelations that the hereafter would be a continuation of life on earth, and that "the same sociality which exists among us here will exist among us there," only with greater glory. He was also pleased to teach certain parents what he had learned—especially those parents who had suffered as he and Emma had with the deaths of their own children—"Yes, Mothers, you will have your children."

Joseph taught one Sunday, April 16, 1843, after learning of the death of a missionary overseas: "God has revealed his Son from the heavens and the doctrine of the resurrection also; and we have a knowledge that those we bury here God will bring up again."

Joseph made a significant contribution to the Saints' understanding of the purpose of prosperity—especially excess money and wealth, undoubtedly any that more than covered one's living expenses and retirement savings: On September 23, 1835, he prayed, "Help me, and I will give to the poor."

On July 1, 1841, Joseph was finally able to share the burden of his responsibility by giving to the Twelve the keys of the kingdom. Helen Kimball, daughter of Heber C., says he excitedly jumped about and clapped his hands like a schoolboy let out to play.

Joseph wanted his people to separate the mistakes he made as a man—such as his occasional temper and resorting to fisticuffs when people became belligerent toward him—from his role as a prophet, in which he had no self-doubt that he was speaking in behalf of the Lord. As late as April 6, 1843, and apparently till the day he died, he never expressed doubt of his prophetic calling. On that date he writes, "If I had not actually got into this work, and been called of God, I would back out. But I cannot back out, I have no doubt of the truth." On a side matter, he would comment once to visitors in the city, "A prophet is only a prophet when he is acting as such."

Joseph overlooked other people's weaknesses and asked that others do the same for him. On November 7, 1841, he spoke after a member of the church criticized the Saints from the pulpit for their lack of temperance and solemnity: "If you will follow the revelations and instructions which God gives you through me, I will take you into heaven as my back load. If you will not accuse me, I will not accuse you. If you will throw a cloak of charity over my sins, I will over yours—for charity covereth a multitude of sins."

### *Joseph Smith*
by David Lindsley

## *Porter Rockwell: A Biography*

by Richard Lloyd Dewey

The epic biography that traces Porter Rockwell from turbulent Eastern beginnings to battles with Midwestern mobs to extraordinary gunfights on the American frontier. Quotes hundreds of journals, letters, and court records. Illustrated by western artist Clark Kelley Price.

Hardcover, $22.95                    ISBN: 0-9616024-0-6

*Look for it in your favorite bookstore,*
*or to obtain autographed copies, see last page.*

*Or order online at:*
**www.stratfordbooks.com**

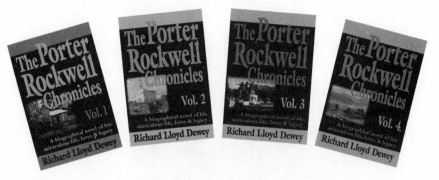

# The Porter Rockwell Chronicles
## by Richard Lloyd Dewey

This best-selling, historically accurate biographical novel series renders Porter's life in riveting story form, bringing it alive for adults and teens alike.

Volume 1 begins with his childhood years in New York where he becomes best friends with the future Mormon prophet Joseph Smith. The story continues through Porter's settlement with the Mormons in Missouri, where he fights against mobs and falls in love with and marries Luana Beebe.

Volume 2 covers the turbulent first four years in Nauvoo, where he continues to fight mobs and becomes Joseph Smith's bodyguard.

The Nauvoo period of his life draws to a close in Volume 3 as his best friend Joseph is murdered and his wife Luana leaves him and remarries, taking his beloved daughter Emily with her. Porter must bid a heartbroken farewell as he and the Mormons are driven from Nauvoo and flee west.

Volume 4 continues with his first ten years in Utah, where he is joyously reunited with his daughter Emily, takes on the U.S. Army in a guerilla war, and enters a new phase of adventures as U.S. Deputy Marshal.

Volume 1 (ISBN: 0-929753-16-X) Hardcover, $26.50
Volume 2 (ISBN: 0-929753-17-8) Hardcover, $26.50
Volume 3 (ISBN: 0-9616024-8-1) Hardcover, $23.88
Volume 4 (ISBN: 0-9616024-9-X) Hardcover, $24.88

*Look for them in your favorite bookstore,*
*or to obtain autographed copies, see last page.*

*Or order online at:*
**www.stratfordbooks.com**

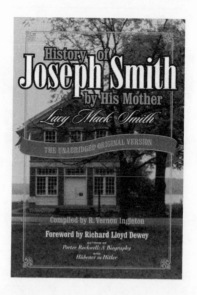

# *History of Joseph Smith by His Mother*
## THE UNABRIDGED ORIGINAL VERSION
## by Lucy Mack Smith

compiled by R. Vernon Ingleton
with foreword by Richard Lloyd Dewey

Of all the versions of Lucy Mack Smith's remarkable history that have appeared since its initial publication a century and a half ago, this is by far the best. For the first time ever, the complete original version is presented, plus the corrections added later by church historians, plus all the facts from the rough draft that have until now been missing from published versions. R. Vernon Ingleton has done a superb job of putting all the elements together to allow Lucy at last to tell her story in its entirety in an easy-to-read format. This is a masterpiece!

Hardcover, $27.95                                ISBN: 0-929753-05-4

*Look for it in your favorite bookstore,*
*or see last page for ordering info.*

*Or order online at:*
**www.stratfordbooks.com**

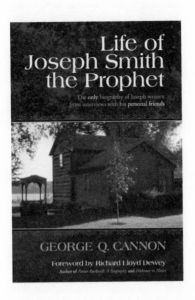

# Life of Joseph Smith the Prophet

by George Q. Cannon
with foreword by Richard Lloyd Dewey

This is the *only* biography about Joseph written from personal interviews with his friends! The author served as First Counselor to four prophets, all of whom knew Joseph. Having full access to Church archives, Cannon weaves the intricate tale of Joseph's intriguing biography in a mesmerizing manner. He stays focused, keeping the reader spell-bound as Joseph has to flee time and again for his life. The reason? Apostates and bigoted religious leaders seek his blood. Seen from an insider's view of what really took place in Nauvoo, Cannon shows how the conspirators worked, even recruiting the governors of two states to get Joseph taken down. But in the end it was Joseph who prevailed spiritually—proven in part by the success of the restored church and its twelve million members today. This must-read biography gives insights, humorous stories and anecdotes with suspenseful plotting rarely seen in this long-out-of-print book that has been republished in clean, modern type for easy reading.

Hardcover, $27.95                    ISBN: 0-929753-09-7

*Look for it in your favorite bookstore,*
*or see last page for ordering info.*

*Or order online at:*
**www.stratfordbooks.com**

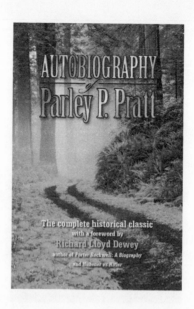

# *Autobiography of Parley P. Pratt*

### Foreword by Richard Lloyd Dewey

Parley P. Pratt's riveting autobiography has thrilled generations of Latter-day Saints. More than just a biography, it is also one of the richest sources of amazing facts from early church history and a treasure trove of classic passages frequently quoted to this day in lessons and over the pulpit. It deserves a place on the bookshelf of every Latter-day Saint and the attention of every student of Mormonism.

Elder Pratt's death was as colorful as the rest of his life. It is generally known that the apostle was assassinated in Arkansas while on a mission, but the fascinating details surrounding this crime of passion are not widely known. In the foreword, bestselling author Richard Lloyd Dewey pulls together the long-obscure historical facts to tell the rest of the story.

In this new edition of Parley P. Pratt's renowned autobiography, spelling, grammar and punctuation have been corrected and modernized so that Pratt's narrative is now easier than ever for readers to enjoy.

Softcover, $19.95

ISBN: 0-929753-12-7

*Look for it in your favorite bookstore,
or see last page for ordering info.*

*Or order online at:*
**www.stratfordbooks.com**

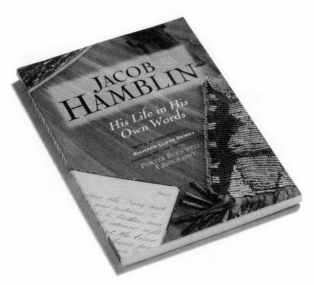

## *Jacob Hamblin:*
## *His Life in His Own Words*

Foreword by Richard Lloyd Dewey

Far from the gun-toting reputation of super-lawman Porter Rockwell, Jacob Hamblin was known in early Western history as the supreme peacemaker.

No less exciting than Porter's account, Jacob's adventures encountered apparent Divine intervention at every turn, a reward seemingly bestowed to certain souls given to absolute faith. And in his faith, like Porter, Jacob Hamblin was one of those incredibly rare warriors who are absolutely fearless.

His migrations from Ohio to Utah with life-and-death adventures at every turn keep the reader spellbound in this unabridged, autobiographical account of the Old West's most unusual adventurer among Native Americans.

In his own words, Jacob Hamblin bares his soul with no pretense, unveiling an eye-witness journal of pioneer attempts to co-exist peacefully with Native brothers, among whom he traveled unarmed, showing his faith in God that he would not be harmed.

Easily considered the most successful—and bravest—diplomat to venture into hostile territory single-handedly, Hamblin takes the reader into hearts of darkness and hearts of light.

Softcover, $10.95                     ISBN: 0-9616024-5-7

*Look for it in your favorite bookstore,*
*or to obtain autographed copies, see last page.*

*Or order online at:*
**www.stratfordbooks.com**

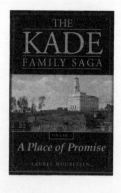

## The Kade Family Saga

### by Laurel Mouritsen

The popular *Kade Family Saga* series of historical novels is steeped in likeable, life-like characters in the fictional story of the Kade family and their adventures spanning from Missouri to the Great Salt Lake.

In Volume 1, *In Quest of Zion*, the saga begins with the romance between the much-travailed Lydia Dawson and the intriguing Christian Kade, who writes for *The Evening and the Morning Star*—controversial newspaper for the Mormons, who have recently arrived in Missouri.

In Volume 2, *A Place of Promise*, the Kade family is in Nauvoo. Young James tries to shield the prophet Joseph from an assassination plot. Meanwhile, his sister Elizabeth is abandoning the faith for a forbidden love. Brother and sister are set on a collision course that will shatter their family and have repercussions for generations of Kades to come.

Volume 3, *Between Two Shores*, continues the breathtaking drama as the Kade family moves west with the saints. James lives the ecstasy and agony of young love in an unyielding desert while sister Elizabeth welters in shattered dreams back in Nauvoo where she has chosen to remain.

Told with the skill of a masterful storyteller against a historically accurate backdrop, the Kade series is at once exciting, heart-wrenching, and very satisfying.

| | |
|---|---|
| Volume 1 (ISBN: 0-929753-07-0) | Hardcover, $19.95 |
| Volume 2 (ISBN: 0-929753-08-9) | Hardcover, $25.95 |
| Volume 3 (ISBN: 0-929753-10-0) | Hardcover, $25.95 |

*Look for it in your favorite bookstore,*
*or see last page for ordering info.*

*Or order online at:*
**www.stratfordbooks.com**

## New Evidences of Christ
## in Ancient America

by Blaine M. Yorgason, Bruce W. Warren, and Harold Brown

In 1947 California lawyer Tom Ferguson threw a shovel over his shoulder and marched into the jungles of southern Mexico. Teamed with world-class scholar Bruce Warren, they found a mountain of evidence supporting Book of Mormon claims. Now the reader can follow their adventure as they unearth amazing archaeological discoveries and ancient writings, all of which shut the mouths of critics who say such evidences do not exist. In this volume, the newest archaeological evidences are also presented.

Endorsed by Hugh Nibley.

Hardcover, $24.95                    ISBN: 0-929753-01-1

# Hübener vs Hitler

## A Biography of Helmuth Hübener,
## Mormon Teenage Resistance Leader

REVISED, SECOND EDITION

by Richard Lloyd Dewey

Nobel Laureate author Günther Grass said Hübener's life should be held up as a role model to every teen in the world. Regional best-selling author Richard Lloyd Dewey (*Porter Rockwell: A Biography*) holds up Hübener's life as a light not only to all teens, but to adults as well.

As an active Latter-day Saint, young Hübener recruited his best friends from church and work and established a sophisticated resistance group that baffled the Gestapo, infuriated the Nazi leadership, frustrated the highest judges in the land, and convinced the SS hierarchy that hundreds of adults—not just a handful of determined teens—were involved!

While other books have told the story of the group of freedom fighters Hübener founded, this tells their complete story from numerous sources, *and* is the first biography of Hübener himself—the astounding young man who led and animated the group. The inspiring, spell-binding, true story of the youngest resistance leader in Nazi Germany.

Hardcover, $27.95                                    ISBN: 0-929753-13-5

*Look for it in your favorite bookstore,*
*or see last page for ordering info.*

*Or order online at:*
**www.stratfordbooks.com**

### *Nauvoo, Illinois, mid-1840s*
#### by Dan Thornton

Art prints of *Nauvoo, Illinois, mid-1840s*, depicted on the dust jackets of Volume 2 of *The Porter Rockwell Chronicles* and of *The Kade Family Saga*, are available from the publisher.

- **Limited Edition** signed and numbered, large size (28.5"w × 19"h) $135.00 each, plus $15.00 shipping & handling (add $1.00 shipping & handling for each additional print sent to same address)

- **Artist's Proof** (same size) $200.00 each, plus $15.00 shipping & handling (add $1.00 shipping & handling for each additional print sent to same address)

- **Greeting Card Packs** unsigned, 10 cards and envelopes $25.00 per pack, plus $3.00 shipping & handling (add $1.00 for each additional pack sent to same address)

As the 860 Limited Edition art prints sell out, the collectors' value may substantially increase.

#### Send check or money order to:
Stratford Books, P.O. Box 1371, Provo, Utah 84603-1371

#### Or order online at:
www.stratfordbooks.com

*Utah residents, add 6.25% sales tax.*

### *Heber C. Kimball Home, Nauvoo*
by Al Rounds

Full-color, 25" × 15" signed-and-numbered, limited-edition art prints of *Heber C. Kimball Home, Nauvoo*, depicted on the dust jacket of Volume 3 of *The Porter Rockwell Chronicles*, are available from the publisher at the price of $150.00 each plus shipping and handling.

Shipping and handling charges are $15.00 for the first print, plus $1.00 additional shipping and handling for each additional print ordered at the same time and shipped to the same address.

As the 700 limited-edition art prints sell out, the collectors' value may substantially increase.

### *Porter Rockwell Returns*
by Clark Kelley Price

This classic color print of the painting by renowned western artist Clark Kelley Price depicts Porter Rockwell coming home at night in a lightning storm through downtown Lehi, Utah.

In this vivid scene, Rockwell is returning from a hard day's work, with an outlaw draped over the horse he has in tow.

36"w x 24"h, $30.00                           ISBN: 0-929753-0-6

*Add $10.00 shipping and handling for first print*
*and $1.00 for each additional print sent to same address.*
*Utah residents, add 6.25% sales tax.*

### Send check or money order to:
Stratford Books, P.O. Box 1371, Provo, Utah 84603-1371

### Or order online at:
www.stratfordbooks.com

*Prices subject to change.*

# Porter Rockwell Limited Edition Prints and Commissioned Paintings

### *Porter's Ranch at Point of the Mountain*
by Clark Kelley Price

Limited-edition art prints of this oil painting, which is featured on the dust jacket of Volume 4 of *The Porter Rockwell Chronicles*, are available at $75 each plus $1 shipping and handling. The edition consists of 880 11" × 14" prints on canvas, signed and numbered by the artist.

Mr. Price's work, found in private collections worldwide, sells in exclusive art galleries and has often been featured on covers of *The Ensign* magazine. A longtime friend of the author, Mr. Price was among the first to inspire Richard Lloyd Dewey about the life of Porter Rockwell. He did the illustrations and back cover painting for Dewey's *Porter Rockwell: A Biography*.

Mr. Price is willing to paint, by commission, additional scenes from Rockwell's life (or any subject that appeals to him) at a minimum size of 24" × 36" (or any dimension of at least 864 square inches) for interested patrons. Commissioned oil paintings are priced at $10 per square inch ($8640 for 24" × 36"). Contact the artist at (307) 883-2322, or P.O. Box 211, Thayne, Wyoming 83127.

The artist requests a lead time of one year. A down payment of 33% is required on the commission. Paintings come on canvas, unframed, and patron pays for shipping.

# ORDERING INFORMATION

**Porter Rockwell: A Biography**                                    $22.95
by Richard Lloyd Dewey. Hardcover, 612 pp. ISBN: 0-9616024-0-6

**The Porter Rockwell Chronicles**
by Richard Lloyd Dewey.

| | | |
|---|---|---|
| **Volume 1** | Hardcover, 486 pp. ISBN: 0-929753-16-X | $26.50 |
| **Volume 2** | Hardcover, 452 pp. ISBN: 0-929753-17-8 | $26.50 |
| **Volume 3** | Hardcover, 527 pp. ISBN: 0-9616024-8-1 | $23.88 |
| **Volume 4** | Hardcover, 570 pp. ISBN: 0-9616024-9-X | $24.88 |

**History of Joseph Smith by His Mother:**                          $27.95
**The Unabridged Original Version**
by Lucy Mack Smith, compiled by R. Vernon Ingleton.
Hardcover, 548 pp. ISBN: 0-929753-05-4

**Life of Joseph Smith the Prophet**                                $27.95
by George Q. Cannon. Hardcover, 615 pp. ISBN: 0-929753-09-7

**Autobiography of Parley P. Pratt**                                $19.95
Softcover, 426 pp. ISBN: 0-929753-12-7

**Jacob Hamblin: His Life in His Own Words**                        $10.95
Foreword by Richard Lloyd Dewey.
Softcover, 128 pp. ISBN: 0-9616024-5-7

**Hübener vs Hitler** (*Revised, Second Edition*)                   $27.95
A biography of Helmuth Hübener, Mormon teenage resistance leader,
by Richard Lloyd Dewey. Hardcover, 594 pp. ISBN: 0-929753-13-5

**The Kade Family Saga**
by Laurel Mouritsen.

**Volume 1: In Quest of Zion**                                      $19.95
Hardcover, 396 pp. ISBN: 0-929753-07-0
**Volume 2: A Place of Promise**                                    $25.95
Hardcover, 389 pp. ISBN: 0-929753-08-9
**Volume 3: Between Two Shores**                                    $25.95
Hardcover, 364 pp. ISBN: 0-929753-10-0

**New Evidences of Christ in Ancient America**                      $24.95
by Blaine M. Yorgason, Bruce W. Warren, and Harold Brown.
Hardcover, 430 pp. ISBN: 0-929753-01-1

FREE SHIPPING & HANDLING
*Utah residents, add 6.25% sales tax.*

*Send check or money order to:*
**Stratford Books**
P.O. Box 1371, Provo, Utah 84603-1371

*Or order online at:*
**www.stratfordbooks.com**

*Prices subject to change.*